Lecture Notes in Artificial Intelligence   3327

Edited by J. G. Carbonell and J. Siekmann

Subseries of Lecture Notes in Computer Science

Yong Shi   Weixuan Xu   Zhengxin Chen (Eds.)

Data Mining and Knowledge Management

Chinese Academy of Sciences Symposium
CASDMKM 2004
Beijing, China, July 12-14, 2004
Revised Papers

Series Editors

Jaime G. Carbonell, Carnegie Mellon University, Pittsburgh, PA, USA
Jörg Siekmann, University of Saarland, Saarbrücken, Germany

Volume Editors

Yong Shi
Graduate University of Chinese Academy of Sciences
CAS Research Center on Data Technology and Knowledge Economy
No. 80 Zhongguancun East Rd., Beijing, China 100080
E-mail: yshi@mail.unomaha.edu
and University of Nebraska at Omaha
College of Information Science and Technology
Omaha, NE 68182, USA
E-mail: yshi@mail.unomaha.edu

Weixuan Xu
Chinese Academy of Sciences, Institute of Policy and Management
55 Zhongguancun Rd., Beijing 100080, China
E-mail: wxu@mail.casipm.ac.cn

Zhengxin Chen
University of Nebraska at Omaha, College of Information Science and Technology
Omaha, NE 68182, USA
E-mail: zchen@mail.unomaha.edu

Library of Congress Control Number: 2004117657

CR Subject Classification (1998): I.2, H.2.8, H.4, J.1

ISSN 0302-9743
ISBN 3-540-23987-1 Springer Berlin Heidelberg New York

Springer is a part of Springer Science+Business Media

springeronline.com

© Springer-Verlag Berlin Heidelberg 2004
Printed in Germany

Typesetting: Camera-ready by author, data conversion by Scientific Publishing Services, Chennai, India
Printed on acid-free paper   SPIN: 11363613   06/3142   5 4 3 2 1 0

Preface

Toward an Integrated Study of Data Mining and Knowledge Management

Data mining (DM) and knowledge management (KM) are two important research areas, but with different emphases. Research and practice in these two areas have been largely conducted in parallel. The Chinese Academy of Sciences Symposium on Data Mining and Knowledge Management 2004 (CASDMKM 2004) held in Beijing, China (July 12–14, 2004) provided a unique opportunity for scholars to exchange ideas in these two areas. CASDMKM is a forum for discussing research findings and case studies in data mining, knowledge management and related fields such as machine learning and optimization problems. It promotes data mining technology, knowledge management tools and their real-life applications in the global economy.

This volume of symposium postproceedings contains 3 invited talks, as well as 25 papers selected from 60 original research papers submitted to the symposium. Contributions in this volume come from scholars within China as well as from abroad, with diverse backgrounds, addressing a wide range of issues. The papers in this volume address various aspects of data mining and knowledge management. We believe the publication of this volume will stimulate the integrated study of these two important areas in the future.

Although both data mining and knowledge management have been active areas in research and practice, there is still a lack of idea exchange between these two camps. CASDMKM aims to bridge this gap. Numerous issues need to be studied in regard to data mining and knowledge management. For example, how to manage the knowledge mined from different data mining methods? From the knowledge management perspective, what kinds of knowledge need to be discovered? What are the similarities and differences for data mining applications and knowledge management applications? What are the issues not yet explored on the boundary of data mining and knowledge management? This list of questions goes on and on. Of course papers in this volume cannot answer all of these questions. Nevertheless, we believe that CASDMKM 2004 served as an exciting platform to foster an integrated study of data mining and knowledge management in the near future.

The papers included in this volume are organized into the following categories:

- *Data mining methods*: Various theoretical aspects of data mining were examined from different perspectives such as fuzzy set theory, linear and non-linear programming, etc.
- *Practical issues of data mining*: Complementary to theoretical studies of data mining, there are also papers exploring aspects of implementing and applying data mining methods.

- *Data mining for bioinformatics:* As a new field, bioinformatics has shown great potential for applications of data mining. The papers included in this category focus on applying data mining methods for microarray data analysis.
- *Data mining applications:* In addition to bioinformatics, data mining methods have also been applied to many other areas. In particular, multiple-criteria linear and nonlinear programming has proven to be a very useful approach.
- *Knowledge management for enterprise:* These papers address various issues related to the application of knowledge management in corporations using various techniques. A particular emphasis here is on coordination and cooperation.
- *Risk management:* Better knowledge management also requires more advanced techniques for risk management, to identify, control, and minimize the impact of uncertain events, as shown in these papers, using fuzzy set theory and other approaches for better risk management.
- *Integration of data mining and knowledge management:* As indicated earlier, the integration of these two research fields is still in the early stage. Nevertheless, as shown in the papers selected in this volume, researchers have endeavored to integrate data mining methods such as neural networks with various aspects related to knowledge management, such as decision support systems and expert systems, for better knowledge management.

September 2004

Yong Shi
Weixuan Xu
Zhengxin Chen

CASDMKM 2004 Organization

Hosted by

Institute of Policy and Management at the Chinese Academy of Sciences
Graduate School of the Chinese Academy of Sciences
International Journal of Information Technology and Decision Making

Sponsored by

Chinese Academy of Sciences
National Natural Science Foundation of China
University of Nebraska at Omaha, USA

Conference Chairs
Weixuan Xu, Chinese Academy of Sciences, China
Yong Shi, University of Nebraska at Omaha, USA

Advisory Committee

Siwei Cheng, Natural Science Foundation, China
Ruwei Dai, Chinese Academy of Sciences, China
Masao Fukushima, Kyoto University, Japan
Bezalel Gavish, Southern Methodist University, USA
Jiali Ge , Petroleum University, China
Fred Glover, University of Colorado, USA
Jifa Gu, Chinese Academy of Sciences, China
Finn V. Jensen, Aalborg University, Denmark
Peter Keen, Delft University, Netherlands
Ralph Keeney, Duke University, USA
Kin Keung Lai, City University of Hong Kong, Hong Kong, China
Alexander V. Lotov, Russian Academy of Sciences, Russia
Robert Nease, Washington University School of Medicine, USA
Hasan Pirkul, University of Texas at Dallas, USA
David Poole, University of British Columbia, Canada
Thomas Saaty, University of Pittsburgh, USA
Mindia E. Salukvadze, Georgian Academy of Sciences, Georgia
Elie Sanchez, University of Mediterranée, France
Prakash P. Shenoy, University of Kansas, USA
Zhongzhi Shi, Chinese Academy of Sciences, China
Jian Song, Chinese Academy of Engineering, China
Ralph E. Steuer, University of Georgia, USA
Peizhuang Wang, Beijing Normal University, China
Andrew B. Whinston, University of Texas at Austin, USA

Po-Lung Yu, National Chiao Tung University, Taiwan, and University of Kansas,USA
Philip S. Yu, IBM T.J. Watson Research Center, USA
Lotfi A. Zadeh, University of California at Berkeley, USA
Milan Zeleny, Fordham University, USA
Hans-Jürgen Zimmermann, Aachen Institute of Technology, Germany

Program Committee

Hesham Ali, University of Nebraska at Omaha, USA
Daobin Chen, Industrial and Commercial Bank of China, China
Jian Chen, Tsinghua University, China
Xiaojun Chen, Hirosaki University, Japan
Zhengxin Chen, University of Nebraska at Omaha, USA
Chao-Hsien Chu, Pennsylvania State University, USA
John Chuang, University of California at Berkeley, USA
Xiaotie Deng, City University of Hong Kong, Hong Kong, China
Jiawei Han, University of Illinois at Urbana-Champaign, USA
Xirui Hao, Vision Software Inc., USA
Chongfu Huang, Beijing Normal University, China
Haijun Huang, Natural Science Foundation, China
Zhimin Huang, Adelphi University, USA
Deepak Khazanchi, University of Nebraska at Omaha, USA
Wikil Kwak, University of Nebraska at Omaha, USA
Heeseok Lee, Korea Advanced Institute of Science and Technology, Korea
Hongyu Li, Fudan University, China
Shanling Li, McGill University, Canada
Keying Ye, Virginia Polytechnic Institute and State University, USA
Yachen Lin, First North American Bank, USA
Jiming Liu, Hong Kong Baptist University, Hong Kong, China
Xiaohui Liu, Brunel University, UK
Yoshiteru Nakamori, Japan Advanced Institute of Science and Technology,
    Japan
David L. Olson, University of Nebraska at Lincoln, USA
Fuji Ren, Tokushima University, Japan
Hongchi Shi, University of Missouri-Columbia, USA
Minghua Shi, Dagong Global Credit Rating Co., China
Chengzheng Sun, Griffith University, Australia
Di Sun, China Construction Bank, China
Minghe Sun, University of Texas at San Antonio, USA
Tieniu Tan, Chinese Academy of Sciences, China
Zixiang Tan, Syracuse University, USA
Xiaowo Tang, Chinese University of Electronic Science and Technology, China
Xijing Tang, Chinese Academy of Sciences, China
James Wang, Pennsylvania State University, USA
Shouyang Wang, Chinese Academy of Sciences, China
Zhengyuan Wang, University of Nebraska at Omaha, USA
Yiming Wei, Chinese Academy of Sciences, China

Table of Contents

Data Mining for Bioinformatics

Data Mining Applications

Knowledge Management for Enterprise

Visualization-Based Data Mining Tool and Its Web Application

Alexander V. Lotov[1], Alexander A. Kistanov[2], and Alexander D. Zaitsev[2]

[1] State University – Higher School of Economics, Moscow, Russia, and
Russian Academy of Sciences, Dorodnicyn Computing Centre, and
Lomonosov Moscow State University
Lotov1@ccas.ru
http://www.ccas.ru/mmes/mmeda/
[2] Lomonosov Moscow State University, Department of Systems Analysis

Abstract. The paper is devoted to a visualization-based data mining tool that helps to explore properties of large volumes of data given in the form of relational databases. It is shown how the tool can support the process of exploration of data properties and selecting a small number of preferable items from the database by application a graphic form of goal programming. The graphic Web application server is considered which implements the data mining tool via Internet. Its current and future applications are discussed.

1 Introduction

Data mining is a well-known approach to studying large volumes of data collected in databases. Statistical methods that are usually used in data mining help to discover new knowledge concerning the data. In this paper we consider a method for data mining that does not use statistical concepts, but supports discovering of new information concerning the data collected in a relational database by computer visualization. Computer visualization of information proved to be a convenient and effective technique that can help people to assess information. Usually one understands visualization as a transformation of symbolic data into geometric figures that are supposed to help human beings to form a mental picture of the symbolic data. About one half of human brain's neurons is associated with vision, and this fact provides a solid basis for successful application of visualization techniques. One can consider computer visualization of information as a direct way to its understanding.

The visualization method considered in this paper is called the Interactive Decision Maps (IDM) technique. Along with other data mining techniques, the IDM technique helps to find a new knowledge in large volumes of data (and even in mathematical models). However, in contrast to usual data mining techniques that reveal some laws hidden in data volumes, the IDM technique provides information on their frontiers. Moreover, being combined with the goal programming approach, the IDM technique helps to select small volumes of data, which correspond to the interests of the user. By this, information on data responsible for the form of the frontiers is discovered. The IDM technique proved to be compatible with the Internet and was implemented in Web in the framework of server-client structure.

Y. Shi, W. Xu, and Z. Chen (Eds.): CASDMKM 2004, LNAI 3327, pp. 1–10, 2004.

The main idea of the IDM technique in the case of large relational databases consists in transformation of the rows of a database into multi-dimensional points, in enveloping them and in subsequent exploration of the envelope. To be precise, it is assumed that the relational database contains a large list of items described by their attributes. Any item is associated with a row of the database, while columns of the database represent attributes. Several (three to seven) numerical attributes specified by the user are considered as the selection criteria. Then, rows are associated with points in the criterion space. The IDM technique is based on enveloping the variety of criterion points (constructing the convex hull of the variety) and on-line visualization of the Pareto frontier of the envelope in the form of multiple decision maps. Applying the IDM technique, the user obtains information on feasible criterion values and on envelope-related criterion tradeoffs.

An interactive exploration of the Pareto frontier with the help of the IDM technique is usually combined with goal identification: the user has to specify the preferable combination of criterion values (the goal). However, due to the IDM technique, the goal can be identified at a decision map directly on display. Then, several rows from the list are provided, which are close to the identified goal (Reasonable Goals Method, RGM).

The IDM/RGM technique was implemented in the form of a graphic Web application server. The Web application server uses the fundamental feature of the IDM technique that consists in separating the phase of enveloping the points from the phase of human study of the Pareto frontier and identification of the goal. Such a feature makes it possible to apply the IDM/RGM technique in the framework of server-client structure. On the Web, such a structure is applied by using the opportunities of Java. Enveloping of the points is performed at the server, and a Java applet provides visualization of the Pareto frontier on-line and identification of the goal at the user's computer.

The idea to visualize the Pareto frontier was introduced by S.Gass and T.Saaty in 1955 [1]. This idea was transformed into an important form of the multi-criteria methods by J.Cohon [2]. The IDM technique was introduced in the 1980s in the framework of the Feasible Goals Method, FGM, and applied in various economic and environmental studies (see, for example, [3-5]). The FGM is usually used to explore the Pareto frontier and select a reasonable decision in the cases where mathematical models can be used. In contrast, the IDM/RGM technique introduced in 1990s [6] is aimed at exploration of relational databases. It was used in several studies including water management in Russia [7] and national energy planning at the Israeli Ministry of National Infrastructures [8]. Other applications of the RGM/IDM technique are possible, too (see, for example, [9]). They are summarized in [5] and include selecting from large lists of environmental, technical, financial, personal, medical, and other decision alternatives.

In this paper we concentrate on Web application of the IDM technique. Experimental application of the IDM technique on Web has started as soon as in 1996 [3]. Its refined version based on Java technology was developed in 2000 in the form of Web application server [10]. The first real-life application of the Web application server is related to supporting of remote negotiations and decision making in regional water management (Werra project, Germany). However, a wide range of applications of such a Web tool can be considered. Actually, any relational database can be now analyzed through Web in a simple way using the IDM/RGM technique. A database may contain statistical data (medical, demographic, environmental, financial, etc.), the results of experiments with technical or natural systems (say, data on a device performance, etc.) or of simulation experiments with models, etc. The Web tool can be applied in e-commerce, too: for example, it can support selecting of goods or services from large lists as lists of real estate, second-hand cars, tourist tours, etc. The IDM/RGM technique can be used for visualization of temporal databases, and so a graphic Web tool can be coded that studies temporal data by animation of the Pareto frontier via Internet. This option can be especially important in financial management.

The concept of the IDM/RGM technique and its Web implementation are described in the paper. First, the mathematical description of the technique is provided. Then, a description of the demo Web application server is given.

2   Mathematical Description

Let us consider a mathematical description of the IDM/RGM technique. We consider a table that contains N rows and several columns, any of which is related to an attribute. Let us suppose that user has specified m attributes to be selection criteria. Then, each row can be associated to a point of the m-dimensional linear criterion space R^m. Criterion values for the row number j are described by the point y^j, which coordinates are $y_1^{\,j}, ..., y_m^{\,j}$. Since N rows are we considered, we have got N criterion points y^1, y^2, ..., y^N. The RGM is based on enveloping of the points, i.e. on constructing the convex hull of them defined as

$$Y_C = \text{conv} \{ y^1, y^2, ..., y^N \}.$$

Let us suppose that the maximization of the criterion values is preferable. In this case, the point y' dominates (is better than) the point y, if $y' \geq y$ and $y' \neq y$. Then, the Paret-efficient (non-dominated) frontier of Y_C is a variety of points of $y \in Y_C$ that are not dominated, i.e.

$$P(Y_C) = \{ y \in Y_C : \{ y' \in Y_C : y' \geq y, y' \neq y \} = \varnothing \}.$$

The Edgeworth-Pareto Hull of the convex hull (CEPH) denoted by Y_C* is the convex hull of the points broadened by the dominated points, i.e.

$$Y_C* = Y_C + (- R_+^m)$$

where R_+^m is the non-negative cone of R^m. It is important that the efficiency frontier of the CEPH is the same as for the convex hull, but the dominated frontiers disappear. For this reason, the RGM applies approximation of the variety Y_C* instead of Y_C. Approximation methods are described in details in [5].

A two-criterion slice of Y_C* passing through a point $y* \in R^m$ is defined as follows. Let us consider a pair of criteria, say u and v. Let $z*$ be the values of the rest of criteria in the point $y*$. Then, a two-criterion slice of the set Y_C* related to the pair

(u, v) and passing through the point $y*$ can be defined as (we do not care about the order of the criteria)

$$G(Y_C *, z *) = \{(u,v) : (u,v,z *) \in Y_C *\}.$$

Collection of slices, for which the value of only one of the rest of criteria can change, constitutes the decision map. To identify the goal directly on the decision map, user has to select a convenient decision map and a slice on it (by this the values $z*$ of all criteria except two are fixed) Then the identification of a goal vector is reduced to a fixation of the values $u*$ of two criteria given on axes. It can be done by a click of the computer mouse. By this the goal vector $y* = (u*, z*)$ is identified.

Several points, which are close to the identified goal, are selected and related rows are provided to user. Different variants of the concept of proximity can be applied. In our recent studies we apply the weighted Tchebycheff metric $\rho_\lambda(y*, y)$ as the measure of distance between the goal $y* = (y_1 *,..., y_m *)$ and a point $y = (y_1,..., y_m)$ where

$$\rho_\lambda(y*, y) = max \{\lambda_i(y_i* - y_i)_+ : i=1,2,...,m\}.$$

Parameters (weights) $\lambda_1,..., \lambda_m$ are non-negative. Tchebycheff metric has the sense of maximal deviation of weighted criterion values. Usually the weighted Tchebycheff metric is applied with given values of parameters $\lambda=(\lambda_1,..., \lambda_m)$ (see [11]). In this case, a point with minimal value of Tchebycheff metric $\rho_\lambda(y*, y)$ is found. Clearly it is non-dominated.

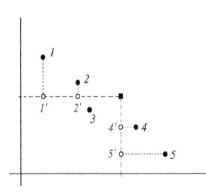

In our case, the only information provided by the user is the goal $y*$. No information about the parameters $\lambda_1,...,\lambda_m$ is supposed to be provided by user. To solve this problem, several approaches could be proposed. Here we described one of them [6], which is used in the Web application server. All points are found that could be optimal if the whole variety of positive parameters $\lambda_1,..., \lambda_m$ is used. Certainly it is impossible to solve the infinite number of optimization problems with all

Fig. 1. Selection procedure of the RGM (it is preferable to increase the criterion values)

different sets of parameters $\lambda_1,..., \lambda_m$. However, the following simple procedure may be used instead of solving an infinite number of optimization problems. In the first step of the procedure, a modified point is constructed for any original point in the following way: if a criterion value in the original point is better than the criterion value in the user-identified goal, the criterion value of the identified goal is substituted for the criterion value of the original point. In the second step of the procedure, Pareto domination rule is applied to modified points. In the result, non-dominated points are selected from the modified points. Finally, the original feasible points that originated the non-dominated modified points are selected. The procedure is illustrated in Fig. 1 for the case of two criteria, which are subject of maximization.

The reasonable goal identified by the user is denoted by the filled square symbol. Original points are represented by the filled circles. For any original point, a modified point is constructed: if a criterion value in an original point is better than in the reasonable goal, the goal value is substituted for the criterion value. Modified points are represented by hollow circles in Fig. 1. So, the feasible point 1 originates the modified point 1', etc. If all criterion values for an original point are less than the aspiration levels (for example, point 3), the modified point coincides with the original one. Then, Pareto domination rule is applied to modified points: non-dominated points are selected among them. Point 2' dominates point 1', and point 4' dominates point 5'. So, three non-dominated modified points are selected: 2', 3, and 4'. Finally, the original feasible points which originated the non-dominated modified points are selected. In Fig. 1, these points are 2, 3 and 4. It is clear that points elected through this procedure represent non-dominated row (in epy usual Pareto sense).

One can see that the approximation of the CEPH and its exploration may be easily separated in time and space in the framework of the RGM/IDM technique. This feature of the RGM/IDM technique is effectively used in the Web application server.

3   Web Application Server

The current Web application server based on the RGM/IDM technique is a prototype version of the future Web application servers that will support easy selection of preferable alternatives from various tables using simple graphic interface. This service can be of a general use suited for any table prepared data or domain specific that enables some useful features and deeper integration with domain data.

Web service implements multi-tier architecture and consists of the calculation server, web server application and graphic presentation.

Calculation server is an executable module coded in C++. It processes given table data and builds the approximation of the CEPH. Calculation server is ANSI C++ compliant so it can be compiled and executed at any platform.

Main graphic presentation window is a Java applet executed inside user browser. MS Internet Explorer, v. 4.0 or higher may be used to display it.

Web application is coded in Java and JSP and serves for several interfacing purposes: it helps user to prepare a table with alternatives, invokes calculation server to process it, displays the applet with calculated data and handles user choice to generate selected alternatives. Web application can be executed on any web server that supports JSP and Java servlets. The Web tool is located at `http://www.ccas.ru/mmes/mmeda/rgdb/index.htm`

The user has first to specify the table to be explored. After the data input is completed and the query is submitted, server envelops the criterion points and sends the Java applet along with the CEPH to computer of the user.

The user can explore the decision maps (Fig. 2) for different numbers of bedrooms and bathrooms by specifying these numbers by moving sliders of the scroll bars. The

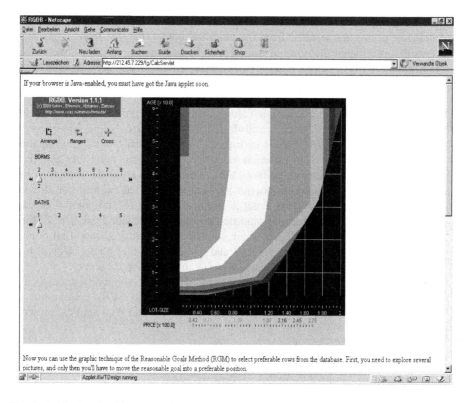

Fig. 2. A black-and-white copy of decision map that describes feasible lot-size and age for several values of price (in color on display and shading here, thousand of US$) for the whole real estate table (as it is specified by scroll bars, not less than two bedrooms and one bathroom are required at the moment)

user may want to use animation (automatic movement of sliders). He/she can see how the numbers of bedrooms and bathrooms influence possible combinations of lot-size, age and price. Using the slider of the color (shading) scroll bar, the user can specify a desired price. The slider is given on the color palette. Colors of the palette are practically not seen in the black-and-white picture given in the paper. Therefore, we propose to visit our Web application server to play with the animation of color decision maps.

To identify a goal, preferred numbers of bedrooms and bathrooms must be identified by the user first. The related decision map given in Fig. 3 differs from one given in previous Fig. 2: several shadings (colors on display) disappeared. Then, the user has to identify a preferable combination of values given of two criteria given in the map. To do it, the user has to use the cross that helps to identify the reasonable goal (Fig. 3). Once again, it is needed to stress that a full freedom of choice with respect to the efficient combinations of criteria is given to the user as it is done in all methods for generating the Pareto-efficient frontier.

After the preferred position of the cross is specified, the user has to use Fixation button. Then, the applet transmits the goal to the server, and the server returns the selected rows to the user.

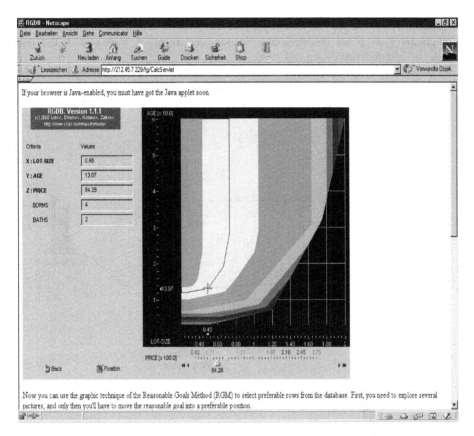

Fig. 3. A decision map for preferred numbers of bedrooms and bathrooms with the cross that helps to identify the goal

The user receives a list of rows that are equal from point of view of the Web server, but surely are not equal to the user. He/she has to choose one of these options by him/herself. Various methods for selecting the criterion points (rows of the table) can be easily applied in customized versions, but they were not included into the demo version.

The demo version is restricted to 500 alternatives and five criteria. The full version can have till seven criteria and several hundreds of thousands of rows. Moreover, matrices of decision maps can be used in a customized version.

Our prototype implements the general approach to exploration of any table data. However this service can be integrated to existing Web sites, Internet stores, online shops, portals etc, everywhere where selection should be performed from large tables of homogenous goods or services.

Integration with other Web sites can be done rather simple by modifying or replacing our Web application tier and integrating it with another one. In this case, data can be prepared or comes from other Web application or Web site, then it is processed via calculation server, examined via our graphic applet, decision is made and selection results are displayed by the means of another Web site and in its context. For example, in most applications a lot of additional information about alternatives as detail descriptions, pictures, etc. must be shown with the list of selected alternatives.

Calculation server (RGDB server) may reside on a special dedicated high-performance server or servers and communicate with Web application via simple external interface. This leads to Application Service Provider (ASP) or Utility architecture.

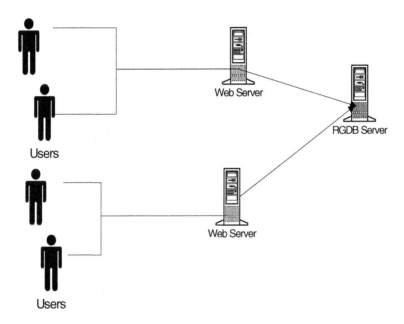

Fig. 4. ASP architecture

There is a server (RGDB server on the Fig. 4) with well-defined interface and users or other programs and web servers that use the server. Hence, Web application becomes independent from calculation server and can be developed and deployed independently.

4   Summary

The RGM/IDM technique helps to explore various relational databases. Due to enveloping, the user has an opportunity to explore the whole variety visually and select several interesting rows by a simple click of the computer mouse. It is important that the RGM procedure is scalable – it can be used in the case of databases that contain even million of rows.

Many applications of the IDM/RGM technique for databases can be found. In addition to e-commerce, problems of e-logistics can be studied (partner selection, etc.). Another network application may be related to supporting the network traders in various exchanges. For example, a day trader can visually monitor technical indicators of stocks provided via network. Graphic display of information of stock may help the trader to be the first to buy an advantageous security during a trade session.

Important applications of the technique may be related to mobile DSS. Visualization provides a natural tool for informing remote users and inquiring concerning their preferences.

Acknowledgments

Fraunhofer Institute for Autonomous Intelligent Systems, Germany, has partially supported coding of the demo version of the Web application server described here. We are grateful to Drs. Hans Voss, Natalia and Gennady Andrienko. Our research was supported by the Russian State Program for Supporting Scientific Schools (grant NSh-1843.2003.1), by Russian Foundation for Basic Research (grant 04-01-00662) and by Program no. 3 for Fundamental Research of Department of Mathematical Sciences of Russian Academy of Sciences.

References

1. Gass, S., Saaty, T. The computational algorithm for the parametric objective function. Naval Research Logistics Quarterly 2 (1955) 39-51
2. Cohon, J.: Multiobjective Programming and Planning, John Wiley, New York (1978)
3. Lotov, A., Bushenkov, V., Chernov, A., Gusev, D. and Kamenev, G.: INTERNET, GIS, and Interactive Decision Maps, in: J. of Geographical Information and Decision Analysis 1 (1997) 119-143 http://www.geodec.org/gida_2.htm
4. Lotov, A., Bushenkov, V., Kamenev, G.: Feasible Goals Method. Mellen Press, Lewiston, NY (1999, in Russian)
5. Lotov, A.V., Bushenkov, V.A., and Kamenev, G.K.: Interactive Decision Maps. Kluwer Academic Publishers, Boston (2004)
6. Gusev, D.V., and Lotov, A.V.: Methods for Decision Support in Finite Choice Problems. In: Ivanilov, Ju. (ed.): Operations Research. Models, Systems, Decisions, Computing Center of Russian Academy of Sciences, Moscow, Russia (1994, in Russian) 15-43
7. Bourmistrova, L., Efremov, R., Lotov, A.: A Visual Decision Making Support Technique and its Application in Water Resources Management Systems. J. of Computer and System Science Int. 41 (2002) 759-769
8. Soloveichik, D., Ben-Aderet, N., Grinman, M., and Lotov, A.: Multi-objective Optimization and Marginal Abatement Cost in the Electricity Sector – an Israeli Case Study. European J. of Operational Research 140 (2002) 571-583

9. Jankowski, P., Lotov, A., and Gusev, D.: Multiple Criteria Trade-off Approach to Spatial Decision Making. In: J.-C. Thill (ed.) Spatial Multicriteria Decision Making and Analysis: A Geographical Information Sciences Approach, Brookfield, VT (1999) 127-148

10. Lotov, A.V., Kistanov, A.A., Zaitsev, A.D.: Client Support in E-commerce: Graphic Search for Bargains in Large Lists. Working Paper N34, Fachbereich Wirtschaftwissenschaften, Institute fuer Wirtschaftsinformatik, University of Siegen, Germany (2001)

11. Steuer, R.E.: Multiple Criteria Optimization. John Wiley, New York (1986).

Knowledge Management, Habitual Domains, and Innovation Dynamics*

P. L. Yu[1] and T. C. Lai[2]

[1,2] Institute of Information Management, National Chiao Tung University, 1001,
Ta Hsueh Road, HsinChu City 300, Taiwan
yupl@mail.nctu.edu.tw, tclai@iim.nctu.edu.tw

Abstract. Knowledge Management (KM) with information technology (IT) has made tremendous progresses in recent years. It has helped many people in making decision and transactions. Nevertheless, without continuous expanding and upgrading our habitual domains (HD) and competence set (CS), KM may lead us to decision traps and making wrong decisions. This article introduces the concepts of habitual domains and competence set analysis in such a way that we could see where KM can commit decision traps and how to avoid them. Innovation dynamics, as an overall picture of continued enterprise innovation, is also introduced so that we could know the areas and directions in which KM can make maximum contributions and create value. KM empowered by HD can make KM even more powerful.

1 Introduction

With rapid advancement of Information Technology (IT), Knowledge Management (KM) has enjoyed its rapid growth [4]. In the market, there are many software available to help people make decisions or transactions, such as supply chain management (SCM), enterprise resource planning (ERP), customer relationship management (CRM), accounting information system (AIS), etc.[3], [7], [12]. In the nutshell, KM is useful because it can help certain people to relieve the pains and frustrations for obtaining useful information to make certain decisions or transactions. For salesperson, KM could provide useful information as to close sales. For credit card companies, KM could provide useful information about card holders' credibility. For supply chain management, KM can efficiently provide where to get needed materials, where to produce and how to transport the product and manage the cash flow, etc.

---

* This research was supported by the National Science Council of the Republic of China. NSC92-2416-H009-009.
[1] Distinguished Chair Professor, Institute of Information Management, National Chiao Tung University, Taiwan and C. A. Scupin Distinguished Professor, School of Business, University of Kansas, Kansas.
[2] Ph. D. Student, Institute of Information Management, National Chiao Tung University, Taiwan.

Y. Shi, W. Xu, and Z. Chen (Eds.): CASDMKM 2004, LNAI 3327, pp. 11–21, 2004.
© Springer-Verlag Berlin Heidelberg 2004

It seems, KM could do "almost everything" to help people make "any decision" with good results. Let us consider the following example.

Example 1: Breeding Mighty Horses. *For centuries, many biologists paid their attention and worked hard to breed endurable mighty working horses so that the new horse could be durable, controllable and did not have to eat. To their great surprise, their dream was realized by mechanists, who invented a kind of "working horse", tractors. The biologists' decision trap and decision blind are obvious.*

Biologists habitually thought that to produce the mighty horses, they had to use "breeding methods" — a bio-tech, a decision trap in their mind. Certainly, they made progress. However, their dream could not be realized.

IT or KM, to certain degree, is similar to breeding, a biotech. One wonders: is it possible that IT or KM could create traps for people as to make wrong decision or transactions? If it is possible, how could we design a good KM that can minimize the possibility to have decision traps and maximize the benefits for the people who use it?

Since humans are involved, habitual domains (HD) and competence set analysis must be addressed as to answer the above questions. We shall discuss these concepts in the next section. As KM is based on IT, its modules can handle only "routine" or "mixed routine" problems. It may help solve "fuzzy problems". But, we must decompose these fuzzy problems into series of routine problems first. For challenge decision problems, their solutions are beyond our HD and KM. Certain insight are needed. We shall discuss these topics in Section 3. Finally, for an enterprise to continuously prosper and be competitive, it needs continuous innovation in technology, management, marketing, financing, distribution logistics, etc. [5]. For a systematic view of the innovation, we introduce "Innovation Dynamics" in Section 4. The introduction will help us to locate which areas and directions that KM can be developed as to maximize its utilization and create its value. At the end, some conclusion remarks will be offered.

2   Habitual Domains and Competence Set Analysis

From Example 1, we see that one's judging and responding could be inefficient or inaccurate if his or her ways of thinking get trapped rigidly within a small domain. To further expound this concept, let us describe the known concept of Habitual Domains. For details, see Refs. [8] and [9].

2.1   Habitual Domains

Each person has a unique set of behavioral patterns resulting from his or her ways of thinking, judging, responding, and handling problems, which gradually stabilized within a certain boundary over a period of time. This collection of ways of thinking, judging, etc., accompanied with its formation, interaction, and dynamics, is called *habitual domain* (HD). Let us take a look at an example.

Example 2: Chairman Ingenuity. *A retiring corporate chairman invited to his ranch two finalists, say A and B, from whom he would select his replacement using a horse* *race. A and B, equally skillful in horseback riding, were given a black and white horse respectively. The chairman laid out the course for the horse race and said, "Starting at the same time now, whoever's horse is slower in completing the course will be selected as the next Chairman!" After a puzzling period, A jumped on B's horse and rode as fast as he could to the finish line while leaving his horse behind. When B realized what was going on, it was too late! Naturally, A was the new Chairman.*

Most people consider that the faster horse will be the winner in the horse race (a habitual domain). When a problem is not in our HD, we are bewildered. The above example makes it clear that one's habitual domain can be helpful in solving problems but it also can come his or her way of thinking. Moreover, one may be distorting information in a different way.

Our habitual domains go wherever we go and have great impact on our decision making. As our HD, over a period of time, will gradually become stabilized, unless there is an occurrence of extraordinary events or we purposely try to expand it, our thinking and behavior will reach some kind of steady state and predictable.

Our habitual domains are comprised of four elements:

1. Potential domain (PD_t). This is the collection of all thoughts, concepts, ideas, and actions that can be potentially activated by one person or by one organization at time t.
2. Actual domain (AD_t). This is the collection of all thoughts, concepts, ideas, and actions, which actually catch our attention and mind at time t.
3. Activation Probability (AP_t). This represents the probability that the ideas, concepts and actions in the potential domain that can be actually activated.
4. Reachable domain (RD_t). This is the collection of thoughts, concepts, ideas, actions and operators that can be generated from initial actual domain.

At any point in time habitual domains, denoted by HD_t, will mean the collection of the above four subsets. That is, $HD_t = (PD_t, AD_t, AP_t, RD_t)$. In general, the actual domain is only a small portion of the reachable domain; in turn, the reachable domain is only a small portion of potential domain, and only a small portion of the actual domain is observable. Note that HD_t changes with time. We will take an example to illustrate PD_t, AD_t, and RD_t.

Example 3. *Assume we are taking an iceberg scenic trip. At the moment of seeing an iceberg, we can merely see the small part of the iceberg which is above sea level and faces us. We cannot see the part of iceberg under sea level, nor see the seal behind the back of iceberg (see Fig. 1). Let us assume t is the point of time when we see the iceberg, the portion which we actually see may be considered as the actual domain (AD_t), in turn, the reachable domain (RD_t) could be the part of iceberg above sea level including the seal. The potential domain (PD_t) could be the whole of the iceberg including those under the sea level.*

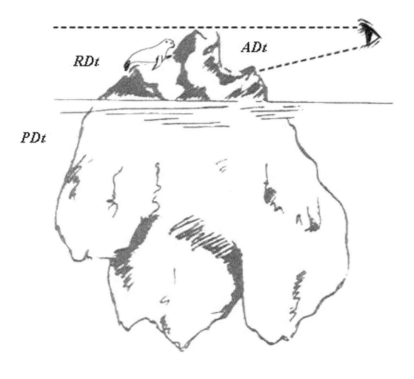

Fig. 1. Illustration of PD*t*, RD*t*, and AD*t*

At time *t*, if we do not pay attention to the backside of the iceberg, we will never find the seal. In addition to this, never can we see the spectacular iceberg if we do not dive into the sea. Some people might argue it is nothing special to see a seal in the iceberg. But, what if it is a box of jewelry rather than a live seal! This example illustrates that the actual domain can easily get trapped in small domain resulting from concentrating our attention on solving certain problems. In doing so, we might overlook the tremendous power of the reachable domain and potential domain.

In the information era, even the advances of IT and KM can help solve people's decision problems, our actual domain could still easily get trapped, leading us to make wrong decision or action.

Example 4: Dog Food. *A dog food company designed a special package that not only was nutritious, but also could reduce dogs' weight. The statistical testing market was positive. The company started "mass production". Its dog food supply was far short from meeting the overwhelming demand. Therefore, the company doubled its capacity. To their big surprise, after one to two months of excellent sales, the customers and the wholesalers began to return the dog food package, because the dogs did not like to eat it.*

Clearly, a decision trap was committed by using statistics on buyers, not on the final users (dogs). The KM used statistical method on "wrong" subject and committed the trap. If the RD (reachable domain) of the KM could include the buyers and the users, the decision traps and wrong decisions might be avoided.

There are many methods for helping us to improve or expand our habitual domains and avoid decision traps. We list some of them in the following two tables. The interested reader is referred to Refs. [8] and [9] for more detail.

Table 1. Eight basic methods for expanding habitual domains

1. Learning Actively
2. Take the Higher Position
3. Active Association
4. Changing the Relative Parameters
5. Changing the Environment
6. Brainstorming
7. Retreat in Order to Advance
8. Praying or Meditation

Table 2. Nine principles for deep knowledge

1. Deep and Down Principle
2. Alternating Principle
3. Contrasting and Complementing Principle
4. Revolving and Cycling Principle
5. Inner Connection Principle
6. Changing and Transforming Principle
7. Contradiction Principle
8. Cracking and Ripping Principle
9. Void Principle

2.2 Competence Set and Cores of Competence Set

For each decision problem or event E, there is a *competence set* consisting of ideas, knowledge, skills, and resources for its effective solution. When the decision maker (DM) thinks he/she has already acquired and mastered the competence set as perceived, he/she would feel comfortable making the decision. Note that conceptually, competence set of a problem may be regarded as a projection of a habitual domain on the problem. Thus, it also has potential domain, actual domain, reachable domain, and activation probability as described in Sec. 2.1. Also note that through training, education, and experience, competence set can be expanded and enriched (i.e. its number of elements can be increased and their corresponding activation probability can become larger) [8, 9, 10, 11].

Given an event or a decision problem E which catches our attention at time t, the probability or propensity for an idea I or element in Sk (or HD) that can be activated is denoted by $P_t(I, E)$. Like a conditional probability, we know that $0 \leq P_t(I, E) \leq 1$, that $P_t(I, E) = 0$ if I is unrelated to E or I is not an element of PD_t (potential domain) at time t; and that $P_t(I, E) = 1$ if I is automatically activated in the thinking process whenever E is presented. Empirically, like probability functions, $P_t(I, E)$ may be estimated by determining its relative frequency. For instance, if I is activated 7 out of 10 times whenever E is presented, then $P_t(I, E)$ may be estimated at 0.7. Probability theory and statistics can then be used to estimate $P_t(I, E)$.

The α-core of competence set at time t, denoted by $C_t(\alpha, E)$, is defined to be the collection of skills or elements of Sk that can be activated with a propensity larger than or equal to α. That is, $C_t(\alpha, E) = \{I | Pt(I, E) \geq \alpha\}$.

3   Classification of Decision Problems

Let the truly need competence set at time t, the acquired skill set at time t, and the α-core of an acquired skill set at time t be denoted by $Tr_t(E)$, $Sk_t(E)$, and $C_t(\alpha, E)$, respectively. Depending on $Tr_t(E)$, $Sk_t(E)$, and $C_t(\alpha, E)$, we may classify decision problems into following categories:

1. If $Tr_t(E)$ is well-known and $Tr_t(E) \subset C_t(\alpha, E)$ with high value of α or $\alpha \to 1$, then the problem is a routine problem, for which satisfactory solutions are readily known and routinely used.
2. Mixed-routine problem consists of a number of routine sub-problems, we may decompose it into a number of routine problems to which the current IT can provide the solutions.
3. If $Tr_t(E)$ is only fuzzily known and may not contained in $C_t(\alpha, E)$ with a high value of α, then the problem is a fuzzy problem, for which solutions are fuzzily known. Note that once the $Tr_t(E)$ is gradually clarified and contained in α-core with a high value of α, the fuzzy problem may gradually become routine problem.
4. If $Tr_t(E) \setminus C_t(\alpha, E)$ is very large relative $C_t(\alpha, E)$ no matter how small is α or $Tr_t(E)$ is unknown and difficult to know, then the problem is a challenging problem.

So far, KM with IT can accelerate decisions for the routine or mixed-routine problems. There still are many challenging problems, which cannot be easily solved by KM with IT. This is because the needed competence set ($Tr_t(E)$) of a challenging problem is unknown or only partially known, especially when humans are involved. The following illustrates this fact.

Example 5: Alinsky's Strategy (Adapted from Alinsky [1]). *In 1960 African Americans living in Chicago had little political power and were subject to discriminatory treatment in just about every aspect of their lives. Leaders of the black community invited Alinsky, a great social movement leader, to participate in their effort. Alinsky clearly was aware of deep knowledge principles. Working with black leaders* *he came up with a strategy so alien to city leaders that they would be powerless to anticipate it. He would mobilize a large number of people to legally occupy all the public restrooms of the O'Hare Airport. Imagine thousands of individuals visit the airport daily who were hydraulically loaded (very high level of charge) rushed for restroom but there would be no place for all these persons to relieve themselves.*

How embarrassing when the newspaper and media around the world headlined and dramatized the situation. As it turned, the plan never was put into operation. City authorities found out about Alinsky's strategy and, realizing their inability to prevent its implementation and its potential for damaging the city's reputation, met with black leaders and promised to fulfill several of their key demands.

The above example shows us the importance of understanding one's potential domain. At the beginning, African Americans did not entirely know the habitual domain of city authorities (a challenging problem). Their campaigns, such as demonstration, hunger strike, etc., failed to reach their goal (an actual domain). Alinsky observed a potentially high level of charge of the city authorities, the public opinion (potential domain), that could force them to act. As a result, the authorities agreed to meet the key demands of the black community, with both sides claiming a victory.

4 Innovation Dynamics

Without creative ideas and innovation, our lives will be bound in a certain domain and become stable. Similarly, without continuous innovation, our business will lose its vitality and competitive edge [2], [6]. Bill Gates indicated that Microsoft would collapse in about two years if they do not continue the innovation.

In this section, we are going to explore innovation dynamics based on Habitual Domains (HD) and Competence Set (CS) Analysis as to increase competitive edge. From HD Theory and CS Analysis, all things and humans can release pains and frustrations for certain group of people at certain situations and time. Thus all humans and things carry the competence (in broad sense, including skills, attitudes, resources, and functionalities). For instance, a cup is useful when we need a container to carry water as to release our pains and frustrations of having no cup.

The competitive edge of an organization or human can be defined as the capability to provide right services and products at right price to the target customers earlier than the competitors, as to release their pains and frustrations and make them satisfied and happy.

To be competitive, we therefore need to know what would be the customers' needs as to produce the right products or services at a lower cost and faster than the competitors. At the same time, given a product or service of certain competence or functionality, how to reach out the potential customers as to create value (the value is usually positively related to how much we could release the customers' pains and frustrations).

If we abstractly regard all humans and things as a set of different CS, then producing new products or services can be regarded as a transformation of the existent CS to a new form of CS. Based on this, we could draw clockwise innovation dynamics as in Fig. 2:

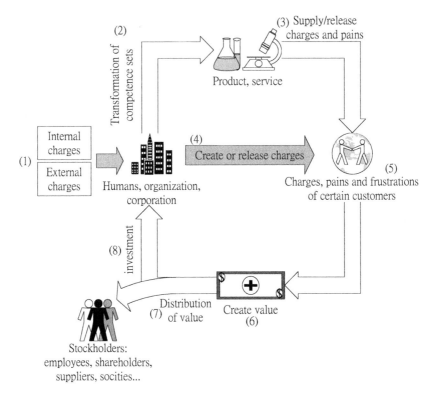

Fig. 2. Clockwise Innovation Dynamics

Although Fig. 2 is self-explaining, the following are worth mentioning: (The numbers are corresponding to that of the figure.)

Note 1: According to HD Theory, when the current states and the ideal goals have unfavorable discrepancies (for instance losing money instead of making money, technologically behind, instead of ahead of, the competitors) will create mental charge which can prompt us to work harder to reach our ideal goals.

Note 2: Producing product and service is a matter of transforming CS from the existing one to a new form.

Note 3: Our product could release the charges and pains of certain group of people and make them satisfied and happy.

Note 4: The organization can create or release charges of certain group of people through advertising, marketing and selling.

Note 5: The target group of people will experience the change of charges. When their pains and frustrations, by buying our products or services, are relieved and become happy, the products and services can create value, which is Note 6.

Note 7 and Note 8 respectively are the distribution of the created value and reinvestment. To gain the competitive edge, products and services need to be continuously upgraded and changed. The reinvestment, Note 8, is needed for research and development for producing new product and service.

In a contrast, the innovation dynamics can be counter-clockwise. We could draw counter-clockwise innovation dynamics as in Fig. 3:

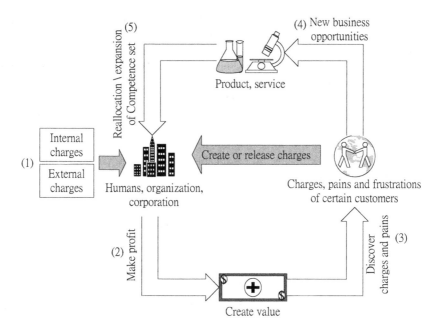

Fig. 3. Counter-clockwise Innovation Dynamic

Note 1: According to HD Theory, when the current states and the ideal goals have unfavorable discrepancies will create mental charge which can prompt us to work harder to reach our ideal goals.

Note 2: In order to make profit, organization must create value.

Note 3: According to CS analysis, all things carry competence which can release pains and frustrations for certain group of people at certain situations and time.

Note 4: New business opportunities could be found by understanding and analyzing the pains and frustrations of certain group of people.

Note 5: Reallocation or expansion of competence set is needed for innovating products or services to release people's pains and frustrations.

Innovation needs creative ideas, which are outside the existing HD and must be able to relieve the pains and frustrations of certain people. From this point of view, the method of expanding and upgrading our HDs becomes readily applicable. Innovation can be defined as the work and process to transform the creative ideas into reality as to create the value expected. It includes planning, executing (building structures, organization, processes, etc.), and adjustment. It could demand hard working, perseverance, persistence and competences. Innovation is, therefore, a process of transforming the existing CS toward a desired CS (product or service).

5 Conclusions

With the advances of information technologies including computer, network, etc. Knowledge Management (KM) has been rapidly innovated in recent years. KM is useless if it cannot help some people release their frustrations and pains, or if it cannot help them make better decisions. The challenging for KM nowadays is how can it be developed to maximize its value to help solve complex problems.

This article discussed four categories of decision problems: routine, mixed-routine, fuzzy, and challenging problems. Many routine problems can be solved by KM/IT. For mixed-routine and fuzzy problems, we may decompose it into a number of solvable routine sub-problems. As to challenging problems, one must expand his/her habitual domain or think deeper into reachable domain even potential domain, to find effective solution and avoid decision traps.

This paper also addressed "Innovation Dynamics" for a systematic view of innovation. Though KM can clarify what are the needed competence set, and may speed up the process of expansion of competence set. KM/IT may also lead us into traps as to make wrong decisions or transactions. This is most likely when we are confronted with challenging problems and we are in a state of high level of charge.

Many research problems are open for exploration. For instance, in the innovation dynamics, each link of Fig. 2 and 3 involves a number of routine, fuzzy and challenging problems. How do use KM/IT, HD, CS to help the decision maker to make good (optimal) decisions easily and quickly, so that we could relieve their pains and frustration, and create value?

References

1. Alinsky, S. D.: Rules for Radicals. Vintage Books, New York (1972)
2. Drucker, P. F.: The Coming of New Organization. Harvard Business Review on Knowledge Management. Boston MA: Harvard Business School Press (1998)
3. Grant, G. G.: ERP & data warehousing in organizations: issues and challenges. IRM Press (2003)
4. Holsapple, C. W.: Handbook on knowledge management. Springer-Verlag, Berlin Heidelberg New York (2003)
5. Ikujiro, N. and Hirotaka, T.: The Knowledge-Creating Company. Oxford University Press, New York (1995)
6. Sharkie, R.: Knowledge creation and its place in the development of sustainable competitive advantage. Journal of Knowledge Management, 7(1) (2003) 20-31
7. Stadtler, H. and Kilger, C.: Supply chain management and advanced planning: concepts, models, software, and case studies. Springer-Verlag, Berlin Heidelberg New York (2002)
8. Yu, P. L.: Forming Winning Strategies – An Integrated Theory of Habitual Domains Springer-Verlag, Berlin Heidelberg New York (1990)
9. Yu, P. L.: Habitual Domains and Forming Winning Strategies. NCTU Press (2002)
10. Yu, P. L. and Chiang, C. I.: Decision Making, Habitual Domains and Information Technology. International Journal of Information Technology & Decision Making, 1 (1) (2002) 5-26

11. Yu, P. L. and Zhang, D.: A foundation for competence set analysis. Mathematical Social Sciences, 20. (1990) 251-299
12. Zikmund, W. G., McLeod, R. and Gilbert, F. W.: Customer relationship management: integrating marketing strategy and information technology. Wiley (2002)

Knowledge-Information Circulation Through the Enterprise: Forward to the Roots of Knowledge Management

Milan Zeleny

Fordham University, New York, USA
Tomas Bata University, Zlín, CR
mzeleny@fordham.edu
mzeleny@quick.cz

Abstract. The field of Knowledge Management (KM) has already completed its initiatory phase, characterized by operational confusion between knowledge and information, stemming from the tenuous notion of "explicit knowledge". Consequently, the progress of KM has been much slower than would the significance of knowledge management in a modern enterprise indicate. Here we propose and discuss four cornerstones for returning to the roots of knowledge management and so moving forward towards a new phase of KM. We discuss the roots of reliable knowledge thinking and theory in economics, management and philosophy. Then we formulate clear, unambiguous and pragmatic definitions and distinctions of knowledge and information, establish simple and natural measures of the value of knowledge and propose the Knowledge-Information (KnowIn) continuum and its circulatory nature in managing knowledge of the enterprise. Autopoietic cycle A-C-I-S is elaborated to that purpose. We conclude the paper by discussing some implications of the new KM for strategy and strategic management.

1 Introduction

The field of Knowledge Management (KM) has already completed its initial cycle of relative euphoria and fashion with rather unimpressive practical results. This is because KM lacked reliable and self-confident definition and differentiation from information, information management and IT applications. This allowed an "easy entry" of a large variety of enthusiasts who were able to interpret "knowledge" in whichever suitable way. Such phenomenon is well documented by an unusual swell of thousands of KM books and articles. Opportunistic entries resulted in equally opportunistic exits. Consequently, the field of KM has lost its ways [8].

Yet, knowledge based strategy and therefore also KM undoubtedly represent one of the most significant advances in economics, management and business enterprise of modern era. The earliest expositions and formulations of Knowledge Management come from the 1980s, as for example in [12, 13].

At least four cornerstones have to be re-established before fully capitalizing on the KM promise of such import and magnitude:

Y. Shi, W. Xu, and Z. Chen (Eds.): CASDMKM 2004, LNAI 3327, pp. 22–33, 2004.

1. Return to the firm *roots* of reliable knowledge thinking and theory in economics, management and philosophy.
2. Formulate clear, unambiguous and pragmatic definitions and *distinctions* of knowledge and information.
3. Establish simple and *natural* measures of the value of knowledge.
4. Propose the Knowledge-Information (*KnowIn*) continuum and its circulatory nature in the enterprise.

Other aspects, like strategy, technology, human resources and organizational environment are also important, but can be more or less *derived* from the above four cornerstones of conceptual foundations of KM. Observe that all four cornerstones are interconnected in a legacy progression, the next always based on the preceding one.

In this paper we concentrate on outlining the four cornerstones, with a short conclusion exploring the nature of strategy and strategic management from the vantage point of the new KM.

1   Forward to the Roots of Knowledge

Although we have to return *back* to the roots [3, 4], in the context of KM such move represents a step *forward*. This apparent contradiction is intentional.

A useful and practical philosophical foundation of knowledge comes from American pragmatists, especially from C. I. Lewis's system of *conceptualistic pragmatism* [5], rooted in the thought of Peirce, James and Dewey[2].

Pragmatist philosophical roots firmly established that knowledge is:

1. Action oriented
2. Socially established
3. Relatively interpreted

First, knowledge is action. This is also echoed in Polanyi's "All knowledge is tacit" [9]. There is no "explicit" knowledge, only information. Second, knowledge is consensually social and without a social context there can be no knowledge. Third, although the "given" of sensory data and experience remains absolute, its classification and *its relation to other things* is relative to a given context of experience *and* intended action.

Lewis captured the social dimension of knowledge through his term *community of action*. Congruity of behavior and *consensual* human cooperation are the ultimate tests of *shared knowledge*. The purpose of *communication* is coordination of action and behavior: It is therefore essential that all of its aspects remain consensual.

Knowledge cannot be separated from the process of knowing (establishing relationships). Knowledge and knowing are identical: *knowledge is process*.

What is meant when we say that somebody knows or possesses knowledge? We imply that we expect one to be capable of coordinated action towards some goals and objectives. Coordinated action is the test of possessing knowledge. Knowledge without action reduces to simple information or data. Maturana and Varela [6] put it very succinctly: *All doing is knowing, and all knowing is doing*.

Clearly, "explicit knowledge", repositories of data and information (data banks, encyclopaedias, expert systems) are only passive recordings, descriptions of knowledge. Only coordinated human action, i. e., process of relating such components into coherent patterns, which turn out to be successful in achieving goals and purposes, qualifies as knowledge.

Among the myriads of possible postulated relationships among objects, only some result in a coordinated action. Every act of knowing brings forth a world. We "bring forth" a hypothesis about the relationships and test it through action; if we succeed in reaching our goal - we know.

Bringing forth a world of coordinated action is human knowledge.

Bringing forth a world manifests itself in all our action and all our being. Knowing is effective [i. e., coordinated and "successful"] action.

Knowledge as an effective action enables a living (human) being to persist in its coordinated existence in a specific environment from which it continually brings forth its own world of action. All knowing is coordinated action by the knower and therefore depends on the "structure" of the knower. The way knowledge can be brought forth in doing depends on the nature of "doing" as it is implied by the organization of the knower and his circumstance (working environment).

3 Definition of Knowledge

Clear, unambiguous and operational definition of knowledge is essential and without it the field of KM cannot progress in either theory or practice.

Based on the preceding philosophical foundations, we can advance the simplest possible definitions for the purposes of effective KM [14].

Knowledge is purposeful coordination of action.

The quality and effectiveness of achieved purpose is the evidence (and measure) of knowledge.

Information is symbolic description of action.

Any action, past, current or future, can be described and captured through symbols. All such descriptions are information. All those rules, formulas, frames, plans, scripts, and semantic networks are information, not forms of knowledge. It is not a set of rules or a formal representation of knowledge, i. e. information, that is critical to intelligence, but rather the mind's coordination of the body's experiences and actions, i. e. knowledge.

Knowledge is rooted in each individual's actions, behavior and experiences and therefore partially embedded in the process that is being coordinated.

The differences between knowledge and information are significant, qualitative and striking – as the differences between action and its description should be. I know because I do. I have information because I describe.

There can be *too much information* (information overload) but there can never be *too much knowledge*: There is no knowledge overload.

Information is only *one of the inputs* into the process coordination. Knowledge is coordination itself. There can be too many inputs, but coordination can only be better or worse. Information can be correct or incorrect, right or wrong, true or misleading. Knowledge can only be more or less effective.

Knowledge is *always gradual*, from less to more (effective). In this sense, it is not correct or incorrect: it is not an input.

Knowledge refers to the processing of inputs through coordination of action. The *rules of coordination* (sequences, patterns, levels of performance), derived from experience, observation, consensus or social prescription, are characteristic of knowledge, not of information. What are these rules and how are they followed are among the determinants of forms of knowledge.

Skills. If the rules are *internally* determined and controlled by the subject, we speak of skills. Skills can be validated by the action's outcome only. There is no need for social sanction or approval of the rules. Robinson Crusoe has skills as all autodidacts have skills. Neither have knowledge.

Knowledge. If the rules adhered to are established *externally*, in a social context and validation, then we can speak of knowledge rather than skills. Knowledge is recognized and validated socially. (One cannot say "I know" – unless one is an autodidact (amateur or diletante) and thus self-exempt from the rules. Only others - family, community or society – can testify to one's knowledge.) One cannot claim knowledge without proper social validation.

Expertise. If the external rules are mastered and performed at a *socially respected* degree and if the actor can reflect upon the rules with respect to their improvement or change, then knowledge becomes expertise. An expert gains socially sanctioned power over the rules so that they no longer need to be obeyed. Expertise is an acquired ability to change the rules.

Observe that the difference between skills and knowledge is not based on the outcome. A skillful person can sometimes achieve a better outcome than a knowledgeable person, but it is not equally socially recognized and valued. Skill is based on the outcome only. Knowledge is based on both the outcome *and* the process leading to it. Expertise is masterful knowledge and cannot grow out of skills.

While skills, knowledge and expertise are all related to *know-how* – how to achieve a given or stated purpose, or to *know-what* – how to state or select a purpose to be pursued, the notion of *wisdom* is related to *know-why*.

Knowledge is related to both *efficiency* (know-how) and *effectiveness* (know-what) while wisdom is related to *explicability* (know-why). Having information is far from being knowledgeable. Being knowledgeable still does not imply wisdom.

One can be knowledgeable without being wise. Many use information and follow given rules efficiently: they acquire dexterity and become *specialists*. Others choose their goals and change the rules with the approval of others – and become *experts*. But even the masters of rules and purposes are not wise if they cannot satisfactorily explain *why* particular purposes, rules or courses of action *should* be chosen or rejected.

Wisdom is socially accepted or experience validated explication of purpose.

Enhancing human wisdom, pursuing practices and systems that are not only efficient or effective, but also wise, i. e., building *wisdom systems*, is the next frontier of the long and tortuous progression from data and information to knowledge and wisdom.

It is probably useful to expand on a definition of *communication*.

Communication is closely related to both knowledge and information. Conventional wisdom would weaken the usefulness of the concept of communication by including any *information transfer* in its domain.

We communicate with each other through language. Language is a system of symbolic descriptions of action. We exchange these symbolic labels (information) in order to coordinate our action and modify behavior. When such coordination or modification occurs, we communicate. When it does not, we just transfer information.

Communication occurs when the result of a particular exchange of information (e. g., linguistic labels) is the coordination of action (doings, operations) or modification of behavior.

Clearly, language is *not* a system of communication, yet communication occurs through language.

What is the difference between action and behavior? *Action* is the result of deliberate decision making [15] within new contexts and circumstances. *Behavior* is a habitual or automated response to repeating circumstances within a known context. Both are affected by communication.

Communication is consequential exchange of information.

4 Natural Measure of Knowledge

Knowledge must be measured in a simple, natural way, not through a complex arificial formula or construct.

Based on the definition of knowledge as purposeful coordination of action, one can derive a natural measure of knowledge as a *value attributed to coordination*.

Knowledge is neither intangible nor abstract and it is *not difficult* to measure. Knowledge produces very tangible outcomes of real value to the approving society. Information, as a *description* of action, may be difficult to measure – it has no tangible outcome per se. The value of information is intangible, unless it becomes an input into measurable action, i. e. knowledge. Action itself (knowledge) is eminently measurable because its outcomes can be observed, measured and valued.

Knowledge is measured by the value that our coordination of effort, action and process adds to inputs of material, technology, energy, services, information, time, etc.

Knowledge is measured by added value.

Value of any produced item, product or service, is a combination of purchased or otherwise externally or internally acquired inputs and work and labor (coordinated performance of operations constituting the process). This value have to be socially recognized and accepted: by the market, by the purchaser, sponsor, peer group, community, family and so on. If nobody wants my product then it is irrelevant how many inputs, how much time and effort have I expended. My knowledge has no value.

If somebody pays for my product (in money or in kind) then its market or social value has been established. To derive the *value of knowledge*, we have to correct the value of product by *subtracting all* (including information) external and internal purchases (their market value) or used and otherwise valued acquisitions. In corporate setting, we also subtract operating cost and general administrative cost.

As a result we obtain added value (to inputs) or added value per hour or worker. Such conceived added value is due to action or process, its performance and coordination. There are three components to added value: labor, work and coordination.

One has to pay wages to labor (performance of externally coordinated operations) and work (internally coordinated operations). In addition, one has to pay salaries for any employed coordination services. Observe that both wages and salaries can only be covered from the added value. Labor, work and management are not (or should not be) inputs, but forms of coordination and performance of the process. If no value has been added, no payment of wages and salaries can be sustained.

"Work" can be defined as economically purposeful activity requiring substantial human coordination of task and action. "Job" designates the kind of work that is performed contractually, that is, explicitly for remuneration and in the employ of others. "Labor" (often used as a synonym for hard work or toil) can more properly be related to performing simplified work-components or tasks without engaging in their substantial coordination towards given purposes. Work often involves labor but not vice versa. Work involves coordination of tasks while labor relates only to their performance. After we subtract from added value the cost of labor (considered material input), what remains is the value of knowledge applied to the process.

Added value measures knowledge, the contribution of coordination of action through work and management.

The *relativity* of the value of knowledge is clear. The same expenditure of coordination effort, time, skills and work can have great value in one context and no value in another. The same level of knowledge can have great value in New York and no value in Prague – and vice versa. All knowledge is relative and its value is derived from the context of its application. This is why knowledge cannot be measured from inputs and through apriori expenditures of time, effort and skills. Knowledge is not primary but secondary, a derived category: derived from the value of its outcome. The amount of knowledge does not determine the value of its outcome, but the value of the outcome determines the value of knowledge applied.

No amount of information, duration of study, hard work or dedicated effort can guarantee the value of knowledge. All such effort has to be socially accepted and sanctioned, its value affirmed and validated. Otherwise it can be wrong, misplaced, unuseful and unvalued – regardless of the effort.

In education we mostly acquire information (description of action), not knowledge (action itself). We study cookbooks but rarely learn to cook. Information is necessary and potentially useful, easy to transmit. But *information is not knowledge.*

In a world of global communications and information sharing we are less and less going to be paid for having information and more and more for knowing, for being able to coordinate action successfully (pay for knowledge). The value of education rooted in information is going to decline, *education for knowledge* is going to rise.

In this context, it becomes apparent that confusing information with knowledge is rapidly becoming counterproductive. After reading hundreds of cookbooks, I am still not a viable chef. I still do not know how to coordinate action, my own or others.

After reading hundreds of textbooks on management, I am still not a manager. I still do not know how to manage enterprise, my own or of others.

One of the cruelest outcomes of education is instilling the feeling that information *is* knowledge in unexperienced novices. Studying description of action does not guarantee knowledge of action.

This is why even the oxymoronic connection "explicit knowledge", implying that somehow a symbolic description is some sort of "knowledge", is not only confusing and unscientific, but also damaging and fundamentally untrue.

Witness K. E. Sveiby [10]: "All knowledge is either tacit or rooted in tacit knowledge. All our knowledge therefore rests in the tacit dimension," or M. Polanyi [9]: "Knowledge is an activity which would be better described as a process of knowing." So it would be. To know is to do.

The field of KM has to abandon its initial cycle and leap forward to its roots.

5 KnowIn Circulatory System

It is important that knowledge and information become inteconnected in an integrated, mutually enhancing system of autopoietic self-production cycle of *KnowIn* circulation.

Clearly, there is a useful connection between action and its description, between knowledge and information. While knowledge management should include information management, information management cannot include knowledge management. Process can include its inputs, but no single input can include its process.

Knowledge produces more knowledge with the help of intermediate information. The purpose is to produce more knowledge, not more information.

In order to do that effectively, we have to integrate knowledge and information (KnowIn) flows into a *unified system of transformations*. It is insufficient, although necessary, to manage, manipulate, mine and massage data and information. It is incomplete and inadequate to manage knowledge without managing its descriptions. Its is both necessary and sufficient to manage integrated and interdependent KnowIn flows.

Purpose of knowledge is more knowledge, not more information.

Useful knowledge is codified into its recording or description. Obtained information is combined and adjusted to yield *actionable* information. Actionable information forms an input into *effective* coordination of action (knowledge). Effective knowledge is then socialized and shared, transformed into *useful* knowledge. In short, the cycle

Knowledge -> Information -> Knowledge

can be broken into its constituent transformations:

1. **Articulation**: knowledge -> information
2. **Combination**: information -> information
3. **Internalization**: information -> knowledge
4. **Socialization**: knowledge -> knowledge

These labels are due to Nonaka's [7] transitions of knowledge: tacit to explicit, Articulation; explicit to explicit, Combination; explicit to tacit, Internalization; and tacit to tacit, Socialization. They are not separate dimensions and should not be separately treated.

The above sequence **A-C-I-S** of KnowIn flows is continually repeated in a circular organization of *knowledge production*.

Every enterprise, individual or collective, is engaged in two types of production:

1. Production of the other (products, services), *heteropoiesis*
2. Production of itself (ability to produce, knowledge), *autopoiesis*

Production of the other is dependent on the production of itself. Any successful, sustainable enterprise must continually produce itself, its own ability to produce, in order to produce the other, its products and services. Production, renewal and improvement of knowledge to produce is necessary for producing anything.

Knowledge production (production of itself) has traditionally been left unmanaged and uncoordinated. The focus used to be on the product or service, on "the other". In the era od global competition the omission of knowledge management is no longer affordable. Knowledge production leads to sustained competitive products and services but not the other way around. Even the most successful products do not guarantee sustained knowledge base and competitiveness of the enterprise.

The A-C-I-S cycle is concerned with *autopoiesis* [18], the production of itself. Traditional management is focused on its products and services, while neglecting its own continued ability to produce requisite knowledge for their production. Therein lies the imperative for knowledge management in the global era: information is becoming abundant, more accessible and cheaper, while knowledge is increasingly scarce, valued and more expensive commodity. There are too many people with a lot of information, but too few with useful and effective knowledge.

A-C-I-S Cycle. We can now characterize all four essential transformations in greater detail:

1. **Articulation:** transformation (knowledge -> information) is designed to describe, record and preserve the acquired, tested and provenly effective knowledge and experience in a form of symbolic description. All such symbolic descriptions, like records, manuals, recipes, databases, graphs, diagrams, digital captures and expert systems, but also books, "cookbooks" and procedures, help to create *symbolic memory* of the enterprise. This phase creates the information necessary for its subsequent combination and recombination into forms suitable for new and effective action.
2. **Combination:** transformation (information -> information) is the simplest as it is the only one taking place entirely in the symbolic domain. This is the content of traditional information management and technology (IT). It transforms one symbolic description into another, more suitable (actionable) symbolic description. It involves data and information processing, data mining, data warehousing, documentation, databases and other combinations. The purpose is to make information actionable, a useful input into coordination process.
3. **Internalization:** transformation (information -> knowledge) is the most important and demanding phase of the cycle: how to use information for effective action, for useful knowledge. Symbolic memory should not be passive,

information just laying about in libraries, databases, computers and networks. Information has to be *actively* internalized in human abilities, coordinations, activities, operations and decisions – in human action. Only through action information attains value, gains context and interpretation and - connected with the experience of the actor – becomes reflected in the quality of achieved results.

4. **Socialization:** transformation (knowledge -> knowledge) is related to sharing, propagating, learning and transfer of knowledge among various actors, coordinators and decision makers. Without such sharing through the community of action knowledge loses its social dimension and becomes ineffective. Through intra- and inter-company communities, markets, fairs and incubators we connect experts with novices, customers with specialists, employees with management for the purposes of learning through example, practice, training, instruction and debate. Learning organization can emerge and become effective only through socialization of knowledge.

The A-C-I-S cycle is continually repeated and renewed on improved, more effective levels through each iteration. All phases, not just the traditional combination of IT, have to be managed and coordinated *as a system*.

Circular KnowIn flows are stimulated, coordinated and maintained by a *catalytic function* of Knowledge Exchange Hub (KEH). This KEH functions under the supervision of KM Coordinator who is responsible for maintaining the four transformations A-C-I-S.

For the first two transformations, Tuggle and Goldfinger [11] developed a partial methodology for externalizing (or articulating) knowledge embedded in organizational processes. Any such externalization produces useful information [1]. It consists of four steps. First, a process important to the organization is selected. Second, a map of the selected process is produced (by specifying its steps and operations and identifying who is involved in executing the process, what are the inputs and the outputs). Third, the accuracy of the *process map* needs to be verified. Fourth, we examine the process map for extracting the embedded information: What does the process reveal about the characteristics of the person executing the process? What about the nature of the work performed? What about the organization in which this process occurs? Why is this process important to the organization in question? What benefit (added value) does the process contribute to the organization?

There are two forms of information extracted from the process mapping. The first extraction produces information about process structure while the second extraction produces information about process coordination. By producing a map of the process, a symbolic description of action, one extracts information about the process. The second extraction works with the process map directly (extracting information from information), i. e. shifting into Combination of A-C-I-S. It describes properties about the agent conducting the process, insights regarding the steps carried out in executing the process, and revealed understandings about the communications going on during the execution of the process.

This methodology involves only the A-C portion of the A-C-I-S cycle. The all important stages of Internalization and Socialization are not yet addressed. This incompleteness is probably due to the Nonaka [7] induced habit of treating the dimensions of A-C-I-S as separate, autonomous and independent. *They form an autopoietic cycle and cannot be separated.*

A-C-I-S cycle has *autopoietic organization* [16, 17], defined as a network of processes of:

1) *Knowledge Production (Poiesis)*: the rules governing the process of creation of new knowledge through Internalization of information.
2) *Knowledge Bonding (Linkage)*: the rules governing the process of Socialization of knowledge within the enterprise.
3) *Knowledge Degradation (Information Renewal and Replenishment)*: the rules associated with the process of transforming knowledge into information through Articulation and Combination.

All three types of constitutive processes must be well *balanced* and functioning *in harmony*. If one of the three types is missing or if one or two types predominate (out-of-balance system), then the organization can either be heteropoietic or allopoietic, i. e., capable of producing only "the other" rather than itself.

Any self-sustaining system will have the processes of production, bonding and degradation concatenated in a balanced way, so that the production rate does not significantly exceed the replenishment rate, and vice versa. *Self-sustaining systems will be autopoietic in an environment of shared or common resources;* such a business enterprise would resemble a living organism rather than mechanistic machinery.

Autopoietic knowledge systems, in spite of their rich metaphoric and anthropomorphic meanings and intuitions, are simply networks characterized by *inner coordination of individual actions achieved through communication among temporary member-agents.* The key words are coordination, communication, and limited individual life span of members. Coordinated behavior includes *both cooperation and competition.*

So we, as individuals, can coordinate our own actions in the environment only if we coordinate it with the actions of other participants in the same, intersecting or shared network. In order to achieve this, we have to in-form (change) the environment so that the actions of others are suitably modified: *we have to communicate.* As all other individuals are attempting to do the same, a *knowledge network of coordination* emerges, and, if successful, it is being "selected" and persists. Such a network then improves our ability to coordinate our own actions effectively. Cooperation, competition, altruism, and self-interest are inseparable. *Business enterprise becomes a living organism.*

Any self-sustainable system must secure, enhance and preserve communication (and thus coordinated action) among its components or agents as well as their own coordination and self-coordination competencies. Systems with limited or curtailed communication can be sustained and coordinated only through external commands or feedback; they are not self-sustaining. *Hierarchies of command are sustainable but not self-sustaining.* Their organization is machine-like, based on processing information, not on producing knowledge.

We have established that consensual (unforced) and purposeful (goal-directed) coordination of action is knowledge. Self-sustainable systems must maintain their ability to coordinate their own actions – producing *knowledge*. Self-sustaining systems must be knowledge producing, not only information, labor or money consuming entities.

6 Knowledge Based Strategy

One of the main implications of the new KM is the realization that strategy should be based on knowledge rather than information and rooted in action rather than its symbolic description.

Traditionally, the organization executives prepare a set of statements, descriptions of future action: mission, vision, set of goals, plan or pattern for action and similar artefacts. Observe that all these statements are nothing but information. It all remains to be translated into action. That is where most organization executives stumble.

How do you transform information into knowledge? How do you carry out the Internalization phase of A-C-I-S? They can all write statements, but can they do? All the statements, from mission to plan are "above the cloud line". They do not see from the high clear skies of information down into the confusing reality of knowledge. So, it does not work.

So, we have to start anew.

Strategy is about what you do, not about what you say you do or desire to do. Strategy is about action, not about description of action. Strategy is about doing, not about talking about it.

Your strategy is what you do. And what you do is your strategy.

All the rest is words.

All organizations do and so all organizations have strategy, whether or not they realize it.

Executives have to stop managing information through issuing statements and start managing knowledge through coordinating action. There are no strategic, tactical and operational levels: everything takes place below the cloud line, separating information from knowledge. Everything useful is operational.

First, one has to create a detailed map of corporate activities to find out what is company doing, reveal its own strategy. Remarkably, many corporations do not know what they do, do not know their own strategy. They only know what they say, their own statements.

Second, after creating activity map, one has to analyze the activities by benchmarking them with respect to competitors, industry standards or stated aspirations.

Third, value-curve maps are created in order to differentiate one's activities from those of competition. *Differentiation, not imitation*, is the key to competitiveness and strategy.

Fourth, selected activities are changed in order to fill the spaces revealed by value-curve maps as most effective for successful differentiatiation.

So, we change our action, and thus our strategy, without ever leaving the action domain. Our strategy remains what we are doing, even though we are doing something else. No need to implement or execute our "strategy" (set of statements) – it has already been enacted.

Executives "execute" their strategic statements. Their strategies are hard to execute. They are probably created "above the cloud line", far removed from the doing, and should not be executed at all. Their effective (forced) execution is likely to damage the corporation and its strategic resilience.

Once we have effectively changed our activities and differentiated our action, there is nothing to prevent excutives from describing the newly created strategy: They can derive their missions and visions as a description of true action, from bottom up, reflecting a real strategy – and take them above the cloud line. Their company will prosper.

Strategic management is all about doing, producing and creating. How do we produce knowledge, capability, core values, alliances, and networks? How do we do?

Therein lies the new promise and challenge of Knowledge Management.

References

1. Desouza, K. C.: Facilitating Tacit Knowledge Exchange. *Communications of the ACM*, 46 (6) (2003) 85-88
2. Dewey, J. And Bentley, A. F.: *Knowing and the Known*, Beacon Press, Boston (1949)
3. Hayek, F. A.: The Use of Knowledge in Society. *The American Economic Review*, 35(1945) 519-530
4. Hayek, F. A.: Economics and Knowledge. *Economica*, February (1937) 33-45.
5. Lewis, C. I.: *Mind and the World-Order* (1929), 2nd ed., Dover Publ., New York, (1956)
6. Maturana H. R. and Varela, F. J.: *The Tree of Knowledge* .Shambhala Publications, Inc., Boston (1987)
7. Nonaka I.: The Knowledge-Creating Company. *Harvard Business Review* 69 (6) Nov. - Dec. (1991) 96-104
8. Prusak, L.: What's up with knowledge management: A personal view. In: Cortada, J. W., Woods, J. A. (eds.): *The Knowledge Management Yearbook 1999-2000*, Butterworth-Heinemann, Woburn, MA (1999) 3-7
9. Polanyi, M.: *The Tacit Dimension*, Routledge and Keoan, London, England (1966) (Peter Smith Publ., June 1983).
10. Sveiby, K. E.: Tacit knowledge. *The Knowledge Management Yearbook 1999-2000*, eds. J. W. Cortada and J. A. Woods, Butterworth-Heinemann, Woburn, MA, 1999, pp. 18-27.
11. Tuggle, F. D., Goldfinger, W. E.: A Methodology for Mining Embedded Knowledge from Process Maps. *Human Systems Management* (2004)
12. Zeleny, M.: Management Support Systems: Towards Integrated Knowledge Management. *Human Systems Management*, 7 (1) (1987) 59-70
13. Zeleny, M.: Knowledge as a New Form of Capital, Part 1: Division and Reintegration of Knowledge. *Human Systems Management*, 8(1) (1989) 45-58; Knowledge as a New Form of Capital, Part 2: Knowledge-Based Management Systems. *Human Systems Management*, 8(2) 1989) 129-143
14. Zeleny, M.: Knowledge versus Information. In: Zeleny, M. (ed.), *IEBM Handbook of Information Technology in Business*, Thomson, London (2000) 162-168
15. Zeleny, M.: *Multiple Criteria Decision Making*. McGraw-Hill, New York (1982)
16. Zeleny M.: *Autopoiesis, Dissipative Structures, and Spontaneous Social Orders*. Westview Press, Boulder, Co. (1980)
17. Zeleny M.: *Autopoiesis: A Theory of Living Organization*. North-Holland, New York (1981)
18. Zeleny, M.: Autopoiesis (Self-Production). In: Zeleny, M. (ed.), *IEBM Handbook of Information Technology in Business*. Thomson, London (2000) 283-290

A Hybrid Nonlinear Classifier Based on
Generalized Choquet Integrals

Zhenyuan Wang[1], Hai-Feng Guo[2], Yong Shi[3], and Kwong-Sak Leung[4]

[1] Department of Mathematics,
University of Nebraska at Omaha, Omaha, NE 68182, USA
[2] Department of Computer Science,
University of Nebraska at Omaha, Omaha, NE 68182, USA
[3] Department of Information Systems and Quantitative Analysis,
University of Nebraska at Omaha, Omaha, NE 68182, USA
{zhenyuanwang, haifengguo yshi}@mail.unomaha.edu
[4] Department of Computer Science and Engineering,
The Chinese University of Hong Kong, Shatin, NT, Hong Kong
ksleung@cse.cuhk.edu.hk

Abstract. In this new hybrid model of nonlinear classifier, unlike the classical linear classifier where the feature attributes influence the classifying attribute independently, the interaction among the influences from the feature attributes toward the classifying attribute is described by a signed fuzzy measure. An optimized Choquet integral with respect to an optimized signed fuzzy measure is adopted as a nonlinear projector to map each observation from the sample space onto a one-dimensional space. Thus, combining a criterion concerning the weighted Euclidean distance, the new linear classifier also takes account of the elliptic-clustering character of the classes and, therefore, is much more powerful than some existing classifiers. Such a classifier can be applied to deal with data even having classes with some complex geometrical shapes such as crescent (cashew-shaped) classes.

1   Introduction

Classification is one of the important methods for pattern recognition [1, 10]. It has been applied in data mining widely. The simplest and fundamental model of classification is the two-class linear classifier that divides the feature space into two parts by a hyperplane. Applying any linear classifier needs a basic assumption that there is no interaction among the strengths of the influences from individual feature attributes toward the classifying attribute, that is, the joint influence from a set of feature attributes toward the classifying attribute is just a linear combination of the influences from individual feature attributes in the set toward the classifying attribute. However, the above-mentioned interaction cannot be ignored in many real problems. Due to the interaction, the geometrical shapes may be various. Some previous works [2, 3, 11, 12] have adopted nonadditive set functions to describe such an interaction among the feature attributes directly and used nonlinear integrals (such as the

Y. Shi, W. Xu, and Z. Chen (Eds.): CASDMKM 2004, LNAI 3327, pp. 34–40, 2004.

Choquet integral [4, 7, 8]) as a projector from the feature space to a one-dimensional space. As a continuation of these previous works, this paper provides a new hybrid model of nonlinear classifier that combines the Choquet deviation and the weighted Euclidean distance. Thus, the new nonlinear classifier also takes account of the elliptic-clustering character of the classes and, therefore, is much more powerful than some existing classifiers. Such a classifier can be applied to deal with data even having classes with some complex geometrical shapes such as crescent (cashew-shaped) classes.

2   Basic Concepts and Notations

Consider m feature attributes, $x_1, x_2, ..., x_m$, and a classifying attribute, y, in a database. Attributes $x_1, x_2, ..., x_m$ are numerical, while y is categorical with a range $C = \{c_1, c_2, ...,c_n\}$ where each c_k, $k = 1, 2, ..., n$, is the indicator of a class and may be symbolic or numerical. Denote $\{x_1, x_2, ..., x_m\}$ by X. The m-dimensional Euclidean space is the feature space. An n-classifier is an n-partition of the feature space with a one-to-one correspondence to C. It should be determined based on a sufficient data set. The data set consists of l observations of $x_1, x_2, ..., x_m$ and y, and has a form as

x_1	x_2	$\cdots$	x_m	y
f_{11}	f_{12}	$\cdots$	f_{1m}	y_1
f_{21}	f_{22}	$\cdots$	f_{2m}	y_2
$\vdots$				
f_{l1}	f_{l2}	$\cdots$	f_{lm}	y_l

where row

f_{i1}	f_{i2}	$\cdots$	f_{im}	y_i

is the i-th observation of attributes $x_1, x_2, ..., x_m$ and y with $f_{ij} \in (-\infty, \infty)$ and $y_i \in C$ for $i = 1, 2, ..., l$ and $j = 1, 2, ..., m$. Positive integer l is called the size of the data, and should be much larger than m. The observation of $x_1, x_2, ..., x_m$ can be regarded as a function $f : X \rightarrow (-\infty, \infty)$. It is a point in the feature space. Thus, the i-th observation of $x_1, x_2, ..., x_m$ is denoted by f_i, and we write $f_{ij} = f_i(x_j)$, $j = 1, 2, ..., m$ for $i = 1, 2, ..., l$. Let $I_k = \{i | y_i = c_k\}$, $k = 1, 2, ..., n$. Then, $\{ I_1, I_2, ..., I_n \}$ is an n-partition of index set $\{1, 2, ..., l\}$.

The interaction among the influences of feature attributes toward the classifying attribute is described by a set function μ defined on the power set of X satisfying the condition of vanishing at the empty set, i.e., μ: $P(X) \rightarrow (-\infty, \infty)$ with $\mu(\emptyset) = 0$. For convenience, we also require that $\mu(X) = 1$. Set function μ may not be additive or nonnegative, or neither. Such a set function is called a pseudo-regular signed fuzzy measure. A pseudo-regular singed fuzzy measure defined on $P(X)$ is identified with a vector of order $2^m - 2$: $(\mu_1, \mu_2, ..., \mu_{2^m-2})$, where $\mu_h = \mu(\bigcup\{x_j\})$ if h is expressed in binary digits as $h_m h_{m-1} \cdots h_1$ for every $h = 1, 2, ..., 2^m - 2$.

The generalized Choquet integral of a function, f, with respect to pseudo-regular signed fuzzy measure μ is defined by

$$\int f \, d\mu = \int_{-\infty}^{0} [\mu(F_\alpha) - 1] d\alpha + \int_{0}^{\infty} \mu(F_\alpha) d\alpha$$

when not both terms on the right-hand side are infinite, where set $F_\alpha = \{x | f(x) \geq \alpha\}$ is called the α-cut set of function f for any $\alpha \in (-\infty, \infty)$. The generalized Choquet integral can be calculated through the following formula:

$$\int f d\mu = \sum_{h=1}^{2^m - 1} z_h \mu_h$$

where

$$z_h = \begin{cases} \min_{h_j=1} f_{\cdot j} - \max_{h_j=0} f_{\cdot j}, & \text{if it is} > 0 \text{ or } h = 2^m - 1 \\ 0, & \text{otherwise} \end{cases} \quad \text{for} \quad h = 1, 2, \ldots, 2^m - 1,$$

and $\mu_{2^m-1} = 1$, in which $f_{\cdot j} = f(x_j)$. In the above expression, a convention that the maximum taken on an empty set has value zero is adopted.

Given two constants c_1 and c_2, functions $a : X \to [0, \infty)$ with $\min_{1 \leq j \leq m} a(x_j) = 0$ and $b : X \to [-1, 1]$ with $\max_{1 \leq j \leq m} |b(x_j)| = 1$, and given a pseudo-regular signed fuzzy measure μ, inequality $c_1 \leq \int (a + bf) d\mu \leq c_2$ represents a subset of the feature space. Such a region can reflect the interaction among the influences from feature attributes toward the classifying attribute and, therefore, can be adopted as a frame to each component of the n-partition of the feature space. Simply, we denote $a(x_j)$ by a_j and $b(x_j)$ by b_j for $j = 1, 2, \ldots, m$, i.e., $a = (a_1, a_2, \ldots, a_m)$ and $b = (b_1, b_2, \ldots, b_m)$.

3   Main Algorithm

(1) Input the data set. Create l, m, n, and nonempty sets I_k, $k = 1, 2, \ldots, n$.
(2) Choose a large prime s as the seed for the random number generator. Set the value for each parameter listed in the following.

λ: The bit length of each gene, i.e., λ bits are used for expressing each gene. It depends on the required precision of the results. e.g., $\lambda=10$ means that the precision is almost 10^{-3}. Its default is 10.
P and q: The population sizes used in GAI and GAII. They should be large positive even integers. Their defaults are 200 and 100 respectively.

α_1, β_1, α_2 and β_2: The probabilities used in a random switch in GAI and GAII to control the choice of genetic operators for producing offspring from selected parents. They should satisfy the condition that $\alpha_i \geq 0$, $\beta_i \geq 0$, and $\alpha_i + \beta_i \leq 1$ for $i = 1,2$. Their defaults are 0.2, 0.5, 0.2, and 0.5 respectively.

ε_1 and ε_2: Small positive numbers used in the stopping controller in GAI. Their defaults are 10^{-6} and 10^{-10} respectively.

t_1 and t_2: The limit numbers of generations that have no significant progression successively in GAI and GAII. Their defaults are 10 and 100 respectively.

w: the weight for using weighted Euclidean distance in GAI. Its default is 0.1.

(3) Let $D_k = \{f_i | i \in I_k\}$, $k = 1, 2, ..., n$. For each D_k, take it as D and run GAI. The obtained result is saved as $a^{(k)}$, $b^{(k)}$, $c^{(k)}$, $\mu^{(k)}$, $f_*^{(k)}$, s_k^2, d_k^2, and σ_k^2.

(4) Rearrange D_k, $k = 1, 2, ..., n$, as D_{p_k}, $k = 1, 2, ..., n$, such that

$$\sigma_{p_1}^2 \leq \sigma_{p_2}^2 \leq \cdots \leq \sigma_{p_n}^2$$

where ($p_1, p_2, ..., p_n$) is a permutation of $(1,2,...,n)$.

(5) From $k = 1$ to $k = n$ successively, taking $D_{p_k}^{(k)}$ as A and $\bigcup_{i>k} D_{p_i}^{(k)}$ as B, and using $a^{(p_k)}$, $b^{(p_k)}$, $c^{(p_k)}$, $\mu^{(p_k)}$, $f_*^{(p_k)}$, $s_{p_k}^2$, and $d_{p_k}^2$, run GAII, where $D_{p_i}^{(k)}$, $i = k, k+1, ..., n$, is the adjustment of D_{p_i}, i.e., the remainder of D_{p_i} by erasing those data that have already been classified into the previous classes $c_{p_{i'}}$, $i' = 1, 2, ..., k-1$. The obtained ξ_0 and η_0 are saved as ξ_{p_k} and η_{p_k}, $k = 1, 2, ..., n$.

(6) Stop.

4   Genetic Algorithm I (GAI for Determining the Location and Shape of Each Class)

Given a nonempty subset of data with a form $D = \{f_i | i \in I\}$, where I is a nonempty index set, its location and shape may be described by vectors a, b, constant c, and pseudo-regular signed fuzzy measure μ. These parameters can be determined according to the criterion that

$$s^2 = \frac{1}{|I|} \sum_{i \in I} [c - \int (a + bf_i) d\mu]^2$$

is minimized, where $|I|$ is the cardinality of I. Constant c is called the Choquet projected mean of D, μ is called the eigenmeasure of D, and $\sigma_*^2 = \min s^2$ is called the Choquet projected variance of D. The Choquet centroid of D is point f_* in the feature space whose j-th coordinate is $f_{*j} = \dfrac{c - a_j}{b_j}$ when $b_j \neq 0$, $j = 1, 2, ..., m$. Any j-th dimension of the feature space with $b_j = 0$ will be rejected and then the Choquet centroid will be considered in the relevant lower-dimensional space. Minimizing s^2 is the main criterion of the optimization. However, another criterion that the data should be as close to the Choquet centroid as possible will be also considered. Thus, a convex combination of s^2 and

$$d^2 = \frac{1}{m|I|} \sum_{i \in I} \sum_{b_j \neq 0} b_j^2 (f_{ij} - f_{*j})^2,$$

that is, $\sigma^2 = (1 - w)s^2 + wd^2$, will be adopted as the objective of the optimization, where $1 - w$ and w are the weights chosen before running the program.

A genetic algorithm [5, 6, 9] is used to determine a, b, c, and μ, with relevant f_*, s^2, and d^2 that minimize σ^2 for the given subset of data, D.

5   Genetic Algorithm II (GAII for Determining the Size of Each Class)

Once the location and the shape of a class are determined, the size of the class that will be adopted for the classification may be described by the relative Choquet deviation

$$\delta_1(f) = \frac{\left| c - \int (a + bf) d\mu \right|}{\sqrt{s^2}}$$

and the relative weighted Euclidean distance from the Choquet centroid

$$\delta_2(f) = \frac{\sqrt{\dfrac{1}{m} \sum_{b_j \neq 0} b_j^2 (f_{\cdot j} - f_{*j})^2}}{\sqrt{d^2}},$$

where f is a point in the feature space. The optimal size of the class will be determined by minimizing the misclassification rate. The problem now is simplified to be a two-class classification, i.e., to determine the best boundaries of the class with data set A, which will be used to distinguish points in this class from the others with data set B. The boundaries are expressed in terms of the relative Choquet deviation and the relative weighted Euclidean distance from the Choquet centroid when the data sets A (or adjusted A) and B are given and the information on A's location and shape is available. A genetic algorithm is used to determine the optimal constants ξ_0 and η_0 for dominating the relative Choquet deviation and the relative weighted Euclidean distance from the Choquet centroid respectively.

6   Application

Once a new observation is available, it can be classified into some class as follows.

(1) Set the value of switch SW. $SW = 0$ means classifying any outlier into some class among $c_1, c_2, \ldots$, and c_n obligatorily, while $SW = 1$ means classifying any outlier into an additional class c_{n+1}. Its default is 1.

(2) Set the value of parameter γ. It is a factor used for balancing the relative Choquet deviation and weighted Euclidean distance to the Choquet centroid of a class when an outlier is obligatory to be classified into one of the given n classes. Its default is 2.

(3) Input the new observation, $f = (f_{\cdot 1}, f_{\cdot 2}, \ldots, f_{\cdot m})$. Based on the result obtained in the main algorithm, according to the order of $p_1, p_2, \ldots, p_n$, f is classified into class c_{p_k} if it has not been classified into previous class and satisfies

$$(c^{(p_k)} - \int (a^{(p_k)} + b^{(p_k)} f) d\mu^{(p_k)})^2 \leq \xi_{p_k} \cdot s_{p_k}^2$$

and

$$\frac{1}{m} \sum_{b_j^{(p_k)} \neq 0} (b_j^{(p_k)})^2 (f_{\cdot j} - f_{*j}^{(p_k)})^2 \leq \eta_{p_k} \cdot d_{p_k}^2 .$$

Then go to step (5). In case no such a k exists for f, go to the next step.

(4) If $SW = 0$, calculate

$$\theta_k^2(f) = \frac{[c^{(k)} - \int (a^{(k)} + b^{(k)} f) d\mu^{(k)}]^2}{s_k^2} + \frac{\sum_{b_j^{(k)} \neq 0} (b_j^{(k)})^2 (f_{\cdot j} - f_{*j}^{(k)})^2}{\gamma \cdot m}$$

for $k = 1, 2, \ldots, n$. Then f is classified into class c_h if

$$\theta_h^2(f) = \min_{1 \leq k \leq n} \theta_k^2(f).$$

If $SW = 1$, classify f into c_{n+1}.

(5) Output $f \in c_h$, where h is one of 1, 2, …, n, and $n+1$. Then stop.

References

1. Devijver, P. A., Kittler, J.: Pattern Recognition: A Statistical Approach, Prentice Hall (1982)
2. Grabisch, M., Nicolas, J. M.: Classification by fuzzy integral: Performance and tests, Fuzzy Sets and Systems, Vol. 65 (1994) 255-271
3. Mikenina, L., Zimmermann, H. -J.: Improved feature selection and classification by the 2-additive fuzzy measure, Fuzzy Sets and Systems, Vol. 107 (1999) 197-218

4. Murofushi, T., Sugeno, M.: An interpretation of fuzzy measure and the Choquet integral as an integral with respect to a fuzzy measure, Fuzzy Sets and Systems, Vol. 29 (1989) 201-227

5. Wang, W., Wang, Z., Klir, G. J.: Genetic algorithm for determining fuzzy measures from data, Journal of Intelligent and Fuzzy Systems, Vol. 6 (1998) 171-183

6. Wang, Z., A new genetic algorithm for nonlinear multiregressions based on generalized Choquet integrals, Proc. FUZZ-IEEE (2003) 819-821

7. Wang, Z., Convergence theorems for sequences of Choquet integrals, Int. j. General Systems, Vol. 26 (1997) 133-143

8. Wang, Z., Klir, G. J.: Fuzzy Measure Theory, Plenum, New York (1992)

9. Wang, Z., Leung, K. S., Wang, J.: A genetic algorithm for determining nonadditive set functions in information fusion, Fuzzy Sets and Systems, Vol. 102 (1999) 463-469

10. Weiss, S. M., Kapouleas, I.: An empirical comparison of pattern recognition, neural nets, and machine learning classification methods, Proc. 11th IJCAI (1989) 781-787

11. Xu, K., Wang, Z., Heng, P. A., Leung, K. S.: Using generalized Choquet integrals in projection pursuit based classification, Proc. IFSA/NAFIPS (2001) 506-511

12. Xu, K., Wang, Z., Leung, K. S.: Classification by nonlinear integral projections, IEEE T. Fuzzy Systems, Vol. 11, No. 2 (2003) 187-201

Fuzzy Classification Using Self-Organizing Map and Learning Vector Quantization

Ning Chen

Faculdade de Ciências e Tecnologia, Universidade Nova de Lisboa, Portugal
Institute of Mechanics, Chinese Academy of Sciences, P. R. China
ningchen74@yahoo.com

Abstract. Fuzzy classification proposes an approach to solve uncertainty problem in classification tasks. It assigns an instance to more than one class with different degrees instead of a definite class by crisp classification. This paper studies the usage of fuzzy strategy in classification. Two fuzzy algorithms for sequential self-organizing map and learning vector quantization are proposed based on fuzzy projection and learning rules. The derived classifiers are able to provide fuzzy classes when classifying new data. Experiments show the effectiveness of proposed algorithms in terms of classification accuracy.

Keywords: fuzzy classification, self-organizing map (SOM), learning vector quantization (LVQ).

1 Introduction

Classification is a supervised machine learning method to derive models between features (independent variables) and class (target variable). In the past decades, classification has been widely applied to solve a great variety of classifying tasks, e.g., product marketing, medical diagnosis, credit approval, image segmentation, qualitative prediction, customer attrition causes analysis. The process of classification is to first produce models from training data in which each sample is assumed to have a predefined class and then use the models to classify new data in which the class label is unknown. Classification can be divided into crisp classification and fuzzy classification. Crisp classification produces a number of classical sets of data, in which an element is classified to only one class. However, there also exist uncertainty cases in which samples are not clear members of any class [4]. Fuzzy classification is advantageous over crisp classification on solving uncertainty problems by assigning a sample to multiple classes with different membership degrees. The membership degrees given by fuzzy classification provide some valuable information, e.g., significance of a sample belonging to a class.

Self-organizing map (SOM) and learning vector quantization (LVQ) are artificial neuron network algorithms. SOM is trained in an unsupervised way. It projects the data into neurons through a topology preserving transformation so that the neurons close to each other have similar features in the input space. Although SOM is an unsupervised learning method by nature, it can be also used for supervised tasks after the map is labeled. LVQ is performed in a supervised way which defines class regions in the data space rather than preserves topological property of data.

Y. Shi, W. Xu, and Z. Chen (Eds.): CASDMKM 2004, LNAI 3327, pp. 41–50, 2004.

Fuzzy SOM and LVQ have been studied in literature. FLVQ [2] is a batch SOM algorithm combining online weight adaptation rule with fuzzy membership assignment. The relative membership is calculated directly from the distances between the input instance and map neurons rather than the topological neighbors. Replacing crisp class with fuzzy class membership for both input samples and map neurons, a fuzzy SOM classifier is presented in [6]. The crisp labels of input samples are fuzzified by a k-nearest neighbor rule. After training, each map neuron is assigned to a class with a membership degree based on the typicalness of patterns projected on it. In this method, the fuzzy paradigm is only used in the labeling phase and has no impact on map organization. Some competitive algorithms: FALVQ 1, FALVQ 2, and FALVQ 3 support fuzzy classification using different membership functions [3]. These algorithms optimize some fuzzy cost functions, formed as the weighted sum of squared Euclidean distances between input vectors and reference vectors of neurons. However, it is noted that the optimization procedures are plagued with local minima.

In this paper, we propose two sequential algorithms for fuzzy classification using SOM and LVQ. Sequential algorithms are 'on-line' in the sense that the neurons are updated after the presentation of each input. Discarding each sample once it has been used, sequential algorithms avoid the storage of complete data set. The fuzzy SOM and LVQ algorithms are based on fuzzy projection, in which the membership values are calculated from the distance between input samples and map neurons. As opposed to [6], the fuzzy paradigm is used in both model training and model classification. In training phase, the neurons are updated according to the membership values. In classifying phase, each instance is assigned to multiple classes with different degrees. Finally, a hybrid classifier is presented combining fuzzy SOM and LVQ to hold both topology preserving property and pattern recognition capability. The performance of proposed fuzzy algorithms is investigated in terms of classification accuracy. In the remaining of the paper, section 2 describes the methodology of fuzzy classification algorithms. Experiments and results are given in section 3. Lastly, section 4 concludes the paper.

2   Fuzzy Sequential SOM and LVQ

2.1   Fuzzy Projection

SOM is an artificial neural network (ANN) which attempts to represent the input data in low dimensional grid space through a topology preserving mapping [5]. The neurons are organized on a regular grid with usually one or two dimensions. Each neuron is associated with input samples by a reference vector and connected to adjacent neurons by a neighborhood function. Suppose x_i is the ith input vector and m_j is the reference vector of the jth neuron. Crisp SOM projects x_i to map unit c which best matches to it, i.e., $c = arg\,min_j d(m_j, x_i)$, where d is the Euclidean distance. Fuzzy SOM projects x_i to m_j with a membership degree ω_{ij}, satisfying $\omega_{ij} \in [0, 1]$ and $\sum_{j=1}^{m} \omega_{ij} = 1$. Given a fuzzy parameter $\alpha \geq 1$ which controls the degree of fuzziness, the membership matrix can be calculated from the distance between input vector and reference vectors [1].

$$\text{If } \alpha = 1: \quad \omega_{ij} = \begin{cases} 1 \; d(x_i, m_j) \le d(x_i, m_l), l \ne j \\ 0 \; \text{otherwise} \end{cases}$$

$$\text{If } \alpha > 1: \omega_{ij} = \begin{cases} 1 & \text{if } x_i = m_j \\ 0 & \text{if } x_i = m_l, l \ne j \\ \dfrac{1}{\sum_{l=1}^{m} \left(\frac{d(x_i, m_j)}{d(x_i, m_l)} \right)^{\frac{1}{\alpha-1}}} & \text{otherwise} \end{cases} \tag{1}$$

2.2   Fuzzy Sequential SOM (FSSOM)

Fuzzy sequential SOM uses fuzzy match instead of crisp match and updates reference vectors according to membership degrees. The map is trained iteratively by updating reference vectors according to input samples. An input vector x_i is assigned to each neuron with a membership degree obtained by Equation 1. Then the units are updated towards the input case with a proportion of the distance between them. The incremental vector is the sum of the neighborhood function values weighted by the exponent on the membership degrees. After training, the neurons become topologically ordered on the map. Finally, the map neurons are labeled by specific classes according to classified samples. For the purpose of constructing a classifier, the fuzzy sequential SOM algorithm for model derivation is described as follows:

Step 1: Initialize the map with a lattice of neurons and reference vectors.
Step 2: Choose a sample x_i from the training data set at time t.
Step 3: Calculate the distances between x_i and reference vectors.
Step 4: Compute the membership degree of neurons with respect to x_i.
Step 5: Update the reference vectors of all neurons using fuzzy update rule:

$$m_p(t+1) = m_p(t) + \Delta m_p(t)$$
$$= m_p(t) + \gamma(t) \sum_{j=1}^{m} h_{jp} \omega_{ij}^{\alpha} (x_i - m_p(t)) \tag{2}$$

where $\gamma(t)$ is the learning rate at time t, and h is the neighborhood function of radius $\delta(t)$. Both $\delta(t)$ and $\gamma(t)$ are non-increasing functions of time.

Step 6: Repeat from Step 2 to Step 5 enough iterations until the status of map is stable.
Step 7: Input the samples of classified data and project them to best-matching units.
Step 8: Label a neuron with the class of maximal frequency occurring in the projected samples.

Usually the neighborhood radius and learning rate are bigger values at first and decrease to zero with training steps [5]. Apparently, when $\alpha = 1$, it produces a hard projection that $\omega_{ic} = 1$ (c is the best-matching unit which has the minimal distance to the input) and $\omega_{ij} = 0$ ($j \ne c$). In such case, FSSOM is equivalent to classic sequential SOM.

2.3   Fuzzy Sequential LVQ (FSLVQ)

Learning vector quantizer (LVQ), a variant of SOM, uses a supervised approach during learning. The map units are assigned by class labels in the initialization and then updated at each training step. The update way depends on the match of class labels between best-matching unit and input. If the unit has the same class to the input, the reference vector is moved close to the input, otherwise, it is moved away from the input. In contrast to crisp LVQ which updates only the best-matching unit, FSLVQ updates all units according to the memberships. As an extension of LVQ1 [5], one of basic LVQ algorithms, the fuzzy sequential LVQ algorithm is described as follows:

Step 1: Initialize the reference vector and class label for each neuron.
Step 2: Choose a sample x_i from the training data set at time t.
Step 3: Calculate the distances between x_i and reference vectors.
Step 4: Compute the membership degree of neurons with respect to x_i.
Step 5: Update the reference vector of all neurons:

$$m_p(t+1) = \begin{cases} m_p(t) + \gamma(t)\omega_{ip}^{\alpha}(x_i - m_p(t)) & \text{if class}(m_p) = \text{class}(x_i) \\ m_p(t) - \gamma(t)\omega_{ip}^{\alpha}(x_i - m_p(t)) & \text{otherwise} \end{cases} \quad (3)$$

Step 6: Repeat from Step 2 to Step 5 enough iterations.

When $\alpha = 1$, only the best-matching unit is updated, so that FSLVQ is essentially equivalent to crisp LVQ1.

2.4   Fuzzy Classifying

Once a map is trained and labeled, it can be used as a classifier for unclassified data. Fuzzy classification offers more insight of class assignment to decision makers. After calculating the membership degrees of a sample with respect to all units, the degree of the sample to one class is calculated as the sum of membership degrees with respect to the units having the same class. When a crisp assignment is needed, the classification can be done according to the class with maximal degree. If there are more than one class having the maximal degree, the first one is chosen. When $\alpha = 1$, it yields to a crisp classification, that simply assigns the input to the class of best-matching unit. Suppose $\{c_1, c_2, \cdots, c_k\}$ is the set of class labels, then the class of sample x_i is determined as follows:

$$P(x_i, c_r) = \sum_{j=1}^{m}(\omega_{ij}|\text{class}(m_j) = c_r)$$

$$class(x_i) = arg\,max_r P(x_i, c_r) \quad (4)$$

3   Experiments and Results

3.1   Hybrid Fuzzy Classifier

Although both SOM and LVQ can be used for classification, they are different in some aspects. Firstly, SOM attempts to approximately preserve the neighborhood relationship of data in a topological order fashion. LVQ tries to recognize the patterns of class with respect to other features; Secondly, SOM is trained from an initial map without class labels. LVQ needs the assignment of labels for neurons in the initialization; Next, SOM is trained in an unsupervised way without the direction of class labels. The training process is extreme data driven based on intrinsic similarity of data. LVQ is trained in a supervised way under the direction of class information. In order to possess both topology preserving property and pattern recognition capability, the unsupervised and supervised scheme can be combined in either simultaneous manner, e.g. LVQ-SOM [5], HLVQ [7], or successive manner [9].

In the hybrid fuzzy classifier, the models are derived using FSSOM followed by FSLVQ. The combination of FSSOM and FSLVQ is inspired by three reasons. First, the local neighborhood properties of trained SOM contribute to easier pattern recognition tasks, hence no pre-classified samples are required in the initial training, and only a limited number of known samples is needed in the labeling phases. This feature makes SOM particularly suitable for classification cases where there are few classified samples and allow users to avoid the expensive and tedious process of known sample collection [9]. Next, the objective of SOM is to preserve topology property of data without any consideration of class assignment. FSLVQ can be used to adjust the map neurons for better performance on pattern recognition. With labels and reference vectors induced from data clustering, FSSOM offers a better starting condition for FSLVQ training than random initialization. Next, FSSOM is very close to FSLVQ in data structure and learning scheme. In fact, to stabilize the status of FSSOM, neighborhood region usually shrinks to zero in fine-tuning step so that it is easy to change to FSLVQ in a straightforward way.

3.2   Effectiveness Study

The proposed classification algorithms are implemented based on SOM & LVQ software [8]. The following experiments are performed on Iris data set in a machine with 256M memory and intel celeron 1.03 GHz processor running windows XP professional operating system. Iris data set has 150 Iris flowers, described by four numeric features: sepal length, sepal width, petal length and petal width. The samples belong to three classes respectively: 'setosa', 'versicolor', and 'virginica'. The experiments are performed in four steps.

Step 1: The performance of proposed algorithms is evaluated using 10-fold cross validation. In each trial, nine folds are used for model exploration and the remaining is for model validation.

Step 2: For each training data, a map is initialized linearly in the two-dimensional subspace corresponding to the largest eigenvalues of autocorrelation matrix of the training data. Afterwards, the map is trained by FSSOM using a variant of fuzzy parameter from 1 to 10 in an unsupervised manner, and then labeled according to the known samples in a supervised manner. After that, FSLVQ is performed on the resultant map with the same parameters as previous training.

Step 3: In the validation, each sample of the test data set is compared to map units and assigned by the label of best-matching unit. Then the accuracy is calculated as the percent of the correctly classified samples.

Step 4: The final accuracy is obtained by calculating the average results on distinct trials.

Table 1 lists the arguments used in the experiment. The intermediate values of learning rate and neighborhood radius are linearly interpolated from the initial values to the

Table 1. Arguments of FSSOM and FSLVQ

parameters	FSSOM	FSLVQ
lattice	hexagonal	-
shape	sheet	-
map size	15×4	-
neighborhood function	gaussian	-
initial radius	2	-
final radius	1	-
training epochs	5	20
initial learning rate	0.5	0.05
learning type	inverse	const

end values. After the labeling phase, some units are not labeled because no sample is projected on them. Although these neurons maybe useful on recognizing uncertain cases in future decision making, the existence of non-labeled neurons will influence the classification accuracy. This problem is exacerbated by big maps which probably result in more unlabeled neurons. Hence, these neurons are discarded before classifying. In Table 2, the average accuracy ratios for three classes and whole test data at a varied fuzzy parameter are given. It was observed that the accuracy of fuzzy configuration has an obvious increase compared to crisp configuration. The overall accuracy increases from 94.67% to 97.33%. Fuzzy parameter over 3 do not end up with any improvement on accuracy. Starting from the resulting map of FSSOM, FSLVQ does not result in significant improvement (less than 1%) on the accuracy. This is due to the fact that Iris data has an almost unmixed cluster formulation of class regions so that FSSOM classifier performs as well as hybrid classifier.

In Figure 1, the test data is projected to a 2-dimensional subspace spanned by its two eigenvectors with greatest eigenvalues using principal component analysis (PCA). Figure 2 is the projection of classified data using crisp SOM. Figure 3 is the projection of classified data using FSSOM at fuzzy parameter of 2. In each visualization, three classes are plotted in different markers: • for 'setosa', × for 'versicolor' and * for 'virginica'. For the sake of easy detection, the misclassified samples are marked by ▶ in the last two figures. Compared to the crisp classifier which misclassifies two samples, fuzzy classifier results in only one error. It was also found that the misclassified samples occur on the boundary of class regions, where uncertain cases usually locate.

3.3   Fuzzy Classifying

In the following experiment, we use a more complex approach to classification phase which takes fuzzy parameter into account. The membership degrees of a sample to the units are calculated by Equation 1 and then the class with maximum degree is obtained by Equation 4. In each trial, a model is trained by FSSOM and FSLVQ using a random fuzzy parameter between 1 and 10 and a map size of $[4 \times 3]$. Each obtained model is validated by the same test data using different fuzzy parameters. Increasing the fuzzy parameter from 1 to 3 with a step of 0.2, the results achieved on test data are listed in Table 3. It was observed the result is quite good when fuzzy parameter is below 3, showing

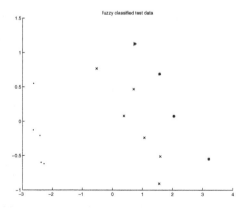

Fig. 1. PCA projection of test data

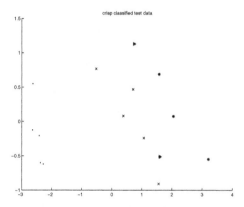

Fig. 2. PCA projection of crisp classified test data (2 errors)

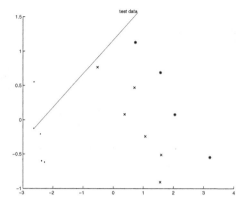

Fig. 3. PCA projection of fuzzy classified test data (1 error)

Table 2. Classification accuracy using FSSOM and FSLVQ

fuzzy	FSSOM (%)				FSSOM + FSLVQ (%)			
	setosa	versicolor	virginica	overall	setosa	versicolor	virginica	overall
1	100	90.06	95.65	94.67	100	93.39	96.90	96.00
2	100	93.81	98.33	97.33	100	93.81	98.33	97.33
3	100	92.14	97.08	96.00	100	92.14	97.08	96.00
4	100	92.14	97.08	96.00	100	92.14	97.08	96.00
5	100	92.14	97.08	96.00	100	92.14	97.08	96.00
6	100	92.14	97.08	96.00	100	92.14	97.08	96.00
7	100	92.14	97.08	96.00	100	92.14	97.08	96.00
8	100	92.14	97.08	96.00	100	92.14	97.08	96.00
9	100	92.14	97.08	96.00	100	92.14	97.08	96.00
10	100	92.14	97.08	96.00	100	92.14	97.08	96.00

that the fuzziness of classification does not degrade the accuracy while providing more information of class assignment.

Figure 4 shows the test data and map neurons in a 2-dimensional subspace. The neurons are displayed in different makers according to their labels and the number of samples is shown. For each sample, the class assignment of crisp classification and class memberships of fuzzy classification ($\alpha=2$) are given in Table 4. From the membership, the significance of an instance belonging to a class is known. Some misclassified samples are classified correctly under fuzzy strategy, for example, sample 8 is misclassified to 'virginica' in crisp case, while it is assigned to 'versicolor' in fuzzy case. Also, sample '4' and '10' are two members of 'setosa', while the latter has bigger membership (0.98) than the former (0.84). In fact, the latter is much closer to the representative neurons of 'setosa' than the former in Figure 4. It can be stated that replacing exact project with fuzzy project at a certain level in classification does not compromise the benefit of models.

Table 3. Fuzzy classification accuracy

fuzzy	FSSOM (%)				FSSOM + FSLVQ (%)			
	setosa	versicolor	virginica	overall	setosa	versicolor	virginica	overall
1.0	100	92.17	85.17	92.67	100	93.83	85.17	93.33
1.2	100	92.17	85.17	92.67	100	93.83	85.17	93.33
1.4	100	92.17	85.17	92.67	100	93.83	85.17	93.33
1.6	100	92.17	85.17	92.67	100	93.83	85.17	93.33
1.8	100	92.17	85.17	92.67	100	93.83	85.17	93.33
2.0	100	92.17	85.17	92.67	100	93.83	85.17	93.33
2.2	100	94.17	85.17	93.33	100	93.83	82.67	92.67
2.4	100	94.17	83.17	92.67	100	95.83	82.67	93.33
2.6	100	94.17	80.67	92.00	100	97.50	82.67	94.00
2.8	100	95.83	78.67	92.00	100	97.50	80.67	93.33
3.0	100	95.83	78.67	92.00	100	97.50	77.42	92.00

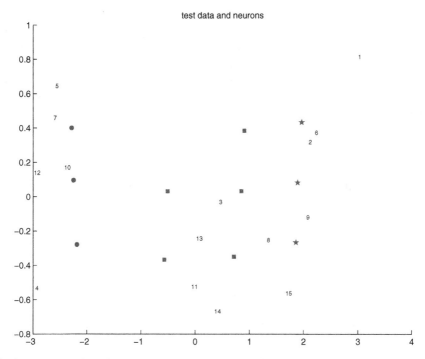

Fig. 4. PCA projection of test data and map neurons in a 2-dimensional subspace. Three classes of neurons are shown in different markers: ● for 'setosa', ■ for 'versicolor' and ★ for 'virginica'. The samples of test data are marked by their numbers

Table 4. Crisp and fuzzy classification

sample	crisp class	fuzzy classification			sample	crisp class	fuzzy classification		
		setosa	versicolor	virginica			setosa	versicolor	virginica
1	virginica	0.04	0.29	0.67	9	virginica	0.01	0.08	0.92
2	virginica	0.01	0.08	0.92	10	setosa	0.98	0.02	0.00
3	versicolor	0.02	0.90	0.08	11	versicolor	0.07	0.85	0.09
4	setosa	0.84	0.13	0.03	12	setosa	0.88	0.10	0.02
5	setosa	0.92	0.07	0.01	13	versicolor	0.05	0.86	0.08
6	virginica	0.01	0.11	0.88	14	versicolor	0.04	0.85	0.11
7	setosa	0.94	0.05	0.01	15	virginica	0.02	0.30	0.68
8	virginica	0.02	0.52	0.46					

4   Conclusion

Fuzzy classification is an extension of crisp classification using fuzzy set theory. In this paper, two fuzzy classification algorithms are proposed using sequential SOM and LVQ based on fuzzy projection. The resulting map of SOM can be used as the initialization of LVQ in a hybrid classifier, which can improve the pattern recognition ability while preserves the topology property approximately. Experimental results show that the proposed algorithms at a certain fuzzy level improve the accuracy of classification compared to crisp algorithms. It could be stated that fuzzy classification solves the uncertainty problem of samples belonging to several classes, and improves classification accuracy in future decision. Future work will mainly focus on the qualitative description of classification models.

Acknowledgements

Parts of this reported work were supported by NSFC-RGC #70201003 from National Science Foundation of China and Head Fund #0347SZ from Institute of Policy and Management, CAS.

References

1. Bezdek, James C.: Pattern recognition with fuzzy objective function algorithms. Plenum Press, New York (1981)
2. Bezdek, James C., Pal, Nikhil R.: Two soft relative of learning vector quantization. Neural Networks **8(5)** (1995) 729-743
3. Karayiannis, Nicolaos B., Pai, Pin-I: Fuzzy algorithms for learning vector quantization: generalizations and extensions. In: Steven K. Rogers (ed.): Applications and Science of Artificial Neural Networks. Proceedings of SPIE, Air Force Institute of Technology, Wright-Patterson AFB, OH, USA **2492** (1995) 264-275
4. Keller, James M., Gary, Michael R., Givens, James A.: A fuzzy k-nearest neighnor algorithm. IEEE Trans. on Systems, Man, and Cybernetics **15(4)** (1985) 580-585
5. Kohonen, T.: Self-organizing maps. Springer Verlag, Berlin, Second edition (1997)
6. Sohn, S., Dagli, Cihan H.: Self-organizing map with fuzzy class memberships. In Proceedings of SPIE International Symposium on AreoSense **4390** (2001) 150-157
7. Solaiman, B., Mouchot, Marie C., Maillard, Eric P.: A hybrid algorithm (HLVQ) combining unsupervised and supervised learning approaches. In Proceedings of IEEE International Conference on Neural Networks(ICNN), Orlando, USA (1994) 1772-1778
8. Laboratory of computer and information sciences & Neural networks research center, Helsinki University of Technology: SOM Toolbox 2.0. http://www.cis.hut.fi/projects/somtoolbox/
9. Visa, A., Valkealahti, K., Iivarinen, J., Simula, O.: Experiences from operational cloud classifier based on self-organising map. In Procedings of SPIE, Orlando, Florida, Applications of Artificial Neural Networks V **2243** (1994) 484-495

Solving Discriminant Models Using Interior Point Algorithm

Siming Huang, Guoliang Yang, and Chao Su

Institute of Policy and Management, Chinese Academy of Sciences,
Beijing 100080, China
simhua@mail.casipm.ac.cn

Abstract. In this paper we first survey the linear programming based discriminant models in the literature. We then propose an interior point algorithm to solve the linear programming. The algorithm is polynomial with simple starting point.

1 Introduction

The two-group discriminant problem has applications in many areas, for example, differentiating between good credit risks and poor ones, between promising new firms and those likely to fail, or between patients with strong prospects for recovery and those highly at risk. The two-group classification problem, sometimes referred to as the two-group discriminant problem, involves classifying an observation into one of two a prior group based on the attributes of the observation.

In some recent papers, Freed and Glover [5], Banks and Abad [2], Lee and Ord [10] proposed some linear programming-based models and some solution algorithms. While the proposed algorithms are promising, it is the objective of this paper to propose a new optimization algorithms to solve the discriminant models.

This paper presents a new efficient LP-based solution algorithms, interior point algorithms for linear programming, to optimally solve some proposed discriminant models due to the efficiency of interior point algorithm. The recent research will be used as a benchmark for the proposed interior point algorithm.

2 Proposed Discriminant Models

In this section a set of proposed discriminant models will be listed and explained.

2.1 MMD (Minimize Maximum Deviation) Model

The first and simplest, hereafter referred to as the MMD models [5], can be summarized as follows:

$$Minimize \quad \alpha$$
$$s.t. \quad A_i x \leq b + \alpha \quad for \quad all \quad A_i \ in \quad group1$$
$$A_i x \geq b - \alpha \quad for \quad all \quad A_i \ in \quad group2$$

Y. Shi, W. Xu, and Z. Chen (Eds.): CASDMKM 2004, LNAI 3327, pp. 51–60, 2004.
© Springer-Verlag Berlin Heidelberg 2004

where $x = [x_1, x_2]^T$, $A_i = [a_{i1}, a_{i2}]$, the variables satisfy:

$$x_1, x_2 \text{ and } b \text{ unrestricted in sign, } a \geq 0.$$

2.2   MSID (Minimize the Sum of Interior Distance) Model

The second LP formulation, hereafter referred to as the MSID model[5], seeks to:

$$Minimize \quad H\alpha - \sum d_i$$

$$s.t. \quad A_i x + d_i \leq b + \alpha \quad for\ all \quad A_i \quad in \quad group\,1$$

$$A_i x + d_i \geq b + \alpha \quad for\ all \quad A_i \quad in \quad group\,2$$

where the variables satisfy:

$$x \text{ and } b \text{ unrestricted in sign, } \alpha \geq 0 \text{ and } d_i \geq 0 \text{ for all } i.$$

The objective is essentially two-fold: Find the discriminant function (x) and the boundary (b) that will minimize group overlap (α) and maximize the total (interior) distance (d_i) of group members from the designated boundary hyperplane ($Ax = b$). A parametric procedure was used to produce the set of ranges on the values of H which would generate the full family of distinct MSID solutions. Thus, a given two-group problem might produce 5 or 6 solutions (i.e., discriminant functions, x), each corresponding to a specific range of values assigned to H.

2.3   MSD (Minimize Sum of Deviations) Model

The third LP model is referred to as the MSD model [5], has the form of:

$$Minimize \quad \sum \alpha_i$$

$$s.t. \quad A_i x \leq b + \alpha_i \quad for \quad all \quad A_i \quad in \quad group\,1$$

$$A_i x \geq b - \alpha_i \quad for \quad all \quad A_i \quad in \quad group\,2$$

where the variables satisfy:

$$x \quad \text{and } b \text{ unrestricted in sign } \alpha_i \geq 0, all \quad i.$$

The objective here focuses on the minimization of total (vs. maximal) group overlap. The objective has value zero when the paired groups can be separated by a hyperplane. This formulation has the advantage (over the preceding formulation) of not requiring parametric adjustment.

2.4   LAD (Least Absolute Deviations) Model

An alternative approach to the least squares method in regression analysis is the LAD method [10]. Instead of minimizing the sum of squares, a linear model is fitted by minimizing the sum of absolute deviations.

For regression analysis, many studies have compared the relative performance of the LAD procedure with the least squares method. In general, these studies suggest that the LAD estimators are more efficient when the error terms have a Laplace or some other heavy-tailed distribution. The LAD approach may be justified directly or by a likelihood argument, as we now demonstrate.

Suppose the error terms ξ_i are independent and follow the double exponential (or Laplace) distribution with zero mean and mean deviation of σ. The functional form is

$$f(\xi_i) = (2\sigma)^{-1} \exp\{-|\xi_i|/\sigma\}, i = 1, 2, ..., n.$$

As before, we consider

$$Y_i = \beta_0 + \beta' X_i + \xi_i,$$

where $Y_i = 0 \ or \ 1$ and the X_i are measured about their mean. From (2), the likelihood is

$$L = \prod_{i=1}^{n} (2\sigma)^{-1} \exp\{-|\xi_i|/\sigma\} = (2\sigma)^{-n} \exp\{-\sum|\xi_i|/\sigma\},$$

By inspection, we see that the likelihood estimators are given by minimizing the sum of the absolute deviations. This may be formulated as the following LP problem with dummy variables d_i^- and d_i^+ :

$$Minimize \qquad \sum_{i=1}^{n}(d_i^+ + d_i^-)$$

$$s.t. \qquad \beta_0^+ - \beta_0^- + \sum_{j=1}^{p}\beta_j^+ X_{ij} - \sum_{j=1}^{p}\beta_j^- X_{ij} + d_i^+ - d_i^- = Y_i$$

where

$$\beta_j^+, \beta_j^- \geq 0, j = 0, 1, 2, ..., p,$$

$$d_i^+, d_i^- \geq 0, i = 1, 2, ..., n.$$

2.5   The Hybrid Discriminant Model

We restrict attention to the two-group discriminant problem, observing that the multigroup problem can be handled by a sequential variant of the two-group approach. Notationally, we represent each data point by A_i, where $i \in G_1$ (Group 1) and $i \in G_2$ (Group 2). We seek a weighting vector x and a scalar b, providing a hyperplane of the form $Ax = b$.(This interpretation arises retrospectively by supposing variables x and b have already been determined and thus may be treated as constants; A is a row vector of variables.) The goal is to assure as nearly as possible that the points of Group 1 lie on one side of the hyperplane and those of Group 2 on the other (e.g., $A_i x < b$ for $i \in G_1$ and $A_i x > b$ for $i \in G_2$). Upon introducing objective function coefficients to discourage external deviations and encourage internal deviations, and defining $G = G_1 \bigcup G_2$, we may express the hybrid model [6] as follows.

$$Minimize \qquad h_0\alpha_0 + \sum_{i \in G} h_i\alpha_i - k_0\beta_0 - \sum_{i \in G} k_i\beta_i$$

$$s.t. \qquad A_i x - \alpha_0 - \alpha_i + \beta_0 + \beta_i = b, \qquad for \quad i \in G_1$$
$$A_i x + \alpha_0 + \alpha_i - \beta_0 - \beta_i = b, \qquad for \quad i \in G_2$$
$$\alpha_0, \beta_0 \geq 0$$
$$\alpha_i, \beta_i \geq 0, i \in G$$
$$x, b = unrestricted\ in\ sign$$

The objective function coefficients are assumed nonnegative. Appropriate values of these coefficients should satisfy $h_i \geq k_i$ for $i = 0$ and $i \in G$, and $\sum_{i \in G} h_i \geq k_0$ and $\sum_{i \in G} k_i \leq h_0$. In general, the coefficients would be chosen to make each of the foregoing inequalities strict. These restrictions can be understood by direct analysis but can also be justified as conditions essential to assuring feasibility of the linear programming dual.

2.6 MIP (Mixed Integer Programming) Model

The MIP model [2] is:

$$Min \qquad Z = \sum_{i=1}^{M_1} R_i + \alpha \sum_{i=M_1+1}^{M_1+M_2} R_i$$

$$s.t.$$

$$\sum_{j=1}^{J} W_j A_{ij} + S_i - T_i = C, \qquad for \quad i = 1, 2, ..., M_1$$

$$\sum_{j=1}^{J} W_j A_{ij} - S_i + T_i = C, \qquad for \quad i = M_1+1, ..., M_1+M_2$$

$$R_i \geq T_i, \qquad for \quad i = 1, 2, ..., M_1+M_2$$

$$T_i \geq Q_i, \qquad for \quad i = 1, 2, ..., M_1+M_2$$

$$\sum_{i=1}^{M_1+M_2} Q_i = 1, \qquad for \quad i = 1, 2, ..., M_1+M_2$$

$$Factor(1-R_i) \geq S_i, \qquad for \quad i = M_1+1, ..., M_1+M_2$$

$$S_i \geq 0 \qquad for \quad i = M_1+1, ..., M_1+M_2$$

$$T_i \geq 0 \qquad for \quad i = M_1+1, ..., M_1+M_2$$

where

A_{ij} =the value for observation i of attribute j ,

C =the unknown cutoff value(unrestricted on sign),

F_p =the prior probability of being from group p

H_p =the cost of misclassifying an observation from group p

M_p =the number of observations in group p

$$Q_i = \begin{cases} 1, \text{ if observation i is the greatest distance from the cutoff hyperplane;} \\ 0, \text{otherwise,} \end{cases}$$

$$R_i = \begin{cases} 1, \text{ if observation i is misclassified;} \\ 0, \text{otherwise,} \end{cases}$$

S_i =the correct classification deviation,

T_i =the misclassification deviation,

W_j =the unknown weight for attribute j (unrestricted on sign),

Z =the value of the objective function,

$$\alpha = (F_2 H_2 / M_2)/(F_1 H_1 / M_1) .$$

The objective function represents the expected cost of misclassification. The R_i terms are 0-1 variables. The value of R_i is to be 1 if observation i is misclassified and 0 if observation i is correctly classified. The R_i / M_p term represents the proportion of misclassifications in sample group p .In order to obtain the expected misclassification proportion for the population, the sample proportions are multiplied by the population prior probabilities of group membership, F_p .Including costs of misclassification, H_p the objective function represents the expected cost of misclassification.

The equivalent linear programming (ELP) model is:

$$Min \quad \sum_{i=1}^{M_1}(\sum_{j=1}^{J}W_jA_{ij}+S_i-C)+\alpha\sum_{i=M_1+1}^{M_1+M_2}(\sum_{j=1}^{J}-W_jA_{ij}+S_i+C)$$

s.t.

$$\sum_{j=1}^{J}W_jA_{ij}+S_i-C\leq 1, \qquad for \quad i=1,2,...M_1$$

$$-\sum_{j=1}^{J}W_jA_{ij}+S_i-C\leq 1, \qquad for \quad i=M_1+1,...,M_1+M_2$$

$$\sum_{j=1}^{J}W_jA_{ij}+S_i-C\geq 0, \qquad for \quad i=1,2,...M_1$$

$$-\sum_{j=1}^{J}W_jA_{ij}+S_i-C\geq 0, \qquad for \quad i=M_1+1,...,M_1+M_2$$

$$S_i\geq 0, \qquad for \quad i=1,2,...,M_1+M_2$$

2.7 PMM (Practical Minimal Misclassifications) Model

The practical minimal misclassifications (PMM) [2] is:

$$Min \quad Z=\sum_{i=1}^{M_1}R_i+\sum_{i=M_1+1}^{M_1+M_2}R_i$$

s.t.

$$\sum_{j=1}^{J}W_jA_{ij}\geq C-PR_i, \qquad for \quad i=1,2,...,M_1$$

$$\sum_{j=1}^{J}W_jA_{ij}\leq C+PR_i, \qquad for \quad i=M_1+1,...,M_1+M_2$$

For at least one i,

$$\sum_{j=1}^{J}W_jA_{ij}\leq C-\xi, \qquad for \quad i=1,2,...,M_1$$

$$\sum_{j=1}^{J}W_jA_{ij}\geq C+\xi, \qquad for \quad i=M_1+1,...,M_1+M_2$$

where

$$R_i=\begin{cases}1,\text{if observation i is misclassified;}\\0,otherwise\end{cases}$$

P = a positive number,

ξ =a small positive number relative to P ,and

W_j, C =are unconstrained on sign.

3 An Infeasible Interior Point Algorithm for Proposed Models

In this section we introduce a homogeneous feasibility model for linear programming for solving the models. Consider the primal and dual linear programming in standard form:
Primal problem(LP):

$$Min \qquad (c^T x)$$

$$s.t.$$

$$Ax = b$$

$$x \geq 0$$

Dual problem(LD):

$$Max \qquad (b^T y)$$

$$s.t.$$

$$s = c - A^T y$$

$$x, s \geq 0$$

We consider the following homogeneous feasibility model (HLP) introduced in Huang [8]:

$$Ax = \tau b$$

$$A^T y + s = \tau c$$

$$b^T y - c^T x = \theta$$

$$x, s, \tau, \theta \geq 0$$

The above model is an extension of the homogeneous and self-dual model for linear programming developed by Goldman and Tucker. A similar formulation was introduced by Potra and Sheng for solving semidefinite programming. It is also closely related to the shifted homogeneous primal-dual model considered by Nesterov. It is easy to see:

$$x^T s + \tau \theta = 0$$

Therefore we can obtain the following theorem immediately.

Theorem 1. The (LP) problem has a solution if and only if the (HLP) has a feasible solution $(x^*, y^*, s^*, \tau^*, \theta^*)$ such that $\tau^* > 0, \theta^* = 0$. .

Let $F_h^0 = R_{++}^n \times R^m \times R_{++}^n \times R_{++} \times R_{++}$, and $(x, y, s, \tau, \theta) \in F_h^0$ be any point, we denote the residual with respect to (HLP) as follows:

$$R_p = \tau b - Ax^0,$$

$$R_d = \tau c - A^T y^0 - s^0$$

$$r = -(\theta^0 - b^T y^0 + c^T x^0)$$

$$u = [(x^0)^T s^0 + \tau^0 \theta^0]/(n+1)$$

We define the infeasible central path neighborhood of the homogeneous problem by

$$N(\beta) = \left\{ (x, y, s, \tau, \theta) \in F_h^0 : \left\| \begin{pmatrix} Xs \\ \tau\theta \end{pmatrix} - ue_{n+1} \right\| \leq \beta u \right\}, \beta \in (0,1).$$

Search direction $(dx, dy, ds, d\tau, d\theta)$ is defined by the following linear system:

$$\begin{cases} Xds + Sdx = \gamma ue - Xs \\ \tau d\theta + \theta d\tau = \gamma u - \tau\theta \\ Adx - bd\tau = (1-\gamma)R_p \\ A^T dy + ds - d\tau c = (1-\gamma)R_d \\ d\theta - b^T dy + c^T dx = (1-\gamma)r \end{cases}$$

where $\gamma \in [0,1]$ is a parameter. It is easy to show that the above linear system has a unique solution.

Let $(dx, dy, ds, d\tau, d\theta)$ be the solution of above linear system with

$$\gamma = 1 - \frac{0.3}{\sqrt{n+1}} \text{ and}$$

$$x^1 = x^0 + dx, \ y^1 = y^0 + dy, \ s^1 = s^0 + ds$$

$$\tau^1 = \tau^0 + d\tau, \theta^1 = \theta^0 + d\theta,$$

We can then prove the following result:

Theorem 2.

(i) $(x^1, y^1, s^1, \tau^1, \theta^1) \in N(0.3)$;

(ii) $u^1 = (1 - \frac{0.3}{\sqrt{n+1}})u$;

(iii) $R_p^1 = (1 - \frac{0.3}{\sqrt{n+1}})R_p^0; R_d^1 = (1 - \frac{0.3}{\sqrt{n+1}})R_d^0; r^1 = (1 - \frac{0.3}{\sqrt{n+1}})r^0$

Corollary 1. Let $(x^k, y^k, s^k, \tau^k, \theta^k)$ be the sequence generated by path-following algorithms, then

$$R_P^k = u_k R_p^0, \quad R_d^k = u_k R_d^0, \quad r_k = u_k r_0.$$

We defined the set of ξ-approximate solutions of (LP)-(LD) by

$$F_\xi = \left\{ (x,y,s) \in R_+^n \times R^m \times R_+^n \mid x^T s \leq \xi, \|b - Ax\| \leq \xi, \|c - A^T y - s\| \leq \xi \right\},$$

and the stopping criterion of the algorithm by

$$E_k = \max\{\|R_p^k\| / \tau^k, \|R_d^k\| / \tau^k, (n+1)u_k / \tau_k^2\} \leq \xi,$$

where ξ is the tolerance.

4 Conclusions

In this paper we introduce an interior point algorithm for solving the linear programming based discriminant models in the literature. The algorithm is polynomial in its complexity with simple start. It has been implemented in practical with good efficiency. Therefore we think it can also solve the LP discriminant models efficiently. We have applied it to some data mining problems (support vector machine) and it showed that the interior point algorithms is one of the best in solving the data mining problems. The result will appear in an up coming paper.

References

[1] Bajgier, S. M., Hill, A. V.: An Experimental Comparison of Statistical and Linear Programming Approaches to the Discriminant Problem. Decision Sciences, 13 (1982) 604-618

[2] Banks, W. J., Abad, P. L.: An Efficient Optimal Solution Algorithms for the Classfication Problem. Decision Sciences, 21 (1991) 1008-1023

[3] Freed, N., Glover, F.: A Linear Programming Approach to the Discriminant Problem. Decision Sciences, 12 (1981) 68-74

[4] Freed, N., Glover, F.: Resolving Certain Difficulties and Improving the Classification Power of LP Discriminant Analysis Formulations. Decision Sciences, 17 (1986) 589-595

[5] Freed, N., Glover, F.: Evaluating Alternative Linear Programming Models to Solve the Two-group Discriminant Problem. Decision Sciences, 17 (1986) 151-162

[6] Glover, F., Keene, S., Duea, B.: A New Class of Models For the Discriminant Problem. Decision Sciences, 19 (1988) 269-280.

[7] Glover, F.: Improved Linear Programming Models for Discriminant Analysis. Decision Sciences 21 (1990) 771-784.

[8] Huang, S.: Probabilistic Analysis of Infeasible Interior-Point Algorithms for Linear Programming. Working Paper, Institute of Policy and Management, Chinese Academy of Sciences, Beijing 100080, China (2003)

[9] Koehler, G. J., Erenguc, S. S.: Minimizing Misclassifications in Linear Discriminant Analysis. Decision Sciences 21 (1990) 62-85

[10] Lee, C. K., Ord, J. K.: Discriminant Analysis Using Least Absolute Deviations, Decision Sciences 21 (1990) 86-96

[11] Markowski, E. P., Markowski, C. A.: Some Difficulties and Improvements in applying linear programming Formulations to the Discriminant Problem. Decision Sciences 16 (1985) 237-247

[12] Ragsdate, G. T., Stam, A.: Mathematical Programming Formulations for the Discriminant Problem: An Old Dog Does New Tricks. Decision Sciences 22 (1991)

[13] Rubin, P. A.: A Comparison of Linear Programming and Parametric Approaches to the Two-Group Discriminant Problem. Decision Sciences 21 (1990) 373-386

[14] Rubin, P. A.: Separation Failure in Linear Programming Discriminant Models. Decision Sciences, 22 (1991) 519-535

[15] Stam, A., Joachimsthaler, E. A.: Solving the classification Problem in Discriminant Analysis Via Linear and Nonlinear Programming Methods. Decision Sciences (1989) 285-293

[16] Yarnold, P. R., Soltsik, R. C.: Refining Two-Group Multivariable Classification Models Using Univariate Optimal Discriminant Analysis. Decision Sciences 22 (1991) 1158-1164

A Method for Solving Optimization Problem in Continuous Space Using Improved Ant Colony Algorithm*

Ling Chen[1,2], Jie Shen[1], Ling Qin[1], and Jin Fan[1]

[1] Department of Computer Science, Yangzhou University, Yangzhou 225009
[2] National Key Lab of Advanced Software Tech, Nanjing Univ. Nanjing 210093
{lchen, yzshenjie, fanjin}@yzcn.net
qllynne@hotmail.com

Abstract. A method for solving optimization problem with continuous parameters using improved ant colony algorithm is presented. In the method, groups of candidate values of the components are constructed, and each value in the group has its trail information. In each iteration of the ant colony algorithm, the method first chooses initial values of the components using the trail information. Then, crossover and mutation can determine the values of the components in the solution. Our experimental results of the problem of nonlinear programming show that our method has much higher convergence speed and stability than that of GA, and the drawback of ant colony algorithm of not being suitable for solving continuous optimization problems is overcome.

1 Introduction

Ant colony algorithm (AC) has emerged recently as a new meta-heuristic for hard combinatorial optimization problems. This meta-heuristic also includes evolutionary algorithms, neural networks, simulated annealing which all belong to the class of problem-solving strategies derived from nature. The first AC algorithm was introduced by Dorigo, Maniezzo, and Colorni[1], using as example the Traveling Salesman Problem (TSP)[2]. With the further study in this area, ant colony algorithm is widely applied to the problems of Job-shop Scheduling[3], Quadratic Assignment Problem (QAP)[4,5], the Sequential Ordering Problem (SOP)[6] and some other NP complete hard problems[7-11]. It demonstrates its superiority of solving complicated combinatorial optimization problems.

The AC algorithm is basically a multi-agent system where low level interactions between single agents, i.e., artificial ants, result in a complex behavior of the whole ant colony. AC algorithms have been inspired by colonies of real ants, which deposit a chemical substance called pheromone on the ground. This substance influences the choices they make: the larger amount of pheromone is on a particular path, the larger

---

* This research was supported in part by Chinese National Science Foundation, Science Foun
dation of Jaingsu Educational Commission, China.

Y. Shi, W. Xu, and Z. Chen (Eds.): CASDMKM 2004, LNAI 3327, pp. 61–70, 2004.

probability is that an ant selects the path. Artificial ants in AC algorithms behave in similar way. Thus, these behaviors of ant colony construct a positive feedback loop, and the pheromone is used to communicate information among individuals finding the shortest path from a food source to the nest. Ant colony algorithm simulates this mechanism of optimization, which can find the optimal solutions by means of communication and cooperation with each other.

Here we briefly introduce AC and its applications to TSP. In the TSP, a given set of n cities has to be visited exactly once and the tour ends in the initial city. We denote the distance between city i and j as d_{ij} ($i,j = 1,2,\ldots, n$). Let $_{ij}(t)$ be the intensity of trail information on edge (i, j) at time t, and use it simulate the pheromone of real ants. Suppose m is the total number of ants, in time t the kth ant selects from its current city i to transit from to city j according to the following probability distribution:

$$
p_{ij}^k(t) = \begin{cases} \dfrac{\tau_{ij}^\alpha(t)\eta_{ij}^\beta(t)}{\sum_{r\in allowedk} \tau_{ij}^\alpha(t)\eta_{ij}^\beta(t)}, & j \in allowed_k \\ 0, & otherwise \end{cases}
\tag{1}
$$

where $allowed_k$ is a set of the cities can be chosen by the kth ant at city i for the next step , η_{ij} is a heuristic function which is defined as the visibility of the path between cities i and j , for instance it can defined as $1/ d_{ij}$, parameters α and β determine the relative influence of the trail information and the visibility. The algorithm becomes a traditional greedy algorithm while $\alpha = 0$, and a complete heuristic algorithm with positive feedback while $\beta = 0$. It will take an ant n steps to complete a tour of traversing all the cities. For every ant its path traversing all the cities forms a solution. The intensity of trail information should be changed by the updating formula:

$$
\tau_{ij}(t+1) = \rho\, \tau_{ij}(t) + \Delta\, \tau_{ij}
\tag{2}
$$

where $\rho \in (0,1)$, and $(1-\rho)$ represents the evaporation of $\tau_{ij}(t)$ between time t and $t+1$, $\Delta\tau_{ij}$ is the increment of $\tau_{ij}(t)$:

$$
\Delta\tau_{ij} = \sum_{k=1}^{m} \Delta\, \tau_{ij}^k
\tag{3}
$$

Here, $\Delta\tau_{ij}^k$ is the trail information laid by the kth ant the path between cities i and j in step t, it takes different formula depending the model used. For example, in the most popularly used model called "ant circle system" it is given as:

$$
\Delta\tau_{ij}^k = \begin{cases} Q/L_k, & if\ the\ k th\ ant\ passes\ edge(i, j)\ in current tour \\ 0, & otherwise \end{cases}
\tag{4}
$$

where Q is a constant, L_k is the total length of current tour traveled by the kth ant. These iterations will end when a certain terminal condition is satisfied.

The essence of the optimization process in ant colony algorithm is that:

1. Learning mechanism: the more trail information a edge has, the more probability it being selected;
2. Updating mechanism: the intensity of trail information on the edge would be increased by the passing ants and decreased by evaporation;
3. Coorperative mechanism: communications and cooperations between individuals by trail information enable the ant colony algorithm to have strong capability of finding the best solutions.

However, the classical ant colony algorithm also has its defects. For instance, since the moving of the ants is stochastic, while the population size is large enough, it could take quite a long time to find a better solution of a path. Based on the algorithm introduced above M.Dorigo et al improved the classical AC algorithm and proposed an much more general algorithm called "Ant-Q System"[12,13]. This algorithm allow the path which has the most intensive trail information to has much higher probability to be selected so as to make full use of the learning mechanism and stronger exploitation of the feedback information of the best solution. In order to overcome the stagnation behavior in the Ant-Q System, T. Stutzle et al presented the MAX-MIN Ant System[14] in which the Allowed range of the trail information in each edge is limited to a certain interval. On the other hand, L.M.Gambardella et al proposed the Hybrid Ant System (HAS)[15]. In each iteration of HAS, local probe is made for each solution by constructed by ants was used so as to find the local optimal. The previous solutions of the ants would be replaced by these local optimal solutions so as to improve the quality of the solutions quickly. Moreover, H.M.Botee et al make a thorough study on the adjustment of the parameter α, β, m and ρ and obtained the optimal combination of these parameters using GA [16]. L. Chen et al also have proposed an ant colony algorithm based on equilibrium of distribution and ant colony algorithm with characteristics of sensation and consciousness [17,18], which enhance the optimization ability of ACA and broaden its application area. The problems of the convergence and parallelization of the ant colony algorithm have also been studied to speedup the ant colony optimization [19,20].

Since the ants can only choose limited and fixed paths at each stage, the ant colony algorithm demand of discrete search space and is not suitable for solving continuous optimization problems such as linear or non-linear programming. The main issue when extending the basic approach to deal with continuous search spaces is how to model a continuous nest neighborhood with a discrete structure. Recently, some research works have extended AC algorithm to real function optimization problems. Bilchev and Parmee [21]. for example, proposed an adaptation of the Ant Colony model for continuous problems. They proposed to represent a finite number of directions whose origin is a common base point called the nest. Since the idea is to cover eventually all the continuous search space, these vectors evolve over time according to the fitness values of the ants. In this paper, we present a new method for solving optimization problem in continuous space. In this method, the set of candidate paths the ants to select is dynamic and unfixed. Since genetic operations of crossover and mutate are used to determine the value of each component, the solutions obtained will tend to be more diverse and global, and the values of the components can be selected in a continuous space. Group of candidate values for each component is constructed and each value in the group has its trail information. In each iteration of the algorithm, the method first chooses initial values of the components from its candidate values using the trail information, then the values of the components in the solution can be determined by the operations of crossover and mutation. Our experimental results on non-linear programming (NLP) problem show that our method has much higher convergence speed and stability than that of GA. Our method can also be applied to other problems with continuous parameters or problems with massive candidates in each stage, it widens the applying scope of ant colony system.

2 Solving Continuous Optimization Problems

In this section, we introduce our method using the following nonlinear programming (NLP) problem as an example:

$$\min G(x_1, x_2, ..., x_n)$$

$$Subject \quad to \quad a_{i1}x_1 + a_{i2}x_2 + ... + a_{in}x_n \geq b_i \quad (i = 1, 2, ..., r)$$

Here, objective function G is a given non-linear function, constraint conditions which represented by a set of inequalities form a convex domain of R^n. We can obtain the minimal n-d hyper-cube which encloses this convex domain by transforming the inequalities. The hyper-cube obtained can be defined the following in equalities :

$$l_i \leq x_i < u_i \quad (i = 1, 2, ..., n)$$

Let the total number of ants in the system be m and the m initial solution vectors are chosen at random. All the ith components of these initial solution vectors construct a group of candidate values of the ith components of solution vector. If we use n vertices to represent the n components and the edges between vertex i and vertex $i+1$ to represent the candidate values of component i, a path from the start vertex to the last vertex represents a solution vector whose n edges represent n components of the solution vector. We denote the jth edge between vertex i and $i+1$ as (i, j) and intensity of trail information on edge (i, j) at time t as $\tau_{ij}(t)$. Each ant start at the first vertex, select n edges in turn according to a certain possibility distribution and reaches the last vertex to complete a tour. In order to enhance the diversity of the component values, we update the selected m values of each component using genetic operations of crossover and mutation. When all components have got their m new values, m new solutions are obtained. Then we update the trail information of the edges on each path. After each iteration, each component will have 2m candidate values which consists of its m former candidate values and its m new values. Then from these 2m values the m new candidate values with higher trail information should be selected to form a new set of candidate values. This process is iterated until a certain terminal condition is satisfied. The framework of our algorithm is described as follows:

1 Generate m initial solutions at random and compute
  their fitness, then construct the groups of candidate values for each component using these m solutions. The initial trail information of each candidate is set just as the fitness value of the corresponding initial solution.

2 While (not the terminal conditions) do
    2.1 for i=1 to n do   /* for n components */
    2.1.1   for k=1 to m do   /* for m ants */
        Select an initial value for the kth ant
        in the group of candidate values of
        component i with the probability p_{ij}^{k}
        (t) given by Eq.(5);
        end for k
    2.1.2   Perform operations of crossover and muta-
        tion on the m values to get m new values ,
        then add the new values to the group of
        candidate values for component i.
        end for i
        Using the component values finding by the m
        ants form m solutions of a new generation,
        then compute the fitness of these m solutions.
        Denote the fitness of the kth solution as f_k
    2.2 for k= 1 to m do
        for i= 1 to n do
        if the kth ant choose the jth candidate
        value from the ith group of component
        then $\tau_{ij} = \tau_{ij} + f_k$
        end for i
        end for k
    2.3 for i= 1 to n do   /* for n components */
        for k= 1 to m do   /* for m ants */
        Add kth solution's ith component into ith
        group of candidate with trail information f_k
        end for i
        end for k
    2.4 for i=1 to n do   /* for n components */
        Choose m values in the ith candidate group
        with highest trail information and construct
        a new group to replace the old one.
        end for i
    end while

In line 2.1.1 of the algorithm, an ant choose the jth value in the candidate group of component i at time t according to the following probability distribution:

$$p_{ij}^k(t) = \frac{\tau_{ij}(t)}{\sum\limits_{r=1}^{m} \tau_{ir}(t)} \tag{5}$$

Here, $\tau_{ij}(t)$ is the intensity of trail information of the jth candidate value of the group for component i at time t, it is changing dynamically.

3 Adaptive Crossover and Mutation

Line 2.1.2 of the algorithm introduced above is to have crossover and mutation on the m values selected for component i. To get high speed of convergence and avoid excessive local optimization, we adopt self-adaptive crossover and mutation operations. The probabilities of operations and the range of values are determined dynamically by the quality of solutions.

Suppose $x_i(1)$ and $x_i(2)$ are two initial values of component i which is going to be crossovered, the fitness of the two solutions they belonged to are f_1, f_2. Assume the crossover probability set by the system is p_{cross}, then the actual crossover probability for $x_i'(1)$ and $x_i'(2)$ is as $p_c [x_i'(1), x_i'(2)] = p_{cros}(1 - \dfrac{f_1 + f_2}{2f_{max}})$, here f_{max} is the maximal fitness of the current generation. The higher fitness the two solutions $x_i'(1)$, $x_i'(2)$ have, the lower $p_c [x_i'(1), x_i'(2)]$ is. Generate a random number $p \in [0,1]$, the crossover operation could be carried out only if $p > p_c$. In the operation of crossover, we first generate two stochastic numbers c_1 and $c_2 \in [-b, b]$ so that $c_1 + c_2 = 1$ here $b = 2 \bullet (1 - \dfrac{f_1 + f_2}{2f_{max}})$. The results of the crossover operation $x_i'(1)$ and $x_i'(2)$ can be obtained by the following affine combination of $x_i(1)$ and $x_i(2)$:

$$x_i'(1) = c_1 x_i(1) + c_2 x_i(2)$$

$$x_i'(2) = c_2 x_i(1) + c_1 x_i(2)$$

It can easily be seen that the lower fitness $x_i(1)$ and $x_i(2)$ have, the larger value range crossover operation has.

In the mutation of a component value x, the real mutate probability p_m is determined according to the fitness f of the solution where x belongs to. Suppose the mutation probability set by the system is p_{mutate}, we let $p_m = p_{mutate}(1 - f / f_{max})$. If a solution has much higher fitness f, its values of components will have much lower mutate probability p_m, and the values of components in better solutions would has greater chance to be preserved. Generate a random number $p \in [0,1]$, mutate operation is implemented only if $p > p_m$. Suppose x_i will transformed into x_i' after mutation and $l_i \leq x_i \leq u_i$, to ensure $x_i' \in [l_i, u_i]$, define $r_i = (u_i - l_i)/2$, $d_i = |x_i - r_i|$, and x_i' can be obtained by:

$$x_i^{'} = x_i + sign(x_i - l_i - r_i)\sigma(f,t)(d_i + r_i)$$

Here, $\delta(f, t)$ is a stochastic number between [-1,1], and it has greater chance of the tendency to be 0 with the increment of the value of fitness f and generation number t, $\delta(f, t)$ is determined by this formula:

$$\sigma(f,t) = re^{-\lambda tf}$$

Here r is also a stochastic number between [-1,1], λ is the parameter who decides the extent of diversity and adjusts the area of local probe, it can be selected between 0.005 and 0.01. As a result, the component values derived from a solution with higher fitness f will have smaller mutate scope and causes a local probe. On the contrary, the process becomes a global probe when f is large and the mutate scope is wide enough. The mutate scope of the component value is reduced gradually while the number of iterations is increased. In this way, the convergent process could be controlled when generation number is very large so as to accelerate the speed of convergence.

4 Experimental Results

The algorithm presented in this paper was coded in C language performed on a Pentium PC. The computational testing of the new algorithm was carried out applying the code to the standard test problems G1 to G5 from the literature, and comparing the results to those of GA algorithm, under identical experimental conditions. We let $m=25$, $p_{cross} = 0.9$, $p_{mutate}=0.05$ and perform 20 trials on each problem. The data given as follows is the average numbers of iteration required to find the best solution.

Table 1. Comparision of our algorithm with GA applied to NLP instances

instance	iteration numbers to find the best solution		the time to find the best solution(s)	
	GA	Our algorithm	GA	Our algorithm
G1	924.03	674.97	73.52	66.36
G2	4846.36	3480.13	365.65	245.83
G3	5673.21	4945.66	478.45	370.85
G4	5283.67	3126.61	433.86	269.01
G5	4698.15	3767.32	336.51	252.23
average	4285. 084	3198. 938	337.598	240.856

Table 1 shows us that, the average number of iterations to reach the best solution on G1 to G5 using GA is 4285.084, the average number is 3198.938 while using our algorithm. This fact shows that our algorithm has a stronger capability of finding optical solutions than GA, and it saves much more computing time. The experimental results illustrate that our algorithm is very effective solving continuous optimization problems.

Fig.1 shows the process of the best solution of G1 using both our algorithm and GA. It is obvious that the speed of reaching the best solution using our algorithm is higher than that of using GA. In our algorithm, after reaching the best solution, the curse fluctuates within a very narrow scope around the best solution, this confirms the conclusion that our algorithm has a good convergence. We also test G1 and G2 with our algorithm and GA on 10 trials each of which have 500 iterations on G1 and 1500

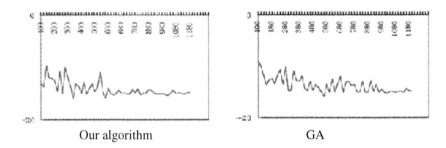

| Our algorithm | GA |

Fig. 1. The process of the best solution

Table 2. The best objective function values obtained by our algorithm and GA on G1, G2

instance	optimal	method	iteration	the best solution	average	SD
G1	-15.000	GA	500	-12.389 -11.668 -14.325 -13.678 -14.172 -14.741 -10.426 -14.128 -13.546 -13.96	-13.303	1.302
		Our method	500	-14.912 -12.028 -14.565 -14.999 -14.004 -13.905 -14.516 -13.237 -14.971 -14.608	-14.175	0.889
G2	7049.331	GA	1500	7790.456 9000.892 8670.341 7343.457 7523.292 8345.125 7393.463 8919.336 7600.835 8346.263	8093.346	606.434
		Our method	1500	8001.275 7623.291 7232.513 7813.922 8417.061 7576.237 7018.501 7936.463 7113.901 7026.182	7575.935	449.627

iterations on G2. The best objective function values of each trial, their average value, and their standard deviation (SD), are listed in table 2.

The experimental results of 10 trials show that the standard deviation is much lower using our algorithm than that of using GA, this demonstrates that our algorithm is superior in stability. The reason our algorithm has much higher convergence and stability is that component values of the solutions are obtained by genetic operations on the values of the components of different solutions in the previous generation, this leads to solutions of new generation be more diverse and global so as to avoid the prematurity. On the other hand, since each component chooses its values of the next generation from a group of candidate values in which most of the component values evolved are from solutions with better fitness, this makes the new solutions have strong capability of optimization in all directions so that better solutions can be constructed in a short period of time.

5   Conclusions

To overcome the drawback of classical ant colony algorithm of not being suitable for continuous optimizations, a method for solving optimization problem with continuous parameters using improved ant colony algorithm is presented. In the method, the candidate paths to be selected by the ants is changing dynamically rather than being fixed, and the solutions will tent to be diverse and global by means of using genetic operations on the component values of the paths at every stage. Groups of candidate values of the components are constructed, and each value in the group has its trail information. In each iteration of the algorithm, the method first chooses initial values of the components using the trail information. Then, crossover and mutation can determine the values of the components in the solution. This enables us to select the component values from a continuous space. Thus, our method can solve continuous optimization problems using ant colony algorithm successfully. Our experimental results of the problem of nonlinear programming show that our method has much higher convergence speed and stability than that of GA. Furthermore, our method can also be applied to other problems with continuous parameters.

References

1. Dorigo, M., Maniezzo, V., Colorni A.: Ant system: Optimization by a colony of coorperating agents. *IEEE Trans. On SMC*, 26(1) (1996) 28-41
2. Dorigo, M, Gambardella, L. M.: Ant Colony System: A cooperative learning approach to the traveling salesman problem. *IEEE Trans. On Evolutionary Computing*, 1(1) (1997) 53-56
3. Colorni, A., Dorigo, M., Maniezzo, V.: Ant colony system for job-shop scheduling. *Belgian J. of Operations Research Statistics and Computer Science*, 34(1) (1994) 39-53
4. Maniezzo V, Exact and approximate nonditerministic tree search procedures for the quadratic assignment problem. *INFORMS J. Comput.* 11 (1999) 358-369
5. Maniezzo V, Carbonaro A.: An ANTS heuristic for the frequency assignment problem, *Future Generation Computer Systems,* 16 (2000) 927-935

6. Gambardella, L. M., Dorigo, M.: HAS-SOP: An Hybrid Ant System for the Sequential Ordering Problem. Tech. Rep. No. IDSIA 97-11, IDSIA, Lugano, Switzerland (1997)
7. Hadeli, Valckenaers, P., Kollingbaum, M., Van Brussel, **H.:** Multi-agent coordination and control using stigmergy. *Computers in Industry,* 53(1) (2004) 75-96
8. Eggers, J., Feillet, D., Kehl, S., Wagner, M. O., Yannou, **B.:** Optimization of the keyboard arrangement problem using an Ant Colony algorithm. *European Journal of Operational Research,* 148(3) (2003) 672-686
9. Gravel, M., Price, W. L., Gagné, C.: Scheduling continuous casting of aluminum using a multiple objective ant colony optimization metaheuristic. *European Journal of Operational Research,* 143(1) (2002) 218-229
10. Shelokar, P. S., Jayaraman, V. K., Kulkarni, B. D.: An ant colony classifier system: application to some process engineering problems, *Computers & Chemical Engineering,* 28(9) (2004) 1577-1584
11. Scheuermann, B., So, K., Guntsch, M., Middendorf, M., Diessel, O., ElGindy, H., Schmeck, H.: FPGA implementation of population-based ant colony optimization , *Applied Soft Computing, 4*(3) (2004) 303-322
12. Gambardella, L., Dorigo, M.: Ant-Q: A reinforcement learning approach to the traveling salesman problem. *Proceedings of the 11th International Conference on Evolutionary Computation* (1996) 616-621
13. Dorigo, M, Luca, M.: A study of Ant-Q. *Proceedings of 4th International Conference on Parallel Problem from Nature*, Springer Verlag, Berlin (199) 656-665
14. Stutzle, T., Hoos, H. H.: Improvements on the Ant System: Introducing the MAX-MIN Ant System. *Artificial Neural Networks and Genetic Algorithms.* Springer Verlag, New York (1988) 245-249
15. Gambaradella L.M., Dorigo M.: HAS-SOP: Hybrid ant system for the sequential ordering problem. *Technical Report,* IDSIA (1997)
16. Botee H. M., Bonabeau E.: Evolving ant colony optimization. *Adv. Complex Systems*, 1 (1998) 149-159
17. 17 Chen, L., Shen, J., Qin, L.: An Adaptive Ant Colony Algorithm Based on Equilibrium of Distribution. *Journal of Software,* 14(6) (2003) 1148-1151
18. Chen, L., Qin, L. et al. Ant colony algorithm with characteristics of sensation and consciousness. *Journal of System Simulation*, 15(10) (2003) 1418-1425
19. Gutjahr, W. J.: ACO algorithms with guaranteed convergence to the optimal solution. *Information Processing Letters,* 82(3) (2002) 145-153
20. Randall, M., Lewis, A.: A Parallel Implementation of Ant Colony Optimization. *Journal of Parallel and Distributed Computing,* 62(9) (2002) 1421-1432
21. Bilchev, G., Parmee, I. C.: The ant colony metaphor for searching continuous design spaces. In: Fogarty, Y., ed., Lecture Notes in Computer Science 993, (1995) 25-39.
22. Shen, J., Chen, L.: A new approach to solving nonlinear programming, *Journal of Systems Science and Systems Engineering,* 11(1) 2002 (28-36)

Data Set Balancing

David L. Olson

University of Nebraska, Department of Management, Lincoln, NE 68588-0491 USA
dolson3@unl.edu

Abstract. This paper conducts experiments with three skewed data sets, seeking to demonstrate problems when skewed data is used, and identifying counter problems when data is balanced. The basic data mining algorithms of decision tree, regression-based, and neural network models are considered, using both categorical and continuous data. Two of the data sets have binary outcomes, while the third has a set of four possible outcomes. Key findings are that when the data is highly unbalanced, algorithms tend to degenerate by assigning all cases to the most common outcome. When data is balanced, accuracy rates tend to decline. If data is balanced, that reduces the training set size, and can lead to the degeneracy of model failure through omission of cases encountered in the test set. Decision tree algorithms were found to be the most robust with respect to the degree of balancing applied.

1 Introduction

Data mining technology is used increasingly by many companies to analyze large databases in order to discover previously unknown and actionable information that is then used to make crucial business decisions. This is the basis for the term "knowledge discovery". Data mining can be performed through a number of techniques, such as association, classification, clustering, prediction, and sequential patterns. Data mining algorithms are implemented from various fields such as statistics, decision trees, neural networks, fuzzy logic and linear programming. There are many data mining software product suites, to include Enterprise Miner (SAS), Intelligent Miner (IBM), Clementine (SPSS), and Polyanalyst (Megaputer). There are also specialty software products for specific algorithms, such as CART and See5 for decision trees, and other products for various phases of the data mining process.

Data mining has proven valuable in almost every academic discipline. Understanding business application of data mining is necessary to expose business college students to current analytic information technology. Data mining has been instrumental in customer relationship management [1] [2], financial analysis [3], credit card management [4], banking [5], insurance [6], tourism [7], and many other areas of statistical support to business. Business data mining is made possible by the generation of masses of data from computer information systems. Understanding this information generation system and tools available leading to analysis is fundamental for business students in the 21st Century. There are many highly useful applications in practically every field of scientific study. Data mining support is required to make sense of the masses of business data generated by computer technology.

Y. Shi, W. Xu, and Z. Chen (Eds.): CASDMKM 2004, LNAI 3327, pp. 71–80, 2004.

A major problem in many of these applications is that data is often skewed. For instance, insurance companies hope that only a small portion of claims are fraudulent. Physicians hope that only a small portion of tested patients have cancerous tumors. Banks hope that only a small portion of their loans will turn out to have repayment problems. This paper examines the relative impact of such skewed data sets on common data mining algorithms for two different types of data – categorical and continuous.

2 Data Sets

The paper presents results of experiments on outcome balancing using three simulated data sets representative of common applications of data mining in business. While simulated, these data sets were designed to have realistic correlations across variables. The first model includes loan applicants, the second data set insurance claims, and the third records of job performance.

2.1 Loan Application Data

This data set consists of information on applicants for appliance loans. The full data set involves 650 past observations, of which 400 were used for the full training set, and 250 for testing. Applicant information on age, income, assets, debts, and credit rating (from a credit bureau, with red for bad credit, yellow for some credit problems, and green for clean credit record) is assumed available from loan applications. Variable Want is the amount requested in the appliance loan application. For past observations, variable On-Time is 1 if all payments were received on time, and 0 if not (Late or Default). The majority of past loans were paid on time.

Data was transformed to obtain categorical data for some of the techniques. Age was grouped by less than 30 (young), 60 and over (old), and in between (middle aged). Income was grouped as less than or equal to $30,000 per year and lower (low income), $80,000 per year or more (high income), and average in between. Asset, debt, and loan amount (variable Want) are used by rule to generate categorical variable risk. Risk was categorized as high if debts exceeded assets, as low if assets exceeded the sum of debts plus the borrowing amount requested, and average in between. The categorical data thus consisted of four variables, each with three levels. The continuous data set transformed the original data to a 0-1 scale with 1 representing ideal and 0 the nadir for each variable.

2.2 Insurance Fraud Data

The second data set involves insurance claims. The full data set includes 5000 past claims with known outcomes, of which 4000 were available for training and 1000 reserved for testing. Variables include claimant age, gender, amount of insurance claim, number of traffic tickets currently on record (less than 3 years old), number of prior accident claims of the type insured, and Attorney (if any). Outcome variable Fraud was 0 if fraud was not detected, and 1 if fraud was detected.

The categorical data set was generated by grouping Claimant Age into three levels and Claim amount into three levels. Gender was binary, while number of tickets and prior claims were both integer (from 0 to 3). The Attorney variable was left as five discrete values. Outcome was binary. The continuous data set transformed the original data to a 0-1 scale with 1 representing ideal and 0 the nadir for each variable.

2.3 Job Application Data

The third data set involves 500 past job applicants, of which 250 were used for the full training set and 250 reserved for testing. This data set varies from the first two in that there are four possible outcomes (unacceptable, minimal, adequate, and excellent, in order of attractiveness).

Some of these variables were quantitative and others are nominal. State, degree, and major were nominal. There is no information content intended by state or major. State was not expected to have a specific order prior to analysis, nor was major. (The analysis may conclude that there is a relationship between state, major, and outcome, however.) Degree was ordinal, in that MS and MBA are higher degrees than BS. However, as with state and major, the analysis may find a reverse relationship with outcome.

The categorical data set was created by generating three age groups, two state outcomes (binary), five degree categories, three majors, and three experience levels. The continuous data set transformed the original data to a 0-1 scale with 1 representing ideal and 0 the nadir for each variable.

3 Experiments

These data sets represent instances where there can be a high degree of imbalance in the data. Data mining was applied for categorical and continuous forms of all three data sets. For categorical data, decision tree models were obtained using See5, logistic regression from Clementine, and Clementine's neural network model applied. For continuous data sets, See5 was used for a regression tree, and Clementine for regression (discriminant analysis) and neural network. In each case, the training data was sorted so that a controlled experiment could be conducted. First, the full model was run. Then the training set was reduced in size by deleting cases with the most common outcome until the desired imbalance was obtained.

The correct classification rate was obtained by dividing the correctly classified test cases by the total number of test cases. This is not the only useful error metric, especially when there is high differential in the cost by error type. However, other error metrics would yield different solutions. Thus for our purposes, correct classification rate serves the purpose of examining the degradation of accuracy expected from reducing the training set in order to balance the data.

3.1 Loan Data Results

The loan application training set included 45 late cases of 400, for a balance proportion of 0.1125 (45/400). Keeping the 45 late cases for all training sets, the training set size was reduced by deleting cases with on-time outcomes, for late-case proportions of 0.15 (300 total), 0.2 (225 total), 0.25 (180 total), and 0.3 (150 total). The correct classification rates and cost results are shown in Tables 1 through 6.

The first test is shown in Table 1, using a decision tree model on categorical data.

Using the full training set had a relatively low proportion of late cases (0.1125). This training set yielded a model predicting all cases to be on-time, which was correct in 0.92 of the 250 test cases. As the training set was balanced, the correct classification rate deteriorated, although some cases were assigned to the late category. Note that this trend was not true throughout the experiment, as when the training set was reduced to 150 cases, the correct classification rate actually increased over the results for training set sizes of 180 and 225.

Table 2 shows the results of the logistic regression model on categorical data.

Here the full training set was again best. Balancing the data yielded the same results from then on.

Table 3 shows the results for a neural network model on categorical data.

Table 1. Categorical Loan Data, Decision Tree

Train	Proportion Late (0)	Predict 0 = 1	Predict 1 = 0	Correct
400	0.1125	20	0	0.920
300	0.1500	20	0	0.920
225	0.2000	9	39	0.808
180	0.2500	9	39	0.808
150	0.3000	9	32	0.836

Table 2. Categorical Loan Data, Logistic Regression

Train	Proportion Late (0)	Predict 0 = 1	Predict 1 = 0	Correct
400	0.1125	17	6	0.908
300	0.1500	9	34	0.828
225	0.2000	9	34	0.828
180	0.2500	9	34	0.828
150	0.3000	9	34	0.828

Table 3. Categorical Loan Data, Neural Network

Train	Proportion Late (0)	Predict 0 = 1	Predict 1 = 0	Correct
400	0.1125	20	0	0.920
300	0.1500	15	17	0.872
225	0.2000	13	26	0.844
180	0.2500	13	26	0.844
150	0.3000	9	43	0.792

The results for this model were consistent with expectations. Reducing the training set to balance the outcomes yielded less and less accurate results.

Tests were also conducted on continuous data with the same three algorithms. Table 4 gives the results for a linear regression model on continuous data. These results were similar to those obtained with categorical data. Here there was an anomaly with the training set of 180 observations, but results were not much different from expectations.

Table 5 shows results for a discriminant analysis model applied to the continuous data.

These results were slightly better than those obtained for categorical data, exhibiting the expected trend of decreased accuracy with smaller training set.

Table 6 shows the results for the neural network model applied to continuous data.

Table 4. Continuous Loan Data, Regression Tree

Train	Proportion Late (0)	Predict 0 = 1	Predict 1 = 0	Correct
400	0.1125	20	0	0.920
300	0.1500	15	15	0.880
225	0.2000	8	46	0.784
180	0.2500	9	41	0.800
150	0.3000	8	46	0.784

Table 5. Continuous Loan Data, Discriminant Analysis Regression

Train	Proportion Late (0)	Predict 0 = 1	Predict 1 = 0	Correct
400	0.1125	20	0	0.920
300	0.1500	19	1	0.920
225	0.2000	16	7	0.908
180	0.2500	13	20	0.868
150	0.3000	11	28	0.844

Table 6. Continuous Loan Data, Neural Network

Train	Proportion Late (0)	Predict 0 = 1	Predict 1 = 0	Correct
400	0.1125	19	2	0.916
300	0.1500	17	10	0.892
225	0.2000	11	28	0.844
180	0.2500	9	33	0.832
150	0.3000	8	46	0.784

The neural network model for continuous data was slightly less accurate than the results obtained from applying a neural network model to categorical data. The trend in accuracy was as expected.

As expected, the full training set yielded the highest correct classification rate, except for two anomalies. Data mining software has the capability of including a cost function that could be used to direct algorithms in the case of decision trees. That was not used in this case, but it is expected to yield parallel results (greater accuracy according to the metric driving the algorithm would be obtained with larger data sets). The best of the six models was the decision tree using categorical data, pruning the training set to only 150 observations.

Continuous data might be expected to provide greater accuracy, as it is more precise than categorical data. However, this was not borne out by the results. Continuous data is more vulnerable to error induced by smaller data sets, which could have been one factor.

3.2 Fraud Data Set

The fraud data set was more severely imbalanced, including only 60 late cases in the full training set of 4000. Training sets of 3000 (0.02 late), 2000 (0.03 late), 1000 (0.06 late), 600 (0.1 late), 300 (0.2 late), and 120 (0.5 late) were generated. Table 7 shows the decision tree model results.

Only two sets of results were obtained. The outcome based on larger training sets was degenerate – assigning all cases to be OK (not fraudulent). This yielded a very good correct classification rate, as only 22 of 1000 test cases were fraudulent.

Table 8 gives results for the logistic regression model.

Table 7. Fraud Data Set, Categorical Data, Decision Tree

Train	Proportion Fraud (1)	Predict 0 = 1	Predict 1 = 0	Correct
4000	0.015	22	0	0.978
3000	0.020	22	0	0.978
2000	0.030	22	0	0.978
1000	0.060	17	8	0.975
600	0.100	17	8	0.975
300	0.200	17	8	0.975
120	0.500	17	8	0.975

Table 8. Fraud Data Set, Categorical Data, Logistic Regression

Train	Proportion Fraud (1)	Predict 0 = 1	Predict 1 = 0	Correct
4000	0.015	20	2	0.978
3000	0.020	19	2	0.979
2000	0.030	19	2	0.979
1000	0.060	17	9	0.974
600	0.100	17	9	0.974
300	0.200	16	34	0.950
120	0.500	11	229	0.760*

*Model with 120 in training set included 31 null predictions, due to no training case equivalent to test case

Balancing the data from 4000 to 3000 training cases actually yielded an improved correct classification rate. This degenerated when training file size was reduced to

1000, and the model yielded very poor results when the training data set was completely balanced, as only 120 observations were left. For the logistic regression model, this led to a case where the test set contained 31 cases not covered by the training set.

Table 9 shows results for the neural network model applied to categorical data. The neural network model applied to categorical data was quite stable until the last training set where there were only 120 observations. At that point, model accuracy became very bad.

Table 10 displays results for the regression tree applied to continuous data.

The regression tree for continuous data had results very similar to those of the decision tree applied to categorical data. For the smaller training sets, the continuous data yielded slightly inferior results.

Table 11 gives results for the discriminant analysis model.

Table 9. Fraud Data Set, Categorical Data, Neural Network

Train	Proportion Fraud (1)	Predict 0 = 1	Predict 1 = 0	Correct
4000	0.015	20	1	0.979
3000	0.020	20	2	0.978
2000	0.030	20	2	0.978
1000	0.060	19	2	0.979
600	0.100	19	2	0.979
300	0.200	17	17	0.966
120	0.500	10	461	0.529

Table 10. Fraud Data Set, Continuous Data, Regression Tree

Train	Proportion Fraud (1)	Predict 0 = 1	Predict 1 = 0	Correct
4000	0.015	22	0	0.978
3000	0.020	22	0	0.978
2000	0.030	22	0	0.978
1000	0.060	20	8	0.972
600	0.100	17	18	0.965
300	0.200	17	18	0.965
120	0.500	15	57	0.928

Table 11. Fraud Data Set, Continuous Data, Discriminant Analysis Regression

Train	Proportion Fraud (1)	Predict 0 = 1	Predict 1 = 0	Correct
4000	0.015	22	0	0.978
3000	0.020	22	0	0.978
2000	0.030	22	0	0.978
1000	0.060	17	18	0.965
600	0.100	17	18	0.965
300	0.200	17	18	0.965
120	0.500	13	265	0.722

The discriminant analysis model using continuous data had results with fewer anomalies than logistic regression obtained with categorical data, but was slightly less accurate. It also was not very good when based upon the smallest training set. The neural network model based on continuous data was not as good as the neural network model applied to categorical data, except that the degeneration for the training set of 120 was not as severe.

Table 12 shows relative accuracy for the neural network model applied to the continuous data.

Table 12. Fraud Data Set, Continuous Data, Neural Network

Train	Proportion Fraud (1)	Predict 0 = 1	Predict 1 = 0	Correct
4000	0.015	22	0	0.978
3000	0.020	22	0	0.978
2000	0.030	22	1	0.977
1000	0.060	20	9	0.971
600	0.100	19	10	0.971
300	0.200	17	23	0.960
120	0.500	10	334	0.656

Overall, application of models to the highly imbalanced fraud data set behaved as expected for the most part. The best fit was obtained with logistic regression and neural network models applied to categorical data. Almost all of the models over the original data set were degenerate, in that they called all outcomes OK. The exceptions were logistic regression and neural network models over continuous data. The set of runs demonstrated the reverse problem of having too small a data set. The neural network models for both categorical and continuous data had very high error rates for the equally balanced training set, as did the logistic regression model for categorical data. There was a clear degeneration of correct classification rate as the training set was reduced, along with improved cost results, except for these extreme instances.

3.3   Job Applicant Data Results

This data set was far more complex, with correct classification requiring consideration of a four by four outcome matrix. The original data set was small, with only 250 training observations, only 7 of which were excellent (135 were adequate, 79 minimal, and 29 unacceptable). Training sets of 140 (7 excellent, 66 adequate, 38 minimal, and 29 unacceptable), 70 (7 excellent and 21 for each of the other three categories), 35 (7 excellent, 10 adequate, and 9 for the other two categories), and 28 (all categories 7 cases) were generated. Results are shown in Table 13.

The proportion correct increased as the training set size increased. This was because there were three ways for the forecast to be wrong. A naïve forecast would be expected to be correct 0.25 of the time. The correct classification rate was more erratic in this case. Smaller training sets tended to have lower correct classification rates, but the extreme small size of the smaller sets led to anomalies in results from the decision tree model applied to categorical data. The results from the logistic regression model were superior to that of the decision tree for the training sets of size 250 and 140. The other results, however, were far inferior, and for the very small training sets were degenerate with no results reported. Neural network model results over categorical data were quite good, and relatively stable for smaller data sets. There was, however, an anomaly for the training data set of 70 observations.

Table 13. Job Applicant Data Set, Categorical Data, Decision Tree

	28 training	35 training	70 training	140 training	250 training
Proportion excellent	0.25	0.20	0.10	0.05	0.028
Decision tree	0.580	0.584	0.444	0.508	0.508
Logistic regression	degenerate	Degenerate	0.400	0.588	0.608
Neural net – categorical	0.416	0.448	0.392	0.604	0.604
Regression tree	0.484	0.484	0.444	0.556	0.600
Discriminant analysis	0.508	0.544	0.520	0.572	0.604
Neural net - continuous	0.432	0.516	0.496	0.592	0.588

Results for the regression tree model applied to continuous data was inferior to that of the decision tree applied to categorical data except for the largest training set (which was very close in result). Discriminant analysis applied to continuous data also performed quite well, and did not degenerate when applied to the smaller data sets. The neural network model applied to continuous data was again erratic. Neural network models worked better for the data sets with more training observations.

4 Results

The logistic regression model had the best overall fit, using the full training set. However, this model failed when the data set was reduced to the point where the training set did not include cases that appeared in the test set. The categorical decision tree model was very good when 140 or 250 observations were used for training, but when the training set was reduced to 70, it was very bad (as were all categorical models. The decision tree model again seemed the most robust. Models based upon

Table 14. Comparison

Factor	Positive Features	Negative Features
Large data sets (unbalanced)	Greater accuracy	Often degenerate (decision tree, regression tree, discriminant model)
Smaller data sets (balanced)	No degeneracy	Can miss test instances (logistic) May yield poor fit (categorical neural network model)
Categorical data	Slightly greater accuracy (but mixed results)	Less stable (small data set performance often the worst)

continuous data did not have results as good as those based on categorical data for most training sets. Table 14 provides a comparison of data set features based upon these results.

5 Conclusions

Key findings are that when the data is highly unbalanced, algorithms tend to degenerate by assigning all cases to the most common outcome. When data is balanced, accuracy rates tend to decline. If data is balanced, that reduces the training set size, and can lead to the degeneracy of model failure through omission of cases encountered in the test set. Decision tree algorithms were found to be the most robust with respect to the degree of balancing applied.

Simulated data sets representing important data mining applications in business were used. The positive feature of this approach is that expected data characteristics were controlled (no correlation of outcome with gender or state, for instance; positive correlations for educational level and major). However, it obviously would be better to use real data. Given access to such real data, similar testing is attractive. For now, however, this set of experiments has identified some characteristics data mining tools with respect to the issue of balancing data sets.

References

1. Drew, J.H., Mani, D.R., Betz, A.L., Datta, P.: Targeting customers with statistical and data-mining techniques, *Journal of Service Research* **3**:3 (2001) 205-219.
2. Garver, M.S.: Using data mining for customer satisfaction research, *Marketing Research* **14**:1 (2002) 8-17.
3. Cowan, A.M.: Data mining in finance: Advances in relational and hybrid methods, *International Journal of Forecasting* **18**:1 (2002) 155-156.
4. Adams, N.M., Hand, D.J., Till, R.J.: Mining for classes and patterns in behavioural data, *The Journal of the Operational Research Society* **52**:9 (2001) 1017-1024.
5. Sung, T.K., Chang, N., Lee, G.: Dynamics of modeling in data mining: Interpretive approach to bankruptcy prediction, *Journal of Management Information Systems* **16**:1 (1999) 63-85.
6. Smith, K.A., Willis, R.J., Brooks, M.: An analysis of customer retention and insurance claim patterns using data mining: A case study, *The Journal of the Operational Research Society* **51**:5 (2000) 532-541.
7. Petropoulos, C., Patelis, A., Metaxiotis, K., Nikolopoulos, K., Assimakopoulos, V.: SFTIS: A decision support system for tourism demand analysis and forecasting, *Journal of Computer Information Systems* **44**:1 (2003), 21-32.

Computation of Least Square Estimates Without Matrix Manipulation

Yachen Lin[1] and Chung Chen[2]

[1] JPM Chase, Division of Private Label Cards, 225 Chastain Meadows Ct,
Kennesaw, GA 30152, USA
Yachen_Lin@fnanb.com
[2] School of Management, Syracuse University,
Syracuse, NY 13244, USA

Abstract. The least square approach is undoubtedly one of the well known methods in the fields of statistics and related disciplines such as optimization, artificial intelligence, and data mining. The core of the traditional least square approach is to find the inverse of the product of the design matrix and its transpose. Therefore, it requires storing at least two matrixes - the design matrix and the inverse matrix of the product. In some applications, for example, high frequency financial data in the capital market and transactional data in the credit card market, the design matrix is huge and on line update is desirable. Such cases present a difficulty to the traditional matrix version of the least square approach. The reasons are from the following two aspects: (1) it is still a cumbersome task to manipulate the huge matrix; (2) it is difficult to utilize the latest information and update the estimates on the fly. Therefore, a new method is demanded. In this paper, authors applied the idea of CIO-component-wise iterative optimization and propose an algorithm to solve a least square estimate without manipulating matrix, i.e. it requires no storage for the design matrix and the inverse of the product, and furthermore it can update the estimates on the fly. Also, it is rigorously shown that the solution obtained by the algorithm is truly a least square estimate.

1 Introduction

In recent years, e-commerce has grown exponentially. As the amount of information recorded and stored electronically grows ever large, it becomes increasingly useful and essential to develop better and more efficient ways to store, extract, and process information. In fact, it is clear that so far our achievements on acquiring data and storing data have been far more ahead than those on analyzing data. With the availability of huge information, it has been found in many cases that the well-known methodologies have shown difficulties to be applied directly because of the size of information being processed or because of the way of information being utilized. Such difficulties in the real applications present an uncompromising challenge for academic researchers and practitioners. At the same time, business and industry have been demanding new tools for their tasks of in-depth data analysis. The born of a

Y. Shi, W. Xu, and Z. Chen (Eds.): CASDMKM 2004, LNAI 3327, pp. 81–89, 2004.
© Springer-Verlag Berlin Heidelberg 2004

research area called data mining is partially due to the demands of this kind. People, in the field of data mining, have no longer confined themselves with assumptions of the underlying probability space and distributions. They only treat the data as a set of close related objects for given tasks; certainly, some tasks may take the same statistical settings of assumptions.

Why dose the size of data bring such a revolutionary change? In statistical text books, a nice result is usually obtained when the sample size tends to infinity under regular assumptions such as a given probability space and an underlying distribution. People may tend to think it is fine to apply the asymptotic results when the sample size is larger than a few hundreds. Indeed it is maybe useful, in many cases, to apply the asymptotic results when the sample size is larger than a few hundreds and smaller than a few hundred thousands, but may not be useful at all for the case that the sample size is larger than few millions (Lin (2001)) for some problems. The fact is that the size matters! A penny may not be significant, but when it is amplified by millions, it becomes significant. Such an effect of large quantities in business is called the Gigabyte effect due to the fact that information recorded and processed needs a few Giga bytes to store. The phenomenon that from the change of quantity to the change of quality reveals an underlying truth that the assumption of a given probability space and distribution is not sufficient. This insufficiency, we believe, is partially caused by entangled signals in the data. When the size becomes extremely large, the entangled signals will be significant not only in the desirable dimension but also in unexpected dimensions.

The size of data being processed for a regular OLAP (On-Line Analytical Processing) task in a credit card issuer of medium size is usually about a few million observations. An OLAP task may come from one of the following categories: (1) decisions for potential customers; (2) decisions for existing non-default customers; (3) decisions for default customers. The first category focuses on whether or not to extend credit, and if yes, by how much, which is known as acquisition decision making. The second category is for those decisions including increasing or lowering the credit limit, authorization, reissue, and promotion. The third category contains several decisions regarding to delinquent or default customers, which is known as collection or recovery, such as making a computer generated letter, a phone call, or sending a business or an attorney letter, assigning to an external collection agency. Any action taken will be based on the assessment of risk or profit on the individual account level and is usually including those like computing the values from predictive models. There are three categories of predictive models in terms of the final outcomes: (a) predicted likelihood, (b) expected values, and (c) real values. The last two categories usually involve the computing for the estimates of real values, and for these cases, the least square approach is often one of the preferred. Considering transactional based real value predictive models, which are used to directly predict the profit or revenue of accounts or used in updating the profiles of accounts, millions of transactions are processed through these models in each single day. If the traditional least square approach were used in the computation, it would cost (1) larger computing resources due to the stored matrixes, (2) unstable results in some cases due to the singularity of matrixes, and (3) virtually impossible to update the least square estimates on the fly due to the lack of such an algorithm. Therefore, the natural question is raised: how can we overcome the barriers of the traditional matrix version of the least square approach and find a least square solution without these problems?

In order to answer the question, we need to re-exam the core of the traditional least square approach: it is to find the inverse of the product of the design matrix and its transpose. In such an approach, it requires at least to store two matrixes - the design matrix and the inverse matrix of the product (many variations of matrix manipulation for least square estimates in the literature all require to store these matrixes, although the sizes of the matrixes have been reduced and varied due to the improvement of the algorithms). As such, we can say that the core in the heart of the traditional least square approach is the matrix manipulation, which, although is neat, brings with the potential problems stated above in computing resources, in stability, and in on-going updating when the size of matrix is large. Based on these observations, the new algorithms should come from the category of the non-matrix version, that is, algorithms without matrix manipulation.

In the current study, we propose an algorithm to solve a least square estimate without manipulating matrix, i.e. it requires no storage for the design matrix and the inverse of the product, and furthermore it can update the estimates on the fly. The algorithm proposed is based on the principle, as we called - CIO, the component-wise iterative optimization, which will become clear in the next section. Section 3 gives a theoretical proof that indeed the proposed algorithm generates a least square solution.

2   The Component-Wise Iterative Optimization and Algorithm

Given a linear model,

$$y_i = \beta_0 + \beta_1 x_1 + \cdots + \beta_p x_p + \varepsilon_i, \tag{2.1}$$

where ε_i is a random term, $i = 1, 2, \cdots, n$, and its objective function is

$$S(\beta_0, \beta_1, \ldots, \beta_p) = \sum_{i=1}^{n} (y_i - \beta_0 - \beta_1 x_{i1} - \cdots - \beta_p x_{ip})^2. \tag{2.2}$$

A least square estimate $\hat{\beta}$ of $\beta = (\beta_0, \beta_1, \cdots, \beta_p)^t$ is defined as a solution of

$$S(\hat{\beta}_0, \hat{\beta}_1, \ldots, \hat{\beta}_p) = \min_{\beta \in R^p} S(\beta_0, \beta_1, \ldots, \beta_p)$$

$$= \min_{\beta \in R^p} \sum_{i=1}^{n} (y_i - \beta_0 - \beta_1 x_{i1} - \cdots - \beta_p x_{ip})^2.$$

Theoretically, $\hat{\beta}$ has a nice closed form in terms of X and Y, where X and Y are the design matrix and response vector, respectively. It is well-known that $\hat{\beta} = (XX')^+ X'Y$. In theory, we have solved the problem. But in practice, we still need to find the inverse, $(XX')^+$. Thus, there are many algorithms proposed to solve the inverse due to different conditions. However, all those algorithms, no matter how different they appeared, have the following two items in common: (1) all observations need to present in memory, (2) the inverse of the matrix needs to be in memory also. Due to the above two constrains, the OLAP task using the current algorithms for least square solutions has to be kept for a relatively small to a medium size of data, i.e. up to a few hundred thousands observations. Also to update the least square estimate, we have to make all the observations available at the time when a transaction occurred. For a relative large credit card issuer, this means huge memory and CPU resources and sometimes non-practical. Considering the current approaches, the key is the matrix manipulations. If we can find a way around this, we may be able to save memory and CPU resources and make the approach more applicable. To avoid storing a huge matrix, we have to explore a totally new way to solve the least square problem.

Starting from the early 80's, the Gibbs sampling has been drawn on much attention and later has been developed into a field called MCMC. The idea in the Gibbs sampling is that the underlying population may be either unknown or very complicated, however, given any component, the conditional distribution is known or relatively easy to simulate. They basic procedure is the following:

Step 0. Pick $x_0 = (x_{01}, x_{02}, \cdots, x_{0k})$ in the support of $F(X) = F(x_1, x_2, \cdots, x_k)$, the underlying population.

Step 1. Compute $x_1 = (x_{11}, x_{12}, \cdots, x_{1k})$ in the following way:

(1) Draw x_{11} from the distribution of $x_1 | (x_2 = x_{02}, \cdots, x_k = x_{0k})$,

(2) Draw x_{12} from the distribution of $x_2 | (x_1 = x_{11}, x_3 = x_{03}, \cdots, x_k = x_{0k})$, ...,

   continue the same procedure to the last component.

(3) Draw x_{1k} from the distribution of $x_k | (x_1 = x_{11}, x_2 = x_{12}, \cdots, x_{k-1} = x_{1k-1})$.

Thus, the first cycle of Gibbs sampling is achieved and we can update $x_0 = (x_{01}, x_{02}, \cdots, x_{0k})$ to the $x_1 = (x_{11}, x_{12}, \cdots, x_{1k})$. Repeat the Step 1 for n-1 times, and then get to Step n.

Step n. Following the same procedure, we can get $x_n = (x_{n1}, x_{n2}, \cdots, x_{nk})$.

By some regular assumptions, we can prove that $x_n \xrightarrow{\ F\ } x$ in distribution.

These steps of Gibbs sampling present a typical procedure of CIO-the component-wise iterative optimization. The idea of CIO can also be seen from many other topics such as EM algorithms. In the E-step, the conditional expectation of the missing component given the likelihood of the complete data is calculated with respect to the observed data. In the M-step, it maximizes for the underlying model. The CIO proposes a principle that the complicated problem can be solved iteratively by a series of relatively simple solutions. A general study has been carried out, and some fruitful results can be found in (Lin (2003)), which includes more rigorous studies on its theoretical foundation.

Applying the idea of CIO to the problem of the matrix version of the least square approach discussed in the beginning of this section, we proposed the following algorithm. From this algorithm, readers can get a much clearer picture about how the procedure of CIO can pave the way to propose a new algorithm.

Non-matrix Version of Algorithm for Solving the Least Square Estimates
Given (2.1) and (2.2), the following algorithm generates a solution of least square estimates for $\beta = (\beta_0, \beta_1, \cdots, \beta_p)^t$.

Step 1: Objective Function: Take $S(\beta_0, \beta_1, ..., \beta_p) = \sum_{i=1}^{n} (y_i - \beta^t X_i)^2$,

the sum of squares as the objective function, , the goal is to find a solution of $\hat{\beta}$ of $\beta = (\beta_0, \beta_1, \cdots, \beta_p)^t$ such that

$$S(\hat{\beta}_0, \hat{\beta}_1, ..., \hat{\beta}_p) = \min_{\beta \in R^p} S(\beta_0, \beta_1, ..., \beta_p).$$

Step 2. Initial Value: Choose an initial value of $\beta^{(0)} = (\beta_0^{(0)}, \beta_1^{(0)}, \cdots, \beta_p^{(0)})^t$ for β randomly or by certain optimal rules.

Step 3. Updating the Intercept: (1) Given the ith pattern of $(y_i, x_{i1}, \cdots, x_{ip})$ and the kth iterations for updating β, take the value for the intercept at k^{th} iterations as $\beta_0^{(k)}(i) = y_i - \sum_{j=1}^{p} \beta_j^{(k-1)} x_{ij}$.

(2) Repeat (1) of Step 3 for all sample patterns $\beta_0^{(k)}(i)$, $i = 1, \cdots, n$,   and let

$$\beta_0^{(k)} = \frac{1}{n} \sum_{i=1}^{n} \beta_0^{(k)}(i).$$

Step 4. Updating the Slops: (1) Given the ith pattern of $(y_i, x_{i1}, \cdots, x_{ip})$ and the kth iterations for updating β, take the value for the slop β_l, $l = 1, \cdots, p$, at k^{th} iterations as

$$\beta_l^{(k)}(i) = \left(y_i - \beta_0^{(k)} - \sum_{j=1}^{l-1} \beta_j^{(k)} x_{ij} - \sum_{j=l+1}^{p} \beta_j^{(k-1)} x_{ij} \right) / x_{il}.$$

(2) Repeat of (1) Step 4 for all patterns $\beta_l^{(k)}(i)$, $i = 1, \cdots, n$,   and let

$$\beta_l^{(k)} = \sum_{i=1}^{n} \frac{x_{il}^2}{\sum_{i=1}^{n} x_{il}^2} \beta_l^{(k)}(i), \quad l = 1, 2, \cdots, p.$$

Step 5. Updating β: Set $\beta \leftarrow \beta^{(k)} = (\beta_0^{(k)}, \beta_1^{(k)}, \cdots, \beta_p^{(k)})^t$.

Remarks: (1) From the algorithm, we can see that it follows exactly the procedure of CIO. Each component of the parameter is optimized iteratively given others and then finally the whole parameter optimized.

(2) Each updating cycle or iteration is finished by updating the components one by one. Up to certain cycles, say k^{th}, $\beta^{(k)}$ and $\beta^{(k-1)}$ generate the similar values for the given objective function. If we change the size of sample patterns, we have a series of estimates $\left\{\beta^{(k)}_{(n)}\right\}$.

(3) The implementation can be in a much simpler way:

$$\beta_0^{(k)} = \frac{1}{n}\sum_{i=1}^{n}\left(y_i - \sum_{j=1}^{p}\beta_j^{(k-1)}x_{ij}\right)$$

$$\beta_l^{(k)} = \sum_{i=1}^{n}\frac{x_{il}}{\sum_{i=1}^{n}x_{il}^2}\left(y_i - \beta_0^{(k)} - \sum_{j=1}^{l-1}\beta_j^{(k)}x_{ij} - \sum_{j=l+1}^{p}\beta_j^{(k-1)}x_{ij}\right), \quad l=1,2,\cdots,p.$$

Thus, the case of x_{il} being zero is no longer an issue.

3   The Proposed Algorithm Generates a Least Square Solution

From the last section, we have mentioned that the proposed algorithm possesses some useful asymptotic properties such as strong consistence and asymptotic normal. In this section, we will prove that the proposed algorithm generates a least square solution computationally. From the proof, readers will have a chance to appreciate insightful nature of the procedure of CIO.

Theorem. Given the setting of (2.1) and the objective function of (2.2), in the kth and $k+1^{th}$ iterations for estimating β using the proposed algorithm of Section 2, where $\beta^{(k)} = (\beta_0^{(k)}, \beta_1^{(k)}, ..., \beta_p^{(k)})^t$ and $\beta^{(k+1)} = (\beta_0^{(k+1)}, \beta_1^{(k+1)}, ..., \beta_p^{(k+1)})^t$ denote the estimates in the kth and $k+1^{th}$ iterations, respectively, we have that

$$S(\beta_0^{(k)},\beta_1^{(k)},\cdots,\beta_p^{(k)}) \geq S(\beta_0^{(k+1)},\beta_1^{(k+1)},\cdots,\beta_p^{(k+1)}) \tag{3.1}$$

where the equality holds if and only if $\beta_i^{(k)} = \beta_i^{(k+1)}$, $i=0,1,...,p$. Under the equality, $\beta^{(k)} = (\beta_0^{(k)}, ..., \beta_p^{(k)})^t$ are least square estimates.

Proof. Two parts of the proof will be carried out: (1) to prove (3.1) to be true for any k. If (3.1) is true, then it implies that either improvement will be made for each iteration or equality holds. If a significant improvement still presents after k^{th} iterations, then more iterations are needed. (2) If equality holds or non-significant improvement presents after k^{th} iterations, then it means that $\beta_i^{(k)} = \beta_i^{(k+1)}$, $i=0,1,...,p$. At this point, the $\beta^{(k)} = (\beta_0^{(k)}, ..., \beta_p^{(k)})^t$ will be a least square solution.

In order to prove (3.1) to be true, by mathematical induction, it is sufficient to prove it to be true when $k=0$. That is

$$S(\beta_0^{(0)}, \beta_1^{(0)}, \cdots, \beta_p^{(0)}) \geq S(\beta_0^{(1)}, \beta_1^{(1)}, \cdots, \beta_p^{(1)}) \qquad (3.2)$$

By the procedure of CIO, we optimize one component at each time in the proposed algorithm. Thus, to prove (3.2) to be true, we will prove the following sequence of inequalities holds:

$$S(\beta_0^{(0)}, \beta_1^{(0)}, \cdots, \beta_p^{(0)}) \geq S(\beta_0^{(1)}, \beta_1^{(0)}, \cdots, \beta_p^{(0)}),$$

$$S(\beta_0^{(1)}, \beta_1^{(0)}, \cdots, \beta_p^{(0)}) \geq S(\beta_0^{(1)}, \beta_1^{(1)}, \cdots, \beta_p^{(0)}) \qquad (3.3)$$

$$S(\beta_0^{(1)}, \beta_1^{(1)}, \cdots, \beta_{p-1}^{(1)}, \beta_p^{(0)}) \geq S(\beta_0^{(1)}, \beta_1^{(1)}, \cdots, \beta_{p-1}^{(1)}, \beta_p^{(1)})$$

First, we prove that

$$S(\beta_0^{(0)}, \beta_1^{(0)}, \cdots, \beta_p^{(0)}) \geq S(\beta_0^{(1)}, \beta_1^{(0)}, \cdots, \beta_p^{(0)})$$

where $\quad \beta_0^{(1)} = \dfrac{1}{n} \sum_{i=1}^{n} \beta_0^{(1)}(i), \quad \beta_0^{(1)}(i) = y_i - \sum_{j=1}^{p} \beta_j^{(0)} x_{ij}, \quad$ and

$i=0,1, \ldots, n$ and by (2) of Step 3 in the proposed algorithm. That is

$$\sum_{i=1}^{n} \left(y_i - \sum_{j=1}^{p} \beta_j^{(0)} x_{ij} - \beta_0^{(0)} \right)^2 \geq \sum_{i=1}^{n} \left(y_i - \sum_{j=1}^{p} \beta_j^{(0)} x_{ij} - \beta_0^{(1)} \right)^2, \qquad (3.4)$$

Let LHS and RHS denote the left-hand side of (3.4) and the right hand side of (3.4), respectively. To prove that $LHS \geq RHS$, considering the following expansion of the equivalent forms:

$$LHS = \sum_{i=1}^{n} \left(y_i - \sum_{j=1}^{p} \beta_j^{(0)} x_{ij} \right)^2 - 2 \beta_0^{(0)} \sum_{i=1}^{n} \left(y_i - \sum_{j=1}^{p} \beta_j^{(0)} x_{ij} \right) + n\beta_0^{(0)\,2}$$

$$= \sum_{i=1}^{n} \left(\beta_0^{(1)}(i) \right)^2 - 2 \beta_0^{(0)} \sum_{i=1}^{n} \left(\beta_0^{(1)}(i) \right) + n\beta_0^{(0)\,2},$$

$$RHS = \sum_{i=1}^{n} \left(\left(y_i - \sum_{j=1}^{p} \beta_j^{(0)} x_{ij} \right) - \beta_0^{(1)}(i) - \left(\frac{1}{n} \sum_{i=1}^{n} \beta_0^{(1)}(i) - \beta_0^{(1)}(i) \right) \right)^2$$

$$= \sum_{i=1}^{n} \left(\frac{1}{n} \sum_{i=1}^{n} \beta_0^{(1)}(i) - \beta_0^{(1)}(i) \right)^2 = \sum_{i=1}^{n} \left(\beta_0^{(1)}(i) \right)^2 - \frac{1}{n} \left(\sum_{i=1}^{n} \beta_0^{(1)}(i) \right)^2.$$

Combining LHS and RHS, we can have the following equivalent inequalities:
LHS $\geq$ RHS

$$\Leftrightarrow -2 \beta_0^{(0)} \left(\sum_{i=1}^{n} \beta_0^{(1)}(i) \right) + n\beta_0^{(0)\,2} \geq -\frac{1}{n} \left(\sum_{i=1}^{n} \beta_0^{(1)}(i) \right)^2$$

$$\Leftrightarrow \left(\sum_{i=1}^{n} \beta_0^{(1)}(i) - n\beta_0^{(0)} \right)^2 \geq 0 \Leftrightarrow \left(\beta_0^{(1)} - \beta_0^{(0)} \right)^2 \geq 0$$

The last inequality holds, therefore, we have proved that (3.4) is true. Furthermore, the equality of (3.4) holds if and only if $\beta_0^{(0)} = \beta_0^{(1)}$.

Next, we prove the following inequality holds:

$$S(\beta_0^{(1)}, \beta_1^{(0)}, \cdots, \beta_p^{(0)}) \geq S(\beta_0^{(1)}, \beta_1^{(1)}, \beta_2^{(0)}, \cdots, \beta_p^{(0)}), \tag{3.5}$$

where $\beta_1^{(1)} = \sum_{i=1}^{n} \dfrac{x_{i1}}{\sum_{i=1}^{n} x_{il}^2} \left(y_i - \beta_0^{(1)} - \sum_{j=2}^{p} \beta_j^{(0)} x_{ij} \right)$,   by (2) of Step 4 in the

proposed algorithm.

Let $\Omega_1(i) = \left(y_i - \beta_0^{(1)} - \sum_{j=2}^{p} \beta_j^{(0)} x_{ij} \right)$, then $\beta_1^{(1)} = \sum_{i=1}^{n} \dfrac{x_{i1}}{\sum_{i=1}^{n} x_{il}^2} \Omega_1(i)$.

Let LHS and RHS denote the left-hand side of (3.5) and the right hand side of (3.5), respectively. It is easy to see that

$$LHS = \sum_{i=1}^{n} \left((\Omega_1(i))^2 - 2\Omega_1(i)\beta_1^{(0)} x_{i1} + (\beta_1^{(0)} x_{i1})^2 \right)$$

and

$$RHS = \sum_{i=1}^{n} \left((\Omega_1(i))^2 - 2\Omega_1(i)\beta_1^{(1)} x_{i1} + (\beta_1^{(1)} x_{i1})^2 \right).$$

Combining LHS and RHS, we can have the following equivalent inequalities:

LHS $\geq$ RHS

$$\Leftrightarrow -2\beta_1^{(0)} \sum_{i=1}^{n} \frac{x_{i1}}{\sum_{i=1}^{n} x_{i1}^2} \Omega_1(i) + (\beta_1^{(0)})^2 \geq -2\beta_1^{(1)} \sum_{i=1}^{n} \frac{x_{i1}}{\sum_{i=1}^{n} x_{i1}^2} \Omega_1(i) + (\beta_1^{(1)})^2$$

$$\Leftrightarrow -2\beta_1^{(0)} \beta_1^{(1)} + (\beta_1^{(0)})^2 \geq -2\beta_1^{(1)} \beta_1^{(1)} + (\beta_1^{(1)})^2$$

$$\Leftrightarrow \left(\beta_1^{(1)} - \beta_1^{(0)} \right)^2 \geq 0.$$

The last inequality holds, therefore, we have proved that (3.4) is true. Furthermore, the equality of (3.5) holds if and only if $\beta_1^{(1)} = \beta_1^{(0)}$. Using the same reasoning, it is easy to prove that for any j we have the following equivalent inequalities:

$$S(\beta_0^{(1)},\beta_1^{(1)},\cdots,\beta_{j-1}^{(1)},\beta_j^{(0)}\cdots,\beta_p^{(0)}) \geq S(\beta_0^{(1)},\beta_1^{(1)},\cdots,\beta_j^{(1)},\beta_{j+1}^{(0)}\cdots,\beta_p^{(0)})$$

$$\Leftrightarrow \left(\beta_j^{(1)}-\beta_j^{(0)}\right)^2 \geq 0,$$

where $j = 2,\ldots, p$. It is clear that the equality holds if and only if $\beta_j^{(1)} = \beta_j^{(0)}$. Thus, we have proved that (3.3) holds. Therefore, (3.2) holds.

For the second part of the proof: we assume that $\beta^{(1)} = \beta^{(0)}$, we prove $\beta^{(1)}$ is a solution of least square normal equations.

If we assume that $\beta_1^{(1)} = \beta_1^{(0)}$, then

$$\beta_1^{(0)}\sum_{i=1}^{n} x_{i1}^2 =$$

$$\sum_{i=1}^{n}(x_{i1}-\overline{x_{\bullet 1}})(y_i-\overline{y})-\sum_{j=2}^{p}\beta_j^{(0)}\sum_{i=1}^{n}(x_{i1}-\overline{x_{\bullet 1}})(x_{ij}-\overline{x_{\bullet j}})+n\beta_1^{(0)}\overline{x_{\bullet 1}}^2,$$

which is equivalent to

$$\sum_{i=1}^{n}\left((y_i-\overline{y})-\sum_{j=1}^{p}\beta_j^{(0)}(x_{ij}-\overline{x_{\bullet j}})\right)x_{i1} = 0. \qquad 3.6$$

Similarly, if $\beta_j^{(1)} = \beta_j^{(0)}$, we have

$$\sum_{i=1}^{n}\left((y_i-\overline{y})-\sum_{j=1}^{p}\beta_j^{(0)}(x_{ij}-\overline{x_{\bullet j}})\right)x_{ij} = 0. \qquad (3.7)$$

(3.6) and (3.7) are simply normal equations for the least square solutions. Therefore, we come to the conclusion that if $\beta^{(1)} = \beta^{(0)}$, and then $\beta^{(1)}$ is a least square solution.

Remark: In real applications, it may require a few more iterations rather than one iteration.

References

1. Lin, Y.: Success or Failure? Another look at the statistical significant test in credit scoring, Technical report, First North American National Bank (2001)
2. Lin, Y.: Introduction to Component-wise Iterative, Technical report, First North American National Bank (2003)
3. Lin, Y.: Estimation of parameters in nonlinear regressions and neural networks, Invited talk in 2nd North American New Researchers' Meeting in Kingston, Canada during July 5 – July 8 (1995)
4. Lin, Y.: Feed-forward Neural Networks-Learning Algorithms, Statistical Properties, and Applications, Ph. D. dissertation, Department of mathematics, Syracuse University (1996)
5. Lin, Y.: Statistical Behavior of Two-Stage Learning for Feed-forward Neural Networks with a Single Hidden Layer, 98's proceeding of American Statistical Association (1998)

Ensuring Serializability for Mobile Data Mining on Multimedia Objects

Shin Parker[1], Zhengxin Chen[1], and Eugene Sheng[2]

[1] Department of Computer Science,
University of Nebraska at Omaha,
Omaha, NE 68182-0500
zchen@mail.unomahe.edu
[2] Department of Computer Science,
Northern Illinois University,
DeKalb, IL 60115
sheng@cs.niu.edu

Abstract. Data mining usually is considered as application tasks conducted on the top of database management systems. However, this may not always be true. To illustrate this, in this article we examine the issue of conduct data mining in mobile computing environments, where multiple physical copies of the same data object in client caches may exist at the same time with the server as the primary owner of all data objects. By demonstrating what can be mined in such an environment, we point out the important connection of data mining with database implementation. This leads us to take a look at the issue of extending traditional invalid-access prevention policy protocols, which are needed to ensure serializability involving data updates in mobile environments. Furthermore, we provide examples to illustrate how such kind of research can shed light on mobile data mining.

1 Introduction

We start this paper with the following interesting question related to data mining:

- *For (database-centric) data mining, is it always a task of database application? In other words, is data mining always restricted to a front-end tool?*

A more general form of this question is:

- *Could data mining be related to database implementation in any way?*

In this paper we will address these issues by taking a look at the case of mobile data mining, which is concerned with conducting data mining in a mobile computing environment. We present our opinion on these questions, arguing that there is a need to consider issues related to data mining and implementation of database management systems (DBMSs). As an example of our viewpoint, we first review a recent work for extending serializability support to handle multiple copies of objects so that concurrent execution of multiple transactions is conflict equivalent to serial execution of these transactions. We then examine the indication of this work to data mining.

Y. Shi, W. Xu, and Z. Chen (Eds.): CASDMKM 2004, LNAI 3327, pp. 90–98, 2004.

The balance of this paper is organized as follows. In Section 2 we provide example to illustrate the need for examining the relationship between data mining and DBMS implementation. This leads us to take a look at the general data management issues for mobile data mining in Section 3. In order to deal with problems raised in Section 2, we examine the problem of ensuring serializability in mobile computing environment in Section 4, and further discuss the indications of this research to mobile data mining in Section 5. We conclude the paper in Section 6, where related future research work is discussed.

2   Mobile Data Mining and DBMS Implementation

Mobile data mining can be considered as a special case of distributed data mining (DDM) [7, 9], which is concerned with mining data using distributed resources. However, there are unique features for mobile data mining, and researchers have started exploring this area (e.g., [12]). One interesting issue of data mining in mobile computing environment is related to mining on mobile users, such as their behavior in mobile environments. The importance of using mobile user movement data to *derive knowledge about mobile users* in the e-commerce application domain have been noticed [8].

So what is the role of DBMS in mobile data mining? Techniques for mobile query processing and optimization, such as location-dependent query processing [14], have been addressed by various researchers. Since mobile data mining can take advantage of such kind of technical advance, it seems not too difficult to argue that query processing can contribute to mobile data mining.

But how about the relevance of other aspects in DBMS implementation, such as transaction processing? The connection between mobile data mining and transaction processing seems to be quite remote. However, consider the following scenario. In order to derive knowledge about mobile users in the e-commerce application domain, if the same multimedia object is accessed or even updated by different mobile users, then in order to mine the user profiles, shopping habit or other useful knowledge about users, it is crucial to handle multiple copies of objects correctly. Such a prerequisite can be stated as a problem of ensuring serializability in mobile client-server environment, a problem within the realm of transaction processing. For example, we may want to know what kind of mobile users are interested in certain kind of video, or what kind of video are interested by certain kind of mobile users. It is thus important to recognize multiple versions of the same mobile object. Mobile data mining community has the responsibility to identify such kind of problems to be dealt with.

Furthermore, mobile mining community may even have to develop solutions for some problems identified by themselves (rather than just waiting for solutions provided by other people such as DBMS developer), because such requirements may be closely integrated into the data mining task at hand. For example, we may want to know which kind of message boards (or some other shared objects) is updated most frequently by mobile users; in this case, we need to trace and count the version numbers of the object. Therefore, although version numbers are usually handled by database implementation, mobile data mining algorithms may have to do something about them.

3 Data Management Issues for Mobile Data Mining

In order to understand the importance of our observation made in Section 2, we can cooperate it into the general discussion of data management issues for mobile data mining as identified by Lim et al. [8]:

- *Developing infrastructure for mobile data mining,* to explore the design issues involving a warehouse for mobile data. This may include the algorithms for efficient aggregation and transformation of mobile data. The challenge in this case is to deal with the heterogeneous data format from different mobile devices at different locations with different bandwidth and computing resources.
- *Developing algorithms for mobile data mining,* such as to develop algorithms to find knowledge to improve the efficiency of mobile applications/queries.
- *Incorporating mobile mining results into operational systems,* to integrate knowledge obtained from data mining with the operational systems. The challenge is to develop algorithms that evaluate which are the 'actionable' data mining results, and then apply them in a timely fashion to ensure the effectiveness of the mobile data mining system.
- In addition to above issues raised in [8], we also advocate the study of the following aspect: *Conducting research in support of query processing/optimization and transaction processing,* so that mobile data mining can be effectively conducted.

The rest of this paper is to further examine this last issue.

4 Extending Invalid-Access Prevention Policy

As a concrete example of conducting research on transaction processing for mobile data mining, we now get back to the question raised in Section 2, namely, how to correctly handle multiple object copies so that serializability can be ensured in mobile computing environments. One approach could be attaching an additional field in each record of the system log so that the identifier of the mobile user who has accessed (or even updated) can be recorded along with the object itself. However, this approach may not be realistic, because the introduction of such additional field may not be justified by other system applications (i.e., such information may not be useful for other applications). Therefore, in the rest of this paper we consider how to extend a recent work of study on extending traditional invalid-access prevention policy for mobile data mining concerning multiple-copy objects. This is done in two steps. First, in this section (Section 4) we provide a discussion of the extension process itself (based on the discussion of Parker and Chen 2004) without addressing any issues directly related to mobile computing. Then in Section 5, we revisit the issue of mobile data mining concerning multiple-copy objects by pointing out how we can take advantage of results obtained in this section.

4.1 Review of Traditional Invalid-Access Prevention Policy

In a typical client/server computing architecture, there may exist multiple physical copies of the same data object at the same time in the network with the server as the primary owner of all data objects. The existence of multiple copies of the same multimedia object in client caches is possible when there is no data conflict in the network. In managing multiple clients' concurrent read/write operations on a multimedia object, no transactions that accessed the old version should be allowed to commit. From this basis of the *invalid-access prevention policy*, several protocols have been proposed. The purpose of these protocols is to create an illusion of a single, logical, multimedia data object in the face of multiple physical copies in the client/server network when a data conflict situation arises. When the server becomes aware of a network-wide data conflict, it initiates a cache consistency request to remote clients on behalf of the transaction that caused the data conflict. The basic ideas of three known protocols under this policy are summarized below (for a summary of these methods, see [11]; for other related work, see [2,3,4,5,6,10,13,15]).

Server-Based Two-Phase Locking (S2PL): The S2PL uses a detection-based algorithm and supports inter-transaction caching. It validates cached pages synchronously on a transaction's initial access to the page. Before a transaction is allowed to commit, it must first access the primary copies from the server on each data item that it has read at the client. The new value must be installed at the client if the client's cache version is outdated. The server is aware of a list of clients who requested locks only, and no broadcast is used by the server to communicate with clients. The client is aware of a list of object version numbers, and no local lock is used by the client. This protocol carries no overhead in page table maintenance at the price of not being able to detect multiple versions in a network.

Call-Back Locking (CBL): CBL is an avoidance-based protocol that supports inter-transactional page caching. Transactions executing under an avoidance-based scheme must obey the read-once write-all (ROWA) replica management approach, which guarantees the correctness of data from the client cache by enforcing that all existing copies of an updated object have the same value when an updating transaction commits. Therefore an interaction with the server is required only at client cache-miss or for updating its cache copy. The global nature of ROWA implies that consistency actions may be required at one or more remote clients before the server can register a write permit for a local client. An update transaction cannot commit until all of the necessary consistency operations have been completed at remote clients. When all consistency operations are complete, there exist only two copies of the multimedia object, a primary copy in the server and a secondary copy in the client with a write permit, to get ready for a commit. Note that a write-write data conflict does not exist in the CBL. In the process of securing a write permit for a local client, all remote clients' cache copies were invalidated and no new download is possible while the write permit locks the row in the database.

Optimistic Two-Phase Locking (O2PL): This is avoidance-based and is more optimistic about the existence of data contention in the network than CBL. It defers the write intention declaration until the end of a transaction's execution phase. Under the ROWA protocol, an interaction with the server is required only at client cache-miss or for committing its cache copy under the O2PL. As in CBL, all clients must inform the server when they erase a page from their buffer so that the server can update its page list.

All three of the above invalid-access prevention policy protocols ensure that any update transactions that previously accessed the old version data be aborted by the server. A general difference among them is the varying degree in the number of client messages sent to the server and the server's abort frequency.

4.2 What's New in Mobile Computing Environment?

The inherent limitations of mobile computing systems present a challenge to the traditional problems of database management, especially when the client/server communication is unexpectedly severed from the client site.

From the summary presented in Section 3, we can provide the following observations. In a S2PL network, multiple versions of the same object ID can exist in the network due to automatic and as-needed replications without the server's overall awareness of data conflicts in the network. This may result in frequent transaction aborts in the S2PL protocol. In a CBL or O2PL network, during a brief slice of time when an object is being committed to the database by a row-server with a write lock, there exists only one physical copy at the primary site and one copy at the secondary site if all cached clients have invalidated their locally cached copies. However, some cached mobile clients may not have the opportunity to invalidate their obsolete copies or replicate updated copies due to their disconnection from the network while the object is being committed by another node. This causes the existence of multiple cached versions of the same object ID in the network when the disconnected clients return to the network. This is not desirable in applications requiring the ROWA protocol.

Serializability is the most commonly used correctness criterion for transactions in database applications for concurrent transaction execution at a global level. The standard policy does not enforce the serializability to the mobile computing environment. Transactions executing under an avoidance-based scheme must obey the (ROWA) principle, which guarantees the correctness of the data from the client cache under the CBL or the O2PL protocol. The standard CBL and O2PL protocols cannot guarantee the currency of the mobile clients' cache copies and to prevent serializability violations when they reconnect to the network. Figures 1 illustrates how error condition (appearing toward the end of the figure) arises in CBL environment after mobile clients properly exit the client application.

4.3 Extended Invalid Access Prevention Protocols for Mobile Environment

To prevent the serializability failure scenario described above, the extended invalid access prevention policy protocols are proposed here for the mobile client/server environments that guarantee the serializability. Extended invalid-Access Prevention

Policy should include additional attributes such as version numbers, recreate/release page table rows, relinquish unused locks at sign-off, and maximum lock duration.

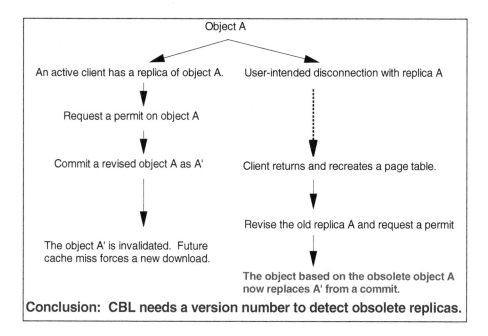

Fig. 1. CBL Failure Analysis Tree in Mobile Environment

With the four extended attributes, all disconnected mobile clients' obsolete cached copies during their absence from the network are logically invalidated while a connected client updates the same multimedia object. The logical invalidation is accomplished via the first two attributes, implementing sequential version numbers in the CBL and O2PL protocols and recreating page table entries only when the version number is current. The remaining two attributes, relinquishing unused permits or locks at exit or shutdown from the client application and the maximum lock duration to help server recover from indefinite stalls, are to handle the effects of normal and abnormal program terminations so that the server does not wait indefinitely to hear from its constituent clients after multicasts. With the implementation of version numbers in CBL and O2PL protocols, the server can now determine which cached objects of returning mobile clients are obsolete and can discard the corresponding page table entries, both from the client and the server page tables.

Experiments have shown that extended invalid-access prevention policy algorithms enforce a guaranteed serializability of multimedia objects in RDBMS applications under a mobile client/server environment. For more details, see [11].

Figure 2 depicts a proper page table procedure for logical invalidations to deal with serializability problem through page table consistency check.

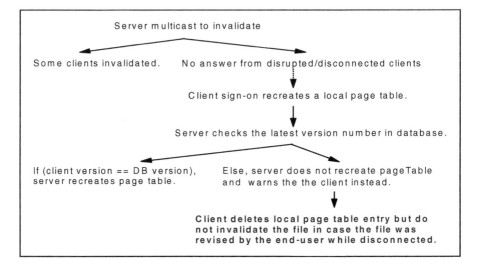

Fig. 2. Consistency check of the page table

5 Potential Contribution of Extended Invalid Access Prevention Protocols to Mobile Data Mining

Based on our discussion presented above, we can now revisit the issues raised earlier, to analyze scenarios and answer queries like following:

- What kind of mobile users is interested in certain kind of video? What kind of video is interested by certain kind of mobile users?
- Which kind of message boards (or some other shared objects) is updated most frequently by mobile users?
- What kind of mobile users (i.e., characteristics) have accessed and updated most frequently on a particular object?
- What kind of multimedia objects (i.e., characteristics) have the largest number of copies at the same time?
- What kind of multimedia objects are likely to be updated as a consequence of updating some other multimedia objects?

To answer these questions and many other questions we need some details of database implementation as discussed earlier. For example, in order to find out "what kind of mobile users is interested in certain kind of video," we need to count the frequency of certain video to be accessed by mobile users. Although in this kind of application a user may not be able to update the contents of video and thus not be able to create new versions of an object, in many other cases (such as the case of dealing with the message board) updates do occur and multiple versions of objects do exist. Therefore, the research work presented in Section 4 may have important contribution in the related data mining tasks.

6   Conclusions and Future Research

In this paper we raised and discussed these issues by examining the case of mobile data mining. Data mining may not be limited to "front end" applications. To the best of our knowledge, these have not been discussed before, but these are issues worthy exploring. In particular, we have focused on how to ensure serializability in dealing with multiple copies of multimedia objects as an example to illustrate the relationship between mobile data mining and DBMS transaction processing. For more details of our proposed approach, see [11].

There are many outstanding research issues that need to be addressed before data mining in mobile environment can be effectively used. Although we have addressed the issues of ensuring the serilizability of large multimedia objects, in doing so will inevitably invalids many transactions that access modified objects. To relieve such problem, we need an elaborate scheme to divide the large object into smaller pieces and subsequently effectively organize and manage these pieces. This will allow multiple users (transactions) to simultaneously update different parts of the same objects without being rollback. Another related issue that needs to be further studied is how to address serializability if we are mining from different data sources.

References

1. Barbara, D.: Mobile Computing and Databases – A Survey. IEEE Transactions on Knowledge and Data Engineering, 11(1) (1999) 108-117
2. Breitbart, Y., Komondoor, R., Rastogi, R., Seshadri, S., Silberschatz, A.: Update Propagation Protocols for Replicated Databases. Proceedings ACM SIGMOD (1999) 97-108
3. Dunham, M. H., Helal, A., Balakrishnan, T.: Mobile transaction model that captures both the data and movement behavior. Mobile Networks and Applications, 2(2) (1997)149-162.
4. Franklin, M. J., Carey, M. J., Livny, M.: Transactional client-server cache consistency: alternatives and performance. ACM Transactions on Database Systems, 22(3) (1997) 315-363.
5. Holiday, J., Agrawal, D., Abbadi, A.: Disconnection Modes for Mobile Databases. Wireless Networks (2002) 391-402
6. Jensen, C. S., Lomer, D. B.: Transaction Timestamping in Temporal Databases. Proceedings of the 27th International Conference on Very Large Data Bases (2001) 441-450
7. Kargupta, H., Joshi, A.: Data Mining "To Go": Ubiquitous KDD for Mobile and Distributed Environments, KDD Tutorial. (2001)
8. Lim, E.-P., Wang, Y., Ong, K.-L., Hwang, S.-Y.: In Search of Knowledge about Mobile Users, Center for Advanced Information Systems at Nanyang Technological University, Singapore. (2003) http://www.ercim.org/publication/Ercim_News/enw54/lim.html.
9. Liu, K., Kargupta, H., Ryan, J.: Distributed data mining bibliography, University of Maryland Baltimore County. (2004)
http://www.cs.umbc.edu/~hillol/DDMBIB/ddmbib.pdf
10. Pacitti, E., Minet, P., .Simon, E.: Fast Algorithms for Maintaining Replica Consistency in Lazy Master Replicated Databases. Proceedings of the 25th International Conference on Very Large Data Bases (1999) 126-137.

11. Parker, S., Chen, Z.: Extending Invalid-Access Prevention Policy Protocols for Mobile-Client Data Caching. Proc. ACM SAC (2004) 1171-1176
12. Saygin, Y., Ulusoy, Ö.: Exploiting Data Mining Techniques for Broadcasting Data in Mobile Computing Environments. IEEE TKDE (2002)1387-1399.
13. Schuldt, H.: Process Locking: A Protocol based on Ordered Shared Locks for the Execution of Transactional Processes. Proceedings of the 20th ACM SIGMOD SIGACT SIGART Symposium on Principles of database systems (2001) 289-300
14. Seydim, A. Y., Dunham, M. H., Kumar, V.: Location dependent query processing. Proceedings of the 2nd ACM international workshop on Data engineering for wireless and mobile access (2001) 47-53
15. Shanmugasundaram, J., Nithrakashyap, A., Sivasankaran R., Ramamritham. K.: Efficient Concurrency Control for Broadcast Environments. *Proceedings of the 1999 ACM SIGMOD International Conference in Management of Data* (1999) 85-96

"Copasetic Clustering": Making Sense of Large-Scale Images

Karl Fraser*, Paul O'Neill*, Zidong Wang, and Xiaohui Liu

Department of Information Systems and Computing, Brunel University,
Uxbridge, Middlesex, UB8 3PH, U.K.
{karl, paul, zidong, hui}@ida-research.net

Abstract. In an information rich world, the task of data analysis is becoming ever more complex. Even with the processing capability of modern technology, more often than not, important details become saturated and thus, lost amongst the volume of data. With analysis problems ranging from discovering credit card fraud to tracking terrorist activities the phrase "a needle in a haystack" has never been more apt. In order to deal with large data sets current approaches require that the data be sampled or summarised before true analysis can take place. In this paper we propose a novel *pyramidic* method, namely, copasetic clustering, which focuses on the problem of applying traditional clustering techniques to large-scale data sets while using limited resources. A further benefit of the technique is the transparency into intermediate clustering steps; when applied to spatial data sets this allows the capture of contextual information. The abilities of this technique are demonstrated using both synthetic and biological data.

1   Introduction

In order to deal with large data sets, current clustering approaches require that the data be sampled or summarised before true analysis can take place. In this paper we deal with the problem of applying clustering techniques to large-scale data sets when subjected to limited resources. The technique was designed such that traditional clustering metrics could not only be applied to large-scale data sets, but would also produce results that were comparable to their un-scaled relatives on appropriately small data sets. This novel technique also gives the advantage of rendering transparent the 'internal decision processes' of the clustering methods. When applied to spatial data sets this results in the capture of contextual information that traditional methods would have lost, producing a far more accurate output. This improved accuracy is shown to exist when the copasetic clustering techniques abilities are applied to both synthetic and biological data sets.

Clustering [1] is a prominent unsupervised technique used for segmentation that allows us to search for and classify the similarity between many thousands

---

* The authors contributed equally to the research held in this paper.

Y. Shi, W. Xu, and Z. Chen (Eds.): CASDMKM 2004, LNAI 3327, pp. 99–108, 2004.
© Springer-Verlag Berlin Heidelberg 2004

of 'objects'. Techniques such as k-means [2] and fuzzy c-means [3] are good representatives of the clustering ideology and are still in widespread use today. k-means for example partitions data by initially creating k random cluster centres which define the boundaries for each partition in the hyper-volume. Fuzzy logic based algorithms [3] on the other hand, were specifically designed to give computer based systems the ability to account for the grey or fuzzy decision processes that are often seen in reality. Fuzzy logic based clustering therefore offers inherent advantages over non-fuzzy methods, as they can cope with problem spaces which have no well defined boundaries.

Like many other techniques, the two clustering methods mentioned suffer a variety of problems: they are heavily influenced by initial starting conditions, can become trapped in local minima, do not lend themselves to distributed processing methods and are restricted in their application to the memory resources of a single workstation. Pavel Berkhin [1] detailed these issues and classified the current solutions into three groups; incremental mining [4], data squashing [5] and reliable sampling [6] methods. The main problem with these implementations is that by reducing the number of elements in the data sets, important data will have been lost and so there is a need for developing techniques that can be scaled to these problems.

This paper focuses on solutions to two of the key challenges in the clustering field. The first of these is associated with the scaling issue of current techniques and thus attempts to meet the demand of modern image sets. Secondly we detail a method whereby rather than discarding the wealth of spatial image information we harness it. The next section then describes the process whereby existing techniques are scaled to larger data sets, not only making their application feasible but also providing extra information about the internal clustering decision process that would traditionally be unavailable. The proposed solution is then tested on both synthetic and real-world biological data, with the results described in detail and the proposed algorithm showing great promise.

2   Copasetic Clustering

The Copasetic Clustering (CC) method is a technique which facilitates the application of tradition clustering algorithms to large-scale data sets; it also has the additional ability of capturing spatial information allowing the refinement of groupings. Initially it arbitrarily divides up the image into spatially related areas (normally very small grid squares). Each of these areas is then clustered using a traditional technique such as k-means [2] or fuzzy c-means [3], and the result is stored. Then representatives are calculated for each of the clusters that exist, these are then further clustered in the next generation. Such a process is repeated until all sub-clustered groups have been merged. The final result is that every pixel will have been clustered into one of n groups and on small data sets the output is comparable with traditional techniques. The aforementioned idea can be illustrated using the conceptual diagram shown in Fig. 1. In the input, we can see twelve items which are to be clustered. Creating two groups with traditional clustering methods would compare all twelve shapes and is likely to output one group of triangles and one containing a mixture of circles and crosses as shown Fig. 1 (left). CC, on the other hand, would divide this set into sub-groups of a given size, in this example, into three sets of four as Fig. 1 (right) shows. Each of these sub-groups would be clustered into one of two classes (represented by the checkerboard pattern or lack thereof, within the layer '0' under each shape). In layer 1, the previously generated representatives for each of these groups have been clustered together. The final result can now be calculated by re-traversing the pyramid structure and tracking the shaded members.

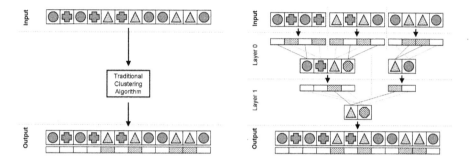

Fig. 1. Conceptual diagram of traditional clustering techniques (left) and CC (right)

Studying the three groups in this example closely, it can be seen that the shapes were chosen to illustrate how this sub-clustering can provide useful contextual information. The first group of circles and crosses can easily be clustered as two separate shape classes with no problems (as shown in layer 0). With the introduction of triangles in the second group, we see that the circle and cross are now clustered together; here this is the optimum arrangement due to shape similarity. By layer 1, the groups are the same as a traditional clustering algorithm, with all circles and crosses in one group and triangles in the other. Unlike a traditional clustering algorithm, information from previous layers can now be used to ascertain the fact that in some situations certain items should not have been grouped together. Here the circles and crosses could have formed two distinctive groups if it were not for the presence of the triangles. Note that this information is context specific, and relies on a spatial data set, an order dependent vector or image for example.

A pseudo-code implementation of the CC algorithm is described in Fig. 2. For clarity, this implementation has been based around clustering an image utilising traditional techniques into two groups containing either signal or noise elements; although the implementation can easily be modified to work with multiple groups. As mentioned, one of the fundamental strengths of the CC approach over traditional clustering techniques is that CC effectively renders transparent

Inputs
Image: The n bit tiff image
WindowSz: The size of the window to use when sub-dividing each level
ClusterMetric: traditional clustering metric {*k*-means, PAM, fuzzy *c*-means, ...}

Outputs
Signal, Noise: Mutually exclusive co-ordinate lists for every pixel in Image

```
Function CopaseticCluster(Image,WindowSz):Signal,Noise
    Width=Image.width
    Height=Image.height
    FirstPass=true

    While (Width > 1 AND Height >1) do
            NewWidth=Width/WindowSz; If (NewWidth<1) Then NewWidth=1
            NewHeight=Height/WindowSz; If (NewHeight<1) Then NewHeight=1
            Create Signal[NewWidth][NewHeight] as empty Co-ordinate list
            Create Noise[NewWidth][NewHeight] as empty Co-ordinate list
            For (y=1 to NewHeight)
                For (x=1 to NewWidth)
                    If (FirstPass=true) then
                        Resultant=ClusterMetric(Image,x,y,x*Window,y*Window)
                        FirstPass=false
                    Else
                        Resultant=ClusterMetric(Signal,Noise,x,y,x*Window,y*Window)
                    Signal[x][y]=Resultant.Signal
                    Noise[x][y]=Resultant.Noise
                    Width=NewWidth
                    Height=NewHeight
                End For
            End For
    End While
End Function
```

Fig. 2. Copasetic clustering pseudo code description

the 'internal decision processes'. This is achieved by way of the *pyramidic* layering concept giving the ability to review historical information which enables the improvement of the final output. Traditional clustering algorithms lack this information and the problems that arise from this can be illustrated with a simple test image which has a gradient (realistic) based background. The left of Fig. 3 shows an image with well defined signal (the arrows) throughout. However, towards the bottom of the image the local noise tends to the signal and will therefore be grouped with this noise element. Note the question mark signifies the complete lack of internal knowledge available from the traditional clustering techniques.

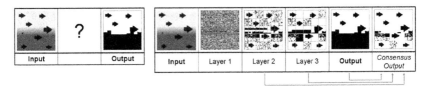

Fig. 3. Traditional clustering (left) and CC's result including historical data (right)

The right of Fig. 3 shows the various layers of the CC algorithm, where we can clearly see there are three intermediate layers between the input and output data. This diagram illustrates two ways the raw output from CC can be used. The simplest method is to take the final layer results and use them directly; which is equivalent to traditional clustering techniques. An alternative way would be to harness the information from all these layers, producing an amalgamated result from a consensus of the previous layers. This result shows more details are accounted for from the original input, than would have otherwise been possible using traditional methods. The consensus layer was generated by calculating the mean value for each pixel across the previous layers and then discretised using a threshold of 0.66 (i.e. agreement between two thirds of the layers). For a data set which consists of two or more clusters a median could be used to the same effect, although the use of more complex methods of forming an agreement are not ruled out.

3   Results

This section details the results of numerous experiments which test the CC technique using both k-means and fuzzy c-means clustering when applied to various data sets. The first set of experiments consists of a series of synthetic imagery, designed to emphasise both the weaknesses and strengths of each technique. These methods are then, applied to biological gene expression analysis data with comparisons drawn between the two clustering results and that of the human expert.

3.1   Synthetic Data Set Experiments

Fig. 4 illustrates a selection of images with various degrees of solid white noise. In the *uniform* set of images the objects have been rendered with an intensity value of 50% while the background was originally set to 0%. Over the course of the series the background noise steadily increased in increments of 5%. The *gradient* set of images is based on the aforementioned set with the obvious difference being that average intensity of the background is gradually increased down the image surface. This has the effect of making lower region background pixels more similar to the signal of the objects than the background in the upper region. As we know the true morphology for the imagery involved, the techniques can be evaluated by calculating the percentage error. Here this percentage error is defined as:

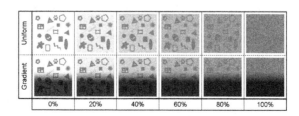

Fig. 4. Two example data sets shown with varying intensities of solid white noise

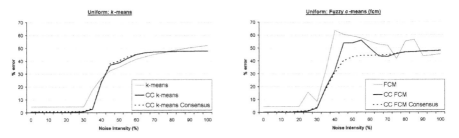

Fig. 5. Results for the uniform synthetic data, k-means (left) and fuzzy c-means (right)

$$\%error = \frac{\sum abs(p_{signal} - p_{mask})}{N} \tag{1}$$

where N is the number of pixels in p_{signal} and p_{mask} such that $p = 1, 2, , N$ for the images *signal* and *mask*. Fig. 5 shows the absolute error results when using the images with a uniform background as plotted against the intensity of the noise for both k-means and fuzzy c-means. Each graph consists of three plots: the grey line shows the traditional clustering technique when applied to each image, the black line shows the performance obtained when CC is applied and finally, the dotted line shows the results when a consensus of the historical CC information is utilised.

Generally all three methods perform admirably producing comparable results. However, the consensus implementation of CC appears to degrade more gracefully as noise levels increase. As this data set contains a uniform spread of noise elements it was envisioned that the results of the experiment would be similar between the techniques. Due to this uniformity of the background, foreground pixels are clearly defined and hence easier to cluster. However in many real data sets this would not be the case, rather, variations in background would mean pixels could only be classified correctly when taken in the context of their local region. Currently traditional clustering techniques fail in this situation, due to the fact that every pixel is treated in isolation, inherently CC is spatially aware and therefore able to capture this contextual information.

Fig. 6 shows the percentage error when the same techniques are applied to the gradient based synthetic data which represents a more realistic scenario. As before, both traditional clustering and CC have performed on a par with one another, which is the expected result. However, for this data set the historic information plays a much bigger role and it can be seen that there is a substantial improvement across the entire series. To further illustrate this some example images are shown in Fig. 7. In these images the benefit of using historical information can clearly be seen. Although there is still a lot of noise present, the objects in the image have been clearly defined and could be used for further analysis such as edge detection. In contrast, the traditional clustering results have lost this information completely and nothing further can be done to clarify the lower region without reanalysis.

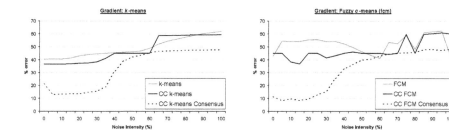

Fig. 6. Results for the gradient synthetic data for k-means (left) and fuzzy c-means (right)

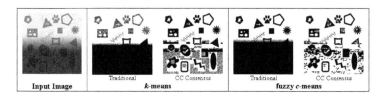

Fig. 7. Representative clustering results of processes

3.2   Microarray Data Set Experiments

The final set of results represent a real-world image analysis problem in the biological domain more specifically that associated with microarray data. Until recently, when biologists wanted to discover which genes were being used in a given process, they would have to focus on one gene at a time. The ability to analyse genes in this manor is extremely useful, but due to the lack of functional knowledge for the majority of genes this is pragmatically restrictive. With the use of Microarray technology [7], biologists can analyse many thousands of genes simultaneously on a single chip. For a detailed explanation readers may find references [8] and [9] of interest. An example usage of this technology is the comparison between cells for a patient before and after infection by disease. If particular genes are used more (highly expressed) after infection, it can be surmised that these genes may play an important role in the life cycle of this disease. This is then digitised using a dual laser scanning device, producing a 5000×2000, two channel 16-bit grey-scale images, an example of which is shown in the left of Fig. 8.

One of the mainstream methods used to analyse microarrays is that provided by Axon Instruments in their package GenePix®. Initially the operator defines a template of gene spot locations, which the package then uses to define the centre of a circle that is then applied to every gene with a simple threshold used to calculate its diameter. All of these are then manually checked and re-aligned if necessary, with the median value of these pixels used as the intensity of the gene spot. The technique samples the surrounding background by placing four rectangular regions in the diagonal space between this and adjacent spots

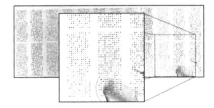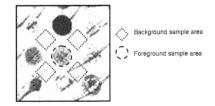

Fig. 8. Example microarray images (left). Template example based on method employed by GenePix® (right)

(valleys). Again the median values of all pixels within these valleys are taken to be background. The final stage is to subtract the background from the foreground domain. The right of Fig. 8 shows an example of this template based approach.

This process makes the assumption there is little variation both within the gene spot and the surrounding background. Unfortunately, this is not always the case as various types of artefacts are commonly found as can be seen in the background regions of Fig. 8. Yang et al. [10] present a review of this and other manual methods as applied to microarray analysis. Rather than this template approach, a better method of dividing the foreground and background domains would be that of clustering. To this end we have investigated a technique that could facilitate the requirement of automatic full-slide processing, while avoiding the associated overheads. Using CC, the entire microarray image can be classified in terms of signal and noise, which can be used to help distinguish the gene spot boundaries. Having calculated a mask for the gene spots across the entire slide, they can be verified using the peak signal-to-noise ratio ($PSNR$) [11] against human defined areas for each of the gene spots. This metric is defined for grey-scale images as:

$$PSNR = 20\log_{10}\left(\frac{1}{RMSE}\right)(\text{dB}) \qquad (2)$$

where the $RMSE$ (root mean squared error) represents the norm of the difference between the original signal and the mask. The $PSNR$ is the ratio of the mean squared difference between two images and the maximum mean squared difference that can exist between them. Therefore the higher the $PSNR$ value, the more accurately the mask fits the raw imagery (for all images present the proposed framework gave more accurate results). This gives a measure of the accuracy between the signal as defined by a trained biologist and the signal defined by the clustering technique. From Fig. 9, we directly compare $PSNR$ values determined by GenePix® and CC for the individual images and on average CC has shown a marked 1 - 3dB improvement over that of the template approach. Essentially the CC process has consistently outperformed the human expert using GenePix® in terms of gene spot identification. We have shown above that the CC technique can apply clustering methods to data sets that are traditionally infeasible while also producing a significant improvement over the manually guided process.

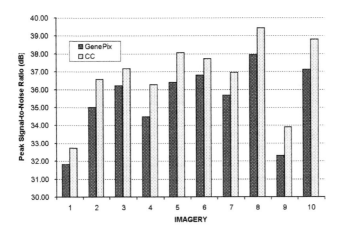

Fig. 9. $PSNR$ Comparison between GenePix® and CC Results

4   Conclusions

This paper presented a new method which can be used to scale existing clustering techniques so that they can process larger images. The proposed method is based entirely on the distribution of the images pixel intensities and thus immune to spatial and morphological issues. With this approach, we have shown that the copasetic clustering algorithm can improve the spatial classification results over those as derived from traditional techniques on both real and synthetic image data. Through this technique's inherent transparency we have also shown that more detail is captured by the method when compared to the traditional techniques on which they are based. In future we would like to further refine the historical capabilities in order to maximise the benefits of the approach. When applied to microarray imagery, this improved accuracy in the classification of the slide surface reduces the difficulty in defining the structural composition.

In this paper we focused primarily on applying the copasetic clustering algorithm in order to ascertain how it compares to traditional techniques with a view to scalability. From the promising results presented here, the next step will be to explore the direct effect that 'window size' has on the resulting quality. At present we have used the smallest 'window size' ($WindowSz = 2$) with a view to high quality output, however, this may not be practical for real-world applications due to their dimensionality; this parameter will always be a trade off between quality and speed. This leads to another important issue, that of resource allocation such as memory and processor load compared to traditional techniques. Currently, copasetic clustering takes significantly longer to process than traditional techniques. However, in its present form the code is un-optimised and should be taken in the context that it is able to process data sets which are several orders of magnitude larger. Our ultimate goal is to develop these techniques into a truly automated microarray processing system. This study brings that goal one step closer as it addresses the challenging issues associated with the initial stages of analysis.

Acknowledgements

For kindly providing the data sets used, the authors would like to thank Paul Kellam from the Dept. of Immunology and Molecular Pathology, University College London.

References

1. Berkhin, P.: Survey of clustering data mining techniques, Accrue Software, San Jose, CA, (2002).
2. McQueen, J.: Some methods for classification and analysis of multivariate observations. Proceedings of the 5th Berkeley Symposium on Mathematical Statistics and Probability, (1967) 281–297.
3. Dunn, C. J.: A fuzzy relative of ISODATA process and its use in detecting compact well-separated clusters, Cybernetics Vol. 3, No. 3, (1974) 32–57.
4. Wann, D. C., Thomopoulos, A. S: A comparative study of self-organising clustering algorithms Dignet and ART2. Neural Networks, Vol. 10, No. 4, (1997) 737–743.
5. DuMouchel, W., Volinsky, C., Johnson, T., Cortes, C., Pregibon, D.: Squashing flat files flatter. Proceedings of the 5th ACM SIGKDD, (1999) 6–15.
6. Motwani, R., Raghavan, P.: Randomised algorithms, Cambridge University Press, (1995)
7. Moore, K. S.: Making Chips, IEEE Spectrum, (2001) 54–60.
8. Orengo, A. C., Jones, D., T., Thorton, M. J.: Bioinformatics: Genes, proteins & computers, BIOS scientific publishers limited, (2003) 217–244.
9. The chipping forecast II.: Nature Genetics Supplement, (2002) 461–552.
10. Yang, H. Y., Buckley, J., M., Dudoit, S., Speed, P. T.: Comparison of methods for image analysis on cDNA microarray data, J. Comput. Graphical Stat., Vol 11, (2002) 108–136.
11. Netravali, N. A., Haskell, G. B.: Digital pictures: Representation, compression and standards (2nd Ed), Plenum Press, New York, NY, (1995).

Ranking Gene Regulatory Network Models with Microarray Data and Bayesian Network

Hongqiang Li, Mi Zhou, and Yan Cui[*]

Department of Molecular Sciences,
Center of Genomics and Bioinformatics,
University of Tennessee Health Science Center,
Memphis, TN 38163, USA
{Hli7, Mzhou3, Ycui2}@utmem.edu

Abstract. Researchers often have several different hypothesises on the possible structures of the gene regulatory network (GRN) underlying the biological model they study. It would be very helpful to be able to rank the hypothesises using existing data. Microarray technologies enable us to monitor the expression levels of tens of thousands of genes simultaneously. Given the expression levels of almost all of the well-substantiated genes in an organism under many experimental conditions, it is possible to evaluate the hypothetical gene regulatory networks with statistical methods. We present RankGRN, a web-based tool for ranking hypothetical gene regulatory networks. RankGRN scores the gene regulatory network models against microarray data using Bayesian Network methods. The score reflects how well a gene network model explains the microarray data. A posterior probability is calculated for each network based on the scores. The networks are then ranked by their posterior probabilities. RankGRN is available online at [http://GeneNet.org/bn]. RankGRN is a useful tool for evaluating the hypothetical gene network models' capability of explaining the observational gene expression data (i.e. the microarray data). Users can select the gene network model that best explains the microarray data.

1 Introduction

The gene expression programs encoded in DNA sequences determine the development of the organisms and their responses to the external stimuli at cellular level. These programs are executed via the gene regulatory networks. The gene regulatory network is a group of gene that interact through directed transcriptional regulation.[1,2] Many diseases are related to malfunctions of part of the gene regulatory network. Better understandings of the structures of gene regulatory networks will improve our understanding of the complex processes involved in higher order biological functions and will affect the researches on many diseases profoundly.

The structures of gene regulatory networks of eukaryotes remain largely unknown, except for a few intensively studied pathways. Recently, the applications of microarray technologies have generated huge amounts of gene expression data,

---

[*] To whom correspondence should be addressed.

Y. Shi, W. Xu, and Z. Chen (Eds.): CASDMKM 2004, LNAI 3327, pp. 109–118, 2004.
© Springer-Verlag Berlin Heidelberg 2004

therefore have made it practical to discover gene regulatory relations through statistical and computational approaches.

Researchers often have several different hypothesises on the possible structures of gene regulatory network underlying the biological model they study. It will be very helpful to be able to rank the hypothesis using existing data.[3]

Bayesian Network methods[4] have been used to infer the structures of gene regulatory networks from microarray data[5-8, 21-28]. In the previous works, Bayesian networks were used mainly for reconstructing the gene regulatory networks without the prior knowledge on the possible structures of the networks. Due to the huge numbers of possible networks need to be evaluate and the limited amount of microarray data, it is impractical to learning the whole gene regulatory network only form microarray data. However, it is much more feasible to evaluate a number of alternative hypothesises about the structure of a regulatory network against microarray data. In this work, we developed a web-based program that ranks gene network models with Bayesian Network methods.

2 Methods

2.1 Data Preparation

Huge amount of microarray data have been stored in public databases, for example, Gene Expression Omnibus (GEO),[9] Stanford Microarray Database,[10,11] ArrayExpress[12] and ExpressDB.[13,14] As of July 3, 2003, microarray data of 6,418 samples using 229 platforms is available at GEO. The most frequently used platform for Human and Mouse microarray data in GEO are Affymetrix GeneChip Human Genome U95 Set HG-U95A (290 samples, 4/30/2003) and Affymetrix GeneChip Murine Genome U74 Version 2 Set MG-U74A (476 samples, 4/30/2003). We downloaded and compiled the microarray datasets of HG-U95A (Human) and MG-U74Av2 (Mouse) from GEO.[9] We also downloaded the Estimated relative abundances (ERAs) for 213 yeast conditions from ExpressDB.[13,14] The downloaded microarray data was then normalized, discretized (see the Method section for details) and saved in a local database. The transformed microarray data is used for scoring hypothetic gene networks.

We first normalize the gene expression data for each sample to having same mean and standard deviation. Then the microarray data are discretized into three levels. We calculate the mean (μ) and standard deviation σ for each gene's expression values. If an expression value is less than $\mu - \sigma$, it belongs to level 0; If an expression value is between $\mu \pm \sigma$, it belongs to level 1; If an expression value is larger than $\mu + \sigma$, it belongs to level 2.

2.2 Bayesian Network

RankGRN uses Bayesian Network methods to rank hypothetical gene networks. A Bayesian network[4] is a probabilistic graphical model of dependencies between multiple variables. It has been considered as an effective tool for learning the genetic networks from gene expression profiles.[19] Directed acyclic graphs are used to depict the dependencies and conditional independencies between variables, in our case, the expression levels of the genes. Causal interpretation for Bayesian networks has been proposed[20] -- the parents of a variable are its immediate causes. The structure of Bayesian networks can be learned from microarray data. [5-8, 21-28] Given the microarray dataset D, we want to find which hypothetical gene regulatory network best matches D. We used a Bayesian score to evaluate a network G:[7]

$$S(G:D) = \log P(G \mid D) \tag{1}$$

The Bayesian score for the entire network is decomposable as a sum of scores for each edge (parent-child relationship) under the assumption of complete data. Thus, the score can be written as:[7]

$$S(G:D) = \sum_i S_{local}(X_i, Pa^G(X_i):D) \tag{2}$$

where X_i is the expression level of Gene i, $Pa^G(X_i)$ are the expression levels of the regulators (i.e. the parents) of Gene i according to the network G. The contribution of each gene to the total score depends only on Gene i and its regulators.

In the case of a discrete Bayesian network with multinomial local conditional probability distributions, the local contributions for each gene can be computed using a closed form equation[7, 29]

$$S_{local}(X_i, Pa^G(X_i):D) =$$

$$\log P(Pa_i = U) + \log \left[\frac{\Gamma(\alpha_{ij})}{\Gamma(\alpha_{ij} + N_{ij})} \cdot \prod_{k=1}^{r_i} \frac{\Gamma(\alpha_{ijk} + N_{ijk})}{\Gamma(\alpha_{ijk})} \right] \tag{3}$$

where $\alpha_{ijk} = \dfrac{1}{q_i r_i}$ is (non-informative) parameter prior, N_{ijk} is the number of occurrences of gene i in state k given parent configuration j, $N_{ij} = \sum_{k=1}^{r_i} N_{ijk}$ and $\alpha_{ij} = \sum_{k=1}^{r_i} \alpha_{ijk}$, $\Gamma(\cdot)$ is the gamma function, the first term is the prior probability assigned to the choice of the set U as the parents of X_i. RankGRN uses uniform structure prior.

The posterior probability of a hypothetical network G_i is

$$P(G \mid D) = \frac{e^{S(G_i:D)}}{\sum_{j=1}^{N} e^{S(G_j:D)}} \tag{4}$$

where N is the number of hypothetical networks.

2.3 Visualization of Gene Networks

The Dot program in the Graphviz,[30] an open source graph drawing software, was used to visualize the gene regulatory networks.

3 Results

3.1 Gene Network Model Selection

RankGRN takes as input hypothetical gene networks in the format of a network description file. For example, six hypothetical yeast gene network structures are described in the following format:

```
LEU3
BAP2
GDH1
LEU2
TOA2
#1
LEU3    BAP2
LEU3    GDH1
LEU3    LEU2
TOA2    LEU2
#2
GDH1    LEU3
GDH1    BAP2
LEU3    LEU2
TOA2    LEU2
#3
BAP2    LEU3
BAP2    GDH1
LEU3    LEU2
TOA2    LEU2
#4
BAP2    LEU3
LEU2    BAP2
LEU3    GDH1
LEU2    TOA2
#5
BAP2    LEU3
LEU3    GDH1
LEU3    LEU2
LEU2    TOA2
#6
LEU3    BAP2
LEU3    GDH1
LEU3    LEU2
TOA2    LEU2
BAP2    TOA2
```

The hypothetical networks consist of five genes that are listed at the top of the file. Each network is a directed graph. The directed edges may represent either positive regulatory relations (activation) or negative regulatory relations (repression). The starting (left, the regulator) and ending (right, the target gene) point of each directed edges is listed in the file. Thus, the structures of the hypothetical networks are completely determined by the network description file. RankGRN first parses the network description file, then scores each hypothetical gene network against microarray data using Bayesian Network methods (See Methods section). The score allows us to directly compare the merits of alternative models.[15] A posterior probability is calculated for each network based on its score. The posterior probability reflects our confidence in the hypothetical network given the microarray data. The hypothetical gene networks are then ranked by their posterior probabilities. The structures of the six networks are shown in Fig. 1.

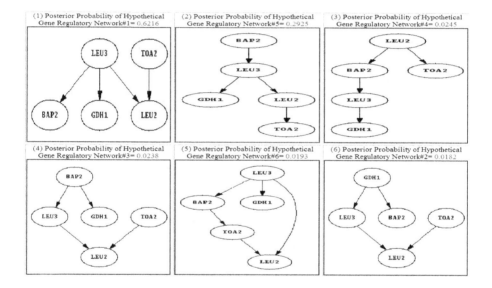

Fig. 1. Six yeast gene regulatory network models and their posterior probabilities

The networks contain five genes – Leu3, encodes zinc finger transcription factor of the Zn(2)-Cys(6) binuclear cluster domain type which regulates genes involved in branched chain amino acid biosynthesis and in ammonia assimilation; Bap2, encodes amino acid permease for leucine, valine, and isoleucine (putative); Gdh1, NADP-specific glutamate dehydrogenase; Leu2, encodes beta-IPM (isopropylmalate) dehydrogenase which is involved in leucine biosynthesis; Toa2 encodes transcription factor IIA subunit beta.[16] Four regulatory relations (between the five genes) are found by searching TransFac database[17] – Leu3 regulates Bap2, Gdh1 and Leu2; Toa2 regulates Leu2.

We assembled hypothetical gene network#1 (Fig. 1) using the four regulatory relations. The other five hypothetical gene networks are constructed using both true and false regulatory relations (Fig. 1).

RankGRN assigns uniform prior probability to all hypothetical networks. The prior probability reflects our confidence in the hypothetical gene network before observing microarray data. We use uniform prior probability because we do not want to bias any network. The probability of the networks may increase or decrease after considering microarray data. The updated probability is called posterior probability. As shown in Fig. 1, the most likely gene network is the network#1 (with the largest posterior probability), which contains and only contains regulatory relations extracted from TransFac database.

In a previous work, Boolean Network model and Genetic Algorithms were used to evaluate the hypothetical models of gene regulatory network.[3] The advantage of Bayesian Network is that the gene expression levels are modelled as random variable which can naturally deal with the stochastic aspect of the gene expression and measurement noise.[19]

4   Discussion

Bayesian network is a powerful tool for ranking hypothetical gene regulatory networks using microarray data. However, it cannot distinguish equivalent networks. In general, two network structures are equivalent if and only if they have the same undirected structures and the same v-structure. A v-structure is an ordered tuple (X, Y, Z) such that there is a directed edge from X to U and from Z to Y, but no edge between X and Z.[18] For example, in Fig. 2, the first five networks (network#1, 7, 8, 9, 6) are equivalent.

RankGRN takes probe set IDs as input because each gene may be represented by more than one probe sets in Affymetrix gene chips. Here we list the genes represented by the five probe set IDs in this figure:

92271_at: Pax6, paired box gene 6
98027_at: Col9a2, procollagen, type IX, alpha 2
102168_at: Gabbr1, gamma-aminobutyric acid (GABA-B) receptor, 1
100154_at: Tapbp, TAP binding protein
92674_at: Foxn1, forkhead box N1

Among them, the network#1 contains and only contains regulatory relations retrieved from TransFac database. The other four equivalent networks are constructed by reversing one of the directed edges in network#1 respectively. If some hypothetical networks are equivalent, they will have same posterior probabilities (Fig. 2). RankGRN cannot tell which one (of the five equivalent networks) is better. However, we can use model averaging to evaluate the features of the networks. Specifically, we calculated a posterior probability for each regulatory relation. An indicator function f was introduced, if a network G contains the regulatory relation, $f(G)=1$, otherwise, $f(G)=0$. The posterior probability of a regulatory relation is

$$P(f(G)\,|\,D) = \sum_G f(G)P(G\,|\,D) \qquad (5)$$

where $P(G\,|\,D)$ is the posterior probability of network G. There are 12 regulatory relations in the 9 gene network models shown in Figure 2. The posterior probabilities of the 12 regulatory relations are listed in Table 1. The first four regulatory relations were retrieved from TransFac database. The posterior probabilities of the four true regulatory relations (>0.79) are significantly higher than the false regulatory relations (<0.21).

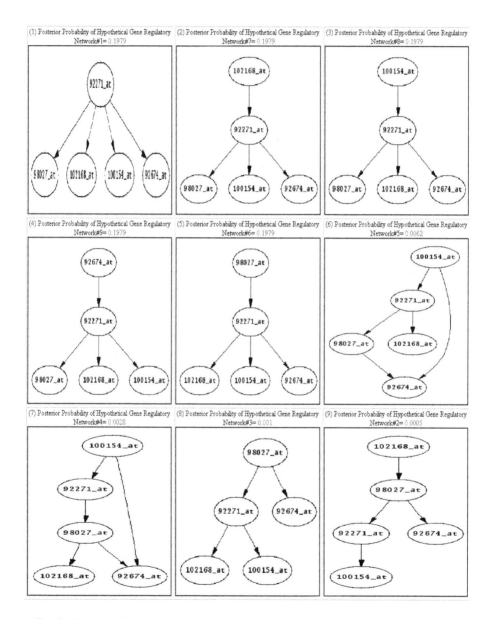

Fig. 2. Nine hypothetical mouse gene regulatory networks and their posterior probabilities

Table 1. Posterior probabilities of the regulatory relations in the nine gene network models in Figure 2

Regulatory Relations	Posterior Probability
92271_at-->98027_at	0.8006
92271_at-->102168_at	0.7988
92271_at-->100154_at	0.7931
92271_at-->92674_at	0.7916
100154_at-->92271_at	0.2069
98027_at-->92271_at	0.1994
102168_at-->92271_at	0.1979
92674_at-->92271_at	0.1979
98027_at-->92674_at	0.0105
100154_at-->92674_at	0.009
98027_at-->102168_at	0.0028
102168_at-->98027_at	0.0005

4   Conclusions

RankGRN is a useful tool for evaluating the merits of different hypothesises on the structure of gene regulatory network using existing microarray data. It ranks the hypothetical gene network models based on their capability of explaining the microarray data. It can be used for selecting the best hypothesis for further investigation.

References

1. Lee, T.I., Rinaldi, N.J., Robert, ., F., Odom, D.T., Bar-Joseph, Z., Gerber, G.K., Hannett, N.M., Harbison, C.T., Thompson, C.M., Simon, I., Zeitlinger, J., Jennings, E.G., Murray, H.L., Gordon, D.B., Ren, B., Wyrick, J.J., Tagne, J.B., Volkert, T.L., Fraenkel, E., Gifford, D.K., Young, R.A.: Transcriptional Regulatory Networks in Saccharomyces cerevisiae. *Science* **298** (2002) 799-804
2. Guelzim, N., Bottani, S., Bourgine, P., Kepes, F.: Topological and causal structure of the yeast transcriptional regulatory network. *Nat. Genet.* **31** (2002) 60-63
3. Repsilber, D., Liljenströmb, H., Anderson, S.G.E.: Reverse engineering of regulatory networks: simulation studies on a genetic algorithm approach for ranking hypotheses. *Biosystems* **66**(1-2) (2002)) 31-41
4. Pearl. J.: Probabilistic Reasoning in Intelligent Systems. *Morgan Kaufmann Publishers* (1988)
5. Freidman, N., Linial, M., Nachman, I., Peer, D.: Using Bayesian Networks to Analyze Expression Data. *J. Comput. Biol.* **7** (2000) 601-620

6. Spirtes, P., Glymour, C., Scheines., R., Kauffman, S., Aimale, V., Wimberly, F.: Constructing Bayesian Network Models of Gene Expression Networks from Microarray Data. *Proceedings of the Atlantic Symposium on Computational Biology,* Genome Information Systems and Technology (2001)

7. Peer, D., A. Regev, G. Elidan and N. Friedman, "Inferring subnetworks from perturbed expression profiles," *Bioinformatics* **17**, S215-S224 (2001)

8. Chu, T. Glymour, C., Scheines, R., Spirtes, P.: A Statistical Problem for Inference to Regulatory Structure from Associations of Gene Expression Measurement with Microarrays. *Bioinformatics* **19** (2003) 1147-1152

9. Gene Expression Omnibus [http://www.ncbi.nlm.nih.gov/geo/]

10. Stanford Microarray Database [http://genome-www5.stanford.edu/MicroArray/SMD/]

11. Gollub, J., Ball, C.A., Binkley, G., Demeter, J., Finkelstein, D.B., Hebert, J. M., Hernandez-Boussard, T., Jin, H., Kaloper, M., Matese, J.C., Schroeder, M., Brown, P.O., Botstein, D., Sherlock, G.: The Stanford Microarray Database: data access and quality assessment tools. *Nucleic Acids Res* **31**(1) (2003) 94-6

12. ArrayExpress at EBI [http://www.ebi.ac.uk/arrayexpress/]

13. ExpressDB [http://arep.med.harvard.edu/ExpressDB/]

14. Aach, J., Rindone, W., Church, G.M.: Systematic management and analysis of yeast gene expression data. *Genome Res.* **10**(4) (2000)) 431-45

15. Hartemink, A. J.: Principled Computational Methods for the Validation and Discovery of Genetic Regulatory Networks. PhD thesis, MIT (2001)

16. Saccharomyces Genome Database [http://www.yeastgenome.org/]

17. BIOBASE, GmbH Databases Transfac Professional Suite [http://www.cognia.com/]

18. Heckerman, D.: A tutorial on learning with Bayesian networks," In: *Learning in Graphical Models* (M, I. Jordan ed.) (1998) 301-354

19. de Jong, H. Modeling and Simulating of Genetic Regulatory Systems: A Literature Review. *J. Comput. Biol.* **9** (2002) 67-103

20. Pearl, J.: *Causality: Models, Reasoning, and Inference.* Cambridge University Press, Cambridge (2000)

21. Segal, E., Shapira, M., Regev, A., Pe'er, D., Botstein, D., Koller, D., Friedman, N.: Module networks: identifying regulatory modules and their condition-specific regulators from gene expression data. *Nat. Genet.* **34**(2) (2003) 166-176

22. Bockhorst, J., Craven, M., Page, D., Shavlik, J., Glasner, J.: A Bayesian network approach to operon prediction. *Bioinformatics.* **19**(10) (2003) 1227-1235

23. Sabatti, C. , Rohlin, L. , Oh, M.K., Liao, J.C.: Co-expression pattern from DNA microarray experiments as a tool for operon prediction. *Nucleic Acids Res* **30**(13) (2002) 2886-2893

24. Savoie, C.J., Aburatani, S., Watanabe, S., Eguchi, Y., Muta, S.,. Imoto, S., Miyano, S., Kuhara, S., Tashiro, K.: Use of gene networks from full genome microarray libraries to identify functionally relevant drug-affected genes and gene regulation cascades. *DNA Res.* **10**(1) (2003)) 19-25

25. Smith, V.A., Jarvis, E.D., Hartemink, A.J.: Influence of network topology and data collection on network inference. *Pac Symp Biocomput.* (2003) 164-75

26. Ong, I.M., Glasner, J.D., Page, D.: Modelling regulatory pathways in E. coli from time series expression profiles. *Bioinformatics*, **Suppl 1** (2002) ,S241-8

27. Imoto, S., Goto, T., Miyano, S.: Estimation of genetic networks and functional structures between genes by using Bayesian networks and nonparametric regression. *Pac Symp Biocomput*, (2002) 175-86

28. Shmulevich, I., Dougherty, E.R., Kim, S., Zhang, W.: Probabilistic Boolean Networks: a rule-based uncertainty model for gene regulatory networks. *Bioinformatics*, **18**(2) (2002)) 261-74
29. Heckerman, D., Geiger, D., Chickering, D.M.: Learning Bayesian networks: The combination of knowledge and statistical data. *Machine Learning* **20**(3) (1995) 197-243
30. "Graphviz", [http://www.research.att.com/sw/tools/graphviz]

On Efficiency of Experimental Designs for Single Factor cDNA Microarray Experiments

Xiao Yang[1] and Keying Ye[2]

[1] Monsanto Company, 800 N. Lindbergh Blvd., St. Louis, MO 63167
xiao.yang@monsanto.com
[2] Department of Statistics, Virginia Tech, Blacksburg, VA 24061-0439
keying@vt.edu

Abstract. Microarray experiments are used to perform gene expression profiling on a large scale. The focus of this study is on the efficiency of statistical design for single factor cDNA two-color microarray experiments. Relative efficiencies of proposed designs in Yang ([13]) are studied within the framework of incomplete block designs as well as row-column designs. Such efficiencies are investigated under fixed and mixed analysis of variance models. Furthermore, a real data analysis is conducted.

1 Introduction

Microarray experiments are used to perform gene expression profiling on a large scale (e.g., see [3] and [5]). Due to various experimental conditions, performing and interpreting cDNA microarray experiments is not efficient without statistical support at each step of the process. One important objective of microarray experiments is to detect differential expressions among genes between varieties. For instance, researchers would like to know whether and how many genes are expressed differentially between cancerous and normal populations. Assuming analysis of variance (ANOVA) models satisfying certain appropriate conditions, such differences may be quantified as contrasts in linear models. The goal of an optimal design is to maximize the precisions of the estimates of those contrasts.

Discussions on statistical designs in cDNA microarray experiments are still rather scarce. Sebastiani *et al.* in ([9]) made a good review of the current situation of statistical design problems in microarray experiments. As noted in Smyth *et al.* ([11]), it is not possible to give universal recommendation for all situations but the general principles of statistical experimental design apply to all microarray experiments.

In practice, there are a few designs researchers have been working with. A reference design, which is shown in Table 1 (a), or replicates of such a design is commonly used for a two-color microarray experiment. In this table, b and ν are the number of arrays and the number of varieties, respectively. Variety 0 is usually a reference sample or a pooled average of all the treatment samples. On the other hand, a loop design can be described in Table 1 (b) in which varieties are arranged in a loop fashion. For both diagrams in the table, the top line

Y. Shi, W. Xu, and Z. Chen (Eds.): CASDMKM 2004, LNAI 3327, pp. 119–127, 2004.

represents the samples with the one dye while the bottom line represents the samples with the other dye.

Table 1. Reference and Loop Designs $(b = \nu)$

(a) Reference Design

0	0	0	$\cdots$	0	0
1	2	3	$\cdots$	$\nu - 1$	ν

(b) Loop Design

1	2	3	$\cdots$	$\nu - 1$	ν
2	3	4	$\cdots$	ν	1

Kerr and Churchill in [7] studied the reference design as well as the loop design under fixed effects ANOVA models in the sense of incomplete block design framework. They compared the efficiencies of those designs. Before, due to the limitation of resources and high cost of the experiments, $b = \nu$ is quite common. Since replications (technical and biological) are important in functional genomic studies ([8]), especially for an experiment with more biological replications such as multiple patients, $b > \nu$ is more typical nowadays. Consequently, replications of the reference design, called replicated reference designs, and variations of the replications of loop designs, including interwoven designs, are of interest to researchers. An interwoven design is an extension of a loop design with number of arrays larger than the number of varieties. An example of interwoven design is given in Table 2. Kerr and Churchill in [7] discussed some design optimality properties of interwoven designs in the situation when $b = 2\nu$.

Table 2. An Interwoven Design with $b = 2\nu = 10$

1	2	3	4	5	1	3	5	2	4
2	3	4	5	1	3	5	2	4	1

In Yang (2003), extension of Kerr and Churchill's ([7]) A- and E- optimality results are developed. He considered a two-color microarray experiment with ν number of varieties and b arrays in the cases that $b = k\nu$, where $k = 1, 2, 3, 4$. To investigate optimal designs for such experiments, he first identified optimality in the context of incomplete block designs (with one block) and row-column designs (with two blocks, one being arrays and the other being dyes) using standard statistical A- and E-optimality criteria. Although arrays are usually treated as fixed effects in designs, it is more reasonable to view them as random ([12]) since they are selected from a larger, yet non-fixed population. In this article, we will compare efficiency of the designs proposed in Yang ([13]) within the framework of incomplete block design for fixed (Section 2) and mixed (Section 3) ANOVA models and row-column designs for fixed effects ANOVA model (Section 4). In Section 5, a data analysis is given.

2   Efficiency of Incomplete Block Designs Under Fixed Effects Model

We consider two fixed effects models along with the lines of Kerr and Churchill ([7]). The first model (M1) includes the main effects of arrays (A), dyes (D), varieties (V), genes (G), the variety-by-gene interactions (VG), and the array-by-gene interactions (AG). The second model (M2) omits the D factor and is suitable for analyzing data from a reference design.

$$y_{ijkgl} = \mu + A_i + D_j + V_k + G_g + (AG)_{ig} + (VG)_{kg} + \epsilon_{ijkgl} \tag{M1}$$
$$y_{ikgl} = \mu + A_i + V_k + G_g + (AG)_{ig} + (VG)_{kg} + \epsilon_{ikgl}. \tag{M2}$$

Response y_{ijkgl} usually is the log-transformed fluorescence intensity for array i, dye j, variety k and gene g. There are N genes, b arrays and ν varieties, and ϵ_{ijkgl} are identically and independently normally distributed with mean zero and constant variance σ_e^2. Furthermore, each gene is present only once on any array. We want to make inferences about differential expression of any gene g between any pair of varieties i and j. The test statistic for differential expression between treatments i and j for gene g is based on the contrast $(\hat{V}_i - \hat{V}_j) + ((V\hat{G})_{ig} - (V\hat{G})_{jg})$, where $i \neq j$ and $i, j = 1, 2, ..., \nu$. Note that this contrast differs from that of Kerr and Churchill (2001) for reasons discussed in Black and Doerge ([1]) and Yang ([13]).

We define a measure of performance for two microarray designs d_1 and d_2 by combining the definition of efficiency factor and relative efficiency as follows:

$$RE(d_1 \; to \; d_2) = \frac{Eff(d_1)}{Eff(d_2)}, \tag{1}$$

where the efficiency of design d, $Eff(d)$, is defined under a particular model as:

$$Eff(d) = \left\{ \frac{2}{\nu(\nu - 1)} \sum_{i<j} Var[(\hat{V}_i - \hat{V}_j) + ((V\hat{G})_{ig} - (V\hat{G})_{jg})] \right\}^{-1}. \tag{2}$$

Note that with all genes represented equally on all arrays, $Eff(d)$ needs to be considered only for a single gene g. As a function of the number of genes (N) and the error variance (σ^2), $Eff(d)$ can be evaluated numerically using the information matrix under (M1) or (M2). We also note that the ratio RE in (1) does not depend on N and σ^2. Finally, we note that had we used the comparison criterion of Kerr and Churchill ([7]) instead of (2), the same relative efficiency values would have been obtained.

Table 3 shows several designs proposed in Yang (2003) that can be viewed as a mixture of a loop and a reference component, and we therefore refer to these designs as mixed designs. We distinguish mixed designs by the level of mixing, which is defined as the number of varieties arranged in the loop component. For example, in design (c) of Table 3, the first three varieties are arranged in a loop, hence it is a Mix(3) design. Note that the design (a) in Table 3 is a special mixed

Table 3. Some Mix Designs

(a) Design Mix(1)

1	1	1	1	$\cdots$	1	1
1	2	3	4	$\cdots$	$\nu-1$	ν

(b) Design Mix(2)

1	1	1	$\cdots$	1	1	2
2	3	4	$\cdots$	$\nu-1$	ν	1

(c) Design Mix(3)

1	2	3	1	1	$\cdots$	1
2	3	1	4	5	$\cdots$	ν

design, Mix(1), and the other special case is the loop design, Mix(ν). Kerr and Churchill in [7] referred to Mix(1) as the augmented reference design.

The A- and E- optimality issues have been discussed in Yang ([13]). In Table 4, we evaluate the relative A- efficiency of various designs from the class of mixed designs and for the nonbinary design Mix(1), relative to the optimal design for each value of ν. Columns in Table 4 contain the relative efficiencies of designs Mix(2), Mix(3), Mix(4), loop, and Mix(1), relative to the optimal design. The best designs are generally mixed designs when the number of treatments exceeds 8.

On the other hand, we note that the A- and E-criteria do not agree with each other. The E-optimal designs Mix(2) and Mix(1) are not A-optimal, while Mix(4), although not E-optimal, is A-optimal when $\nu = 9$, 10, 11 (for more discussion see Yang, 2003). This finding leads to question about which optimality criterion should be used when we search for the best design. In general, there is no consensus on this problem. It is a practical issue, which depends on the purpose of the experiment. We also note that the A-optimal designs listed in Table 4 were found using a computer search algorithm, and hence they may not be the actual optimal design, although they are expected to be highly efficient or near optimal.

3   Relative Efficiencies for Incomplete Block Design Under Mixed Effects Models

In Section 2, the relative efficiencies of various designs have been compared under fixed effects ANOVA models. However, the contrasts of interest can also be estimated using additional inter-block information by treating blocks (array) as random. From design optimality point of views, it is hard to theoretically derive optimal designs under criteria such as A- or E- optimality for a mixed model that contains both fixed and random effects. Thus we want to compute the relative efficiencies of the designs considered in Section 2 while the array effects are treated as random.

Now the relative efficiencies of those designs are compared based on mixed effects models, which are obtained by treating A and AG in models (M1) and

Table 4. Relative Efficiency of Certain Mixed Designs for $b = \nu$ and $k = 2$: when $\nu=12$, Mix(3) and Mix(4) are both A-optimal, which is denoted by (*)

ν	Mix(2)	Mix(3)	Mix(4)	Loop	Mix(1)
3	0.7727	1	NA	1	0.5
4	0.7085	0.7895	1	1	0.5555
5	0.7378	0.7894	0.8696	1	0.625
6	0.7933	0.8332	0.8749	1	0.7
7	0.86	0.8936	0.9181	1	0.7779
8	0.9322	0.9619	0.9769	1	0.8572
9	0.9655	0.9914	1	0.9585	0.8987
10	0.9727	0.9954	1	0.8967	0.9135
11	0.9781	0.9983	1	0.8409	0.925
12*	0.9822	1	1	0.7904	0.9339
13	0.9837	1	0.9986	0.7436	0.9396
14	0.9849	1	0.9979	0.7018	0.9446
15	0.9862	1	0.9972	0.6642	0.949
16	0.9875	1	0.9971	0.6306	0.9528
17	0.9881	1	0.9968	0.5999	0.9557
18	0.9888	1	0.9964	0.5717	0.9584
19	0.9898	1	0.9964	0.5462	0.961
20	0.9901	1	0.996	0.5229	0.963
21	0.9908	1	0.9963	0.5015	0.9651
22	0.9911	1	0.9963	0.4814	0.9668
23	0.9918	1	0.9963	0.4631	0.9685
24	0.9922	1	0.9963	0.4461	0.9699
25	0.9922	1	0.9959	0.4303	0.9709

(M2) as random factors, with A_i being iid $(0,\sigma_a^2)$ for all i's, and $(AG)_{ig}$ iid $(0,\sigma_{ag}^2)$ for all i's and g's. Define $\lambda_A = \sigma_a^2/\sigma_e^2$ and $\lambda_{AG} = \sigma_{ag}^2/\sigma_e^2$ to be the relative variabilities in arrays and array-gene interactions with respect to the noise variation, respectively.

There are many parameters to be considered in these designs. Designs may depend on the values of λ_A, λ_{AG}, and even the number of genes in an array since the variance components of the random effects can be better estimated by more number of genes within each array. Nine scenarios are considered ($\lambda_A=0.1$, 1 and 10 and $\lambda_{AG}=0.1$, 1 and 10) for several values of ν and the results of the relative efficiencies among the reference, loop, and mixed designs (for $b = \nu$) are summarized in Figure 1. It should be noted that the numbers obtained in Figure 1 is based on 20 genes and 2 replicates for each configuration.

Although mixed designs are A-better for blocked design when the number of varieties gets larger as discussed in Section 2, they are all inferior to the loop design when λ_{AG} is small to moderate. However, when λ_{AG} gets bigger, efficiency of the loop design starts to decrease as the number of varieties gets larger and mixed designs are all winning in such cases. In regarding to the reference designs,

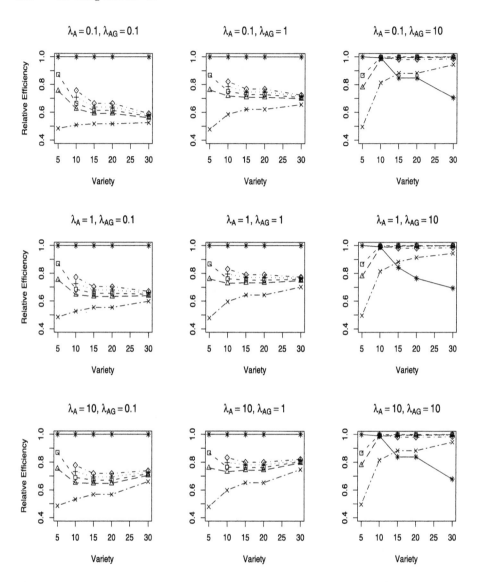

Fig. 1. Relative Efficiencies of Mixed, Loop and Reference Designs under Mixed Effects Model with various λ_A and λ_{AG} settings. In the figure, relative (to the best) efficiencies of mix3, mix4, mix5 and mix6 are denoted by triangle, square, plus and diamond, respectively; the loop design is denoted by star and the reference by strike. The number of genes in each array is 20 with a replication of 2

although it is always A-worse than any of the mixed designs considered in Figure 1, it starts to be better than the loop design when λ_{AG} and ν are large. Our recommendation is to use loop design unless large λ_{AG}^2 is expected.

4   Efficiency for Row-Column Designs

In row-column designs, the experimental units are grouped in two directions, i.e., two blocking factors are used with one factor representing the rows of the design (in our case it is the dye) and the other factor the columns (see [10]). We focus the designs in which each variety is labelled with each dye equally often so that varieties and rows (dyes) are orthogonal. Such a design is called row-orthogonal design ([6]). When there is a balance between dyes and varieties, systematic bias in the red and green intensities can be reduced ([14]). A special case of row-orthogonal design is a dye-swap experiment where gene expressions are compared across two varieties, and the hybridizations are repeated with the dye reversed. The designs considered here have ν varieties arranged in k rows and b columns such that variety i is replicated r_i times. For the design of two-color microarray experiments, the rows represent the two fluorescent dyes and columns represent arrays, and $k = 2$ always in a two-color experiment.

In Yang ([13]), a series of computer-searched optimal designs are discussed. For each of the three scenarios ($b = 2\nu$, $b = 3\nu$, $b = 4\nu$) considered, we compute the relative efficiency of the replicated reference design for each ν, relative to the computer-searched optimal row-column designs. These results are summarized in Figure 2.

In most cases, the efficiency of the replicated reference design is only between one third and one half of the efficiency of the optimal row-orthogonal design, but the relative efficiency of the reference design increases with the number of varieties. For much larger ν, the reference design may again become efficient for a given scenario.

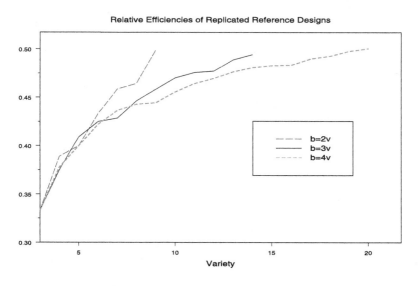

Fig. 2. Relative Efficiencies of Replicated Reference Designs Compared to the Associated Row-column Designs under Three Scenarios of b and ν

In conclusion, when the array effects are treated as fixed, the replicated reference designs are not really efficient in terms of accurately identifying differential gene expressions.

5   An Example

The data set was from a biotechnology company for its bovine embryo classification study to classify developmental competency of NT (nuclear Transfer) embryos against that of IVF (in Vitro Fertilization) embryos. Ten embryos were collected from each cell population (NT or IVF). An interwoven loop design was used, where 2640 genes were spotted twice on each of 100 arrays. The following nested mixed effects model was used for the analysis:

$$y_{ijklmn} = \mu + A_i + D_j + (AD)_{ij} + T_k + E_l(T_k)$$
$$+ G_m + (TG)_{km} + (AG)_{im} + G_m E_l(T_k) + \epsilon_{ijklmn}, \tag{3}$$

where the response y_{ijklmn} was log-transformed intensity from array i, dye j, cell population k, embryo l and gene m. Effects of labelling reactions were estimated with factor AD. Factors A, (AD), (AG), $E(T)$ and $GE(T)$ were assumed random with dispersion assumptions $A_i \sim$ iid N(0,σ_A^2), $(AD)_{ij} \sim$ iid N(0,σ_{AD}^2), $E_l(T_k) \sim$ iid N(0,σ_{ET}^2), $(AG)_{im} \sim$ iid N(0,σ_{AG}^2), $G_m E_l(T_k) \sim$ iid N(0,σ_{EG}^2), and $e_{ijklmn} \sim$ iid N(0,σ_e^2).

The scatter plot of log ratios versus the average of log intensity (RI plots) revealed intensity-dependent biases in the two color channels. The raw data were log-transformed and normalized using LOESS and spatial LOESS functions ([2]). The problem of multiple testing was accounted for by adjusting the raw p-values using Bonferroni and the step-down Bonferroni methods. Nineteen genes were identified to be differentially expressed, and the two methods of adjustments produced the same set of genes.

In the above analysis only a common error was assumed for all genes, implying that the estimates of all contrasts have the same standard error, which seems unrealistic ([4]). Ideally, we could assume an error variance for each gene, but this is computationally prohibitive and unnecessary. In the bovine experiments, groups of genes showed similar variation in expression values, but large variations were observed for highly expressed genes while lowly expressed genes showed much smaller variations. Therefore, models with a common error variance often overestimate the standard errors of contrasts for lowly expressed genes but underestimate standard errors of contrasts for highly expressed genes. Our recommendation is to group genes based on their variations and expression values. For the bovine experiment, we assigned genes into 9 different groups each with a separate error variance based on the first ANOVA results. Initial screening of normalized data revealed that 29 genes were lowly expressed with the average variance of 0.08, 58 genes are highly expressed with average variance of 1.5, and two groups were assigned to these genes. The variation of other genes ranged from 0.11 to 0.98, and were further divided into seven groups with average variance of 0.14, 0.18, 0.22, 0.28, 0.35, 0.45 and 0.62. As a result, 17 of 19 previously reported genes were identified again. The raw data revealed that the two unidentified genes were highly expressed with large variances. Without grouping, their variability was underestimated when a common error variance was assumed. Although the choice of the number of groups is somewhat arbitrary and certainly depends on features of a given data set, we have found the by-group residual plots particularly useful for the visual justification of the grouping.

References

1. Black, M and Doerge, R. (2002). Calculation of the minimum number of replicate spots required for detection of significant gene expression fold change in microarray. *Bioinformatics*, **18**, no. 12, 1609–1616.
2. Cui, X., Kerr, M.K. and Churchill, G. (2002). Data transformations for cDNA microarray data. (http://www.jax.org/research/churchill/pubs/index.html)
3. Derisi, J.L., Iyer, V.R., and Brown, P.O. (1997). Exploring the metabolic and genetic control of gene expression on a genomic scale. *Science* **278**, 680–686.
4. Dudoit, S., Fridlyand, J. and Speed, T.P. (2002). Comparison of discrimination methods for the classification of tumors using gene expression data. *Journal of the American Statistical Association* **97**, 77–87.
5. Eisen, M.B., Spellman, P.T., Brown, P.O. and Botstein, D. (1998). Cluster analysis and display of genome-wide expression patterns. *Proceedings of the National Academy of Sciences* **25**, 14863–14868.
6. John, J.A. and Williams, E.R. (1995). *Cyclic and Computer Generated Designs*. Chapman and Hall, London.
7. Kerr, M. and Churchill, G. (2001). Experimental design for gene expression microarrays. *Biostatistics* **2**, 183–201.
8. Kohane, I.S., Kho, A.T. and Butte, A.J. (2003). *Microarrays for an Integrative Genomics*, The MIT Press, Cambridge, Massachusetts.
9. Sebastiani, P., Gussoni, E., Kohane I.S. and Ramoni, M.F. (2003). Statistical Challenges in Functional Genomics (with discussions). *Statistical Science*, **18**, 33–70.
10. Shah, K.R. and Sinha, B.K. (1989). Theory of Optimal Designs. *Lecture notes in statistics*. Springer-Verlag.
11. Smyth, G. K., Yang, Y.-H. and Speed, T. P. (2002). Statistical issues in microarray data analysis. In: Functional Genomics: Methods and Protocols, M. J. Brownstein and A. B. Khodursky (eds.), Methods in Molecular Biology series, Humana Press, Totowa, NJ, 111–136.
12. Wolfinger, R.D., Gibson, G., Wolfinger, E.D., Bennett, L., Hamadeh, H., Bushel, P, Afshari, C.A. and Paules, R. (2001). Assessing gene significance from cDNA Microarray expression data via mixed Models. *Journal of Computational Biology* **8(6)**, 625–637.
13. Yang, X. (2003). Optimal Design of Single Factor cDNA Microarray Experiments and Mixed Models for Gene Expression Data, Ph.D. dissertation, Department of Statistics, Virginia Tech.
14. Yang, Y.H., Speed, T.P. (2002). Design issues for cDNA microarray experiments. *Nature Reviews* **3**, 579–588.

Data Mining Approach in Scientific Research Organizations Evaluation Via Clustering

Jingli Liu [1,2], Jianping Li [2], Weixuan Xu [2], and Yong Shi [3]

[1] University of Science & Technology of China, Hefei, 230026, P.R.C
[2] Institute of Policy and Management, Chinese Academy of Sciences,
Beijing 100080, P.R.C
{manager, ljp,xwu}@mail.casipm.ac.cn
[3] Graduate School of Chinese Academy of Sciences, Beijing 100039, P.R.C
yshi@unomaha.edu

Abstract. Data mining is a useful tool to draw useful information from large database. In scientific research organizations evaluation, there exists a problem of using the same criteria to evaluate different types of research organizations. In this paper we propose a clustering method to make classification of the scientific research organization of CAS, and then according to this classification we evaluate the scientific research organization using the annual evaluation database of CAS to test our method.

1 Introduction

The evaluation of scientific research organizations has a long history. As early as in the 1930's, the economist in the Soviet Union had tried to make a systematic approach of scientific research evaluation criteria. In Sep. 1968, the Soviet Union constituted a file about how to evaluate the scientific research organization and established the basic indicators and evaluation system. This file was the earliest file in evaluation of scientific organization. In Aug.1973, the Soviet Union established the evaluation system how to evaluate the scientific research organization [1].

The developed countries such as America, Japan, and European Union pay much attention to the evaluation of scientific research organization and have a long research work on the theory and method of how to make proper evaluation of scientific research of organizations. Thus they have made good progress in the evaluation policy, standard and method.

As for China, we didn't pay much attention to the scientific research evaluation until the end of the 20th century. The Chinese Academy of Sciences (CAS) has undergone the evaluation work for several years. As the Knowledge Innovation Project started in 1998, CAS began to make evaluation on the institutes that entered the Innovation base. But according to our experience, we haven't created our own scientific research evaluation theory, method and process. Since CAS has 84 research institutes and the evaluation on them is a big task for us, we need to work hard to build our own theory and method on evaluation of scientific research organizations.

In our evaluation practice, there exist many problems. They are: (1) the classification standard of scientific research organization is ambiguous. Thus in the

Y. Shi, W. Xu, and Z. Chen (Eds.): CASDMKM 2004, LNAI 3327, pp. 128–134, 2004.

evaluation process, the same criteria is adopted while evaluating the different kinds of scientific research organizations. This is sure not reasonable. Of all the 84 institutes of CAS, they are partitioned into four different special bureaus, which are basic bureau, advanced technology bureau, biotechnology bureau and resource and environment bureau. Each bureau leads several institutes. This partition is a very traditional method. With the rapid development of S&T, there are many intersections among various subjects. And the scientific research character is not so pure as before. Those institutes that belong to applied research bureau will also do basic research work. And institutes who belongs to basic research bureau will do applied research work too. This may cause confusion when it comes to evaluation if we still use the same criteria to make evaluation on these institutes. So we need to make new partitions to all the institutes. How to make classification of all the institutes? How to make correct evaluation using right classification? How to judge their real research level? These problems should be solved as early as possible. (2) The evaluation is only to emphasize on quantity not on quality. This makes the researchers do not pay attention to the scientific research quality and hurt their enthusiasm which will leads to lower research level if this situation can't be improved. (3) In the evaluation process, objectivity and impartiality are not in their real state. The evaluation result can't embody the real research level of the researchers because of some personal interruption. This really does harm to the enthusiasm of researchers. (4) There is little attention to the un-cognized scientific research project, which really needs financial support to test their ideas. Most of the time, these projects will not be granted fund. This is really a serious problem in the development of the innovative project. We want more initiative thought, but if they can't get the necessary support, how can it be realized?

In this paper we want to solve the first problem of how to evaluate scientific research organizations according to their classification. So, first we need to make a partition of the scientific research organization, and then evaluate them by different types.

2   The Evaluation of Scientific Research Organizations

2.1   Scientific Research Organization

Scientific research organization is the formal organization that engages in scientific research and training scientific researchers. It is a social unit that brings researchers, material resources and capital together and deals with basic research, applied research and development.

There are different kinds of classification criteria on scientific research organization. One classification method is by the work that scientific research organizations do. According to the research types, they can de divided into three kinds: basic scientific research organization, applied scientific research organization and development scientific research organization. This conforms to three levels of scientific research, which are basic research, applied research and development. Another is by what they belongs. Then they can be divided into state-funded scientific research organization, scientific research organization in college, scientific research organization in companies and non-profitable scientific research organizations.

2.2 Scientific Research Organization Evaluation

Evaluation or assessment of scientific work in scientific research organizations has traditionally been based on a procedure or a system of having equals from the same scientific field or peers to evaluate the quality of the scientific research output, especially the research paper.

Ordinarily, we evaluate scientific research organizations according to their output. The output includes thesis, patent, social and economic benefit, scientific researchers they bring up, the amount of the project they succeeded applied for and the amount of money they get after getting the project granted.

The usual evaluation method will be: First, we set up the evaluation purpose. Generally speaking, the evaluation purpose of the scientific research organization is to take accountability. Since the scientific research organizations have been granted a certain amount of money for their research use, they should be responsible for the taxpayers. At the same time, we would like to check the developing condition of the organization, to review whether the scientific research organization has accomplished its object, to predict the organization's future development.

In the present scientific research organization evaluation, we have mentioned before that there exists a problem of ignoring the organization types. Then the evaluation results obtained by this procedure can't embody the real character of what organizations have done. It is not fair to compare two different kinds of institutes using same evaluation criteria. In order to overcome this problem, we adopt the cluster technique to make a classification of the present institutes. We have used classified evaluation method in scientific research organization evaluation. But this classification has been proved to be not good. So how to classify all the institutes into different groups is a big question.

3   Data Mining

3.1 Introduction to Data Mining

Data mining is a useful tool to discover the interesting data model hidden in the large databases. Thus it can draw meaningful knowledge from the data using such tools as association rule, cluster, neural network, decision tree, etc. It can do classification, prediction, estimation and other works. A general process is illustrated below [2].

3.2 Clustering

Clustering is to group a set of objects into classes of similar objects [2]. It is not like classification for we don't know the class before we make cluster. Cluster is based on the principle of maximizing the similarity of the objects in the same cluster while minimizing the similarity of the objects in the different cluster. Cluster analysis has been widely used in various applications, such as pattern recognition, data analysis, image processing, etc.

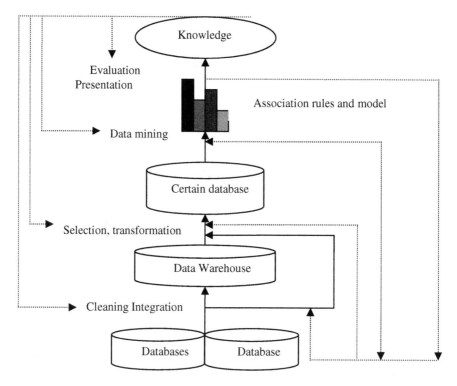

Fig. 1. A General Data Mining Process

How can we evaluate the quality of the cluster? We can define a scoring function that can measure how well the cluster is. We use $d(x, y)$ to represent the distance between x and y, which can measure the compactness of each cluster and the distance of each cluster.

The most popular distance measure is Euclidean distance. Another measure is Manhattan distance. Minkowski distance is a generalization of both Euclidean distance and Manhattan distance. It is defined as

$$d(i, j) = \sqrt{w_1 \left| x_{i1} - x_{j1} \right|^q + w_2 \left| x_{i2} - x_{j2} \right|^q + ... + w_p \left| x_{ip} - x_{jp} \right|^q} \qquad (1)$$

Where $i = (x_{i1}, x_{i2}, ..., x_{ip})$ and $j = (x_{j1}, x_{j2}, ..., x_{jp})$ are two p-dimensional data objects. While in clustering, there are two kinds of standardization of a variable f, they are [2]

1) The mean absolute deviation s_f

$$s_f = \frac{1}{n} \left(\left| x_{1f} - m_f \right| + \left| x_{2f} - m_f \right| + ... + \left| x_{nf} - m_f \right| \right) \qquad (2)$$

2) The standardized measurement

$$z_{if} = \frac{x_{if} - m_f}{s_f} \tag{3}$$

A complete cluster process includes data pre-processing, cluster, using scoring function to test the result of the cluster and make corrections.

4   The Scientific Research Organization Evaluation Via Clustering

Generally, scientific research organizations are evaluated by their outputs. In 2002, there are 84 research institutes to be evaluated according to their output. There are three types of research organizations in the evaluation, basic research, advanced technology and resource & environment. Each institute that belongs to different special bureau was evaluated separately using different indicators. As for basic research organizations, they are evaluated by S&T awards, thesis and literature, S&T person with ability and S&T project outlay. When it comes to advanced technology research institutions, the indicators are S&T awards, thesis and literature, S&T person with ability, patent, project outlay, and project researched. The resource and environment research institutions were evaluated by S&T awards, thesis and literature, S&T person with ability, patent, the amount of project and their corresponding outlay, social benefit.

The research institutes belong to different professional bureau. Every year, the evaluation research center of CAS will make evaluation on the institutes according to which bureau the research institutions belongs to. This evaluation method adopts the concept of classification evaluation, but this classification is based on the factitious partition. After years of organization reform of CAS, the institutes were divided into different types that were under the leadership of certain bureaus. According to our experience, some institutes should be evaluated according to other bureau's evaluation indicators. So we need to make a new partition of all the institutes according to their output for the output of a research institute can represent its character.

Now let us use cluster method on the present 84 institutions of CAS to make a partition.

We use the indicators which were used during the evaluation in 2002. We want to know clearly what the natural states of the institutions are, that is, which institutions should be in one class and which should be in another. After partitioning the institutions into different classes we will use the previous indicators to make evaluation separately.

We use SPSS software to make cluster. The data used are the annual evaluation data of 2002. The indicators used in cluster are thesis, literature, patent, project, scientific research equipment, the material needed for scientific research. The cluster result is listed below.

Table 1. Cluster Result

Class One	62,42,31,36,21,7,75,76,12,15,60,79,48,13,33,45,61,24,81,6,2,30,11
Class Two	34,18,17,39,74,27,49,32,5,35,82,23,40,68,9,77,51,37,22,80,4,41,28,25, 69,19,70,57,10,63,44, 16,55,3,50,64,54,56,46,72,52,53,26,43,66,78
Class Three	67, 81, 20, 71, 73, 14, 65, 58, 47, 29, 38, 59

Remark 1. The number is the table is the serial number of the institutes which we used during the cluster process.

As we can see from the cluster result, the institutions are partitioned into three classes. They are not conforming to the previous classification according to which special bureau the institutes belong to. Each class contains institutes that belong to three special bureaus. This demonstrates that the previous evaluation according to the previous classification is not a good one. The institutes which should be partitioned into the right have been changed. According to this classification, we use the annual evaluation data to make evaluation. It generates a good result, which proves that our classification is right.

5 Conclusion

Scientific research organizations have their own characters. Nowadays countries all over the world pay much attention to the S&T evaluation. In order to make full of our limited scientific research resources we need to make evaluation on them. But how to do evaluation is still a big problem. This needs us understand the different character of the scientific research and its unpredictable output. It is really hard to make an accurate and objective evaluation. In this paper we proposed a method of how to make classification of the different kind of research institutions. We give a preliminary conclusion. Still, this research needs further study on how to make classification more appropriate to generate more accurate and objective evaluation on the institutes.

References

1. Zhang, L.: The Evaluation of Scientific Research Organizations, Colleges Home and abroad. The Impact of Science on Society, Vol.1 (1995) 16-26
2. Han, J., Kanber, M.: Data Ming, Concepts and Techniques. Higher Education press & Morgan Kaufmann Publishers (2001)
3. Gause, J. M., A theory of Organization in Public Administration. Frontiers of Public Administration. University of Chicago Press, Chicago (1936)
4. Hand, D., Mannila, K., Smyth, P.: Principles of Data Mining, China Machine Press, CITIC Publishing House (2003)
5. 2002 Annual Evaluation Report of CAS, Evaluation Research Center of CAS (2002)
6. Zhang, R., Fang, K.: An Introduction to Multi-Statistical Analysis, Science Press (2003)
7. Shi, Z.: Knowledge Discovery, Tsinghua University Press (2002)

8. Hansson, F.: How to Evaluate and Select New Scientific Knowledge by Introducing the Social Dimension in the Evaluation of Research Quality, Paper Presented at the European Evaluation Society 2002 Conference, Seville, Spain, October 10-12th (2002)
9. Echeverria, J.: Science, Technology, and Values: Towards an Axiological Analysis of Techno-Scientific Activity, Technology in Society, 25(2003) 205-215
10. Zhang, Y.: the Research on Chaos Application into Scientific Research Organization Management, PhD dissertation (2004)
11. Ran, Z.: Scientific Research Organization Behavior, S&T Literature Press (1992)
12. Georghiou, L., Roessner, D.: Evaluating Technology Programs: Tools and Methods, Research Policy, 29 (2000) 657-678
13. Doughhery, E. R., Brun, M.: a Probabilistic Theory of Clustering, Pattern Recognition, 37 (2004) 917-925
14. De Smet, Y., Guzman, L. M.: Towards Multi-Criteria Clustering: An Extension of the K-means Algorithm, European Journal of Operational Research (2003)

Heuristics to Scenario-Based Capacity Expansion Problem of PWB Assembly Systems*

Zhongsheng Hua and Liang Liang

School of Business, University of Science and Technology of China,
Hefei, Anhui 230026, P. R. China
{zshua, lliang}@ustc.edu.cn

Abstract. A model of scenario-based line capacity expansion problem for PWB (Printed Wiring Board) assembly systems at the aggregate level is developed. The model synthesizes BOM (Bill Of Material) of product families and machine operation flexibility, thus it is an attempt of integrating strategic capacity planning, aggregate production planning and MPS (Master Production Scheduling), which is an important research topic of production management. Since the resulting model is a large-scale two-stage stochastic mixed integer programming problem, it can not be solved with standard code. An approximate solution procedure is developed, which first reduces the searching space of capacity expansion decision variables to rough addition sets by heuristics, then the rough addition sets are searched through adaptive genetic algorithms. Numerical experiments are presented to show the financial benefit of the model and the feasibility of our approach.

1 Introduction

Electronic systems play an increasingly important role in today's consumer and industrial products. The most common production process for electronic systems is assembling components on a printed wiring board (PWB). Surface mount component (SMC) placement machines are typically among the most important pieces of manufacturing equipment in a surface mount PWB assembly line. In general, an SMC placement machine is composed of a body base, board handling system, component feeders, placement heads, placement tools, and vision system. A machine line consists of different machine types that can produce many types of product families. The range of products that can be built on the line, i.e., the diversity of the allowable process recipes, is a key measure of the flexibility of a machine line. Because of the high cost of a machine line with *total flexibility* (i.e., a machine line that can build all products), most manufacturing firms build *partially flexible* machine lines (i.e., a machine line that can build only a subset of all products).

Making the most of potential benefits of such expensive component placement machines requires well-thought out capacity expansion decision and production planning before it begins production for each upcoming time period. This paper assumes a

---

* This research is supported by NSFC (grant number:70172041).

Y. Shi, W. Xu, and Z. Chen (Eds.): CASDMKM 2004, LNAI 3327, pp. 135–144, 2004.

firm with certain PWB assembly machine lines with installed capacity (termed as the initial capacity layout) to produce specific product families which consist of some part types. The planning horizon is divided into several time periods with equal length. The capacity expansion problem is to determine whether additional capacity should be installed at the beginning of each time period at each machine line because of demand fluctuation.

Capacity expansion for flexible manufacturing systems (FMS) has been intensively investigated since 1990's. Many researches have been worked on optimal capacity acquisition policies (Gaimon, 1994) (Gaimon and Ho, 1994). Eppen etc. (1989) proposed a scenario approach to capacity planning, which addressed the overall capacity, the type of facility (dedicated or flexible) and the location of the capacity for the auto industry. However, flexibility of production process is not involved in their models. Fine (1990) and Van Mieghem(1998) presented optimal line capacity investment (expansion) strategies respectively. Since they addressed choices between dedicated and flexible machine lines, their models and solution methods are not directly applicable to PWB assembly systems. Li and Tirupati (1994) considered the problem and investment planning in an environment characterized by multiple products and dynamic demands, their focus was on the tradeoff between flexible (totally flexible) and dedicated technologies. Benjaafar and Gupta (1998) used a set of models to compare the effect of product variety and process flexibility on performance under varying operating conditions and control policies. It is in spirit similar to our model, but their models do not associate flexibility with the structure of product.

In the environment of multi-product, multi-period, deterministic and dynamic market demand, Hua and Banerjee (2000) made a pioneer attempt to develop a model of capacity expansion for PWB assembly system (a typical FMS), which brings together the feature of structure of product families and machine flexibility. This paper extends the model proposed by Hua and Banerjee (2000) to random market demand and an approximate solution procedure is developed.

The reminder of the paper is organized as follows. In the next section, a cursory statement of capacity expansion problem for PWB assembly systems is presented. Section 3 describes a scenario-based model for the problem. An approximate solution process and relative heuristic algorithms to the model are developed in section 4. The adaptive genetic algorithms (AGA) for searching rough addition sets are introduced in section 5. Numerical experiments in section 6 illustrate financial benefit of the model and the feasibility of the solution approach and algorithms.

2   Capacity Expansion Problem for PWB Assembly Lines

The PWB assembly system consists of inserting or mounting electrical components, such as resistors, transistors and capacitors, into prespecified positions on a PWB. Each machine can insert certain part types on a PWB, some machines form a machine line which can produce some product families, where families are defined as sets of PWB types (items) which share similar operational characteristics and can be easily determined by exploiting special clustering techniques (Van Laarhoven and Zijm,1993). The demand forecast at the family level is suitable and easy to operate for aggregate planning. A machine line makes insertions on PWBs with the only restriction that all the insertions for a product family are done on the same machine line. The placement operations for a given product family are distributed across the available machines in the line. Figure 1 shows an illustration of such a machine line, with four assembly processes. In this example, each machine is capable of assembling two different types of parts from the list of five categories: small chips (SC), large chips (LC), odd-shaped (OS) parts such as connectors and pins, high-precision (HP) placements such as fine-pitch integrated circuits, and direct chip attach (DCA) parts that require an additional flux dispensing operation.

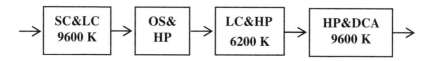

Fig. 1. Illustration of a PWB assembly line

In Figure 1, each text box represents an SMT placement machine. The first machine can insert part types SC and LC. Its designed capacity is 96,00 thousands placements per quarter, and its purchasing cost is 200 k dollars.

The capacity expansion model (Model P_0) is described as follows. Notations in the model are defined in Table 1.

Table 1. Notations

Indices	Cost Parameters
t time periods, $t=1,2,...,T$	$C(t,n,m,l)$ average unit production cost for given m, n , t, l
n demand scenarios, $n=1,2,...,N$	
i part types, $i=1,2,...,I$	$C_{sc}(t,j)$ unit cost of subcontracting product family j in period t
j product families, $j=1,2,...,J$	
m machine types, $m=1,2,...,M$	$C_p(t,m)$ costs of purchase and setup of a machine of type m in period t
l machine lines, $l=1,2,...,L$	

Decision Variables	Capacity and Demand Parameters
$X(t,n,i,j,m,l)$ Number of part type i for product family j produced on machine m in line l under scenario n in period t	$F(i,m)$ capability of machine type m inserting part type i, $F(i,m)=1$ if it can insert part type i; 0, otherwise.
$X_{sc}(t,n,j)$ Amount of subcontracting product family j under scenario n in period t	$Q(m)$ number of insertions machine type m can make in one period
	B capital investment budget
$Y(t,m,l)$ Number of machines of type m added to line l in period t.	$d(t,n,j)$ demand of product family j under scenario n in period t
	$S(i,j)$ number of part type i in each of product family j
	$p(t,n)$ probability that scenario n occurs in period t

(P_0)

$$Min \ Z = \sum_{t,m,l} C_p(t,m)Y(t,m,l) + \sum_{t,n,i,j,m,l} C(t,n,m,l)p(t,n)X(t,n,i,j,m,l)$$

$$+ \sum_{t,n,j} p(t,n)C_{sc}(t,j)X_{sc}(t,n,j) . \tag{1}$$

$$s.t. \ \sum_{j} X(t,n,i,j,m,l) \le \{N(0,m,l) + \sum_{k=1}^{t} Y(k,m,l)\}Q(m)F(i,m) , \tag{2}$$

$$t = 1,...,T, n = 1,...,N, i = 1,...,I, m = 1,...,M, l = 1,...,L$$

$$\sum_{m} X(t,n,i,j,m,l)S(i',j) = \sum_{m} X(t,n,i',j,m,l)S(i,j) , \quad (S(i,j), S(i',j) \ne 0)) \tag{3}$$

$$n = 1,...,N, i,i' = 1,...,I(i \ne i'), j = 1,...,J, l = 1,...,L, t = 1,...,T$$

$$\sum_{i,m,l} X(t,n,i,j,m,l) + S(i,j)X_{sc}(t,n,j) = S(i,j)d(t,n,j) , \tag{4}$$

$$t = 1,...,T, n = 1,...,N, j = 1,...,J$$

$$\sum_{t,m,l} C_p(t,m) * Y(t,m,l) \le B , \tag{5}$$

$$X(t,n,i,j,m,l) \ge 0, X_{sc}(t,n,j) \ge 0, \ integer \ Y(t,m,l) \ge 0 . \tag{6}$$

In the objective function (1), the first term is cost of purchasing and installing machines, the second term is expected production cost, and the third is expected subcontracting cost. Formulae (2) is capacity constraint which ensures that a production assignment does not exceed a machine's capacity of inserting part type i. Formula (3) is machine line constraint that requires all insertions for a product family be completed on one machine line. Formula (4) is demand constraint that requires all demand be met by production or subcontracting. Constraint (5) is the capital investment budget limitation, and formula (6) is nonnegative and integer constraint. Since demand is exogenous, thus from formula (4),

$$S(i,j)X_{sc}(t,n,j) = S(i,j)d(t,n,j) - \sum_{m,l} X(t,n,i,j,m,l) . \tag{7}$$

Since subcontracting cost of product family j in period t is usually determined by its component structure, thus objective function of formula (1) can be rewritten as:

$$Z = \sum_{t,m,l} C_p(t,m)Y(t,m,l) + \sum_{t,n,i,j,m,l} p(t,n)(C(t,n,m,l) - C_{sc}(t,i))X(t,n,i,j,m,l) . \tag{8}$$

Some explanations about the rationale of model P_0 are as follows. (1) Inventory is a good way to smooth demand fluctuating. But for capacity acquisition problem, inventory is usually not involved (Rajagopalan, 1998) etc. (2) Model P_0 is a two-stage stochastic mixed integer programming problem with recourse, which involves two kinds of decisions. Making choice on the number and types of machines to be purchased and added to machine lines to meet capacity demand is the first stage decision. Determining the number and type of parts assigned to each machine in a line for a given product family to meet market demand is the second stage decision. Note that in the above process, a good capacity expansion is complicated by the fact that the total capacity decision affects future production planning. The production planning is further complicated by the fact that the demand is characterized by random variables whose values are revealed after the capacity expansion decision.

3 Reducing Searching Space by a Recursive Planning

Although a realistic capacity expansion problem for PWB assembly system has many integer decision variables, there may be only a few machines to be added to a few machine lines, which implies that the value of most of the integer capacity expansion decision variables is zero. To solve model P_0, we can first to determine a rough set of machines to be added for each machine line in each period (termed rough addition set, an element of the rough addition set represents a possibly compatible machine type with the existing machines in a line in one period) by eliminating part of incompatible capacity expansion decision variables; then the approximate capacity expansion decision is obtained by searching the rough sets with an adaptive genetic algorithm.

Let set $\{A(t,m,l) \mid$ machine type m is possibly compatible with the existing machines in line l in period t, $\forall t$, m, $l\}$ be a rough addition set for machines line l in period t considering all demand scenarios; set $\{B(t,n,m,l) \mid$ machine type m is possibly compatible with the existing machines in line l in period t under demand scenario n, $\forall t$, n, m, $l\}$ be a rough addition set for machines line l in period t considering under demand scenario n. Then the rough addition sets $\{B(t,n,m,l)\}$ can be identified in the way of deterministic demand case (c.f. the Appendix), and the problem now is how to obtain set $\{A(t, m, l)\}$ based on sets $\{B(t,n,m,l)\}$.

An intuition way of determining $\{A(t,m,l)\}$ is as follows:

$$\{A(t,m,l)\} = \bigcup_{n=1}^{N}\{B(t,n,m,l)\} . \tag{9}$$

Formula (9) is actually a way of getting the maximum of rough addition sets under all market demand scenarios (This is termed "Approach 1"). An issue of this approach is, is there any better way to identify the rough addition set $\{A(t, m, l)\}$ considering random market demand? To answer this question, we should go back to looking into continuous demand function and have the following heuristic.

Heuristics: Given cumulative pdf $D(t,x,j)$ (The probability that demand of product family j is less than or equal to x, $1 \leq j \leq J$, $x \geq 0$) of market demand, and $d(t,x,j)$ is its probability density function. Function $d(t,x,j)$ $(1 \leq j \leq J)$ is sampled with small-enough step size and each sample can be treated as a demand scenario. The rough addition sets determined by getting the maximum of rough addition sets under all demand scenarios should also be better for model P_0 than Approach 1.

The rationality of the heuristic is: the rough addition set based on the above heuristic includes that based on Approach 1. It further provides a feasible way to improve Approach 1. Since capacity expansion decision of model P_0 depends on the characteristics of demand density function and the objective function of model P_0 is continuous, thus if $d(t, x, j)$ $(1 \leq j \leq J)$ is sampled with small-enough step size, the maximum of rough addition sets under all demand scenarios will reflect all potential capacity expansion requirement. Therefore, the maximum of rough addition sets under all demand scenarios will reflect all potential capacity expansion requirements on the basis of algorithm in Appendix. It is noteworthy that, because the rough addition sets under deterministic demand based on the algorithm in Appendix does not give its optimal solution definitely, the maximum of rough addition sets does not necessary include the potential optimal solution.

Given demand scenarios $d(t, n, j)$ ($n=1,...,N$, $j=1,...,J$), the algorithm of determining rough addition set for model P_0 can be conceived based on the heuristics as follows (This is termed "Approach 2"):

Algorithm 1: Determine {A(t,m,l)} for Period t Under Random Demand

Step 1. Initializing. $\{A(t,m,l)\}=\phi$, $NN=N$.

Step 2. Order $d(t,nn,j)$ ($nn=1,2,...,N$) from the pessimism case to the optimism case.

Step 3. For all $nn \in \{1,2,...,NN\}$, apply the Algorithm in the appendix to obtain a rough addition set $\{B(t,nn,m,l)\}$ of demand scenario $d(t,nn,j)$.

Step 4. Let $\{A(t,m,l)\} = \{A(t,m,l)\} \cup [\bigcup_{nn=1}^{NN} \{B(t,nn,m,l)\}]$.

Step 5. Generate NN-1 artificial demand scenarios $d'(t,nn,j)$ ($nn=1,2,...,NN$-1) by interpolating demand scenario between adjacent ones.

Step 6. For all $nn \in \{1,2,...,NN$-1$\}$, apply the Algorithm in appendix to obtain a rough addition set $\{B(t,nn,m,l)\}$ of artificial demand scenario $d'(t,nn,j)$.

Step 7. Make the union of $\{B(t,nn,m,l)\}$ ($nn=1,2,...,NN$-1), $\bigcup_{nn=1}^{NN-1} \{B(t,nn,m,l)\}$. If

$$\bigcup_{nn=1}^{NN-1} \{B(t,nn,m,l)\} \subset \{A(t,m,l)\} . \tag{10}$$

go to Step 9; otherwise go to Step 8.

Step 8. Let $\{A(t,m,l)\} = \{A(t,m,l)\} \cup [\bigcup_{nn=1}^{NN} \{B(t,nn,m,l)\}]$.

Let $NN=2NN$-1, go to Step 5.

Step 9. Stop.

Proposition 1. Algorithm 1 is convergent.

Proof. Since (1) $\{A(t,m,l)\}$ is mono-increasing along with the iterations (otherwise Step 7 of the Algorithm will break the iteration process down);(2) There is an upper bound for $\{A(t,m,l)\}$. The upper bound can be expressed as "all M machine types is possibly compatible with the existing machines in all L lines in all T periods".

Therefore Algorithm 1 is convergent.

After the rough addition sets $A(t,m,l)$ ($t=1,...T$,$m=1,...M$,$l=1,...L$) for model P_0 having been obtained, then approximate solutions to model P_0 can be obtained by solving the model P_1, which is the same as model P_0 except for constraint (6) being substituted by :

$$X(t,n,i,j,m,l) \geq 0, X_{sc}(t,n,j) \geq 0, \text{ integer } Y(t,m,l) \in \{A(t,m,l)\} . \tag{6'}$$

4 Searching the Rough Addition Sets with an Adaptive Genetic Algorithm

We apply an adaptive GA to search the rough addition sets. As general GA is quite popular, here we mainly address the definition of the adaptive fitness function.

Denote the minimum and maximum values of the sum of production costs, sub-contracting costs and capacity expansion costs corresponding to all chromosomes (a chromosome represents a capacity expansion decision vector y to model P_1) in one generation as MIN and MAX respectively. The fitness function of decision vector y is defined as follows:

$$f(y) = \begin{cases} \dfrac{Z'(y) - MIN}{MAX - MIN}, & if \sum_{t,m,l} C_p(t,m)*Y(t,m,l) > B \\ \dfrac{Z(y) - MIN}{MAX - MIN}, & if \sum_{t,m,l} C_p(t,m)*Y(t,m,l) \le B \end{cases} \tag{11}$$

In (11), $Z(y)$ is the sum of production costs, subcontracting costs and equipment changeover costs corresponding to solution, $Z'(y)$ is the sum of $Z(y)$ and a penalty factor $P(g,y)$ corresponding to solution y, g is the generation index of GA, i.e.,

$$Z'(y) = Z(y) + P(g, y) . \tag{12}$$

The penalty factor $P(g,y)$ is recursively defined as follows:

$$P(g, y) = \begin{cases} \overline{P}, & if\ g > g_1\ and\ P(g, y) > \overline{P} \\ g^\alpha \beta (\sum_{t,m,l} C_p(t,m)*Y(t,m,l) - \gamma B), & \begin{array}{l} if\ P(g, y) < \overline{P}, g > g_1\ and \\ \sum_{t,m,l} C_p(t,m)*Y(t,m,l) > B \end{array} \\ 0, & others \end{cases} \tag{13}$$

In (13), parameters $\alpha > 0$, $\beta > 0$, γ, $g_1 > 1$ and $\overline{P}$ are adjustable parameters used to control the level of the penalty. Among them, $g_1 > 1$ prevents any penalty of exceeding capital budget, γ is used to strengthen or weaken the impacts of exceeding capital budget, $\alpha > 0$ is used to strengthen the penalty along generations. Parameter $\beta > 0$ is defined to adjust the overall penalty level, and $\overline{P}$ is the penalty's upper bound.

5 Computational Results

The proposed capacity expansion decision procedure for a PWB assembly system is implemented in C and is interfaced with LINDO. LINDO is called when determining the rough addition set and evaluating a solution's fitness in the adaptive GA (In the adaptive GA, let $\alpha = 0$, $\beta = 1$, $\gamma = -1$, $g_1 = 4$, $B = 1.0 \times 10^7 (\$)$, $\overline{P} = 2B$).

A computational study for single period problem was done to evaluate the performance of the algorithm described in Section 3. For description clarity, symbols corresponding to time periods are omitted from all notations in this subsection. Suppose a firm has 12 assembly lines and there are 20 machine types available (the initial line capacity, structures of three product families and machine characteristics are the same as presented in Hua and Banerjee(2000)). The demand for each product family of each experiment is predicted and assumed to be two demand scenarios, i.e. S1 and S2 as shown in Table 2, demand scenarios S3 to S9 are artificial demand scenarios which are generated by applying the algorithm described in Section 3. The addition sets based on S1 to S9 are depicted in Table 3.

Suppose the subcontracting cost for product families depends on part types they are consisted of, and subcontracting costs for SC, LC, OS, HP, DCA are 6.0, 7.0, 9.0, 11.0 and 12.0 (10^3 $/placement) respectively. Cost of installing a machine is $20,000. The probability of market demand scenarios S1 and S2 are 0.35, 0.65 respectively. Capacity expansion decisions based on different rough addition set are shown in Table 4. From Table 4, it can be observed that the recommended rough addition sets lead to less ratio of subcontracting, less expected total cost and higher expected capacity utilization.

Detailed analyses on machine lines (l_2, l_4 and l_7) to which additional machines to be added show some further rationality of algorithm 1. From table 5, it can be observed that capacity expansion decisions for line l_2 are the same, but different for lines l_4 and l_7 based on Approaches 1 and 2. By making comparison of the ratios of capacity utilization of the two Approaches, it can be concluded that machines added to lines l_4 and l_7 improve not only the ratio of capacity utilization of line l_4 and l_7 but the ratio of capacity utilization of line l_2 also. This should be attributed to chaining effect of flexible machine lines (Jordan and Graves,1995).

Table 2. Market (artificial) demand scenarios for the product families (in thousands)

	Demand Scenarios								
	S1	S2	S3	S4	S5	S6	S7	S8	S9
F1	307	437	372	340	405	325	356	389	420
F2	650	420	535	593	477	624	564	506	450
F3	400	700	550	475	625	438	513	588	630

Table 3. Rough addition sets based on Approach 2

Demand Scenarios	Rough addition sets
S1	B(1,1,5,4), B(1,1,6,2)
S2	B(1,2,1,7),B(1,2,5,2), B(1,2,5,4), B(1,2,6,8), B(1,2,8,7)
S3	B(1,3,1,4),B(1,3,5,7), B(1,3,6,2), B(1,3,8,4)
S4	B(1,4,1,4), B(1,4,6,2), B(1,4,8,4), B(1,4,8,7)
S5	B(1,5,5,4), B(1,5,5,7), B(1,5,6,2)
S6	B(1,6,1,4), B(1,6,6,2), B(1,6,8,4), B(1,6,8,7)
S7	B(1,7,5,4), B(1,7,6,2), B(1,7,8,7)
S8	B(1,8,1,4), B(1,8,5,7), B(1,8,6,2), B(1,8,8,4)
S9	B(1,9,1,4), B(1,9,5,7), B(1,9,6,2), B(1,9,8,4)

6 Conclusion

We present a scenario-based model of line capacity expansion problem for PWB assembly systems at the aggregate level. The model brings together the feature of structure of product families and machine flexibility. An approximate solution procedure, which first reduces the searching space of capacity expansion decision variables to rough addition sets by heuristic algorithms and then searches the rough addition sets through adaptive genetic algorithms, is described. Computational studies show that the described algorithm can efficiently drop searching space for the described capacity expansion problem, and the resulting expected ratio of capacity utilization and return of investment based on the described approach are satisfying vowing to quality of the rough addition sets, e.g. assembly lines' chaining effects led by the capacity expansion decisions.

Table 4. Capacity expansion decisions based on different Approaches

Approaches based on which rough addition set for (P_0) is obtained		Approach 1	Approach 2
Rough addition sets $\{A(t,m,l)\}$		{A(1,5,4),A(1,6,2), A(1,1,7),A(1,5,2), A(1,6,8), A(1,8,7)}	{A(1,5,4),A(1,6,2),A(1,1,7), A(1,5,2),A(1,6,8),A(1,8,7),A(1,1,4), A(1,5,7), A(1,8,4)}
Capacity expansion decision		$Y(1,6,2)=1$	$Y(1,1,4)=2, Y(1,5,7)=2,$ $Y(1,6,2)=1$
Ratio of Capacity utilization	Demand realization S1	88.5793%	82.6097%
	Demand realization S2	90.7100%	98.3214%
Expected ratio of capacity utilization		89.9999%	92.8223%
Ratio of sub -contracting	Demand realization S1	7.7292%	7.8822%
	Demand realization S2	17.6578%	4.4577%
Expected total cost*($)		-21995278	-22671219

* Please c.f. the definition of expected total cost which is expressed in formula (9).

Table 5. Comparison of capacity utilization

	Approach 1			Approach 2		
	l_2	l_4	l_7	l_2	l_4	l_7
Capacity after expansion	48000	63000	60000	48000	87000	84000
Production assignment under S1	48000	52440	39330	48000	52440	39330
Ratio of capacity utilization under S1	1.0000	0.8324	0.6555	1.0000	0.6028	0.4682
Production assignment under S2	28200	52440	39330	48000	87000	84000
Ratio of capacity utilization under S2	0.5875	0.8324	0.6555	1.0000	1.0000	1.0000
Expected ratio of capacity utilization	0.7318	0.8324	0.6555	1.0000	0.8610	0.8139

References

1. Benjaafar S, Gupta D. Scope versus focus - issues of flexibility, capacity, and number of production facilities. IIE Transactions 30(1998):413-425
2. Eppen GD, Martin RK, Schrage L. A Scenario Approach to Capacity Planning, Operations Research 37(1989):517-527
3. Fine CH, Freund RM. Optimal Investment in Product-Flexible Manufacturing Capacity, Management Science 36(1990): 449-466
4. Gaimon C. Subcontracting versus Capacity Expansion and the Impact on Pricing of Services, Naval Research Logistics 41(1994): 875-892
5. Gaimon, C., Ho, J.C., Uncertainty and the Acquisition of Capacity - a Competitive Analysis, Computers & Operations Research 21(1994):1073-1088
6. Hua, Z.S., Banerjee, P., Aggregate Line Capacity Design for PWB Assembly Systems, International Journal of Production Research 11(2000):2417-2441
7. Jordan WC, Graves ST. Principles on the Benefits of Manufacturing Process Flexibility, Management Science 41(1995):577-594
8. Li S, Tirupati D. Dynamic capacity expansion problem with multiple products: Technology selection and timing of capacity additions, Operations Research 42(1994): 958-976
9. Rajagopalan S. Capacity Expansion and Equipment Replacement: A Unified Approach, Operations Research 6(1998):846-857
10. Van Laarhoven P, Zijm W. Production Preparation and Numerical Control in PCB Assembly, I. J. of Flexible Manufacturing System 5(1993):187-207
11. Van Mieghem JA. Investment strategies for flexible resources. Management Science 44(1998):1071-1078

Appendix: Algorithm of Determine the Rough Addition Sets for Period t Under Deterministic Demand

Step 1.   Initializing $\{B(t,m,l)\}=\emptyset$;

Step 2.   Establish model P_{1t} for period t; solve model P_{1t} to obtain its convergent solution $X^*(t,i,j,M+1,l)$ $(l=1,2,...,L; i=1,2,...I; j=1,2,...,J)$;

Step 3.   For all $l\in\{1,2,...,L\}$, solve model P_{2t} to get its optimal solution $N_a(t,m,l)$;
For any $m\in\{1,2,...,M\}$, if $N_a(t,m,l)>0$, then $B(t,m,l)=1$ (this indicates that machines type m is necessary to be considered to be added to machine line l in period t);

Step 4. Stop.

Model P_{2t} in the above Algorithm Step 3 is defined as follows:

(P_{2t})

$$\min \sum_m C_p(t,m,l)N_a(t,m,l). \qquad (A1)$$

$$s.t. \ \sum_m N_a(t,m,l)Q(m)F(m,i) \geq \sum_j X^*(t,i,j,M+1,l), \quad (i=1,2,...,I) \qquad (A2)$$

$$\text{integer } N_a(t,m,l) \geq 0. \quad (m=1,2,...,M) \qquad (A3)$$

Where $N_a(t,m,l)$ is the decision variable that indicates the number of machine type m to be added to machine line l in time period t according to $X^*(t,i,j,M+1,l)$. Model P_{2t} has M integer variables. When M is less than 30, the problem is solvable on PC computer by standard code because of its simple model structure.

A Multiple-Criteria Quadratic Programming Approach to Network Intrusion Detection[*]

Gang Kou[1], Yi Peng[1], Yong Shi[1,2], Zhengxin Chen[1], and Xiaojun Chen[3]

[1] College of Information Science and Technology, University of Nebraska at Omaha,
Omaha, NE 68182, USA
{gkou, ypeng, yshi, zchen}@mail.unomaha.edu
[2] Graduate School of Chinese Academy of Sciences, Beijing 100039, China
[3] Faculty of Science and Technology, Hirosaki University, Hirosaki 036-8561, Japan

Abstract. The early and reliable detection and deterrence of malicious attacks, both from external and internal sources are a crucial issue for today's e-business. There are various methods available today for intrusion detection; however, every method has its limitations and new approaches should still be explored. The objectives of this study are twofold: one is to discuss the formulation of Multiple Criteria Quadratic Programming (MCQP) approach, and to investigate the applicability of the quadratic classification method to the intrusion detection problem. The demonstration of successful Multiple Criteria Quadratic Programming application in intrusion detection can add another option to network security toolbox. The classification results are examined by cross-validation and improved by an ensemble method. The results demonstrated that MCQP is excellent and stable. Furthermore, the outcome of MCQP can be improved by the ensemble method.

1 Introduction

Network intrusion refers to inappropriate or malicious activities in the network environment. The number of computer security breaches has risen dramatically in the last couple of years and made network security a crucial issue for companies and organizations [1, 2]. Due to the importance and the complexity of this problem, various data mining methods have been explored and applied to network intrusion detection to identifying misuse and anomaly attacks. The purposes of this study are to formulate a new classification approach: Multiple Criteria Quadratic Programming (MCQP) and investigate the possibility of using MCQP in network intrusion detection.

This paper is organized as follows. Next section is an overview of two-group MCQP model formulation. The third section briefly describes the background information of network intrusion detection. The fourth section presents basic features of the dataset, KDD99, used in this research. The fifth section discusses applying MCQP

[*] This research has been partially supported by a grant of US Air Force Research Laboratory (PR No. E-3-1162) and a grant from the K.C. Wong Education Foundation (2003), Chinese Academy of Sciences.

Y. Shi, W. Xu, and Z. Chen (Eds.): CASDMKM 2004, LNAI 3327, pp. 145–153, 2004.

to network intrusion detection and presenting cross-validated results. The sixth section describes the procedure and outcomes of ensemble analysis. The last section concludes the paper with some remarks.

2 Formulation of a Two-Group Multiple-Criteria Quadratic Programming Model

First, we will introduce the Multiple-Criteria classification problem and its model. Given a set of r variables (attributes), $a = (a_1, ..., a_r)$, let $A_i = (A_{i1}, ..., A_{ir}) \in R^r$ be one of the sample observations of these properties, where $i = 1,..., n$; n represents the total number of observations in the dataset. Suppose we predefine two groups, G_1 and G_2, we can select a boundary b to separate these two groups. A vector $X = (x_1, ..., x_r) \in R^r$ can be identified to establish the following linear inequation [9]:

(Inequation 1) $A_i X < b, \forall A_i \in G_1;$

$A_i X \geq b, \forall A_i \in G_2;$

Where $\forall A_i \in G_j, j = 1, 2$

In a classification problem, $A_i X$ is the score for the ith data record. The final absolute catch rates depend on simultaneously minimize the sum of overlapping (represented by α_i) and maximize the sum of distance (represented by β_i). Introducing α_i and β_i to Inequation 1, and assuming the overlapping function $f(\alpha)$ and distance function $g(\beta)$ be nonlinear, we establish a basic two-criterion non-linear classification model:

(Basic Model) Minimize $f(\alpha)$ and Maximize $g(\beta)$

Subject to:

$$A_i X - \alpha_i + \beta_i - b = 0, \forall A_i \in G_1 \tag{1}$$

$$A_i X + \alpha_i - \beta_i - b = 0, \forall A_i \in G_2 \tag{2}$$

where A_i is given, X and b are unrestricted, and $\alpha = (\alpha_1,...,\alpha_n)^T, \beta = (\beta_1,...,\beta_n)^T; \alpha_i, \beta_i \geq 0, i = 1,...,n$

In order to utilize the computational power of some software packages, we represent next the basic model by norm. Given weights w_α and w_β let $f(\alpha) = \| \alpha \|^p$ and $g(\beta) = \| \beta \|^p$. The two criteria basic model can be converted into a single criterion general non-linear classification model:

(Model 1)   Minimize $w_\alpha \| \alpha \|^p - w_\beta \| \beta \|^p$

Subject to:

$$A_i X - \alpha_i + \beta_i - b = 0, \forall A_i \in G_1$$

$$A_i X + \alpha_i - \beta_i - b = 0, \forall A_i \in G_2$$

Based on Model 1, non-linear classification models with any norm can be defined theoretically. In this study, we formulate a simple quadratic programming model. Let

$$f(\alpha) = \alpha^T H \alpha = \sum_{i=1}^{n} \alpha_i^2 \text{ and } g(\beta) = \beta^T Q \beta = \sum_{i=1}^{n} \beta_i^2 , \text{ where } H \text{ and } Q \text{ are}$$

predefined here as identity matrices. Model 1 now becomes Model 2:

(Model 2) *Minimize* $w_\alpha \sum_{i=1}^{n} \alpha_i^2 - w_\beta \sum_{i=1}^{n} \beta_i^2$

   Subject to:

   $$A_i X - \alpha_i + \beta_i - b = 0, \forall A_i \in G_1$$

   $$A_i X + \alpha_i - \beta_i - b = 0, \forall A_i \in G_2$$

This quadratic model (Model 2) will be utilized in the following sections in network intrusion detection.

Although the notion of MCQP is fresh, it is derived from the Multiple Criteria Linear Programming (MCLP). The fundamental distinction between these two is the different norm values they presume. For MCLP, the norm equals one. While for MCQP, the norm equals two. The most prominent characteristic of MCLP which distinguishes it from traditional linear programming is that it is intended to achieve multiple objectives simultaneously. Inherited this trait, MCQP is attempted to realize multiple objectives at the same time when the norm is two. Further discussion of the differences between MCLP and MCQP exceeds the range of this paper.

3   Network Intrusion Detection

An intrusion is an attempting to break into or misuse network systems [8]. An intrusion detection system is a system for detecting such intrusions. There are two broad types of techniques for network security – protection and detection. Protection techniques are designed to guard hardware, software, and user data against threats from both outsiders and malicious insiders. A common protection device is a firewall that sets up a barrier at the point of connection between the external and the corporate internal networks to ensure only valid data are allowed to pass through. Detection techniques collect information from a variety of systems and network sources, and then analyze the information for signs of intrusion [2].

   Intrusion detection can be classified into two types: misuse detection and anomaly detection [1]. Misuse detection systems detect attacks based on well-known vulnerabilities and intrusions stored in a database. Techniques include rule-based expert systems, model-based reasoning systems, state transition analysis, fuzzy logic, and keystroke monitoring. A major pitfall of misuse detection is that it is trained to recognize existing attacks and has no ability to detect anomaly attacks which are somewhat more serious than known attacks. Anomaly detection systems build predictive models that are capable of distinguishing between normal and abnormal behaviors [8]. Various approaches exist for anomaly detection: statistical analysis, sequence analysis, neural networks, machine learning, and artificial immune systems. Each method has its strengths and weaknesses.

As a new classification scheme, MCQP has not been employed in intrusion detection analysis. It is the aim of this research to test the applicability of MCQP to intrusion detection. The demonstration of successful MCQP application in intrusion detection can add another option to network security toolbox.

4 KDD-99 Dataset

In order to understand the whole detection process, it is important to comprehend the dataset first. This section presents the nature and structure of the network dataset – KDD-99 in detail.

The KDD-99 data set was provided by DARPA in 1998 for the competitive evaluation of intrusion detection approaches. A standard set of data to be audited, which includes a wide variety of intrusions simulated in a military network environment, was provided. A version of this dataset was used in 1999 KDD-CUP intrusion detection contest. After the contest, KDD-99 has become a de facto standard dataset for intrusion detection experiments. Originally, nine weeks of raw TCP dump data for a LAN simulating a typical U.S. Air Force LAN were collected. Multiple attacks were intentionally added to the LAN operation. The raw training data was about four gigabytes of compressed binary TCP dump data from seven weeks of network traffic. A connection is a sequence of TCP packets starting and ending at some well defined times, between which data flows to and from a source IP address to a target IP address under some well defined protocol. Each connection is labeled as either normal, or as an attack, with exactly one specific attack type. Each connection record consists of about 100 bytes. There are four main categories: denial-of-service (DOS); unauthorized access from a remote machine (R2L); unauthorized access to local root privileges (U2R); surveillance and other probing. The training dataset contains a total of 24 attack types while the testing dataset contains an additional 14 types [3].

Because the number of attacks of R2L, U2R, and Probing are small, this paper will focus on comparing Normal category with only one kind of attack: DOS, which has a comparatively large data size. Detection of other attacks will be investigated in the future.

5 Empirical Studies of MCQP and Cross-Validation Results

Cross-validation is utilized to validate the results of MCQP detection rates. By definition, cross-validation is the practice of partitioning a sample of data into sub samples such that analysis is initially performed on a single sub sample, while further sub samples are retained "blind" in order for subsequent use in confirming and validating the initial analysis [4]. There are many cross-validation methods. Due to the enormous size of the dataset, holdout method is applied here. That is, a subset of KDD-99 is randomly selected as a training dataset and the remaining part of KDD-99 serves as a testing dataset. The data computation is performed by the LINGO 8.0, a commercial software package of non-linear programming solvers (http://www.lindo.com/). Our own algorithm to implement MCQP is currently under investigation.

The procedure to select training datasets is described as follows: first, the Normal dataset (812813 records) is divided into 100 intervals (each interval has 8128 records). Within each interval, 20 records are randomly selected. Thus the total of 2000 normal records are obtained after this selection was repeated 100 times. Second, the DOS dataset (247267 records) is divided into 100 intervals (each interval has 2472 records). Within each interval, 20 records are randomly selected. Thus the total of 2000 dos records are obtained after this selection was repeated 100 times. Third, the 2000 Normal and 2000 Dos records are combined to form a single training dataset. Finally, the Normal dataset (812813 records) and DOS dataset (247267 records) become the testing dataset. Repeat this procedure, various training and testing datasets can be obtained. According to this procedure, the total possible combination of this selection is infinitely large. That is, the possibilty to get identical training or testing datasets is approximately zero. Considering the previous detection rates of KDD-99 attacks using other methods were rather high, the across-the-board threshold of 95% for absolute catch rate for both Normal and DOS are set. This threshold is used as a rule to select the experimental results from training and test processes. That is, only those catch rates that are above 95% are considered.

Some samples of the Cross-Validation tests based on Algorithm 1 are summarized in Tables 1.

Under the conditions stated above, the following steps are designed to carry out cross-validation:

Algorithm 1 (Cross Validation)

Step1 Generate the Training set (2000 Normal data+2000 Dos Data) and Testing set (Normal dataset (812813 records) and DOS dataset (247267 records) from the KDD-99 data set.

Step2 Apply the two-group MCQP model to compute the compromise solution $X* = (x_1*, x_2*, \ldots, x_{38}*)$ as the best weights of all 38 variables with given values of control parameters $(b, \alpha*, \beta*)$.

Step3 The classification score $MCQP\ i = AX*$ against of each observation has been calculated against the boundary b to check the performance measures of the classification.

The training and testing datasets have been computed using the above procedure. A part (25 out of the total 300 cross-validation results) of the results against the threshold is summarized. The worst and best classification catch rates for testing sets are 99.18% and 99.88% for Normal, 99.23% and 99.85% for DOS. The result indicates that an excellent separation of Normal versus DOS is observed with this method.

Table 1. Cross-Validation Results

Cross Validation	Testing Set(812813 Normal + 247267 Dos)					
	Normal	Catch Rate	Type II Error	Dos	Catch Rate	Type I Error
DataSet 1	808142	99.43%	0.157%	245998	99.49%	1.863%
DataSet 2	810689	99.74%	0.045%	246902	*99.85%*	0.853%
DataSet 3	807597	99.36%	0.096%	246491	99.69%	2.072%
DataSet 4	808410	99.46%	0.125%	246256	99.59%	1.757%
DataSet 5	810283	99.69%	0.145%	246090	99.52%	1.018%
DataSet 6	809272	99.56%	0.085%	246580	99.72%	1.416%
DataSet 7	806116	*99.18%*	0.129%	246229	99.58%	2.648%
DataSet 8	808143	99.43%	0.157%	245998	99.49%	1.863%
DataSet 9	811806	*99.88%*	0.103%	246433	99.66%	0.407%
DataSet 10	810307	99.69%	0.070%	246702	99.77%	1.006%
DataSet 11	810176	99.68%	0.067%	246726	99.78%	1.057%
DataSet 12	809936	99.65%	0.102%	246442	99.67%	1.154%
DataSet 13	811685	99.86%	0.067%	246722	99.78%	0.455%
DataSet 14	807021	99.29%	0.159%	245980	99.48%	2.300%
DataSet 15	810654	99.73%	0.114%	246340	99.63%	0.869%
DataSet 16	811253	99.81%	0.086%	246569	99.72%	0.629%
DataSet 17	810355	99.70%	0.106%	246406	99.65%	0.988%
DataSet 18	810027	99.66%	0.107%	246400	99.65%	1.118%
DataSet 19	807257	99.32%	0.110%	246382	99.64%	2.205%
DataSet 20	809718	99.62%	0.234%	245366	*99.23%*	1.246%
DataSet 21	807429	99.34%	0.061%	246776	99.80%	2.135%
DataSet 22	811095	99.79%	0.067%	246723	99.78%	0.692%
DataSet 23	810224	99.68%	0.195%	245681	99.36%	1.043%
DataSet 24	809581	99.60%	0.131%	246209	99.57%	1.296%
DataSet 25	806763	99.26%	0.109%	246386	99.64%	2.397%

6 An Ensemble Analysis

An ensemble consists of a set of individually trained classifiers whose predictions are combined when classifying novel instances. There are two fundamental elements of ensembles: a set of properly trained classifiers and an aggregation mechanism that organizes these classifiers into the output ensemble. Normally, the aggregation process will be an average or a simple majority vote over the output of the ensembles [6]. Previous research has shown that an ensemble can help to increase accuracy and stability [6, 7].

There are two basic criterion based on which the ensemble is chosen: first, voters of an ensemble have to satisfy the across-the-board threshold of 95% for absolute catch rate for both Normal and DOS. Second, as the majority vote method is used here, the number of voters in any ensemble must be odd.

From cross-validation, some optimal solutions of MCQP have been computed. Parts of these optimal solutions are selected to form ensembles. Each solution will have one vote for each data record and the final classification result is determined by the majority votes. The numbers of voters to form ensembles are randomly chosen insofar as they are odd. The ensemble analysis process is described in Algorithm 2.

Algorithm 2 (Ensemble Analysis)

Step1 A committee of certain odd number (e.g. 3, 9, 19) of classifiers $X*$ is formed.

Step2 The classification score $MCQPi = AX*$ against of each observation has been calculated against the boundary b by every member of the committee. The performance measures of the classification will be decided by majorities of the committee. If more than half of the committee members succeed in the classification, then the prediction for this observation is successful, otherwise, the prediction is failed.

Step3 The catch rate for each group will be computed by the percentage of successful classification in all observations.

Several results of Algorithm 2 for different ensemble committee size are summarized in Table 2. The results point out three findings: (1) the classification rates are better than cross-validation results; (2) as the number of voter increases, the catch rates increases. When number of voters increased to 11 or more, the change of catch rates is negligible; (3) although the catch rates of ensembles do not outperform the best results of cross-validation, they are more steady than cross-validation.

7 Concluding Remarks

Detecting malicious attacks is an important task in network security. In this paper, MCQP, a novel classification scheme, is employed in detecting DOS attack in

Table 2. Ensemble Results

NO of Voters	Normal	Catch Rate	Type II Error	Dos	Catch Rate	Type I Error
3	810126	99.67%	0.059%	246792	99.81%	1.077%
5	811419	99.83%	0.042%	246930	***99.86%***	0.561%
7	811395	99.83%	0.054%	246830	99.82%	0.571%
9	811486	99.84%	0.058%	246795	99.81%	0.535%
11	812030	99.90%	0.052%	246845	99.83%	0.316%
13	812006	99.90%	0.059%	246788	99.81%	0.326%
15	812089	99.91%	0.056%	246812	99.82%	0.292%
17	812045	99.91%	0.055%	246821	99.82%	0.310%
19	812069	99.91%	0.055%	246817	99.82%	0.301%
21	812010	99.90%	0.054%	246831	99.82%	0.324%
23	812149	***99.92%***	0.055%	246821	99.82%	0.268%
25	812018	99.90%	0.055%	246822	99.82%	0.321%

KDD-99 dataset. The result of cross-validated MCQP indicates that MCQP prediction is stable. In addition, ensemble analysis exhibits that catch rates can be further improved by using ensembles. Due to the space limitation, the content discussed in this paper is brief and in-exhaustive. This limitation is reflected on two major issues. First, the formulation of MCQP model is presented without mentioning the theoretical foundations and justifications. Second, the classification results of applying MCQP on network intrusion detection are delivered directly without specification of how they were accomplished. Although these issues are crucial, discussion of these issues is beyond the scope of this paper. However, these themes will be investigated in the future. The results presented in this paper are merely a beginning. Future research topics may include, not limited to, applying MCQP to real-life network data, integrating MCQP to real-time network intrusion detection systems to provide network administrators the ability to proactively divert attacks, and extending the application of MCQP to other potential fields.

References

1. Zhu, D., Premkumar, G., Zhang, X., Chu, C.H.: Data Mining for Network Intrusion Detection: A comparison of Alternative Methods. Decision Sciences, 32(4) (2001).
2. Lunt, T.F.: A survey of intrusion detection techniques. Computer & Security, 12 (1993).
3. Stolfo, S.J., Fan, Wei., Lee, W., Prodromidis, A., Chan, P.K.: Cost-based Modeling and Evaluation for Data Mining With Application to Fraud and Intrusion Detection: Results from the JAM Project, Proc. DARPA Information Survivability Conference (2000).
4. Plutowski, M.E.: Survey: Cross-Validation in Theory and in Practice. Unpublished manuscript (1996).. Available online at: http://www.emotivate.com/CvSurvey.doc.

5. Gutierrez-Osuna, R.: Selected topics in computer science, Texas A&M University. Available online: http://faculty.cs.tamu.edu/rgutier/courses/cs790_wi02/.
6. Zenobi, G., Cunningham, P.: An Approach to Aggregating Ensembles of Lazy Learners That Supports Explanation. Lecture Notes in Computer Science, Vol. 2416 (2002) 436-447.
7. Opitz, D., Maclin, R.: Popular ensemble methods: an empirical study. Journal of Artificial Intelligence Research 11 (1999) 169-198.
8. Graham, R.: FAQ: Network Intrusion Detection Systems, http://www.robertgraham.com/pubs/network-intrusion-detection.html#0.1,(2004).
9. Shi, Y., Peng, Y., Xu, W., Tang, X.: Data Mining via Multiple Criteria Linear Programming: Applications in Credit Card Portfolio Management, International Journal of Information Technology and Decision Making. 1 (2002) 131-151.

Classifications of Credit Cardholder Behavior by Using Multiple Criteria Non-linear Programming*

Jing He[1,**], Yong Shi[2], and Weixuan Xu[3]

[1] Institute of Systems Science, Academy of Mathematics and Systems Science,
Chinese Academy of Sciences, Beijing 100080, China
hejing@amss.ac.cn
[2] Graduate School of Chinese Academy of Sciences, Beijing 100039, China
yshi@unomaha.edu
[3] Institute of Policy and Management, Chinese Academy of Sciences,
Beijing 100080, China
wxu@mail.casipm.ac.cn

Abstract. Behavior analysis of credit cardholders is one of the main research topics in credit card portfolio management. Usually, the cardholder's behavior, especially bankruptcy, is measured by a score of aggregate attributes that describe cardholder's spending history. In the real-life practice, statistics and neural networks are the major players to calculate such a score system for prediction. Recently, various multiple criteria linear programming based classification methods have been explored for analyzing credit cardholders' behavior. This paper proposes a multiple criteria non-linear programming (MCNP) approach to discovering the bankruptcy patterns of credit cardholders. A real-life credit database from a major US bank is used for empirical study on MCNP classification. Finally, the comparison of MCNP and other known classification methods is conducted to verify the validation of MCNP method.

1   Introduction

Data Mining, an intersection area of human intervention, machine learning, mathematical modeling and databases, is has been used in credit cardholder behavior analysis sicne1960s. Specifically, the purpose of using the classification methods for credit cardholder behavior analysis is to find the common characters and patterns of personal bankruptcy. The process of controlling the bankruptcy risk includes: (1) choosing a training data set for predetermined classes; (2) developing a separation model with rules on the

---

* This research has been partially supported by a grant from National Excellent Youth Fund under (#70028101), National Natural Science Foundation of China and a grant from the K.C. Wong Education Foundation (2003), Chinese Academy of Sciences.
** The corresponding author.

Y. Shi, W. Xu, and Z. Chen (Eds.): CASDMKM 2004, LNAI 3327, pp. 154–163, 2004.

training set; (3) applying the model to classify unknown objects; and (4) discovering knowledge. There are many mathematical methods, including statistics [1], neural networks [2], and multiple criteria linear programming [3, 4, 5] applied in credit card bankruptcy. A common characteristic of these methods is that they first consider the behaviors of the cardholders as two predefined classes: bankrupt accounts and non-bankrupt accounts according to their historical records. Then the methods search for a better-aggregated score separating bankrupt accounts and non-bankrupt accounts in a training set. Finally, the learned classifier is used to produce a "black list" for business decision-making.

Classification of credit cardholder behavior by using multiple criteria linear programming (MCLP) is derived from well-known linear models [6, 7, 8] and the compromise solution in MCLP [3, 4, 5]. In linear discriminant models, the misclassification of data separation can be described by two kinds of objectives in a linear system. In the first, the minimal distances of observations from the critical value are maximized (MMD). The second separates the observations by minimizing the sum of the deviations (MSD) of the observations. This deviation is also called "overlapping." The compromise solution in MCLP locates the best trade-off between linear forms of MMD and MSD as data separation.

This trade-off, however, cannot be justified to lead the best data separation. For example, the MCLP method may fail to predict the status of a determined fraud as potential bankruptcy, which can cause a hug loss of the credit card issuer. The main research problem of this paper is to seek an alternative method with non-linear trade-off of MMD and MSD for possible better data separation result. Since the objective function of the proposed method is non-linear, we shall call it multiple criteria non-linear programming classification (MCNP).

This paper will proceed as follows. Section 2 will review the MCLP compromise solution to data analyses. Section 3 will elaborate the MCNP formulation and algorithm. Section 4 uses a real-life credit database from a major US bank for empirical study which is compared with the results of the other methods, such as MCLP, induction decision tree, and neural networks. The further research problems will be outlined in Section 5.

2   Linear System-Based Classification Models

Research of linear programming (LP) approaches to classification problems was initiated by Freed and Glover [6]. A basic framework of two-class problems can be presented as:

Given a set of r variables (attributes) about a cardholder $a = (a_1, ..., a_r)$, let $A_i = (A_{i1}, ..., A_{ir})$ be the development sample of data for the variables, where $i = 1, ..., n$ and n is the sample size. We want to determine the best coefficients of the variables, denoted by $X = (x_1, ..., x_r)^T$, and a boundary value b (a scalar) to separate two classes: G (Good for non-bankrupt accounts) and B (Bad for bankrupt accounts); that is,

$A_i X \leq b, A_i \in$ G (Good) and $A_i X \geq b, A_i \in$ B (Bad).

To measure the separation of Good and Bad, we define:

α_i = the overlapping of two-class boundary for case A_i (external measurement);
α = the maximum overlapping of two-class boundary for all cases A_i ($\alpha_i < \alpha$);
β_i = the distance of case A_i from its adjusted boundary (internal measurement).
β = the minimum distance for all cases A_i from its adjusted boundary ($\beta_i > \beta$).

A simple version of Freed and Glover's [6] model, which seeks MSD, can be written as:

$$\text{Minimize } \Sigma_i \alpha_i \tag{1}$$
$$\text{Subject to:}$$
$$A_i X \leq b + \alpha_i, A_i \in G,$$
$$A_i X \geq b - \alpha_i, A_i \in B,$$

Where A_i are given, X and b are unrestricted, and $\alpha_i \geq 0$.
The alternative of the above model is to find MMD:

$$\text{Maximize } \Sigma_i \beta_i \tag{2}$$
$$\text{Subject to:}$$
$$A_i X \geq b - \beta_i, A_i \in G,$$
$$A_i X \leq b + \beta_i, A_i \in B,$$

Where A_i are given, X and b are unrestricted, and $\beta_i \geq 0$.

$$A_i X = b$$

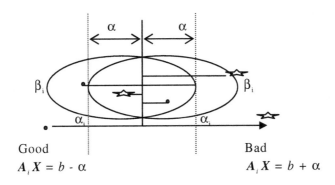

Good
$A_i X = b - \alpha$

Bad
$A_i X = b + \alpha$

Fig. 1. Overlapping Case in Two-class Separation

A graphical representation of these models in terms of α is shown as Figure 1. We note that the key of the two-class linear classification models is to use a linear combination of the minimization of the sum of α_i or/and maximization of the sum of β_i to reduce the two criteria problem into a single criterion. The advantage of this conversion is to easily utilize all techniques of LP for separation, while the disadvantage is that it may miss the scenario of trade-offs between these two separation criteria.

Shi et al. [5] applied the compromise solution of multiple criteria linear programming (MCLP) to minimize the sum of α_i and maximize the sum of β_i simultaneously. A two-criteria linear programming model is stated as:

$$Minimize\ \Sigma_i\alpha_i\ \ and\ \ \ Maximize\ \Sigma_i\beta_i \tag{3}$$
$$Subject\ to:$$

$$A_i X \leq b + \alpha_i - \beta_i, A_i \in B,$$
$$A_i X \geq b - \alpha_i + \beta_i, A_i \in G,$$

where A_i are given, X and b are unrestricted, and α_i and $\beta_i \geq 0$.

In compromise solution approach [10, 11], the *best trade-off* between the linear forms of $-\Sigma_i\alpha_i$ and $\Sigma_i\beta_i$ is identified for an optimal solution. To explain this, assume the "ideal value" of $-\Sigma_i\alpha_i$ be $\alpha^* > 0$ and the "ideal value" of $\Sigma_i\beta_i$ be $\beta^* > 0$. Then, if $-\Sigma_i\alpha_i > \alpha^*$, the regret measure is defined as $-d_\alpha^+ = \Sigma_i\alpha_i + \alpha^*$; otherwise, it is defined as 0. If $-\Sigma_i\alpha_i < \alpha^*$, the regret measure is defined as $d_\alpha^- = \alpha^* + \Sigma_i\alpha_i$; otherwise, it is 0. Thus, the relationship of these measures are (i) $\alpha^* + \Sigma_i\alpha_i = d_\alpha^- - d_\alpha^+$, (ii) $|\alpha^* + \Sigma_i\alpha_i| = d_\alpha^- + d_\alpha^+$, and (iii) $d_\alpha^-, d_\alpha^+ \geq 0$. Similarly, we derive $\beta^* - \Sigma_i\beta_i = d_\beta^- - d_\beta^+$, $|\beta^* - \Sigma_i\beta_i| = d_\beta^- + d_\beta^+$, and $d_\beta^-, d_\beta^+ \geq 0$.

An MCLP model for two-class separation is presented as:

$$Min\ d_\alpha^- + d_\alpha^+ + d_\beta^- + d_\beta^+$$

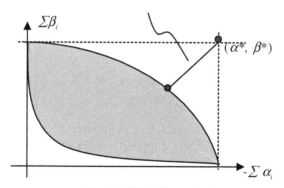

Fig. 2. MCLP Formulation

$$Minimize\ d_\alpha^- + d_\alpha^+ + d_\beta^- + d_\beta^+ \tag{4}$$

$$Subject\ to:$$

$$\alpha^* + \Sigma_i\alpha_i = d_\alpha^- - d_\alpha^+,$$
$$\beta^* - \Sigma_i\beta_i = d_\beta^- - d_\beta^+,$$

$$A_i X \leq b + \alpha_i - \beta_i, \, A_i \in B,$$
$$A_i X \geq b - \alpha_i + \beta_i, \, A_i \in G,$$

where A_i, $\alpha*$, and $\beta*$ are given, X and b are unrestricted, and α_i, β_i, d_α^-, d_α^+, d_β^-, $d_\beta^+ \geq 0$.

Fig.2. the shadow area is shown the criteria space of $-\Sigma_i \alpha_i$ and $\Sigma_i \beta_i$ and $(\alpha*, \beta*)$ is the ideal point to identify the separation. The MCLP compromise approach is to determine the classification of Good and Bad according to the minimization of the linear "distance" function $d_\alpha^- + d_\alpha^+ + d_\beta^- + d_\beta^+$ (which offers the best trade-off of MMD and MSD).

Note that for the purpose of classification, a better classifier must have the higher accuracy rate. Given a threshold of correct classification as a simple criterion, the better classifier can be found through the training process whenever the accuracy rate of the model exceeds the threshold. Suppose that a threshold is given, the next section proposes a heuristic classification method by using the MCNP.

3   Multiple Criteria Non-linear Classification

In general, the overlapping of all α_i and distances of all β_i can be considered as non-linear norms, say $\|\alpha\|^p$ and $\|\beta\|^p$, respectively, where $\alpha = (\alpha_1, ..., \alpha_n)$, $\beta = (\beta_1, ..., \beta_n)$, $p = 1, 2,...,\infty$. When $p = 1$, $\|\alpha\|^p = \Sigma_i \alpha_i$ and $\|\beta\|^p = \Sigma_i \beta_i$. When, $1 < p \leq \infty$, $\|\alpha\|^p$ and $\|\beta\|^p$ have various non-linear formations. As an initial step to MCNP classification for $p = 2$, given n-dimensional parameters w_α and w_β, we consider the following formulation:

$$Minimize \quad w_\alpha \|\alpha\|^2 - w_\beta \|\beta\|^2 \tag{5}$$

Subject to:

$$A_i X \leq b + \alpha_i - \beta_i, \, A_i \in B,$$
$$A_i X \geq b - \alpha_i + \beta_i, \, A_i \in G,$$

Where A_i are given, X and b are unrestricted, and α_i and $\beta_i \geq 0$.

Applying the notation of the diagonal matrix D with +1 & -1 entries to MCNP Problem, the two-class constraints become:

$$A_i X \leq b + \alpha_i - \beta_i, \, D_{ii}=+1 \text{ (Bad)} \tag{6}$$
$$A_i X \geq b - \alpha_i + \beta_i, \, D_{ii}=-1 \text{ (Good)},$$

Then, the MCNP model (M5) can be rewritten as:

$$Minimize \quad w_\alpha \|\alpha\|^2 - w_\beta \|\beta\|^2 \tag{7}$$

Subject to:

$$D(AX-eb) \leq \alpha - \beta, \text{ where } e \text{ is a vector of ones}$$

A heuristic MCNP algorithm can be outlined as:

Algorithm 1.

Step 1. Build a data mart for a task data-mining project.

Step 2. Generate a set of relevant attributes or dimensions from a data mart. Transform the scales of the data mart into the same numerical measurement and determine predefined classes, classification thresholdζ, training set and verifying set.

Step 3. Give a class boundary value b*, use the MCNP model (M5) to learn and compute the overall score Ai X* of the relevant attributes or dimensions over all observations repeatedly (Figure 1).

Step 4. If the accuracy rate of classification exceeds the thresholdζ, go to Step 5, otherwise, go back to Step 3 and choose another boundary value b**.

Step 5. Apply the final learned score X* to predict the unknown data in the verifying set.

4   Experimental Results from a Real-Life Database

Give a set of attributes, such as monthly payment, balance, purchase, and cash advance and the criteria about "bankruptcy", the purpose of data mining in credit card portfolio management is to find the better classifier through a training set and use the classifier to predict all other customer's spending behaviors. The frequently used data-mining model in the business is still two-class separation technique. The key of two-class separation is to separate the "bankruptcy" accounts (called Bad) from the "non-bankruptcy" accounts (called Good) and identify as many bankruptcy accounts as possible. This is also known as the method of "making black list". In this section, a real-life data mart with 65 derived attributes and 1000 records of a major US bank credit database is first used to train the MCNP model classifier. Then, the training solution is employed to predict the spending behaviors of another 5000 customers from different states. Finally, the classification results are compared with that of the MCLP method [3, 4, 5], neural network method [12], and decision tree method [13].

There are two kinds of accuracy rates involved in this section. The first one is the *absolute accuracy rate* for Bad (or Good) which is the number of actual Bad (or Good) identified divided by the total number of Bad (or Good). The second is called *catch rate*, which is defined as the actual number of caught Bad and Good divided by the total number of Bad and Good. Let r_g be the absolute accuracy rate for Good and r_b be the absolute accuracy rate for Bad. Then the catch rate c_r can be written as:

$c_r = (r_g$ x the total of Good $+ r_b$ x the total number of Bad)/the total number of Good & Bad.

The difference of two rates is that the absolute accuracy rate measures the separation power of the model for an individual class while the catch rate represents the overall degree of correctness when the model is used. A threshold τ in this paper is set up against absolute accuracy rate or and catch rate depending on the requirement of business decision making (see Table1.).

4.1   Experimental Results on Unbalanced Data Set

The past experience on classification test showed that the training results of a data set with balanced records (number of Good equals number of Bad) may be different from that of an unbalanced data set. Given the unbalanced 1000 accounts with 860 as Good and 140 as Bad accounts for the training process, suppose w_α and w_β have ½ for each dimension, the MCNP model can be built as follows:

$$Minimize\ 0.5*(\alpha_1^2 +\alpha_2^2+...+\alpha_{1000}^2)- 0.5*(\beta_1^2 +\beta_2^2+...+\beta_{1000}^2) \qquad (8)$$

Subject to:

$$A_1\ X + \alpha_1 - \beta_1 \leq b$$

...

$$A_{840}\ X + \alpha_{840} - \beta_{840} \leq b$$
$$A_{841}\ X + \alpha_{841} - \beta_{841} \geq b$$

...

$$A_{1000}\ X + \alpha_{1000} - \beta_{1000} \geq b$$

Where α_i and $\beta_i \geq 0$, $\mathbf{X} = (x_1, . . ., x_{65})^{T}$ is unrestricted, $\mathbf{A}_i = (A_{i1}, ..., A_{i65})$ are given.

Using a commercial software package, LINGO [17], the learning result learning results of unbalanced 1000 records and the verification of the other 4000 records can be shown as Table 1.

Table 1. Learning Results of Unbalanced 1000 Records

Different b value	Absolute Accuracy Rate by 1000 group			Predict for the other 4000 group		
	Catch			Catch		
	Good	Bad	Rate	Good	Bad	Rate
100	0.990	0.036	0.856	0.957	0.038	0.828
10	0.867	0.329	0.792	0.877	0.330	0.800
-1.1	0.966	0.948	0.963	0.966	0.977	0.967
0	0.002	0.979	0.139	0.020	0.970	0.153
1.1	0.914	0.766	0.894	0.917	0.778	0.897
10	0.837	0.358	0.770	0.866	0.377	0.797
100	0.935	0.027	0.808	0.955	0.028	0.825

From Table 1, if the threshold ζ of finding the absolute accuracy rate of bankruptcy accounts (Bad) is predetermined as 0.85, then the situations when b = 0 and -1.1 are satisfied as better classifiers according to Algorithm 1. The catch rates of the classifier with b = 0 is not as high as that of b = 1.1. This suggests that the classifier with b = -1.1 is the better one, which predicts above 96% accurately for both the bankruptcy accounts (Bad) and non-bankruptcy (Good).

4.2   Experimental Results on Balanced Data Set

A balanced data set was formed by taking 140 Good accounts from 860 of the 1000 accounts used before and combining with the 140 accounts. The records were trained and some of results are summarized in Table 1, where we see that the best catch rate .963 is at b =-1.1. Although the best absolute bad accuracy rate for Bad accounts is .979 at b = 0, the predicting result on Bad accounts for 4000 records is .967 at b =-0.50. If the threshold ζ for all of the absolute accuracy rate of Bad accounts, the absolute accuracy rate of Good accounts and catch rate is set up as 0.95 above, then models of b = -1.10 and b = -1.10 are the two to produce the satisfying classifier by Algorithm 1. However, the predicting result of this case is not the best one (See Table 1).

4.3   Comparisons with Other Data Mining Approaches

Three known classification techniques, decision tree, neural network and multiple criteria linear programming (MCLP) have been used to run the 280 balanced data set and test (or predict) the 5000 credit cardholder records in a major US bank. These results are compared with the proposed MCNP method (see Table 2). The software of decision tree is the commercial version called C5.0 (the newly updated version of C4.5) [14] while software for both neural network and MCLP were developed at the Data Mining Lab, University of Nebraska at Omaha [15, 16].   Note that in both Table 2, the column Tg and Tb respectively represent the number of Good and Bad accounts identified by a method, while the rows of Good and Bad represent the actual numbers of the accounts.

Table 2 shows the predicting (or testing) results on 5000 records by using the classifiers based on the results of 1000 balanced data sets. The MCLP method outperforms others in terms of predicting Good accounts with 3160 out of 4185 (75.51%), but the MCNP method in this paper is the best for predicting Bad accounts with 675 out of 815 (.8282). If the business strategy of making black list on Bad accounts is chosen, then the MCNP method should be used to conduct the data-mining project. Therefore, the MCNP method demonstrated its advantages over the MCLP method and has a certain significance to be an alternative tool to the other well-known data mining techniques in classification (recall the main research problem in Section 1).

Table 2. Comparisons on Prediction of 5000 Records

Decision Tree	Tg	Tb	Total
Good	2180	2005	4185
Bad	141	674	815
Total	2321	2679	5000
Neural Network	Tg	Tb	Total
Good	2814	1371	4185
Bad	176	639	815
Total	2990	2010	5000
MCLP	Tg	Tb	Total
Good	3160	1025	4185
Bad	484	331	815
Total	3644	1356	5000
MCNP	Tg	Tb	Total
Good	2133	2052	4185
Bad	140	675	815
Total	2766	2234	5000

5   Concluding Remarks

In this paper, we have proposed a multiple criteria non-linear programming (MCNP) classification method to discover the bankruptcy patterns of credit cardholders. This approach is based on the developed linear programming (LP) and multiple criteria linear programming (MCNP) classification [3, 4, 5, 6, 7, 8]. Although the mathematical modeling is not new, the framework of MCNP has not considered before. In addition, both empirical training and prediction on a real-life credit database from a major US bank and comparison study have shown that this technique has performed better than is decision tree and neural network in with aspect to predicting the future spending behavior of credit cardholders. It also has a great deal of potential to be used in various data mining tasks. Since the Connection approach is readily implemented by the non-linear programming, any available non-linear programming packages, such as LINGO and Matlab can be used to conduct the data analysis [17, 18]. To verify its application capability, we are currently testing this approach over other real-life databases for more insights.

References

1. Schwalb, O., Lee, T. H., and   Zheng, S.: An Algorithm for score calibration based on cumulative rates. International Journal of Information Technology and Decision Making 2 (1) (2003) 93-103.
2. Lee, T. H. and Zhang, M.: Bias correction and statistical test for developing credit scoring model through logistic regression approach. International Journal of Information Technology and Decision Making 2 (2) (2003) 299-312.
3. Kou, G., Liu, X., Peng, Y., Shi, Y., Wise, M., Xu, W.: Multiple criteria linear programming approach to data mining: models, algorithm designs and software development. Optimization Methods and Software 18 (4) (2203) 453-473.
4. Shi, Y. Peng, Y., Xu, X., Tang, X.: Data mining via multiple criteria linear programming:applications in credit card portfolio management, International Journal of Information Technology and Decision Making 1 (1) (2002) 145-166.
5. Shi, Y., Wise, M., Luo, M., Lin Y.: Data mining in credit card portfolio management: a multiple criteria decision making approach, in: Koksalan, M. and Zionts, S. (Eds.), Multiple Criteria Decision Making in the New Millennium, Springer, Berlin (2001) 427-436.
6. Freed, N., Glover, F.: Simple but powerful goal programming models for discriminant problems, European Journal of Operational Research, 7 (1981) 44-60.
7. Freed, N., Glover, F.: Evaluating alternative linear programming models to solve the two-group discriminant problem, Decision Science, 17 (1986), 151-162.
8. Glover, F.: Improve linear programming models for discriminant analysis, Decision Sciences, 21 (1990) 771-785.
9. Mangasarian, O. L.: Data Mining via Support Vector Machines, in: E. W. Sachs and R. Tichatschke (Eds.), System Modeling and Optimization XX, Kluwer Academic Publishers, Boston (2003) 91-112.
10. Shi, Y., Yu, P. L.: Goal setting and compromise solutions, in: Karpak, B. and Zionts, S. (Eds.), Multiple Criteria Decision Making and Risk Analysis Using Microcomputers,Springer-Verlag, Berlin (1989) 165-204.
11. Shi, Y.: Multiple Criteria Multiple Constraint-levels Linear Programming: Concepts,Techniques and Applications, World Scientific Publishing, River Edge, New Jersey (2001).
12. Guo, H. Gelfand, S. B.: Classification trees with neural network feature extraction, IEEE Transaction on Neural Netwroks 3 (1992) 923-933.
13. Quinlan, J. R.: Induction of decision tree, Machine Learning 1 (1986) 81-106.
14. http://www.rulequest.com/see5-info.html
15. Kou, G., Shi, Y.: Linux based Multiple Linear Programming Classification Program:version 1.0, College of Information Science and Technology, University ofNebraska-Omaha, Omaha, NE 68182, USA, 2002.
16. Yan, N., Shi, Y.: Neural Network Classification Program: version 1.0, A C++ Program run on PC, College of Information Science and Technology, University of Nebraska-Omaha, Omaha, NE 68182, USA, 2003.
17. http://www.lindo.com/
18. http://www.mathworks.com/

Multiple Criteria Linear Programming Data Mining Approach: An Application for Bankruptcy Prediction

Wikil Kwak[1], Yong Shi[2], John J. Cheh[3], and Heeseok Lee[4]

[1] Department of Accounting, College of Business Administration,
University of Nebraska at Omaha, Omaha, Nebraska 68182, U.S.A.
wkwak@mail.unomaha.edu
[2] College of Information Science and Technology, University of Nebraska at Omaha,
Omaha, Nebraska 68182
[3] Accounting and Information Systems, The University of Akron,
College of Business Administration, 259 South Broadway,
Akron, OH 44325-4802
[4] Department of Management and Information System,
Korea Advanced Institute of Science and Technology,
Seoul Korea

Abstract. Data mining is widely used in today's dynamic business environment as a manager's decision making tool, however, not many applications have been used in accounting areas where accountants deal with large amounts of operational as well as financial data. The purpose of this research is to propose a multiple criteria linear programming (MCLP) approach to data mining for bankruptcy prediction. A multiple criteria linear programming data mining approach has recently been applied to credit card portfolio management. This approach has proven to be robust and powerful even for a large sample size using a huge financial database. The results of the MCLP approach in a bankruptcy prediction study are promising as this approach performs better than traditional multiple discriminant analysis or logit analysis using financial data. Similar approaches can be applied to other accounting areas such as fraud detection, detection of tax evasion, and an audit-planning tool for financially distressed firms.

1 Introduction

Data mining is a process of discovering interesting patterns in databases that are useful in business or in other decision making processes [6]. However, not many applications have been tried in accounting businesses, even though accountants deal with a huge amount of transaction and financial data every day. We can try to apply similar approaches that are used in finance or marketing studies to accounting areas such as fraud detection, detection of tax evasion, and an audit-planning tool for financially distressed firms.

The purpose of this study is to propose a multiple criteria linear programming (MCLP) approach to data mining for bankruptcy prediction. Data mining is a tool which can be used to analyze data to generate descriptive or predictive models to solve business problems [7]. The goal of a predictive model like our bankruptcy prediction

Y. Shi, W. Xu, and Z. Chen (Eds.): CASDMKM 2004, LNAI 3327, pp. 164-173, 2004

study is to predict future outcomes based on past data. Bankruptcy prediction is an interesting topic because investors, lenders, auditors, management, unions, employees, and the general public are interested in how bankrupt firms proceed, especially since hearing news about the Enron and United Airline bankruptcy filings.

Wilson and Sharda [32] used the neural networks approach and Sung et al. [31] used the decision tree approach for bankruptcy prediction, but our study is the first one to use the MCLP approach in data mining for bankruptcy prediction.

The challenges may come from creating optimal cost-benefit trade-off mapping between the benefits of quantifying or discretizing financial data and the cost of information loss in the process of granulating financial data for detecting bankruptcy. In computer security detection, the discretization problem may be less severe because of the binary nature of computer virus or security breach that the detectors deal with, whereas financial data are decimal.

On the other hand, as of now, a multiple criteria linear programming data mining approach has been recently applied to credit card portfolio management. This approach has proven to be robust and powerful for even a large sample size using a huge financial database. The results of the MCLP approach in our bankruptcy prediction study are promising as this approach performs better than traditional multiple discriminant analysis or logistic regression analysis using financial data.

Our paper is organized as follows: The next section presents the background of bankruptcy studies. The third section presents a MCLP data mining model. The fourth section describes data collection procedures and reports our empirical results. The last section concludes with a summary of our findings and future research avenues.

2 Background

Altman [1] used multiple discriminant analysis (MDA) by using financial ratios to predict a bankruptcy model. Altman et al. [2] later proposed the ZETA model, but their assumptions of data being normally distributed can be a problem when applying this model.

Beaver [4] used cash flow variables to predict bankruptcy and later studies like Mossman et al. [18] compared financial ratios with cash flow variables and confirmed that cash flow variables are also useful to predict bankruptcy.

Ohlson [20] used a logit model which does not require any assumptions about the prior probability of bankruptcy or the distribution of predictor variables [19]. The assumptions about the knowledge of prior probabilities and group distributions make both of the above techniques very restrictive in bankruptcy prediction studies. In addition, hold-out sample tests are potentially upwardly biased [9] and the differences in the macro economic factors are sensitive to specific time periods [22]. Grice and Ingram [10] empirically tested and reported recently that Altman's [1] study using a small sample of 33 manufacturing firms and the use of equal sample size of bankrupt and non-bankrupt firms using a sample from 1958 to 1961 reported 83.5% overall accuracy. However, Altman's model using the 1988-1991 test period showed that the overall correct classification rate dropped to 57.8%. Begley et al. [5] also reestimated both Altman's [1] and Ohlson's [20] models using 1980's data and reported that Ohlson's model showed a Type-I error rate of 29.2% and the Type-II error rate of 14.9% at the cutoff point of 0.061. They suggested that both models' accuracy rates drop as they are applied in different time periods, but Ohlson's model is a preferred model. Here Type-I error refers to false rejection error. For a bankruptcy prediction model, we reject a firm as a non-bankrupt firm even though this firm is actually a bankruptcy firm. This will be very costly for a decision maker. Type-II error is an opposite case. Type-II error is false acceptance error. For example, we predict a firm as a bankrupt firm even though the actual firm is not a bankrupt firm. In this case, the cost of misclassification is at a minimum. They suggested that both models' accuracy rates drop as they are applied in different time periods, but Ohlson's model is a preferred model.

Freed and Glover [8] proposed linear programming (LP) to minimize misclassifications in linear discriminant analysis. Gupta et al. [11] also proposed linear goal programming as an alternative to discriminant analysis. However, these approaches may not be manageable for the large-scale databases at this time [14].

Pompe and Feelders [24] compared machine learning, neural networks, and statistics using experiments to predict bankruptcy. However, their results are not conclusive to which methods outperform the other methods.

Shin and Lee [30] proposed a genetic algorithm (GA) in bankruptcy prediction modeling using 264 mid-sized Korean manufacturing companies from 1995 to 1997. Their approach is capable of extracting rules that are easy to understand for users like expert systems. Their accuracy rate is 80.8% of both training and hold-out samples. However, this study used only the manufacturing industry and there may be an upward bias for prediction accuracy. In addition, like most GA studies, computational costs of this model can be expensive and there is no guarantee of optimality [31].

Park and Han [21] proposed a case-based reasoning (CBR) with the feature weights derived by an analytic hierarchy process (AHP) for bankruptcy prediction since AHP incorporates both financial ratios as well as non-financial variables into the model. They reported an 84.52% accuracy rate. They also used Korean mid-sized firms from 1995 to 1998. Therefore, we cannot generalize this study to U.S. firms because Korea went through economic turmoil in 1997 [31].

McKee [17] suggested a rough sets theory to develop a bankruptcy prediction model. Neural networks can be characterized as a 'black boxes' model which decision makers may not understand. The rough set model, however, is easily understandable and supported by a set of real examples. Rough sets analysis provides better results when the attributes are continuous variables. In this case, non-financial variables are not easy to incorporate. In addition, his study assumed equal costs for both bankruptcy and non-bankruptcy misclassifications. As Nanda and Pendharkar [19] suggested from their study, GA provides the best performance in terms of reducing Type I error costs. Using 1987-1995 data of 40 sample firms, they reported that using a decision maker explicitly incorporated costs of Type I and Type II errors, goal programming and GA had the highest correct classification rate of 65%. This is a more realistic assumption. In the real world, Type I error costs are much higher than Type II error costs in bankruptcy cases.

Generally, bankruptcy prediction studies as we discussed previously do not have a clear theory. However, this lack of theory is not a major problem in bankruptcy studies since researchers are more interested in prediction of bankruptcy. Bankruptcy prediction models to assess financial distress should attempt to establish criteria that will address the motivation for bankruptcy filing [13]. Platt and Platt [23] propose an inefficiency hypothesis that poses a social issue about future resource allocation. Another hypothesis is equity hypothesis, which worries that junior creditors have too much power in bankruptcy and extract value from senior creditors by threatening to delay legal proceedings following a revision of the Bankruptcy Code in 1979. A fundamental goal of the U.S. Bankruptcy Code is the creation of new 'feasible' companies with manageable debt levels, energized managements and plausible corporate strategies (p. 1210). However, empirical studies show that the bankruptcy process allows inefficient firms to remain in operation. Hotchkiss [12] finds that 40% of her sample emerges from bankruptcies with negative operating incomes and that 32% of post-bankrupt firms are not financially sound. However, bankruptcy is not a simple process as different stakeholders have different motivations.

Recent bankruptcy studies classified and predicted the final bankruptcy resolution using longitudinal study (for example, [3]), but the focus of our study is bankruptcy prediction using past financial data as other previous studies have used these approaches.

3 Models of Multiple Criteria Linear Programming Classification

From the aspect of mathematical tools of data mining, the algorithms of data mining can be implemented by many different types of mathematical techniques. For example, classification or prediction methods can be constructed by decision tree, statistics, and neural networks as previous bankruptcy studies have used [27].

Based on Freed and Glover's [8] linear programming (LP) model, Kou et al. [15] developed a general problem of data classification by using multiple criteria linear programming (MCLP). The basic concept of the formulation can be briefly explained as follows:

Given a set of r variables about the bankrupt or non-bankrupt sample firms in database $a = (a_1, ..., a_r)$, let $A_i = (A_{i1}, ..., A_{ir}) \in R^r$ be the sample observations of data for the variables, where $i = 1, ..., n$ and n is the sample size. We want to determine the coefficients of the variables, denoted by $X = (x_1, ..., x_r)^T$, and a boundary value of b to separate two classes: B(Bankrupt) and N (Non-bankrupt); that is,

(a) $A_i X \leq b, A_i \in$ B (Bankrupt) and $A_i X > b, A_i \in$ N (Non-bankrupt).

Consider now two kinds of measurements for better separation of Bankrupt and Non-bankrupt firms. Let α_i be the overlapping degree with respect to A_i, and β_i be the distance from A_i to its adjusted boundary. In addition, we define α to be the maximum overlapping of two-class boundary for all cases A_i ($\alpha_i < \alpha$) and β to be the minimum distance for all cases A_i from its adjusted boundary ($\beta_i > \beta$). Our goal is to minimize the sum of α_i and maximize the sum of β_i simultaneously. By adding α_i into (a), we have:

(b) $A_i X \leq b + \alpha_i, A_i \in$ B and $A_i X > b - \alpha_i, A_i \in$ N.

However, by considering β_i, we can rewrite (b) as

(c) $A_i X = b + \alpha_i - \beta_i, A_i \in$ B and $A_i X = b - \alpha_i + \beta_i, A_i \in$ N.

Our two-criterion linear programming model is stated as

(d) Minimize $\Sigma_i \alpha_i$ and Maximize $\Sigma_i \beta_i$

Subject to

$$A_i X = b + \alpha_i - \beta_i, A_i \in B,$$
$$A_i X = b - \alpha_i + \beta_i, A_i \in N,$$

Where A_i are given, X and b are unrestricted, α_i and $\beta_i \geq 0$ [28].

The previous MCLP model can be solved in many different ways. One method is to use the compromise solution approach [29];[26] to reform the model (d) by systematically identifying the best trade-offs between $-\Sigma_i \alpha_i$ and $\Sigma_i \beta_i$. To visualize this idea, we assume the ideal value of $-\Sigma_i \alpha_i$ is $\alpha^* > 0$ and the ideal value of $\Sigma_i \beta_i$ is β^* > 0. Then, if $-\Sigma_i \alpha_i > \alpha^*$, we define the regret measure as $-d_\alpha^+ = \Sigma_i \alpha_i + \alpha^*$; otherwise, it is 0. If $-\Sigma_i \alpha_i < \alpha^*$, the regret measure is defined as $d_\alpha^- = \alpha^* + \Sigma_i \alpha_i$; otherwise, it is 0. Thus, we have (i) $\alpha^* + \Sigma_i \alpha_i = d_\alpha^- - d_\alpha^+$, (ii) $|\alpha^* + \Sigma_i \alpha_i| = d_\alpha^- - d_\alpha^+$, and (iii) $d_\alpha^-, -d_\alpha^+$ ≥ 0. Similarly, we derive $\beta^* - \Sigma_i \beta_i = d_\beta^- - d_\beta^+$, $|\beta^* - \Sigma_i \beta_i| = d_\beta^- + d_\beta^+$, and $d_\beta^-, d_\beta^+ \geq 0$. An MCLP model has been gradually evolved as

(e) Minimize $d_\alpha^- + d_\alpha^+ + d_\beta^- + d_\beta^+$

Subject to

$$\alpha^* + \Sigma_i \alpha_i = d_\alpha^- - d_\alpha^+,$$
$$\beta^* - \Sigma_i \beta_i = d_\beta^- - d_\beta^+,$$
$$A_i X = b + \alpha_i - \beta_i, A_i \in B,$$
$$A_i X = b - \alpha_i + \beta_i, A_i \in N,$$

Where A_i, α^*, and β^* are given, X and b are unrestricted, $\alpha_i, \beta_i, d_\alpha^-, d_\alpha^+, d_\beta^-, d_\beta^+ \geq 0$.

The data separation of the MCLP classification method is determined by solving the above problem. Two versions of actual software have been developed to implement the MCLP method on large-scale databases. The first version is based on the well-known commercial SAS platform [25]. In this software, the SAS codes, including SAS linear programming procedure, are used to solve (e) and produce the data separation. The second version of the software is written by C++ language running on Linux platform [16]. The reason for developing Linux version of the MCLP classification software is that the majority of database vendors, such as IBM are aggressively moving to Linux-based system development. This Linux version goes along with the trend of information technology. Because many large companies currently use SAS system for data analysis, the SAS version is also useful to conduct data mining analysis under SAS environment.

4   Data Collection and Research Design

In this paper, we collected bankrupt firms from 1992 to 1998 and an average of 5.84 times more the number of matching control firms by the size and industry to emulate a real world bankruptcy situation. Our financial data are from Research Insight which is a financial database from Standard and Poor's. Among active companies in the

Research Insight (RI) database, we selected companies listed in three major stock exchanges: New York Stock Exchange, American Stock Exchange, and NASDAQ.

In collecting bankrupt firm data from RI and other sources, we first used RI Research (inactive company) data set as the initial screening to find data on bankrupt firms. We also looked at other sources such as the Wall Street Journal Index. However, unless all the financial data are available for our study, such data were not useful. Thus, we used the RI Research data set as our foundation data set.

From this RI research data set, we selected only the inactive firms that were deleted out of the RI active company data set because of bankruptcy. The RI research data set includes financial data of companies with reasons other than bankruptcy that were deleted out of the RI's active data set. Such reasons for deletion include acquisition or merger, liquidation, reverse acquisition, leverage buyout, and privatization. After this initial screening, we verified the bankruptcy data with various other sources such as the Wall Street Journal Index.

We tried to collect bankrupt firm data beyond 1998. However, we found that there were not enough bankrupt companies after 1998 with all the data available for our study. Thus, we decided to include in our sample companies only up to and including 1998 data from 1992. We expected that our analysis from seven years would provide statistically sound evidence, although we found that data on bankrupt firms were scarce as we examined the 1987 and earlier years. For practical reasons, we did not use all available financial data because processing huge amounts of data for such a large number of variables over multiple years is time consuming and inefficient. We ran our model every year since the time period is a factor unless our research design controls all macro economic factors.

In selecting variables, we used Altman's [1] original variables and Ohlson's [20] variables for bankruptcy prediction. Altman used five ratio variables in his study and Ohlson used nine variables in his study. However, with current available data mining tools and computer capabilities, we can handle more variables without difficulty in our model.

We first run our MCLP data mining model using five variables for each year as Altman [1] did in his original study. We want to compare the results of our study with the results of Altman's study to show the prediction accuracy of our study. Then we run our MCLP data mining model using nine variables as Ohlson [20] did in his study. Our goal is to show the effectiveness of our model compared with Ohlson's.

Table 1 presents our MCLP model results using Altman's five variables using overall years. In our study, we tried the MCLP data mining approach using Altman's five variables with more number of control firms since Altman's approach of using the

Table 1. Predictability of the MCLP model using Altman's 5 variables

All Years	N	Number Correct	Percent Correct	Percent Error
Type-I	91	42	46.15	53.85
Type-II	521	500	95.97	4.03
Overall Prediction Rate			88.56%	11.44%

same number of control firms is criticized by Ohlson and others for upward bias of the prediction error rate. The overall prediction rate for all years was 88.56%. Altman reported a 95% prediction rate in his original study, but this rate dropped to 78.4% with 1980's holdout sample [5]. From these results, our MCLP model shows that our approach is a lot more efficient and effective in bankruptcy prediction with current financial data.

Table 2 reports Type I and Type II error rates of the logit model using Ohlson's nine variables for each year and overall years. Here Type I error refers to false rejection error and Type II error refers to false acceptance error. From Table 2, Percent Error reports the Type I error rate and Percent Correct reports the Type II error rate. The lowest prediction rate was 92.5% in 1992 and the highest rate was 100% in 1995. However, the overall prediction rate for all years was 79.6%, which is similar to other previous studies. Begley et al. [5] reported similar results when the re-estimated Ohlson model is applied to the 1980's holdout sample. This table is presented here to compare with results of our MCLP data mining model.

Table 2. Type-I and Type-II errors for re-estimated Ohlson's model using 1990s data

Likelihood Ratio	Year	Percent Correct	Percent Error
38.47	1992	92.5%	7.4%
39.77	1993	96.1	3.7
35.03	1994	98.3	1.7
44.10	1995	100.0	0.0
32.34	1996	93.6	6.1
29.41	1997	94.5	5.5
20.07	1998	93.3	6.7
109.04	all years	79.6	19.7

We applied the MCLP data mining approach using Ohlson's nine variables and their results are reported in Table 3. We tried the Altman's five variables model with equal number of control firms as they did in the original study and their results are reported in Table 3 for comparison purposes.

The Table 3 reports Type I and Type II error rates of both models. If we consider that the costs of Type I errors outweigh the costs of Type II errors in a bankruptcy situation, our focus of prediction error rate should be on the Type I errors. The prediction rate of Type I errors is increasing and the prediction rate of Type II errors is decreasing in Altman's model compared with the model with more number of control firms. This is an interesting result which suggests that Altman's original model could be upward biased and he should use more control firms to represent the real world situation of bankruptcy. However, in the case of Ohlson's nine variables model, the Type I error prediction rate is decreasing and the Type II error prediction rate is stable our MCLP approach. From the results of the overall predication rate, Ohlson's model is similar to Altman's model (86.76% vs. 88.56%) using more control firms, but our MCLP model using Ohlson's nine variables is better than the overall prediction rate of the logit model (79.6%). This sustains our findings in this study. From the above results, our MCLP data mining approach performs better than the Altman's model, but provides similar or better results to the Ohlson's nine variables model.

Table 3. MCLP Data Mining Model

Year		Altman Model			Ohlson Model		
		N	Number Correct	Percent Correct	N	Number Correct	Percent Correct
1992	Type-I	21	15	71%	21	11	52%
	Type-II	21	17	81%	70	66	94%
1993	Type-I	15	13	87%	15	13	87%
	Type-II	15	13	87%	74	72	97%
1994	Type-I	12	8	67%	12	9	75%
	Type-II	12	10	83%	63	62	98%
1995	Type-I	8	8	100%	8	6	75%
	Type-II	8	8	100%	58	57	98%
1996	Type-I	15	14	93%	15	8	53%
	Type-II	15	14	93%	96	93	97%
1997	Type-I	12	10	83%	12	7	58%
	Type-II	12	11	92%	70	69	99%
1998	Type-I	9	7	78%	9	4	44%
	Type-II	9	8	89%	89	87	98%
All data	Type-I	126	109	87%	91	39	43%
	Type-II	91	62	68%	521	492	94%

5 Summary and Conclusions

In this paper we used the MCLP data mining approach to predict bankruptcy and compared our results with the results of Altman's and Ohlson's models using 1992-1998 financial data. The MCLP data mining approach has recently been applied to credit card portfolio management [27]. This approach has proved to be robust and powerful even for a large sample size using a huge financial database. The results of the MCLP approach in our bankruptcy prediction study are promising as this approach performs better than the traditional multiple discriminant analysis of Altman's [1] or Ohlson's [20] logit analysis using financial data. Similar approaches can be applied to other accounting areas such as fraud detection, detection of tax evasion, and an audit-planning tool for financially distressed firms.

Our next research will compare our MCLP data mining approach with the decision tree approach to see which approach is more efficient and effective in bankruptcy prediction.

References

1. Altman E.: Financial Ratios, Discriminant Analysis and the Prediction of Corporate Bankruptcy. *The Journal of Finance* 23 (3) (1968) 589-609

2. Altman E., Haldeman, R. G., Narayanan, P.: ZETA Analysis: A New Model to Identify Bankruptcy Risk of Corporations. *Journal of Banking and Finance,* 1(1) (1977) 29-54
3. Barniv R., Agarwal, A., Leach, R.: Predicting Bankruptcy Resolution. *Journal of Business Finance & Accounting* 29 (3/4) (2002) 497-520
4. Beaver, W.:Financial Rations as Predictors of Failure. Empirical Research in Accounting, Selected Studies. *Supplement to the Journal of Accounting Research* (1966) 71-111
5. Begley J., Ming, J., Watts, S. : Bankruptcy Classification Errors in the 1980s: An Empirical Analysis of Altman's and Ohlson's Models.*Review of Accounting Studies* 1 (1996) 267-284
6. Bose, I., Mahapatra, R. K.: Business Data Mining—A Machine Learning Perspective. *Information and Management* 39 (2001) 211-225
7. Chan C., Lewis, B.: A Basic Primer on Data Mining. *Information Systems Management* (Fall 2002) 56-60
8. Freed N, Glover, F.: Evaluating Alternative Linear Programming Models to Solve the Two-Group Discriminant Problem. *Decision Sciences* 17 (1986) 151-162
9. Grice J. S., Dugan, M. T.: The Limitations of Bankruptcy Prediction Models: Some Cautions for the Researcher. *Review of Quantitative Finance and Accounting* 17 (2001) 151-166
10. Grice J. S., Ingram, R. W.: Tests of Generalizability of Altman's Bankruptcy Prediction Model. *Journal of Business Research* 54 (2001) 53-61
11. Gupta Y. P., Rao, R. P. Baggi, P. K.: Linear Goal Programming as an Alternative to Multivariate Discriminant Analysis: A Not. *Journal of Business, Finance, and Accounting* 17 (4) (1990) 593-598
12. Hotchkiss, E. S.: Post-Bankruptcy Performance and Management Turnover. *Journal of Finance* 50 (1) (1995) 67-84
13. Jones, F. L.: Current Techniques in Bankruptcy Prediction. *Journal of Accounting Literature* 6 (1987) 131-164
14. Koehler, G. J., Erenguc, S. S.: Minimizing Misclassifications in Linear Discriminant Analysis. *Decision Sciences* 21 (1990) 63-85
15. Kou, G., Liu, X., Peng, Y., Shi, Y., Wise, M., Xu, W.: Multiple Criteria Linear Programming Approach to Data Mining: Models, Algorithm Designs and Software Development. *Optimization Methods and Software* 18 (2003) 453-473
16. Kou, G., Shi, Y.: Linux based Multiple Linear Programming Classification Program: version 1.0. College of Information Science and Technology, University of Nebraska-Omaha, Omaha, NE 68182, USA (2002)
17. McKee, T. E.: Developing a Bankruptcy Prediction Model via Rough Sets Theory. *International Journal of Intelligent Systems in Accounting, Finance & Management* 9 (2000) 159-173
18. Mossman, C., Bell, G., Swartz, L. M., Turtle, H.: An Empirical Comparison of Bankruptcy Models. *Financial Review* 33 (1998) 35-53
19. Nanda S., Pendharkar, P.: Linear Models for Minimizing Misclassification Costs in Bankruptcy Prediction. *International Journal of Intelligent Systems in Accounting, Finance & Management* 10 (2001) 155-168
20. Ohlson J.: Financial Ratios and the Probabilistic Prediction of Bankruptcy. *Journal of Accounting Research* 18 (1)(1980) 109-131
21. Park, C. S., Han, I.: A Case-Based Reasoning with the Feature Weights Derived by Analytic Hierarchy Process for Bankruptcy Prediction. *Expert Systems with Applications* 23,3 (2002) 255-264
22. Platt, D. H., Platt, M. B.: Development of a Class of Stable Predictive Variables: The Case of Bankruptcy Prediction. *Journal of Business Finance & Accounting* (Spring 1990) 31-51

23. Platt, D. H., Platt, M. B.: A Re-Examination of the Effectiveness of the Bankruptcy Process. *Journal of Business Finance & Accounting* 29 (9/10) (Spring 2002) 1209-1237
24. Pompe, P. P. M., Feelders, J.: Using Machine Learning, Neural Networks, and Statistics to Predict Corporate Bankruptcy. *Microcomputers in Civil Engineering* 12 (1997) 267-276
25. SAS/OR User's Guide, SAS Institute Inc., Cary, NC (1990)
26. Shi, Y.: *Multiple Criteria multiple Constraint-Levels Linear Programming: Concepts, Techniques and Applications* (World Scientific Publishing, River Edge, New Jersey) (2001)
27. Shi, Y., Peng, Y., Xu, W., Tang, X.: Data Mining via Multiple Criteria Linear Programming: Applications in Credit Card Portfolio Management," *International Journal of Information Technology & Decision Making* 1, 1 (2002) 131-151
28. Shi, Y., Wise, M., Luo, M., Lin, Y.: Data Mining in Credit Card Portfolio Management: A Multiple Criteria Decision Making Approach. In: Koksakan, M. and Zionts, S. (Eds.), *Multiple Criteria Decision Making in the New Millennium*, 427-436 (2001)
29. Shi, Y., Yu, P. L.: Goal Setting and Compromise Solutions. In: Karpak, B. and Zionts, S. (Eds.), *Multiple Criteria Decision Making and Risk Analysis Using Microcomputers*, (Springer-Verlag, Berlin) (1989) 165-204
30. Shin, K. S., Lee, Y. J.: A Genetic Algorithm Application in Bankruptcy Prediction Modeling. *Expert Systems with Applications* 23 (3) (2002) 321-328
31. Sung, T. K., Chang, N., Lee, G.: Dynamics of Modeling in Data Mining: Interpretive Approach to Bankruptcy Prediction. *Journal of Management Information Systems* 16 (1) (1999) 63-85
32. Wilson R. L. Sharda, R.: Bankruptcy Prediction using Neural Networks. *Decision Support Systems* 11(1994) 545-557

Coordination and Cooperation in Manufacturer – Retailer Supply Chains

Zhimin Huang and Susan X. Li

School of Business, Adelphi University, Garden City, New York 11530, U.S.A.
{huang, li}@adelphi.edu

Abstract. In this paper, we explore the role of vertical cooperative (co-op) advertising efficiency of transactions between a manufacturer and a retailer. We address the impact of brand name investments, local advertising, and sharing policy on co-op advertising programs. Game theory concepts form the foundation for the analysis. We begin with the classical co-op advertising model where the manufacturer, as the leader, first specifies its strategy. The retailer, as the follower, then decides on its decision. We then relax the assumption of retailer's inability to influence the manufacturer's decisions and discuss full coordination between the manufacturer and the retailer on co-op advertising. Two alternative bargaining models are employed to select the best co-op advertising scheme for achieving full coordination.

1 Introduction

Vertical co-op advertising is an interactive relationship between a manufacturer and a retailer in which the retailer initiates and implements a local advertisement and the manufacturer pays part of the costs. It is often used in consumer goods industries and plays a significant role in market strategy for many companies. In 1970, estimated co-op advertising expenditures spent by U.S. companies are up to $3 billion (Wolfe and Twedt 1974). In 1980, it was estimated that approximately $5 billion was used in co-op advertising (Advertising Age 1981), a 67% increase compared with 1970. More recently, estimates for 1986 co-op advertising expenditures amounted to $10 billion (Somers, Gupta and Herriott 1990), a 100% increase compared with 1986 and a 233% increase with 1970.

The main reason for a manufacturer to use co-op advertising is to motivate immediate sales at the retail level (Hutchins 1953). The manufacturer's national advertising is intended to influence potential consumers to consider its brand and to help develop brand knowledge and preference, and is also likely to yield benefits beyond sales from an individual retailer. Retailer's local advertising gets people into the store and, with the passage of time, brings potential consumers to the stage of desire and action and gives an immediate reason to buy (brands being offered, specific prices, store location, etc.). Co-op advertising provides consumers the information needs when they move through the final stages of purchase and a congruence of information and information needs that would be impossible if the manufacturer uses only

Y. Shi, W. Xu, and Z. Chen (Eds.): CASDMKM 2004, LNAI 3327, pp. 174–186, 2004.

national advertising (Young and Greyser 1983). In addition to the same objective of immediate sales at the retail level as the manufacturer, the retailer utilizes co-op advertising to reduce substantially its total promotional expense by sharing the cost of advertising with the manufacturer.

Most studies to date on vertical co-op advertising have focused on a relationship where the manufacturer is a leader and the retailer is a follower, which implies that the manufacturer dominates the retailer. The design and management is the main subject (see, for example, Crimmins 1970 & 1985, Berger 1972, Fulop 1988, Hutchins 1953, Somers, Gupta and Herriott 1990, Young and Greyser 1983). Little attention has been given to the recent market structure in which retailers retain equal or more power than manufacturers do in retailing. This paper is intended to discuss the relationship between co-op advertising and the efficiency of manufacturer-retailer transactions. The results lead to the development of game theory structure that enables us to examine the problem of coordination in co-op advertising. Focusing on coordinately organizational economics between the manufacturer and the retailer differentiates this research from previous studies in the literature. In order to avoid the distraction of multiple products, multiple manufacturers, or multiple retailers, a system composed of a single manufacturer and a single retailer is selected to investigate the basic efficiency issue of coordination. Once the methodology is developed and basic issues are initially investigated, further research can be pursued to generalize the model to include multiple manufacturers and/or retailers.

In Section 2 we begin by delineating the assumed relationship and decision variables of the manufacturer and the retailer. The sales response function of the product at the retail level is assumed explicitly nonlinear in the manufacturer's brand name investments and the retailer's local advertising level which is different from the literature where the retailer's local advertising level is the only factor.

Section 3 formulates the relationship between the manufacturer and the retailer as a classical "leader-follower" two stage game. In this classical co-op advertising structure, the manufacturer, as the leader, first specifies the brand name investments and the co-op reimbursement policy. The retailer, as the follower, then decides on the local advertising level. The Stackelberg equilibrium is achieved.

We address our analysis of fully coordinated co-op advertising in Section 4. We relax the leader-follower structure by assuming a symmetric relationship between the manufacture and the retailer. We focus on the discussion of the transactions-efficiency for co-op advertising. We show that, (i) all Pareto efficient co-op advertising schemes are associated with a single local advertising level and a single brand name investment quantity; (ii) among all possible co-op advertising schemes, the system profit (the sum of the manufacturer's and the retailer's profits) is maximized for every Pareto efficient scheme, but not for any other schemes; (iii) the system profit at any Pareto efficient scheme is higher than at Stackelberg equilibrium; (iv) the manufacturer's brand name investments at full coordination is higher than at Stackelberg equilibrium; (v) the local advertising level at full coordination is higher than at Stackelberg equilibrium; and (vi) there is a subset of Pareto efficient co-op advertising schemes on which both the manufacturer and the retailer achieve higher profits than at Stackelberg equilibrium and which are determined by the sharing policy of the local advertising expenditures between the manufacturer and the retailer.

Among those feasible Pareto efficient co-op advertising schemes, the question is which one is the best (sharing policy) for both system members. We address this issue and consider the Nash bargaining model for determining the best sharing policy. The Nash model predicts that both the manufacturer and the retailer should equally share the system additional profits.

Concluding remarks are in Section 5. All proofs of results are in the Appendix.

2 Assumptions

(i) The retailer's sales response volume function of the product, S, is assumed to be affected mainly by the retailer's local advertising level, a, and the manufacturer's national brand name investments, q, which include national advertising and control of implementing co-op advertising agreement between the manufacturer and the retailer. As Young and Greyser (1983) point out that co-op advertising is used to attract the attention of customers near the time of actual purchase and therefore it is to stimulate short-term sales. The manufacturer's brand name investments such as the national advertising is intended to take the potential customers from the awareness of the product to the purchase consideration. The function of the local advertising is to bring potential customers to the stage of desire and action, to give reasons such as low price and high quality to buy, and to state when and where to obtain the product. Therefore, the manufacturer's brand name investments and the retailer's local advertising perform different but complementary functions which have positive effects on the ultimate product sales. Saturation may be reached when both or either the local advertising efforts and the brand name investments are increased. Since co-op advertising is intended to generate short-term sales, we may consider one-period sales response volume function as $S(a, q) = \alpha - \beta a^{-\gamma} q^{-\delta}$, where $\alpha > 0$ is the sales saturate asymptote and β, γ, and δ are positive constants. There is a substantial literature on the estimation of sales response volume functions (see, for example, Little 1979), but all of them consider only the local advertising effect, not others such as national advertising on the volume of sales.

(ii) The manufacturer's dollar marginal profit for each unit to be sold is ρ_m, and the retailer's dollar marginal profit is ρ_r.

(iii) The fraction of total local advertising expenditures which manufacturer agrees to share with retailer is t, which is the manufacturer's co-op advertising reimbursement policy.

(iv) The manufacturer's, retailer's and system's profit functions are as the following:

$$\pi_m = \rho_m (\alpha - \beta a^{-\gamma} q^{-\delta}) - t a - q, \tag{1}$$

$$\pi_r = \rho_r (\alpha - \beta a^{-\gamma} q^{-\delta}) - (1 - t) a, \tag{2}$$

$$\pi = \pi_m + \pi_r = (\rho_m + \rho_r)(\alpha - \beta a^{-\gamma} q^{-\delta}) - a - q. \tag{3}$$

3 Classical Co-op Advertising Model

In this section, we model the relationship between the manufacturer and the retailer as a two-stage game with the manufacturer as the leader and the retailer as the follower. The solution of the game is called Stackelberg equilibrium. This relationship may be explained as follows. The original idea of co-op advertising came from the demands of the retailer's promotional help from the manufacturer in order to increase the retailer's advertising budgets without spending more of retailer's own funds. In the absence of the manufacturer's co-op advertising funds, the retailer will usually spend less money on the local advertising than the amount that is optimal from the manufacturer's point of view. The manufacturer can use co-op advertising subsidization policy to induce the retailer to increase its local advertising expenditure at a level that results in additional sales of the product to the retailer and, thereby, to the manufacturer. The determination of the level of local advertising expenditures depends on how much the manufacturer is willing to subsidize the retailer. The manufacturer may set up some requirements on the co-op advertising such as the size of the advertisement, the display of the manufacturer's brand name, and certain product features. The manufacturer, as the leader, first declares the level of brand name investments and the co-op advertising policy. The retailer, as the follower, then decides on the quantity of products to be purchased from the manufacturer taking into account the total local advertising expenditures to be spent. In other words, the retailer takes the (Stackelberg) equilibrium local advertising expenditures into account in deciding the volume of product to be ordered. The manufacturer on the other hand maximizes its profits by specifying the level of brand investments and co-op advertising reimbursement taking the behavior of the retailer into account.

In order to determine Stackelberg equilibrium, we first solve for the reaction functions in the second stage of the game. Since π_r is a concave function of a, the optimal value of the local advertising expenditures is determined by setting the first derivative of π_r with respect to a to be zero:

$$\frac{\partial \pi_r}{\partial a} = \gamma \rho_r \, \beta \, a^{-(\gamma+1)} \, q^{-\delta} - (1-t) = 0 \tag{4}$$

Then, we have

$$a = \left(\frac{\gamma \rho_r \beta}{(1-t) \, q^{\delta}} \right)^{1/(\gamma+1)} . \tag{5}$$

Equation (5) describes positively and negatively changes in responding to the changes in manufacturer's co-op advertising reimbursement policy and brand name investments. These can be seen by observing that

$$\frac{\partial a}{\partial t} = \frac{1}{\gamma+1} \left(\gamma \beta \rho_r \, / \, q^{\delta} \right)^{1/(\gamma+1)} (1-t)^{-(2+\gamma)(\gamma+1)} > 0, \tag{6}$$

$$\frac{\partial a}{\partial q} = -\frac{\delta}{\gamma + 1}\left(\gamma\beta\rho_r / (1-t)\right)^{1/(\gamma+1)} q^{-(\gamma+\delta+1)(\gamma+1)} < 0. \tag{7}$$

Equation (6) tells us that the more the manufacturer is willing to share the cost of local advertising, the more the retailer will spend on the local advertising. Therefore, the manufacturer's co-op advertising policy can be used as an indicator of the amount of money that the retailer would spend on local advertising. The manufacturer can use this indicator to induce the retailer to increase local advertising expenditure at a level that the manufacturer expects. It also shows that greater manufacturer's share of local advertising spending would lead to more retailer's spending for local advertising with the ultimate result of increased sales for both the retailer and the manufacturer. Equation (7) tells us that in this leader-follower relationship, if the retailer is to capitalize effectively on the brand awareness created by the manufacturer's national advertising, he/she might to increase or decrease local advertising expenditures in accordance with the effect of national advertising. In other words, the retailer has strong incentive to spend less money on the local advertising if the manufacturer increases the level of brand name investments. The amount of money spent by the manufacturer on national advertising can be used as another indicator of the amount of money that the retailer would spend on local advertising.

An analysis of influence of the manufacturer (leader)'s brand name investments and co-op advertising policy on the retailer (follower)'s local advertising is very important. This analysis may allow the manufacturer to measure the effects of changes in manufacturer's brand name investments and co-op advertising policy from one period to another period retailer local advertising. The manufacturer can use it to determine (a) when to do national advertising, (b) how long the national advertising would affect the retailer's local advertising efforts, (c) when to introduce new products, and (d) the total budgets of brand name investments and co-op advertising reimbursement.

Next, the optimal values of q and t are determined by maximizing the manufacturer's profit subject to the constraint imposed by (5). Hence, the manufacturer's problem can be formulated as

$$\operatorname*{Max}_{q,\, t} \pi_m = \rho_m (\alpha - \beta\, a^\gamma q^\delta) - t\, a - q \tag{8}$$

s.t.

$$0 \le t \le 1, q \ge 0,$$

where $a = \left(\dfrac{\gamma\rho_r\beta}{(1\text{-}t)\, q^\delta}\right)^{1/(\gamma+1)}.$

Substituting $a = \left(\dfrac{\gamma\rho_r\beta}{(1\text{-}t)\, q^\delta}\right)^{1/(\gamma+1)}$ into the objective yields the following optimization problem for the manufacturer:

$$\text{Max } \pi_m = \rho_m \left[\alpha - \beta (\gamma \rho_r \beta)^{-\gamma/(\gamma+1)} (1-t)^{\gamma/(\gamma+1)} q^{-\delta/(\gamma+1)} \right]$$

$$- (\gamma \rho_r \beta)^{1/(\gamma+1)} t(1-t)^{-1/(\gamma+1)} q^{-\delta/(\gamma+1)} - q \tag{9}$$

s.t.

$0 \le t \le 1, q \ge 0$.

Theorem 1. Let

$$a^* = \left[\delta^{-\delta} \beta \gamma^{\delta+1} (\rho_m - \gamma \rho_r) \right]^{1/(\delta+\gamma+1)}, \tag{10}$$

$$t^* = (\rho_m - (\gamma+1)\rho_r)/(\rho_m - \gamma \rho_r), \tag{11}$$

$$q^* = \left[\delta^{\gamma+1} \beta \gamma^{-\gamma} (\rho_m - \gamma \rho_r) \right]^{1/(\delta+\gamma+1)}. \tag{12}$$

Then (a^*, t^*, q^*) is the equilibrium point of the two-stage game.

From the above optimal formulations, the fraction level t^* is positively and negatively correlated to changes in manufacturer's marginal profits and retailer's marginal profits, respectively. These are because of

$$\frac{\partial t^*}{\partial \rho_m} = \frac{\rho_r}{(\rho_m - \gamma \rho_r)^2} > 0, \tag{13}$$

$$\frac{\partial t^*}{\partial \rho_r} = \frac{-\rho_m}{(\rho_m - \gamma \rho_r)^2} < 0. \tag{14}$$

For manufacturer, if his marginal profit is high (for instance, those manufacturers who produce infrequently purchased good such as appliances and linens), he/she knows that infrequently purchased products are not very standing out most noticeably to most consumers, except at the time of purchase or need. Once consumer decides to purchase this kind of product, one always or often makes an overt search among local sources of information, seeking specific product information. In order to give the retailer more incentive to attract consumers, the manufacturer should share more local advertising expenditures with the retailer. On the other, if retailer's marginal profit is high, at this situation retailer has strong incentive to spend money in local advertising to attract consumers to buy these products, even though the manufacturer only shares a small fraction of local advertising expenditures.

4 Full Coordinated Vertical Co-op Advertising Model

In previous section, we focused on the equilibrium results for a two-stage game structure. We assumed that the manufacturer as the leader holds extreme power and has almost complete control over the behavior of the retailer. The retailer is presumably powerless to influence the manufacturer. The relationship is that of an employer and an employee. The fact that, in many industries, manufacturing and retailing are vertically separated makes the effective implementation of the manufacturer's co-op advertising program difficult. The manufacturer who can best implement a national advertising campaign to promote brand awareness may not know the local market and the retailer's advertising behavior. The manufacturer can only provide such a co-op advertising program to the retailer and the retailer who knows the local market and can best advertise to create immediate sales decides whether the offer is taken advantage of and to what extent. In other words, it is the retailer, not the manufacturer, decides how much, if any, of the manufacturer's money is spent. As Crimmins (1973) points out that approximately one third to one half of the manufacturer's money allocated through co-op advertising allowances is not used by its retailers.

Recent studies in marketing have demonstrated that in many industries retailers have increased their power relative to manufacturers over the past two decades. The shift of power from manufacturers to retailers is one of the most significant phenomena in manufacturing and retailing. In consumer goods industries, one of the most influence of a retailer on the market performance of the manufacturer is the differentiation of the manufacturer's product. The retailer controls some of the attributes of the product which the consumer may desire. The product's quality and image may be reflected by the retailer's store reputation and image. It is also true that the retailer can influence the sales of the manufacturer's product through local advertising and other selling efforts such as a selling presentation, personal recommendation or advice solicited by the consumer, which provide enough information about the product (Porter 1974). The retailer transfers product information about reliability, features and method of use that may not be available from the manufacturer's national advertising efforts and other sources. Especially, for durable goods such as appliances and automobiles, the retailer has more influence on the consumer's purchase decision. Although the manufacturer's national advertising can lead the consumer to consider a particular brand, the retailer's local advertising and sales efforts can be used to negate the effect of national advertising by changing the consumer's mind. The retailer is able to withhold its selling efforts which includes local advertising for a particular brand and to influence the consumer to purchase another brand. It is clear that as the retailer's influence on product differentiation increases, the retailer's bargaining power relative to the manufacturer increases. This enables the retailer to exercise its enhanced retailing power in order to extract local advertising allowances and additional discounts from the manufacturer. Many retailers actually use manufacturers' allowances and co-op advertising programs for their own purposes, and in process reduce their dependence on the manufacturers (see, for example, Achenbaum and Mitchel 1987, Buzzell et al. 1990, Fulop 1988, and Olver and Farris 1989).

In this section, we relax the leader-follower relationship and assume a symmetric relationship between the manufacturer and the retailer. We will discuss the efficiency of manufacturer and retailer transactions in vertical co-op advertising agreements. Similar approaches have been used in distribution channels, franchising arrangements and inventory control systems (Charnes, Huang and Mahajan 1995, Jeuland and Shugan 1983, Kohli and Park 1989, and Li and Huang 1994).

Now, let's consider Pareto efficient advertising schemes in our co-op advertising arrangements. A scheme (a_0, t_0, q_0) is called Pareto efficient if one cannot find any other scheme (a, t, q) such that neither the manufacturer's nor the retailer's profit is less at (a, t, q) but at least one of the manufacturer's and retailer's profits is higher at (a, t, q) than at (a_0, t_0, q_0). More precisely, (a_0, t_0, q_0) is Pareto efficient if and only if $\pi_m(a, t, q) \geq \pi_m(a_0, t_0, q_0)$ and $\pi_r(a, t, q) \geq \pi_r(a_0, t_0, q_0)$ for some (a, t, q) implies that $\pi_m(a, t, q) = \pi_m(a_0, t_0, q_0)$ and $\pi_r(a, t, q) = \pi_r(a_0, t_0, q_0)$.

Since π_m and π_r are quasi-concave, the set of Pareto efficient schemes consists of those points where the manufacturer's and the retailer's iso-profit surfaces are tangent to each other, i.e.,

$$\nabla \pi_m(a, t, q) + \mu \nabla \pi_r(a, t, q) = 0, \tag{16}$$

for some $\mu \geq 0$ (see Charnes et al. (1990)), where $\nabla \pi_m = \left[\dfrac{\partial \pi_m}{\partial a}, \dfrac{\partial \pi_m}{\partial t}, \dfrac{\partial \pi_m}{\partial q} \right]$

stands for the gradient of π_m. This leads to the following theorem.

Theorem 2. The collection of Pareto efficient schemes is described by the set

$$Y = \left\{ (\overline{a}^*, t, \overline{q}^*) \colon 0 \leq t \leq 1 \right\}, \tag{17}$$

Where

$$\overline{a}^* = \left[\delta^{-\delta} \beta \gamma^{\delta+1} (\rho_m + \rho_r) \right]^{1/(\delta+\gamma+1)} \text{ and } \overline{q}^* = \left[\delta^{\gamma+1} \beta \gamma^{-\gamma} (\rho_m + \rho_r) \right]^{1/(\delta+\gamma+1)}.$$

This theorem tells us that all Pareto efficient schemes are associated with a single local advertising expenditure $\overline{a}^*$ and a single manufacturer's brand name investment $\overline{q}^*$ and with the fraction t of the manufacturer's share of the local advertising expenditures between 0 and 1. The locus of tangency lies on a vertical line segment at $(\overline{a}^*, \overline{q}^*)$ in (a,t, q) space because the expressions for both iso-profit surfaces contain only linear fraction variable t, so that vertically shifting an iso-profit surface yields another iso-profit surface. When a pair of tangent iso-profit surfaces shift vertically, the tangent point also shifts vertically so that the locus of tangency traces a vertical line.

Theorem 3. An advertising scheme is Pareto efficient if and only if it is an optimal solution of

$$\overline{\pi}^* = \underset{a,t,q}{\text{Max}} \ \pi = \pi_m + \pi_r \tag{18}$$

s.t.
$$0 \leq t \leq 1, q \geq 0, a \geq 0.$$

This theorem tells us that, among all possible advertising schemes, the system profit (i.e., the sum of the manufacturer's and the retailer's profits) is maximized for every Pareto efficient scheme, but not for any other schemes. The following theorem implies that Pareto efficiency yields (1) higher system profit than at Stackelberg equilibrium, (2) higher manufacturer's brand name investment than at Stackelberg equilibrium, and (3) higher local advertising expenditures than at Stackelberg equilibrium.

Theorem 4.

$$\overline{\pi}^* > \pi^*, \overline{q}^* > q^*, \overline{a}^* > a^*, \tag{19}$$

where "-*" and "*" represent coordination and Stackelberg equilibrium, respectively.

Theorem 4 leads to the possibility that both the manufacturer and the retailer can gain more profits compared with Stackelberg equilibrium. It should be noted that not all Pareto efficient schemes are feasible to both the manufacturer and the retailer. Neither the manufacturer nor the retailer would be willing to accept less profits at full coordination than at Stackelberg equilibrium. An advertising scheme $\left(\overline{a}^*, t, \overline{q}^*\right) \in Y$ is called feasible Pareto efficient if

$$\Delta\pi_m(t) = \pi_m\left(\overline{a}^*, t, \overline{q}^*\right) - \pi_m^* \geq 0 \text{ and} \tag{20}$$

$$\Delta\pi_r(t) = \pi_r\left(\overline{a}^*, t, \overline{q}^*\right) - \pi_r^* \geq 0, \tag{21}$$

since only schemes satisfying (20) and (21) are acceptable for both the manufacturer and the retailer when they do coordinate. We then call

$$Z = \left\{\left(\overline{a}^*, t, \overline{q}^*\right): \Delta\pi_m(t) \geq 0, \Delta\pi_r(t) \geq 0, \left(\overline{a}^*, t, \overline{q}^*\right) \in Y\right\} \tag{22}$$

the feasible Pareto efficient set of advertising schemes.
Let

$$k_1 = \beta\rho_m\left[(a^*)^{-\gamma}\left(q^*\right)^{-\delta} - (\overline{a}^*)^{-\gamma}\left(\overline{q}^*\right)^{-\delta}\right] + (q^* - \overline{q}^*) + a^* t^*, \tag{23}$$

$$k_2 = \beta\rho_r\left[(a^*)^{-\gamma}(q^*)^{-\delta} - (\overline{a}^*)^{-\gamma}(\overline{q}^*)^{-\delta}\right] + (a^* - \overline{a}^*) - a^* t^*, \tag{24}$$

$$t_{min} = -k_2 / \overline{a}^*, \text{ and} \tag{25}$$

$$t_{max} = k_1 / \overline{a}^*. \tag{26}$$

Here we suppose $k_2 < 0$. Then $\Delta\pi_m(t) = k_1 - \overline{a}^* t$, $\Delta\pi_r(t) = k_2 + \overline{a}^* t$, and Z can be simplified as

$$Z = \left\{\left(\overline{a}^*, t, \overline{q}^*\right): t_{min} \leq t \leq t_{max}\right\}. \tag{27}$$

It can be shown that $1 > t_{max} > t_{min} \geq 0$ (see the Appendix). Therefore, for any given t which satisfies $t_{min} < t < t_{max}$, $\Delta\pi_m(t) > 0$ and $\Delta\pi_r(t) > 0$. This simply implies that there exist Pareto efficient advertising schemes such that both the manufacturer and the retailer are better off at full coordination than at Stackelberg equilibrium. We are interested in finding an advertising scheme in Z which will be agreeable to both the manufacturer and the retailer. According to Theorem 4, for any Pareto scheme $\left(\overline{a}^*, t, \overline{q}^*\right), \Delta\pi_m\left(\overline{a}^*, t, \overline{q}^*\right) + \Delta\pi_r\left(\overline{a}^*, t, \overline{q}^*\right) = \Delta\pi$ where $\Delta\pi = \overline{\pi}^* - \pi^*$ is a positive constant. We refer $\Delta\pi$ as the system profit gain since it is the joint profit gain achieved by the manufacturer and the retailer by moving from a Stackelberg advertising scheme to a Pareto efficient advertising scheme. This property implies that the more the manufacturer's share of the system profit gain, the less the retailer's share of the system profit gain, and vice versa. The property that all feasible efficient transactions occur at $\left(\overline{a}^*, \overline{q}^* \right)$ implies that the manufacturer and the retailer will agree to change the local advertising expenditures to $\overline{a}^*$ from a^* and the brand name investments to $\overline{q}^*$ from q^*. However, they will negotiate over the manufacturer's share of the local advertising expenditures t.

Assume that the manufacturer and the retailer agree to change local advertising expenditures to $\overline{a}^*$ and brand name investments to $\overline{q}^*$ from $a*$ and $q*$, respectively, and engage in bargaining for the determination of reimbursement percentage to divide the system profit gain. A fraction closer to t_{max} is preferred by the retailer, and a fraction closer to t_{min} is preferred by the manufacturer. Let us utilize Nash (1950) bargaining model in our co-op advertising model. Since our entire problem is deterministic, we assume both the manufacturer and retailer's utility functions, u_m and u_r, over $\Delta \pi_m$ and $\Delta \pi_r$ are linear. Without loss of generality, we assume $u_m(\Delta \pi_m) = \Delta \pi_m$ and $u_r(\Delta \pi_r) = \Delta \pi_r$.

According to Nash model, the best Pareto efficient advertising reimbursement, t, is obtained by the following problem:

$$\text{Max } \Delta \pi_m(t) \, \Delta \pi_r(t) \tag{27}$$

s.t.

$$t_{min} \leq t \leq t_{max}$$

Since $\Delta \pi_m(t) \, \Delta \pi_r(t) = (k_1 - \overline{a}^* t)(k_2 + \overline{a}^* t)$, setting the first derivative of $\Delta \pi_m(t) \, \Delta \pi_r(t)$ to be zero, we have

$$\overline{t}^* = (t_{min} + t_{max})/2 \tag{28}$$

Substitute (28) into $\Delta \pi_m(t)$ and $\Delta \pi_r(t)$, we have

$$\Delta \pi_m(\overline{t}^*) = \Delta \pi_r(\overline{t}^*) = \Delta \pi / 2 \tag{29}$$

Therefore, the Nash model predicts that both the manufacturer and the retailer should equally share the system additional profits.

5 Concluding Remarks

This paper attempts to investigate the efficiency of transactions for the system of manufacturer-retailer co-op advertising in the context of game theory. Two co-op advertising models are discussed and compared. The first is the classical leader-follower advertising model where the manufacturer is the leader and the retailer is the follower. The second advertising model assumes the symmetric positions of the manufacturer and the retailer in the decision making process and discusses efficient co-op advertising schemes. The Nash bargaining model is utilized to select the best co-op advertising expenditure sharing rule between the manufacturer and the retailer.

There are three possible avenues for future research. First, the manufacturer-retailer relationship is multi-dimensional, including wholesale and retail price, credit terms, shelf-space, contributions towards special sales, treatment of competitors product and policy with respect to house brands. It may hard, but should very interesting to take all or many of these factors into consideration in the future research. Second, the single manufacture-retailer system assumption can be relaxed to a duopoly situation of manufacturers who sell their products through a common monopolistic retailer who sells multiple competing brands with varying degrees of substitutability. It would be interesting to discuss the impact of duopolistic manufacturers' brand name investments, monopolistic retailer's local advertising level, and advertising sharing rules among manufacturers and retailer on co-op advertising expenditures. Finally, in our analysis we employed nonlinear sales response function to satisfy the saturation requirement. As indicated in the literature of channel studies, many important results in equilibrium analyses depend on the shape of the product demand function (Moorthy 1988 and Shugan 1985). Therefore, the use of a linear sales response function may yield different and interesting results in the analysis for vertical co-op advertising agreements.

References

1. Achenbaum, A. A., Mitchel, F. K.: Pulling Away from Push Marketing. Harvard Business Review, (May-June, 1987), 38-40
2. Advertising Age: Partnership Perks Up Profits. (August 17, 1981), S-1
3. Berger, P. D.: Vertical Cooperative Advertising Ventures. Journal of Marketing Research, 9 (1972), 309-312
4. Buzzell, R. D., Quelch, J. A., Salmon, W. J.: The Costly Bargain of Trade Promotion. Harvard Business Review, (March-April, 1990), 141-149
5. Charnes, A., Huang, Z. M., and Mahajan, V.: Franchising Coordination with Brand Name Considerations. Research in Marketing, 12 (1995), 1-47
6. Charnes, A., Huang, Z. M., Rousseau, J. J., Wei, Q. L.: Cone Extremal Solutions of Multi-Payoff Games with Cross-Constrained Strategy Sets. Optimization, 21 (1990), 51-69
7. Crimmins, E. C.: A Co-op Myth: It Is a Tragedy That Stores Don't Spend All Their Accruals. Sales and Marketing Management, (February 7, 1973)
8. Crimmins, E. C.: A Management Guide to Cooperative Advertising. New York: Association of National Advertisers (1970)
9. Crimmins, E. C.: Cooperative Advertising. New York: Gene Wolf & Co. (1985).
10. Fishburn, P.: Utility Theory for Decision Making. John Wiley & Sons, Inc. (1970).
11. Fulop, C.: The Role of Advertising in the Retail Marketing Mix. International Journal of Advertising, 7 (1988), 99-117
12. Hutchins, M. S.: Cooperative Advertising. New York: Roland Press (1953).
13. Jeuland, A. P., Shugan, S. M.: Managing Channel Profits. Marketing Science, 2 (1983), 239-272
14. Kohli, R. and Park, H.: A Cooperative Game Theory Model of Quantity Discounts. Management Science, 35 (1989), 693-707
15. Li, X. S., Huang, Z. M.: Managing Buyer-Seller System Cooperation with Quantity Discount Considerations. Computers and Operations Research, 22 (1995), 947-958
16. Little, J. D. C.: Aggregate Advertising Models: The State of the Art. Operations Research, 27 (1979), 629-627

17. Moorthy, K. S.: Strategic Decentralization in Channels. Marketing Science, 7 (1988) 335-355
18. Nash, J. F.: The Bargaining Problem. Econometrica (1950)155-162
19. Olver, J. M., Farris, P. W.: Push and Pull: A One-Two Punch for Packaged Products. Sloan Management Review, (Fall, 1989) 53-61
20. Porter, M. E.: Consumer Behavior, Retailer Power and Market Performance in Consumer Goods Industries. Review of Economics and Statistics, LVI (1974), 419-436
21. Shugan, S.: Implicit Understandings in Channels of Distribution. Management Science, 31 (1985) 435-460
22. Somers, T. M., Gupta, Y. P., Herriott, S. R.: Analysis of Cooperative Advertising Expenditures: A Transfer-Function Modeling Approach. Journal of Advertising Research, (October/November, 1990), 35-45
23. Wolfe, H. D., Twedt, D. W.: Essentials of The Promotional Mix. New York, Appleton Century Crofts (1974)
24. Young, R. F., Greyser, S. A.: Managing Cooperative Advertising: A Strategic Approach. Lexington Books (1983)

Appendix-Proof of Results

Proof of Theorem 1:
Solving the first-order conditions of π_m with respect to t and q yields

$$t^* = \frac{\rho_m - (1 + \gamma) \rho_r}{\rho_m - \gamma \rho_r} \text{ and} \tag{A1}$$

$$q^* = \left[\delta^{\gamma+1} \beta \gamma^{-\gamma} (\rho_m - \gamma \rho_r) \right]^{1/(\delta+\gamma+1)} \tag{A2}$$

Substitute (A1) and (A2) into (5), we have

$$a^* = \left[\delta^{-\delta} \beta \gamma^{\delta+1} (\rho_m - \gamma \rho_r) \right]^{1/(\delta+\gamma+1)} \tag{A3}$$

Hence, (a^*, t^*, q^*) is the optimal solution of (9). □

Proof of Theorem 2:
Since

$$\nabla \pi_m(a, t, q) = \left(\beta \gamma \rho_m a^{-(\gamma+1)} q^{-\delta} - t, -a, \beta \delta \rho_m a^{-\gamma} q^{-(\delta+1)} - 1 \right) \tag{A4}$$

$$\nabla \pi_r(a, t, q) = \left(\beta \gamma \rho_r a^{-(\gamma+1)} q^{-\delta} - (1-t), -a, \beta \delta \rho_r a^{-\gamma} q^{-(\delta+1)} - 1 \right), \tag{A5}$$

utilizing (16) we can get $\mu = 1$, $\overline{a}^*$ and $\overline{q}^*$ in (17) and with t between 0 and 1. □

Proof of Theorem 3:
Since $\pi = (\rho_m + \rho_r) (\alpha - \beta a^{-\gamma} q^{-\delta}) - a - q$ does not contain the variable t, any value of t between 0 and 1 can be a component for any optimal solution.

Taking the first derivatives of π with respect to a and q, and setting them to 0, we have

$$\overline{a}^* = \left[\delta^{-\delta} \beta \gamma^{\delta+1} (\rho_m + \rho_r) \right]^{1/(\delta+\gamma+1)} \text{ and}$$

$$\overline{q}^* = \left[\delta^{\gamma+1} \beta \gamma^{-\gamma} (\rho_m + \rho_r) \right]^{1/(\delta+\gamma+1)}. \text{ Therefore, } \left(\overline{a}^*, t, \overline{q}^* \right) \text{ for any } t \text{ in } [0, 1] \text{ is}$$

an optimal solution of (18). □

Proof of Theorem 4:

(i) Proof of $\overline{\pi}^* > \pi^*$:

Let

$$f(x) = \left(\gamma + \delta + 1\right) x + (\gamma + 1)\, \rho_r/(\rho_m + \rho_r) - \left(\gamma + \delta + 1\right) x^{(\gamma + 1)/(\gamma + \delta + 1)}.$$

Since $\pi^* =$

$$\alpha\,(\rho_m + \rho_r) - \left[(\gamma + \delta + 1)(\rho_m - \gamma\rho_r) + (\gamma + 1)\rho_r\right]\left[(1/\delta)^{\delta} \beta \gamma^{-\gamma}(\rho_m - \gamma\rho_r)^{-(\gamma + \delta)}\right]^{1/(\gamma + \delta + 1)}$$

and

$$\overline{\pi}^* = \alpha\,(\rho_m + \rho_r) - (\delta + \gamma + 1)\,(\rho_m + \rho_r)\left[(1/\delta)^{\delta} \beta\,\gamma^{-\gamma}(\rho_m + \rho_r)^{-(\gamma + \delta)}\right]^{1/(\delta + \gamma + 1)},$$

we have

$$\overline{\pi}^* - \pi^* =$$

$$(\rho_m + \rho_r)(\rho_m - \gamma\rho_r)^{-(\gamma + \delta)/(\gamma + \delta + 1)}\left[(1/\delta)^{\delta}\beta\gamma^{-\gamma}\right]^{1/(\gamma + \delta + 1)} f((\rho_m - \gamma\rho_r)/(\rho_m + \rho_r)).$$

Since $f'(x) = \left[(\gamma + \delta)(\gamma + \delta + 1)\right] x^{-(\gamma + \delta + 2)/(\gamma + \delta + 1)} > 0$ for $x > 0$, $f(x)$ is a strictly convex function.   Solving $f'(x) = 0$, we know that the minimum point is $y = \left[(\gamma + \delta)(\gamma + \delta + 1)\right]^{\gamma + \delta + 1}$. Since $f(y) = (\gamma + 1)\,\rho_r/(\rho_m + \rho_r) - 1/(1 + 1/(\gamma + \delta))^{\gamma + \delta} > 0$, we have $f((\rho_m - \gamma\rho_r)/(\rho_m + \rho_r)) > 0$, i.e., $\overline{\pi}^* - \pi^* > 0$.

(ii) Proof of $q^* < \overline{q}^*$:

$$\overline{q}^* - q^* = \left[(\delta\,)^{\gamma + 1} \beta\,\gamma^{-\gamma}(\rho_m + \rho_r)\right]^{1/(\gamma + \delta + 1)} \left\{1 - ((\rho_m - \gamma\rho_r)/(\rho_m + \rho_r))^{1/(\gamma + \delta + 1)}\right\}$$
$$> 0.$$

(iii) Proof of $\overline{a}^* > a^*$:

$$\overline{a}^* - a^* = \left[(1/\delta)^{\delta} \beta\,\gamma^{\delta + 1}\,(\rho_m + \rho_r)\right]^{1/(\gamma + \delta + 1)} \left\{1 - ((\rho_m - \gamma\rho_r)/(\rho_m + \rho_r))^{1/(\gamma + \delta + 1)}\right\}$$
$$> 0.$$ □

Proof of $1 > t_{max} > t_{min} \geq 0$:

Since $t_{max} - t_{min} = (k_1 + k_2)/\overline{a}^* = \Delta\pi/\overline{a}^* > 0$, we have $t_{max} > t_{min}$.
Now let's show $t_{max} < 1$.
Let

$$\Phi(x) = (\delta + \gamma)\, x^{1/(\delta + \gamma + 1)} + (\rho_m/(\rho_m - \gamma\rho_r))\, x^{-(\delta + \gamma)/(\delta + \gamma + 1)} - (\delta + \gamma + 1)$$

Since

$$\Phi'(x) = ((\delta + \gamma)/(\delta + \gamma + 1))\, x^{-(2\delta + 2\gamma + 1)/(\delta + \gamma + 1)} \left\{x - (\rho_m/(\rho_m - \gamma\rho_r))\right\}$$
$$> 0 \quad \text{when } x > \rho_m/(\rho_m - \gamma\rho_r),$$

we have $\Phi((\rho_m + \rho_r)/(\rho_m - \gamma\rho_r)) > \Phi(\rho_m/(\rho_m - \gamma\rho_r))$.
After rearrangement of above inequality, we have $t_{max} < 1$.   □

Development of Enterprises' Capability Based on Cooperative Knowledge Network

Junyu Cheng and Hanhui Hu

Research Center for Industrial Organization, Southeast University,
2 Si Pai Lou, Nanjing, 210096, P. R. China
chengjunyu@yahoo.com.cn, huhh@seu.edu.cn

Abstract. How to develop the capability of an enterprise is a vital problem to many knowledge based enterprises. This paper argues that an enterprise can achieve dynamic development of its capabilities by constructing cooperative knowledge network (CKN). The network can provide the enterprise with multiple learning opportunities and the enterprises in the network can dig out, acquire and exploit all kinds of knowledge resources in the network. Development of the enterprise's capability needs an established basic capability as the foundation together with sustainable learning ability and transformation capability. Based on theoretical analysis, a case is discussed about a high-tech enterprise, Nanjing SVT Group, constructing the CKN for IC design. The paper concludes that construction of CKN is an effective way to acquire internal and external knowledge to improve the capability of the enterprise.

1   Capability Development Based on Knowledge Flow in CKN

An enterprise can achieve dynamic development of its capabilities by constructing cooperative knowledge network (CKN). It must start with its own strategic knowledge, that is, its fundamental abilities which are special and difficult to be imitated. In order to attain a sustainable competitive position and long-run high return, the enterprise needs to continuously obtain new knowledge based on the fundamental abilities it has already possessed. First of all, organizational learning is an important factor. In its development, the enterprise is faced up with new market, new social culture, new competitors and new competition environment, which provide it with various learning opportunities. While fundamental ability is a basic requirement for the enterprise to explore market opportunities, learning ability is necessary for the enterprise to reduce uncertainties in extending its market. The second important factor is how to integrate newly acquired knowledge and capabilities with its existing capability system to achieve the development of its ability. The enterprise needs to possess this kind of ability of reallocation and transformation. That is, the ability to associate external learning with internal resources and capabilities and apply them in competitive environment to develop its existing capability. This transformation ability is crucially important for the enterprise to keep a sustainable competitive advantage.

Y. Shi, W. Xu, and Z. Chen (Eds.): CASDMKM 2004, LNAI 3327, pp. 187–194, 2004.
© Springer-Verlag Berlin Heidelberg 2004

Therefore the development of enterprise capability is a process of acquiring new knowledge via continuous organizational learning on the bases of its existing resources and capabilities and then reallocating and transforming the newly acquired knowledge. This capability development in CKN can be divided into three parts: basic capabilities (enterprises possess key technologies and can operate them to produce cash flow), learning ability (to the source, it is a process of knowledge confusion and transformation; to the recipient, it is a dynamic organizational learning process), and transformation capability (reallocation and transformation of the capability). These three parts are basic elements supporting the operation of the whole enterprises. Meanwhile, it is also a basis for our consideration about the mode choice in construction of the enterprise's knowledge network.

1.1   Knowledge Basis of an Enterprise

Knowledge basis of an enterprise is its key assets, knowledge and capabilities, which are firm specific and hard to imitate. For example, key resource of the Coco-Cola Company is its Coco-Cola prescription, which can give its sustainable leading position in the market rather than its skillful feeding technology.

In a highly labor divided and specialized economic system, despite possessing specific knowledge basis, none of the enterprises have all the knowledge that needs to be used in providing specific product or service to customers. So an enterprise needs to construct its knowledge network to obtain all kinds of knowledge it needs. Because of the phenomenon of knowledge market failure, it seems that knowledge exchange can only be conducted in the way of "labor exchange", that is, the enterprise must have its own knowledge basis to exchange with others. From this point, we can see that the knowledge basis of the enterprise is not only the starting point of the development of its capability, but also the groundwork on which it can construct knowledge network and attain profits.

1.2   Learning Ability in CKN

Different from enterprises outside CKN, enterprises in the network need extra knowledge managing process and organizational learning, thus they must possess stronger learning capacity. CKN enable the enterprises to contact with many differentiated markets and to transact and cooperate with different customers, suppliers and middlemen. This provides them with multiple learning opportunities. If the enterprise in the network can effectively manage its learning process, it will be able to acquire more updated and much more knowledge than enterprises outside the network, which may bring about substantial competitive advantage.

The distinguished feature of acquiring knowledge in CKN lies in three relevant questions. Firstly, the specific knowledge of the enterprise is definitely related to certain kind of knowledge. This requires that the enterprise consider how to construct CKN to attain complementary knowledge. Secondly, the enterprise should learn how to control the whole knowledge network for the network itself has internal and external complexity. Last but also the most important, CKN is not only a tool to use knowledge, but also an organization to generate new knowledge. Knowledge innovation needs communication, integration and complementing of different kinds of knowledge. Through cooperation, network knowledge can be created among the organizations (Nonaka & Takeuchi, 1995), which is new to all the participants. Thus, knowledge innovation is realized in the cooperation of the enterprises. Just as Shan, Walker and Kogut (1994) pointed out, cooperation interface of the enterprises in biotechnology industry is where technology innovations take place.

In CKN, learning is a relative concept. Enterprises are both the source and the recipient of the knowledge. On the one hand, the enterprise needs to transfer its own knowledge to other enterprises in the network to prepare for integration and transformation of its own knowledge and the knowledge from other enterprises; On the other hand, the enterprise also needs to obtain knowledge from other enterprises to accomplish its organizational learning.

From the view of knowledge transfer, Wernerfelt (1984) pointed out that in a competitive environment, if an enterprise can construct a proper mode to apply its resources in dynamic internal and external environment, the resources would bring it with more competitive advantages.   According to transaction theory, when strategic resources of an enterprise diffuse in a market with high uncertainty, the enterprise usually acts with more caution (Williamson, 1985). So, when the enterprise is faced up with an unfamiliar, changeable and unpredictable network, it tends not to transfer large amount of its knowledge to the network. But if the network may bring about a huge market potential, then it is necessary for the enterprise to properly transfer its knowledge for the purpose of occupying new market and getting profits in the growing market. In this case, the enterprise needs to analyze the opportunities and the risks they are faced up with and evaluate whether potential profits will overweight potential risks. They should decide with caution if they are able to manage the risks. Controlling knowledge transfer can serve as an important mechanism of balancing risks and opportunities. If potential profits from a market will exceed the potential risks it can bear, then knowledge transfer is necessary. If the enterprise needs to seek for long-run market opportunities and profits from a network, then knowledge transfer is of crucial importance.

From the view of knowledge learning, enterprises tend to obtain external knowledge by constructing knowledge network. Hamel (1991) pointed out that the chief drive of cooperation is to learn specific new knowledge and capabilities of other enterprises. Nowadays, more and more organizations are fusing into alliance to get new knowledge and practical skills. Even though they are forming alliance for other purposes, new knowledge is also a satisfying by-product of their cooperation. Just as Inkpen (1998) commented, alignment creates a precious learning opportunity for the cooperators when it puts enterprises with different skill and knowledge basis into one unit.

The biggest advantage of the knowledge network lies in that the enterprises can not only get external coded knowledge but also acquire tacit knowledge of other organizations, and then turn them into their own organizational knowledge. Core knowledge and tacit knowledge are highly asset proprietary and knowledge specific. They are hard to obtain through market transaction. Only through long run cooperation can that knowledge be obtained on the basis of mutual trust. Researchers find out that cooperation is a basic way and tool to improve learning ability and obtain knowledge (Mowery, 1996). In fact, cooperation among enterprises is to open a window through which the cooperator has an opportunity to enter its partner's core knowledge field (Lei, 1992).

1.3   Transformation Capability in CKN

In CKN, development of new capabilities consists of two stages. First, it is a stage of acquiring new knowledge through organizational learning or transferring knowledge among participants. Second, it is a stage of knowledge integration. That is to absorb, assimilate the learned skills and knowledge and then transform them into new ability to complete the development of the enterprise's capability. This, in fact, is to internalize the new knowledge in the organization. The enterprise acquires new knowledge through organizational learning. But this does not guarantee development of the enterprise's capability. Only through integration of the new knowledge with current knowledge and capability system of the enterprise and applying them in market competition, can the enterprise really transform the new knowledge into its new capability.

Transformation capability in CKN is not only relative to knowledge basis and prior experience of the enterprise, but also relative to the similarity between knowledge of different enterprises, for the new knowledge may contradict with prior routines of the enterprise. This kind of conflicts is quite obvious in multinational companies. From the point of corporation culture, this kind of conflicts in multinational companies mainly comes from the process of absorbing, applying and sharing the knowledge that are transferred across international boundary. As pointed out by Forsgren (Forsgren, 1997), the more various different subsidiaries' business backgrounds are, the more bright future the multinational company will have in developing new knowledge internally. However, the more various their business backgrounds are, the more difficult it is for them to exploit the new knowledge extensively.

Because of these conflicts, enterprises need a transformation process after they have learned new knowledge. The new knowledge has to be integrated to change into internal capabilities of the enterprises. In fact, global corporation culture does not conflict with local needs of the host country. On the contrary, global culture can serve as a path and mode of cooperation and integration between overseas business units. It can create a value system being shared by managers all over the world, which will promote reallocation and transformation of multinational company's key capabilities globally. Finally it is hoped that organizational units distributed all over the world could create and share the same mode of observation and the same approach of thinking.

In CKN, whether the newly acquired knowledge can be quickly transformed in the organization is of great influence to the efficiency of enterprise's capability development. Once acquired, the new knowledge should be integrated with current skills and knowledge and be modified and improved in practice. In the process of transformation, the enterprise needs to construct both an efficient information transmission system and an organization structure, which can provide incentives to experiments and trial errors. They are both essential to sustainable development of enterprise's capability.

1.4   Enterprise's Capability Development in CKN

Basic capability, learning ability and transformation capability are three constituents of enterprise's capability development. Among them, basic capability is the core capability of the enterprise, while learning ability and transformation capability are subsidiary capabilities that can help the enterprise to develop its basic capability. Development of the enterprise's capability needs an established basic capability as the foundation together with sustainable learning ability and transformation capability. This logic can be used to describe the process of knowledge transfer among network nodes to realize the development of the enterprise's capability. First of all, we assume that two enterprises construct a knowledge network in the way of both investing in a new entity. The two enterprises conduct their knowledge learning and transfer through the network node--the new entity. We refer the two enterprises as core enterprises or key enterprises, the new entity as the node enterprise.

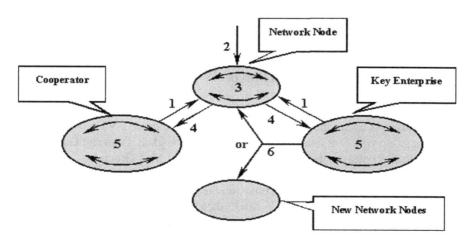

Fig. 1. Capability development based on CKN

As shown in figure 1, the two enterprises first transfer their knowledge to the node enterprise, which conducts its own organizational learning in this process (process 1). Meanwhile, the node enterprise continuously gets new knowledge through organizational learning when it closely contacts with new customers, suppliers, cooperators and the government in its new business (process 2). It then reallocates and integrates the newly acquired knowledge, the basic knowledge and capabilities of the core enterprises and the knowledge from other cooperators to develop its new capability (process 3). After that, the core enterprises need to timely transfer the new capability of the node enterprise to their own enterprises (process 4). Having accepted the new capability, the core enterprises transform it into new basic capability through certain integration process (process 5). Finally, the core enterprises balance the risks and profits carefully and then decide whether to construct new network node based on the new capability or to transfer the new capability to the original network node to start a new cycle of capability development (process 6).

Undoubtedly, effective transfer and learning of knowledge and capability among network nodes is important to the development of enterprise's capability.   It is also an effective approach to sustain and strengthen the competitive advantage of the enterprise in a dynamic environment. If the core enterprises and the node enterprises can perform the 6-process activities continuously to form a sound cycle, knowledge and capabilities will be created and shared in the whole network and continuous learning will be achieved. In CKN, each of the six processes is helpful in maintaining and increasing knowledge and capability of the whole network. This model in fact demonstrates the process that the core enterprises learn, create and transfer knowledge and capability via network nodes in the whole network.

It is only the first step of network learning strategy for the core enterprises to learn and absorb new knowledge creatively via network nodes in the whole network. What is more important is how the core enterprises can make best use of this system to effectively integrate all of the new knowledge and capability from the network nodes to develop capability of the enterprises. This is the significance of capability development based on CKN.

2   Case Study: Construction of SVT's CKN

Founded in 1992, SVT Group used to be SVT High Technology Innovation Limited Enterprise. As one of the starting civil technology enterprise, SVT now has developed into a group with four headquarters in Nanjing, Shanghai, Xi'an and Guangzhou and more than 30 member firms. The basic capability of SVT Group lies in its ability to practice technology innovation to meet market demand. The first success of SVT group came from the production of the first generation counterfeit money identification machine in 1992. Since then, it has continuously got first hand information from the market to closely connect its technology innovation with the market. Consequently, it has introduced many new products into the market.

As for its technology, SVT has successfully developed about one hundred technologies in the field of telecommunications and power system in the last decade. As it is well known that the great support of technology innovation is human resources. Besides a large group of outstanding experts, professors and engineers attracted by its flexible mechanism specific to civil enterprises, SVT established the first post-doctor workstation of civil technology enterprise in 2000 in China. In the next two years, with help of Nanjing University, Science and Technology University of China and Southeast University, SVT has recruited more than ten post-doctoral researchers in information and telecommunications engineering, electronic engineering, electric engineering and other six subjects. SVT assigns them research tasks according to its market research information. Thus the workstation provides support and guarantee to technology innovation in related fields in the group.

As for its management, the idea of "internal customer relation management" is carried out inside SVT. The essence of market economy is introduced into the enterprise, which emphasizes the importance of customers, so that a good internal management can be achieved.

Good culture atmosphere is another important constituent of the enterprise's capability. Inside SVT, a learning culture is created with responsibility as core, innovation as essence, understanding as link and learning as drive. This culture has been gradually formed in the long term business operation and is deeply rooted inside. With this culture, the enterprise encourages innovation, accepts errors and failures, and supports cooperation. Its employees always work together to overcome difficulties, either in product generation and improvement or in production and trial.

Since 2001, SVT started to construct CKN for IC design to integrate both national and overseas knowledge with the purpose of developing the enterprise's capability with help of external knowledge. The main approach it takes is to integrate universities' resources and construct international strategic alliance.

In recent years, through the way of investment control by its subsidiaries, SVT Group managed to cooperate with some universities and research institutes which have the first class technology in IC design in China, such as Southeast University, Hefei Industry University, Shanghai Jiao Tong University, and to set up quite a few high-tech companies controlled by SVT, including Jiangsu Dong Da IC System Engineering Technology Company, Hefei Gong Da Xian Xing Micro-electronic Technology Limited Company, Shanghai Jiao Tong Chuangqi Information Security Chip Limited Company, etc. In this way, SVT, in a short period, has got hold of a large quantity of first class talents in IC design that have both specialty strength and experience.

We should notice that the way SVT constructing its knowledge network is not only limited in modes of controlling or forming alliance. It also applies direct introduction of advanced technology etc.

3   Conclusion

In such a short period of two years, SVT uses its extraordinary dynamic capability and flexible ways of controlling or forming alliance to integrate its own knowledge with that of multinational companies, well-known universities and research institutions, and constructs a first class IC design knowledge network in both scale and technology in domestic market. In this process, SVT not just invested in some companies, it, with the aim of improving China's IC key technology, integrated advantage resources of human capital and technology by means of international cooperation and capital operation. It has built up a knowledge chain in China's IC high-end technology products. This obviously demonstrates SVT's dynamic capability of digging, acquiring and applying new knowledge quickly to get the advantage position in a new industry.

From the process of SVT setting foot in IC design area and successfully constructing IC industrial network, we can find out that dynamic capability is also an operation capability. It plays an important role in the development of an enterprise's capability. SVT Group has good basis in strategic factors such as technology, organization, talents and culture. It also has strong capability in technology innovation according to market demand. But this capability is only limited in innovation of non-core technology, and it can only guarantee the competitive advantage in limited area and time. Meanwhile, this kind of technology innovation has strong rigidity due to its specialized labor division. To achieve further development of the capability, it has to stand in front of the whole industry to get advanced knowledge through the way of constructing knowledge network.

Although SVT has succeeded in getting advanced knowledge, we wait to see whether it can integrate and make full use of that knowledge and complete the capability development and value creation. It is out of question that, in such a short period of two years, SVT has grown into a force that we cannot neglect in domestic IC design industry. SVT's behavior will inevitably influence the competition structure of IC design industry deeply and profoundly.

References

1. Forsgren, M.: The Advantage Paradox of the Multinational Corporation. The Nature of the International Firm, Copenhagen: Copenhagen Business School Press, (1997) 69-85
2. Hamel, G.: Competition for Competence and Inter-partner Learning within International Strategic Alliances. Strategic Management Journal, 12(1991) 83-103
3. Inkpen, A. C.: Learning and Knowledge Acquisition through International Strategic Alliances. Academy of Management Executive, 12 (4)(1998) 69-80
4. Lei, D. & Slocum, J.W.: Global Strategy, Competence Building and Strategic Alliances. California Management Review, Fall (1992) 81-97
5. Mowery, D. C., Oxley, J. E. & Silverman, B. S.: Strategic Alliances and Inter-firm Knowledge Transfer. Strategic Management Journal, Winter Special Issue, 17 (1996) 77-91
6. Nonaka, I. & Takeuchi, H.: The Knowledge-Creating Company: How Japanese Companies Create the Dynamics of Innovation. London: Oxford University Press, (1995)
7. Shan, W. J., Walker & Kogut, B.: Interfirm Cooperation and Startup Innovation in the Biotechnology Industry, Strategic Management Journal, 15(5) (1994) 387-394
8. Wernerfelt, B.: A Resource-Based View of the Firm. Strategic Management Journal, 5(1984) 171-180
9. Williamson, O.: The Economic Institutions of Capitalism: Firms, Markets, Relational Contracting. New York: Free Press, (1985)

Information Mechanism, Knowledge Management and Arrangement of Corporate Stratagem

Zhengqing Tang[1], Jianping Li[2], and Zetao Yan[2]

[1] Guanghua School of Management, Peking University,
Beijing 100871, P. R. China
hfahtzq@tom.com
[2] Institute of Policy & Management Science, Chinese Academy of Sciences,
Beijing 100871, P. R. China
{ljp, ztao}@mail.casipm.ac.cn; jianpingli@yahoo.com

Abstract. General application of information technology leads to modern corporate information mechanism. With this mechanism corporation can make full use of knowledge resource, improve managing efficiency and make corporate performance better. But on the other hand, competition among corporations also becomes more drastic under the unifying trend of global economy.

This paper gives a brief view of some characteristics of knowledge and information. We show what constitutes corporate stratagem. In our analysis, corporate dominance comes from knowledge management and knowledge innovation. All of it involves collecting, processing, innovating and utilizing information and knowledge resource. To success, corporation must turn to knowledge management and knowledge innovation. From this point of view, we put forward two arrangements for corporation to win dominance in drastic market competition. The first is about practice of knowledge management in corporate activity. The other is strategic framework of corporate management and competition based on knowledge management.

1 Introduction

1.1 Development of Modern Economic Structure

We are now living through a period of knowledge capitalism. The developing trend of knowledge and information society began in 1980s. Application of modern information technology clears up communicating baffle of information (see Porter and Millar 1985). It reduces information's producing cost and strengthens our ability of exploiting knowledge and information. In this way can we be able to make full use of information resource and make knowledge innovation.

Knowledge and information can improve economic efficiency, promoting economic development   and social evolution. According to the statistic of worldbank report, now production value based on utilization of knowledge and information resource has taken a big share of GDP in many countries. A new economic structure called knowledge economy comes into being after agriculture economy and industry

Y. Shi, W. Xu, and Z. Chen (Eds.): CASDMKM 2004, LNAI 3327, pp. 195–203, 2004.

economy. OECD points out in its report of 1996 that knowledge and information has become the driving power for social and economic development.

Table 1. Comparative analysis of three economic structure

Economy	Agriculture	Industry	Knowledge, Information
Pattern	Autarky	Resource Consuming	Knowledge Innovation
Basis	Land	Machine	Human
Point	Land, labor	Material, Technology	Management, Knowledge
Dominance	Amount, Gift	Quality, Price	Speed, Service

We compare different points of three economies in list 1. As we see, knowledge economy breaks limitation of resource economy compared to agriculture economy or industry economy. It is a creative economy supported by knowledge and information resource. In this economic structure, knowledge and information is producing factor more important than material resource. It is element of management, support of decision-making, decisive factor of corporate competition. Innovation, communication and application of knowledge is dominant power in economic development.

1.2 Function of Knowledge and Information

Bell (1973) and Freeman (1982) consider knowledge as a key factor in the production and reproduction of economies and societies. The function model about relation between knowledge and economic growth can be expressed as:

$$Y = F(C, \ KL)$$

Y: Production, C: Capital, K: Knowledge, L: Labor.

In modern economic growth theory, growth of production lies on three factors: capital stock, labor input, knowledge and learning effect. In knowledge society knowledge is the most influential resource among the three factors (see Drucker 1993). Burton-jones (1999) stress that much attention has been given to the growing economic importance of technology, information, business processes, quality control, human capital, and corporate capabilities and competencies — all knowledge-related factors over recent years. To sum up, knowledge and information will promote social and economic development in the following fields:

- It solves resource problem in economy. Natural resource is limited and social evolution can't fully depend on natural resource supply. So the best potential power comes from exploration of knowledge and information. With this kind of resource can we realize technical innovation, design new product and offer better service. To meet social demand we must pay attention to processing, innovating and utilizing of knowledge resource.
- As a kind of immaterial capital, knowledge and information resource is public, nondepletable and nonrivalous. It is public product as well as social product. The cost of producing knowledge is very low while the profit of applying knowledge is considerable. So every one can easily make use of it and benefit from it.

- Structure of knowledge economy is consistent with the unifying trend of global economy. Modern information technology solves limitation of space and time. Now it is possible for all kinds of economic activities to synchronously span countries and regions, such as global capital flow, production, market and conference. It is clear that under some disciplines such as geography, sociology, economy, culture, management and so on, there is growing acceptance that flow of knowledge is integral to understanding contemporary global capitalism.
- Agglomeration, innovation and spread of knowledge and information becomes decisive power in corporate reform. It promotes innovation of corporate managing mechanism, organizational structure and competing stratagem. Teece (1982), Winter (1987), Nonaka (1991), Senge (1990) give a whole range of studies on the importance of knowledge as a vital aspect of corporate competence.

2 Information Mechanism in Corporate Competition

2.1 Development of Modern Corporate Competition

2.1.1 Unifying Trend of Global Corporate Competition

Bryson (2000) presents both a major theoretical statement and an empirical exemplification of the power of knowledge in shaping spaces and places of today and society. In global economy, there is no limitation on product market and capital flow. Nowadays industry, finance, investment, transportation, communication of every country and every region is only one part of the unified global economic system. The typical characteristics of our society in this period include the unified economy, high-tech of corporate product, multiple market demand and drastic corporate competition.

With advanced transporting and communicating tools, corporation can finish production, sale, management and all kinds of corporate activities on basis of optimal resource allocation in the unified global economy.Application of modern information technology not only has great influence on corporation and market, but also leads to great change in modern corporate management and competition. On the one hand it accelerates connection and cooperation among different corporate inner departments, breaking distance between corporation and client. On the other hand it also intensifies competition among corporations.

2.1.2 Incentive for International Corporate Competition

General application of information technology leads to establishment of modern corporate information mechanism. It is an evolutionary period that corporation explores its information resource, improves managing efficiency and makes corporate performance better. It is also a necessary course for corporation to take part in international competition.

Development of global economy and international competition shows importance of corporate innovation. To win in drastic international competition, corporation must change its old operating pattern by innovation of management. Corporation will realize business reform, adopt electronic business and expand market network. All of these arrangements depend on new corporate information mechanism.

2.2 Information Mechanism in Corporate Operation

David and Foray (1995) show that underpinning the knowledge economy is the increasing use of information and communication technologies (ICTs) that have a profound effect on the generation, distribution and exploitation of knowledge. Combination of modern information mechanism with corporate management brings a new comprehensive management of corporate material flow, capital flow, information flow and human flow. This promotes a new style of corporate stratagem.

2.2.1 Foundation of New Information Mechanism

The new corporate information mechanism is made up of Internet, intranet, MIS and software. It is a process strategy or method by which actors (individuals, organizations) attempt to enroll others in a network. Progress of information-processing technology solves technical limitation on management. With general application of distributed-managing system, database, OA system, MIS and professional managing software, corporation can speedup working efficiency such as information collecting, processing, communicating and utilizing.

Goddard(1995) examines the impact of information and communication technologies (ICTs) and find that the successful implementation of telematics widens the locational repertoires available to corporation. Computer and network work in all activities of corporate business. With help of new corporate information mechanism, corporation could improve management of finance, market, stock and human resource. ERP, electric business and network marketing develops rapidly. The new style of operation has replace traditional trade style gradually.

2.2.2 Reconstruction of Corporate Organization and Management

This new information mechanism is more powerful, open and timely in corporate operation. Now all departments of corporation located in different places can exchange information synchronously. They can connect more closely and work more efficiently. With this mechanism, more work can be finished and less middle management is needed between the leader and the employee. So corporation is more successful and more sensitive to respond to any information and any change.

In addition, it causes reform of corporate business flow and reconstruction of organization. Bryson (1997) sums up some of the recent attempts to explain the spatial reorganization of production and finds that there is a blurring of the organizational boundary of the business corporation. Bloomfield, Coombs and Owen (1993) point out that ICTs emerges as a new resource in the struggle for reallocation of power in corporate organization.

Great change is happening in corporate organizational structure. A mutual network structure based on information mechanism has replaced the former structure. In general, reconstruction of corporate organization and management is showed in following fields:

- Refinement of corporate departments
- Multi-task for corporate departments

- Synchronizing trend of different corporate departments
- Mutual exchange between management and implementation

2.3   Function of Knowledge in Corporate Competition

2.3.1   Element of Modern Corporate Competition

Now product and service market give priority to consumer. Client's demand for product and service depends on multiple characteristics that corporation can supply, such as quality, amount, speed, reputation, extra value, speed and so on.

In fact corporate competitive dominance is a comprehensive advantage. It doesn't run in some one part but in many fields that may be corporate management, organizational structure, strategic framework, business flow, financial operation, market power and so forth. It comes from extra technology, producing ability, human resource, marketing method and so on. All these can't go without information mechanism and knowledge management.

Table 2. Product/Market decision in corporate competition

Marketing Research	Strategic decision	Tactical decision	Implementation
Consumer analysis	Market choice	Product	Organizing
Channel analysis	Discrimination	Price	Managing
Competitor analysis	Orientation	Advertisement	Feedback
Self analysis	Reputation	Spot	Adjusting

From table 2, we can find out the role of corporate information mechanism and knowledge management. Corporation needs all kinds of information including market sorts, producing ability, growth, cost, quality, material supply, reputation, market network, R&D, core ability, feedback. A series of corporate decision need refinement, spread and utilization of this information. Knowledge and information is the most important element of corporate competition.

2.3.2   Reform of Corporate Competitive Stratagem

Corporate dominating element changed two times in the evolution of economy. The first change is from price and amount to quality and reputation. The second change is from quality and reputation to information and speed. In the old corporate opinion, what' most important is product that meets market demand. Now modern conception pays attention to knowledge and information. Practice shows the favorite corporation is the one that can provide both product and knowledge. Corporation owning learning ability will success in application of new knowledge in operation.

With development of high-tech industry and application of advanced tools in different fields, it's possible for corporation to provide consumer more product and service with high extra value. This leads to more drastic corporate competition. It is no longer under limitation of cost, discrimination and market location. Information mechanism and knowledge management are expansion of corporate competitive factors. The new competitive stratagem based on knowledge management and knowledge innovation has been generally applied by corporations.

3 Arrangement of Corporate Strategic Framework

3.1 Combination of Knowledge Management with Corporate Competition

Hamel and Prahalad (1994) insist that corporation must hold its own competence. Coyle (1997), Drucker (1993) give some discussion on the growing significance of knowledge in contemporary capitalism. Corporate competence is now bound up not with new material per se but with new ways of producing, using and combining diverse knowledge. The key to our competence is how we can combine, marshal and commercialise our knowledge.

The direct goal of corporate information mechanism and knowledge management is to establish corporate information dominance. Its strategic goal is to win the competitive dominance. Corporate information mechanism can improve business process and management efficiency. The heart of information mechanism lies in processing, producing, exchanging and applying information and knowledge. Realization of information automation is only the first step of its tasks. In the competence respective, the corporation is essentially a rearrangement of skill, experience and knowledge, rather than a set of response to information or transaction. By this token, knowledge management is exactly the stage that corporation adjusts itself to knowledge economy and social environment. It is important for us to see that corporation must get competitive dominance by information dominance.

Corporate business and management must be combined with modern information technology. Thus corporation could make full use of advantage of knowledge management and be able to change it into corporate competitive dominance. Knowledge management in corporation is closely connected with a series of corporate arrangements, such as strategic plan, business process, organizational structure and management mode. It involves production, finance, market, human management and many other fields. We must pay attention to some factors that have great influence on corporate operation and management. The first factor we should notice is widespread application of information technology. The second factor is reform of corporate stratagem caused by drastic market and complex environment.

3.2 Factor Arrangement for Knowledge Management

The core of corporate knowledge management focuses on establishment of innovating system supported by knowledge management. Corporation can realize knowledge production and knowledge innovation on basis of information mechanism and knowledge-managing system. Sundo (1998) give a coherent analysis about development of innovation theory. Innovation is the source of corporate competitive dominance. It is a course of reproducing new knowledge and technology with application of original knowledge and information resource. Corporation can advance management level, expand global market and win corporate comprehensive dominance.

Table 3. Corporate competition based on knowledge management

Ability	Advantage	Method
Utilization of information network; Implement knowledge management; Implement knowledge innovation; Ability of adjustment to market competition; Improve knowledge content in product and service;	Technology; Market power Cost; Size; Speed; Management; Knowledge;	Producing multiple product; Reduce cost; Make discrimination; Change knowledge into corporate ability; Explore new business mode;

We give a brief view of corporate competition in table 3. It includes three parts that are ability, show and method. All of these factors work on basis of corporate knowledge management and innovation. In fact, the course in which corporation gets competitive dominance is also a course of carrying out knowledge management and innovation. Castells (1996) give prominence to importance of innovation, knowledge and learning in a globalizing, rapidly evolving economy.

According to demand of corporate competition, usually operation of knowledge management should include the following tasks:

- Combination of macroscopical stratagem with local arrangements,
- Working out tactics and plan of organization,
- Fluent business process and corporate operation,
- Good learning environment,
- Harmonious fellowship,
- Training of employee's ability.

To realize the above achievement, we will stress corporate learning skill here. Corporation must provide training of learning skill for itself. This is an absolutely necessary stage of knowledge management that produces corporate own knowledge capital.

3.3 Strategic Framework Based on Knowledge Management

As we have expressed in introduction, knowledge and information is the most important resource for corporate competition compared to other resources. Market competition in modern economy is very drastic. Development of corporation mainly depends on efficiency of corporate management and decision-making. But to complete this achievement, corporation must have enough valuable information and could change it into knowledge capital that corporation wants urgently. From this point of view, what knowledge management should do is to collect information rapidly, process it precisely and explored it effectively. Corporation must design its stratagem under the consideration of knowledge management.

As a whole, competitive dominance comes from the comprehensive ability of corporate management. Corporate transformation requires exposure to flows of knowledge either in the form of direct or indirect movement of ideas between departments and places or through knowledge situated in manufactured items that out compete existing products. What we showed in figure 1 is the strategic framework of corporate management system According to analysis from different attitude, location and task, the framework can be divided into three parts which are made up of six fields. First, management of production, finance, market and human belongs to microcosmic fields of corporate management. It is located at the tactical level. On the other hand management of decision-making belongs to macroscopical field of corporate management. It is consist of strategic arrangements. Between them are knowledge management and knowledge innovation that unite all parts of corporate management like a bridge. Knowledge management and information mechanism dealing with corporate information and knowledge resource pay more attention to reprocessing, innovation and exploration. With effective information mechanism, knowledge management can finish rearrangement of competitive factors, provide knowledge support for decision-making, explore potential of corporate management and win competitive dominance.

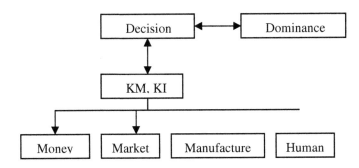

Fig. 1. Strategic framework of corporate competition

4 Summary

We present some discussion about information mechanism and knowledge management in corporate development in our paper. But we notice establishment of corporate dominance is a systematic work. Our statement is imperfect. More detailed research and work can be carried on from different point of view, such as:

- Training of corporate learning skill,
- Implementation of corporate stratagem,
- Evolution of corporate organization,
- Particular innovation drove by knowledge.

Modern society operates on basis of information network. In knowledge economy, corporation must respond rapidly to market demand, implement knowledge management and innovation, avoid uncertainty and risk in corporate decision-making and establish comprehensive stratagem of corporate development. In the long run, the basic idea is that corporation must win dominance from knowledge management.

References

1. Bell, D.: The coming of Post-Industrial Society: A venture in Social Forecasting. New York: Basic Books (1973)
2. Bell, H.: Measuring and managing knowledge. George Werthman (2001)
3. Bloomfield, B.P., Coombs, R., and Owen, J.: The social construction of information systems: The implications for management control. Internal Paper. Manchester School of Management, University of Manchester (1993)
4. Bryson, J.R.: Business service firms, service space and the management of change, Entrepreneurship and Regional Development.9 (1997) 93-111
5. Bryson, J.R., Daniels, P.W., Henry, N.,& Pollard, J.: -Knowledge-Space-Economy. Routledge (2000)
6. Burton-jones, A.: Knowledge capitalism: Business, working, and learning in the new economy. Oxford (1999)
7. Castells, M.: The Information Age: Economy, Society and Culture. Volume I: The Rise of the Network Society. Oxford: Blackwell (1996)
8. Coyle, D.: The Weightless World: Strategies for Managing the Digital Economy. Oxford: Capstone (1997)
9. David, P.A., Foray, D.: Accessing and expanding the science and technology knowledge base. STI Review 16 (1995) 13-68
10. Drucker, P.: Post-capitalist Society, Oxford: Butterworth-Heinemann (1993)
11. Freeman, C.: The Economics of Industrial Innovation. 2nd, edn, London: Pinter (1982)
12. Goddard, J.B.: Telematics and employment: What jobs, where? Paper presented to the National Program for information and Communication Technologies (PICT) Conference. 11 May. London: Department of Industry, Economic and Social Research Council (1995)
13. Hamel, G., Prahalad, C. K.: Competing for the Future, Boston: Harvard Business School Press. (1994)
14. Nonaka, I.: The knowledge-creating company, Harvard Business Review 69 (1991) 96-104
15. OECD Report (1996)
16. Porter,R. E. and Millar V.E.: How information gives you competitive advantage. Reprinted in Porter, M. E. 1998, Boston: Harvard Business School Press (1985)
17. Senge, P.: The leader's new work: building learning organizations. Sloan Management Review 32 (1990) 7-23
18. Sundo, J.: The theory of innovation. Edward Elgar (1998)
19. Teece, D. J.: Towards an economic theory of the multiproduct firm, Journal of Economic Behaviour and Organization 3 (1982) 39-63
20. Winter, S.: Knowledge and competence as strategic assets. In: Teece. D. (ed) The Competitive Challenge: Strategies for Industrial Innovation and Renewal. Cambrideg, MA: Ballinger (1987) 159-84

An Integrating Model of Experts' Opinions*

Jun Tian, Shaochuan Cheng, Kanliang Wang, and Yingluo Wang

Management School of Xi' an Jiaotong University,
No.28 West Xianning Road, Xi'an, Shaanxi province, China 710049
{tianjun, sccheng, klwang, ylwang}@mail.xjtu.edu.cn

Abstract. The paper presents a framework for integrating experts' opinions from the view of systematic optimization, considering factors of consistency or harmony and reliability of all experts' opinions. The characteristics of consistence of experts' opinions are defined based on statistics. The reliability function of expert's opinion is designed and the measurement of the reliability of integration result of all experts' opinions was then conducted. A non-liner programming model is set up to get the optimal scheme to correspond to the different experts' opinions that consider systematically influences of the consistency, harmony and reliabilities at the same time. The independence of each expert's opinion were not only kept but also, well preserved.

1 Introduction

The integration of experts' opinions is a key step in Group Support System (GSS) that helps decision-makers to bring experts' ideas into a good decision conclusion. The study of the methods and mechanisms of integrating experts' opinions is an important area in the research of GSS, synthesis evaluation, and expert systems. It has an important theoretical and practical application values in using experts' intelligences and experiences to deal with complex problems in society and economy.

Delphi Inquiry Method is a typical method in integrating expert's opinions [1]. It provides us with a convergence mechanism of expert's opinion from disperses to consistence with cyclic communication to experts by the procedure of "collecting, statistic and feed backing". However, this system has a defect in that it influences the independent thinking of experts by the production of statistics and feed back process. The mechanism also has ventures that the procedure couldn't get convergence if some experts insisted on their judgments. The research on models of integrating experts' opinions includes: the aggregation of information [2], utility theory of group [3], AHP [4], Byes probability [5, 6] and fuzzy evaluation [7]. In the measurement of consistency, Kacprzyk proposed an operator of "OWA"[8]. Chi proposed a KBS checking based on knowledge management systems [9]. The Nash equilibrium of Game Theory was used to solve the conflict situations. The measurement of the reliability of aggregation result can be got through setting up the model for the system-

---

* Supported by NSFC of China (code:70271024) and soft-science funds of shaanxi province (code:2003KR67).

Y. Shi, W. Xu, and Z. Chen (Eds.): CASDMKM 2004, LNAI 3327, pp. 204–212, 2004.

atic reliability [10] or the model of error transformation in hierarchy judgment matrix [11].

It is necessary to study the effective integrating mechanism and method of experts' opinions systematically in order to remedy the deficiency in Delphi Method or other methods. This paper set up a framework for non-liner programming model to search the total optimal conclusion, which considers both factors of consistence (or correspondence) and reliabilities.

2 The Framework of Integrating Expert's Opinions

The purpose of integrating expert's opinions is to find ways of forming consistent suggestions, So as to get the group's satisfied or optimal solution. Thus, the integration of expert's opinions can be realized through optimization search. The framework of optimization search is set up based on the quantitative evaluation of experts' opinions.

The appraisal value of an expert given represents the most possible value that the expert thinks. Because of the influence of different factors such as the complexities of the problem, the deviations of expert's subjective judgments, the restrictions of expert's knowledge and ability, and so on, the expert's judgment value is adjustable by a certain degree in most situations. The adjustability would be permitted if the expert took the attitude of cooperation. That is the appraisal value each expert gave can be adjusted properly in order to obtain convergence of the opinions of the group. But the range of adjustment is inversing to the reliability of the value. Adjusting an expert's opinion might reduce its reliability as cost spending. That is, the more distance adjusted the lower the reliability is. Furthermore, each expert can restrict the limit of the adjustment range.

The integration of expert's opinions is the searching for the best scheme to adjust all experts' opinions that meet the needs of consistency, harmony and reliability. The objective of the adjusting scheme is to obtain the maximum reliability while minimizing the quantities of the whole adjustment. The last conclusion can be got through statistics of the best-adjusted scheme.

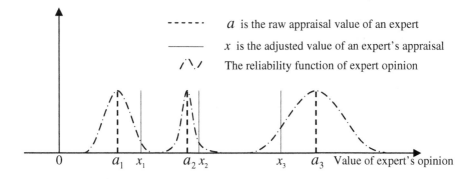

Fig. 1. The integrating process of experts' opinions

3 Definition of Expert's Opinions

3.1 Hypothesis

(1) Expert opinion is given as the quantitative form. It may be a value of evaluation or judgment given by the expert.

(2) Full communication and discussion were carried out between the group experts before each opinion was given. Each expert's opinion was based on the independent thinking at an adequate period of time. Thus the result represented the expert's essential view.

(3) As the complexity of the object problem and the uncertainty in the environment and the limitations of expert's ability, each expert accepts that his (or her) opinion has a little deviation from the practice. He (or she) takes the attitude of cooperation, and permits adjustment of his (or her) opinion while integrating them. But this adjusting reduces dependability as the cost expends. The further the adjusted distance is, the lower the dependability is. A certain kind of distribution function can be structured to describe the dependability based on an expert's opinion.

(4) The restricts of adjustable degree can be given by the expert at the time when his opinion was given, or by the statistics person according to the authority of the expert in the research area or historical records of the expert. The value shows a degree of insistence by expert for his opinion.

3.2 Definitions

[Def.1] Set of expert group, $E = \{E_1, E_2, \cdots E_n\}$. E_i $(i = 1, 2, \ldots, n)$ is the i-th expert.

[Def.2] Set of the appraisal, $A = \{(a_1, r_1), (a_2, r_2), \cdots, (a_n, r_n)\}$. $(a_i\ r_i)$ is the primitive value given by the i-th expert. a_i ---- is the appraise value given by the i-th expert, r_i ----is the absolute value of maximum adjustable degree permitted. $r_i \geq 0$, $i = 1, 2, \ldots, n$.

[Def.3] Set of experts' opinions being optimally adjusted. $\vec{x} = \{x_1, x_2, \cdots, x_n\}$. It is gathered by optimal search from experts' primitive opinions. It meets the requirement of convergence and reliability of the group and it's used for calculating the final integrating result of group's opinions. x_i $(i = 1, 2, \cdots, n)$ is the i-th expert's opinion adjusted within the range of permitted adjustment.

[Def.4] Function of Reliability on an expert's opinion. $\zeta(x)$ is a continuous function defined on $(-\infty, +\infty)$ which has four characteristics:

(1) A boundary of. $0 \leq \zeta(x) \leq 1$.

(2) Symmetry. The figure of $\zeta(x)$ is symmetrical about the beeline of $x=a$. that is: $\zeta(a - \xi) = \zeta(a + \xi)$, among them $\xi = |x - a|$.

(3) $\zeta(x)$ is consistently increasing at the subsection of $(-\infty, a)$ and consistently decreasing at the subsection of $(a, +\infty)$. There is an only maximum value in the point of $x=a$.

(4) Lubricity. $\zeta(x)$ is differential coefficient at the range of $x \in (-\infty, +\infty)$.

3.3 Description of the Integrated Result of Expert's Opinions for the Group

[Def.5] Mean Value Weighted. $U(\vec{x}) = \sum_{i=1}^{n} p_i \cdot x_i$, p_i is the weight of the i-th expert.

[Def.6] Standard Deviation. $\sigma(\vec{x}) = \sqrt{D(\vec{x})}$. In it: $D(\vec{x}) = \sum_{i=1}^{n} (x_i - U(\vec{x}))^2 p_i$.

[Def.7] Credibility of the group's opinions integrated. $\psi(\vec{x}) = \min_i \zeta(x_i)$.

$\varsigma(x_i)$ is the reliability of the i-th expert' s opinion.

[Def. 8] K-power of Central Distance $E|x - U(\vec{x})|^k = \sum_{i=1}^{n} (x_i - U(\vec{x}))^k p_i$.

[Def.9] Kurtosis. $E_k = \dfrac{\mu_4(\vec{x})}{\{\sigma(\vec{x})\}^4} - 3$. In it: $\mu_4(\vec{x}) = \sum_{i=1}^{n} (x_i - U(\vec{x}))^4 p_i$, that

is the 4-power of central distance.

[Def.10] Leaning Degree. $S_k = \dfrac{\mu_3(\vec{x})}{\{\sigma(\vec{x})\}^3}$. In it: $\mu_3(\vec{x}) = \sum_{i=1}^{n} (x_i - U(\vec{x}))^3 p_i$,

that is the 3-power of central distance.

[Def.11] Coefficient of Variation. $V = \dfrac{\sigma(\vec{x})}{U(\vec{x})}$.

The above-mentioned indicators describe a concentrated or scattered degree of experts' opinions of the group. The Kurtosis represents the consistency of the group opinions, and the Coefficient of Variation represents the harmony of the group opinions. The indicators can be used as the parameters to set up the optimization model. The Leaning Degree represents the symmetry degree of the group opinions about the Mean Value Weighted. It can be used to further and deeply analyze or explain the integrated result.

3.4 Design of the Reliability Function for a Single Expert Opinion

According to Def.4, the Reliability of the expert opinion is a function of the distribution of the expert's opinion. It is satisfied using continuity, boundary, symmetry, subsection uniformity and other different characteristics. The distribution of reliability function can be described by the normal function as:

$$F(x) = \Phi\left(\frac{x-a}{\sigma}\right) = \int_{-\infty}^{x} \frac{1}{\sqrt{2\pi}\sigma} e^{-\frac{(t-a)^2}{2\sigma^2}} dt \tag{1}$$

The reliability function can be designed as the S of the area (shadow in the **fig**.2).

$$\zeta(x) = 1 - P\{|x-a| < \xi\} = 1 - \{F(a+\xi) - F(a-\xi)\}$$

$$= 1 - \int_{a-\xi}^{a+\xi} \frac{1}{\sqrt{2\pi}\sigma} e^{-\frac{(t-a)^2}{2\sigma^2}} dt \tag{2}$$

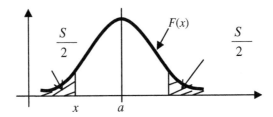

Fig. 2. Sketch map of reliability function on a single expert's opinion (appraisal)

The reliability can be thought of as smaller than 5% when adjusted range is over the expert's permission. That is: $\zeta(x)|_{\tau=a-r} \le 5\%$. Thus we can confirm the parameter σ of the reliability function.

Because $\int_{a-2\sigma}^{a+2\sigma} \frac{1}{\sqrt{2\pi}\sigma} e^{-\frac{(t-a)^2}{2\sigma^2}} dt = 0.954 = 95.4\%$ according to the characteristics of normal function. That is to say $\zeta(a \pm 2\sigma) = 4.6\%$. To simplify the calculation, we take the equation approximately $2\sigma = r$. So we can get:

$$\sigma = \frac{1}{2}r \tag{3}$$

4   The Optimization Model of Integrating Expert's Opinions

4.1   The Objective

The objective of the problem is to minimize the adjusted amount of all experts' opinions, while search for the optimal adjustment scheme of the group opinions within permissible range. The objective is:

$$Min \; f(\vec{x}) = \sum_{i=1}^{n} \left| x_i - a_i \right| \tag{4}$$

4.2 The Constraints

(1) Consistency: According to the theory of Great Amount [12], the values of group expert's opinions obey a normal distribution approximately when they are consistent and the group is large enough. The standard normal distribution can be used to check the convergency of the opinions. Since the Kurtosis of standardized normal distribution is zero, so the condition that the group opinions are consistent is:

$$E_k \geq 0 \tag{5}$$

(2) Harmony: The coefficient of harmony is smaller than or equal to the advanced setting of standard harmony. That is:

$$V \leq V_0 \tag{6}$$

V_0---- Advanced setting of standard harmony.

(3) Credibility: The credibility of integrated result is more than the advanced setting of standard credibility. That is:

$$\zeta(\vec{x}) = \min_{i=1}^{n}\{\zeta(x_i)\} \tag{7}$$

$\zeta(\vec{x})$ must meet the needs of advanced requirement.

$$\zeta(\vec{x}) \geq \psi_0 \tag{8}$$

In it: ψ_0 ---- Advanced setting of standard credibility.

4.3 Optimization Model: Non-liner Programming Model

From formula (4) to (8), can we get the non-liner programming model as below:

$$\min \; f(\vec{x}) = \sum_{i=1}^{n} \left| x_i - a_i \right| \cdot p_i$$

$$s.t \begin{cases} \zeta(\vec{x}) = \min_{i=1}^{n}\{\zeta(\vec{x}_i)\} \\ \zeta(\vec{x}) \geq \psi_0 \\ E_k \geq 0 \\ V = \dfrac{\sigma(\vec{x})}{U(\vec{x})} \leq V_0 \\ \sigma_i = \dfrac{r_i}{2} \end{cases} \tag{9}$$

The requirement for consistency in integration process can be realized through the reduction of credibility step by step. Generally, It is very good when the credibility of the result is above 85%, satisfactory when the credibility of the result is 70% - 84% and acceptable when the credibility is 55% - 69%. There exist great differences in the opinions when the credibility is less than 55%. Here, clustering followed by the integration of the different kinds of opinions is needed. The decision for choosing one from the different integrated results must be made lastly.

4.4   The Flow Chart of Integrating Experts' Opinions

The flow chart of integrating experts' opinions is shown in Fig. 3.

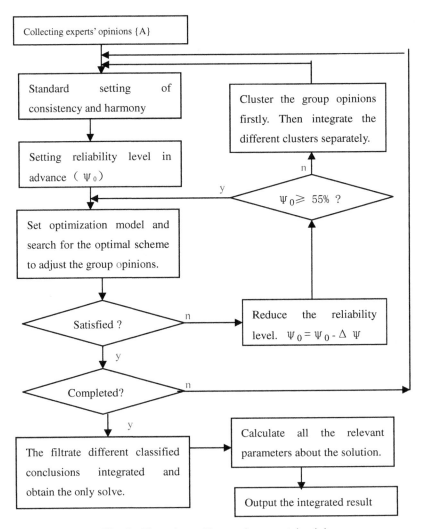

Fig. 3.   Flow chart of integrating experts' opinions

5 Demonstration Analysis

A case of prediction can be used to test our model. The task is to predict the ability of making benefits when a new product is put on sale. A group of experts made up of 15 people were involved. Each expert gave out his prediction after adequate communication with each other (see the left part of **Table 1**). We set the integration model introduced above and solved it using genetic algorithm. The standard setting of variation coefficient is 5% (generally, it was thought be good when the coefficient of variation is smaller than 10%.). The optimal scheme to adjust the experts' opinions was obtained as shown in the right side of **Table 1**. Thus the final integrated result is 2014.47. The reliability is 81%. The Leaning Degree is negative which shows the result leaning to right. That is to say that the most opinions are upper the integrated result. Using Delphi Method, the final result was 2014.7 after three rounds statistics and feedbacks. This value is approximately equal to the mean value of the first round. The real result of this problem is 2014.75. This proves that the integration model have better effects. It can be used to synthesize and coordinate experts' opinions with high efficiency and can provide indictors of credibility that increases the reliability of the integrated result.

Table 1. Analytical table of prediction value of expert

	The value present by expert			The result of optimal search		
Expert	Weight	Predict value	r	σ	Adjusted value	Credibility
E1	1/15	2008	10	5	2009.202	81%
E2	1/15	2012	10	5	2013.202	81%
E3	1/15	2015	10.5	5.25	2014.470	91%
E4	1/15	2007	9.5	4.75	2008.142	81%
E5	1/15	2014	11	5.5	2014.470	93%
E6	1/15	2016	11.5	5.75	2014.470	81%
E7	1/15	2020	7.5	3.75	2019.199	81%
E8	1/15	2018	8	4	2017.138	81%
E9	1/15	2020	11.5	5.75	2018.168	81%
E10	1/15	2017	10	5	2015.798	81%
E11	1/15	2010	10.5	5.25	2011.262	81%
E12	1/15	2017	9	4.5	2015.912	81%
E13	1/15	2015	11.5	5.75	2014.470	92%
E14	1/15	2014	12	6	2014.470	90%
E15	1/15	2018	11	5.5	2016.678	81%
Mean		2014.7			2014.470	
Standard Deviation		3.1720			2.9523	
Kurtosis		-0.19			0.05	
Credibility		100%			81%	
Variation Coefficient		15.7%			0.15%	
Leaning Degree					-0.885 (lean right)	

6 Conclusion

It is feasible to set up the optimization model for integrating experts' opinions not only in theory but also in practice. The integration framework given in this paper can help us to obtain the precise conclusion including reliability indictor from raw experts' opinions. The process kept the independence of each expert's opinion as much as possible. And the efficiency of integration progressed largely. This framework is also applicable to different problems and at a changed environment. Through several experiments, we also found that it is difficult to get an ideal result when the number of experts is lower than 10. It is, therefore, suggested that the number of expert be equal to or more than 10 when this model is used.

References

1. http://www.book888.com.cn/study/means/02/02004.htm,Delphi method. 10. 9. (2001)
2. Yang, L., Xi, Y.: The study of probability aggregation in rational group decision. Theory and Practice of System Engineering, 4 (1998) 90-94
3. Huang, D., Hu, Y.: Group decision and its characteristics. Chinese Journal of decision reference. 4 (1997) 44-46.
4. Lootsma, F., A.: Scale sensitivity in the multiplicative AHP and SMART. Journal of multi-criteria decision analysis, 2 (1993) 87-110
5. Li, H., Fan, Z.: The integrated method of two different bias information in group decision. Transactions of Northeast University, 21(3) (2000) 336-338
6. Bordly, R F.: A Multiplicative Formula for Aggregation Probability Estimates. Management Science, 28(10) (1982).
7. Chiclana F, et al.: Integrating three representation models in fuzzy multipurpose decision-making based on fuzzy preference relation. Fuzzy sets and systems, 97 (1998) 33-48
8. Kacprzyk, J.: Supporting consensus reaching under fuzziness via ordered weighted averaging (OWA) operators. Soft Computing in Intelligent Systems and Information Processing (1996) 453-458
9. Chi, S. C., Benjamin C. O.: A GDSS for locating manufacturing facilities, 6th industrial engineering research conference proceedings. (1997) 169-174
10. Huang, D., Hu, Y.: Research of credibility in GDSS. Journal of Kunming University of Science & Technology, 97, 24(3) (1997) 1-4
11. Wang, Y.: The algorithm of optimal transformation matrix in group judgment and weighted vector. Theory and Practice of System Engineering, 4 (1991)70-74
12. Zhou, G.: Probability and Statistics, Higher Education Publisher (1984)

Cartographic Representation of the Uncertainty Related to Natural Disaster Risk: Overview and State of the Art*

Junxiang Zhang [1,2] and Chongfu Huang [1,2]

[1] College of Resources Science & Technology, Beijing Normal University,
No.19 Xinjiekouwai Street, Beijing 100875, China
[2] Key Laboratory of Environmental Change and Natural Disaster,
Ministry of Education of China,
Beijing Normal University, Beijing 100875, China
{zhangjx, nortzw}@ires.cn

Abstract. There is no believable risk map because of the tremendous imprecision of the risk assessment due to the incomplete-data set. To improve the probability estimation, the fuzzy set methodology was introduced into the area of risk assessment with respect to natural disasters. A fuzzy risk represented by a possibility-probability distribution, which is calculated by employing the interior-outer-set model, can represent the imprecision of risk assessments with a small sample. Thus, by using the fuzzy set methodology, we can provide a soft risk map which can accommodate the imprecision of risk assessment. Soft risk map can be adopted as a useful tool for the representation and reasoning of uncertainty of risk assessments due to incompleteness in real-world applications.

1 Introduction

Natural disaster risk assessment is a typical issue with imprecision, uncertainty and partial truth. The two basic forms of uncertainty related to natural disaster risk assessment are randomness caused by inherent stochastic variability and fuzziness due to macroscopic grad and incomplete knowledge sample [1]. In many literatures, risk is regarded as a product of severity of loss and likelihood of loss and the likelihood is measured by probability [2]. In fact, the probabilistic method effectively ignores fuzziness of risk assessment with incomplete data sets. As a result, it is impossible to accurately estimate the risks of natural disasters within a specified error range. That is, any risk assessment from a small sample must be imprecise. Consequently, currently used methods for cartographical portrayal of natural disaster risks by using the technique of probabilistic risk maps [3] are inadequate and this inadequacy may cause serious information loss and inaccuracy in analysis with adverse consequences in the decision-making process. To overcome this, a possible means for improving the

---

*Project supported by National Natural Science Foundation of China, No. 40371002.

Y. Shi, W. Xu, and Z. Chen (Eds.): CASDMKM 2004, LNAI 3327, pp. 213–220, 2004.

expressive ability of risk maps is to use an alternative concept in which fuzzy imprecision can be accommodated. The fuzzy risk theory and techniques [1] based fuzzy set theory [4] provides an alternative. More importantly it provides flexibility in the way risk information is conveyed.

Our interest here is to find a more effective way for expressing the vagueness and imprecision of natural disaster risk assessments and to find an acceptable way for communicating these imprecision to map users. In the case of that the data set used to assess risk is incomplete, fuzzy probabilities would be used to represent fuzzy risks and give a new risk map called soft risk map, which can accommodate imprecision of natural disaster risk assessments.

2 Uncertainty Due to an Incomplete-Data Set

When we study a natural disaster risk system, we sometimes meet small sample problems [5], where the data is too scanty to make a decision in any classical approach. For example, destructive earthquakes are infrequent events with very small probability of occurrence. Therefore, the size of a sample observed in a seismic zone must be insufficient. Therefore, it is difficult to avoid the so-called incompleteness [6] when we study a natural disaster risk system. If we study an incomplete sample, we cannot avoid its fuzziness. In general, uncertainty feature of risk is concerned with both of randomness and fuzziness. For example, the occurrence of earthquake is a random event, however, the earthquake intensity is a fuzzy concept. In the process of risk evaluation, the randomness is due to a large amount of unknown factors existing, and the fuzziness has concern with the fuzzy information that is associated with an incomplete data set with respect to scarcity. This kind of fuzzy information is called mass-body fuzzy information [1]. The feature of mass-body fuzzy information is that each of the data may be crisp but its aggregation or collective, as a whole, has uncertainty different from randomness and carries fuzziness when we employ them to recognize a relation. The main task of processing the mass-body fuzzy information is to unearth (or mine) fuzzy information, which is buried in an incomplete data set. In many cases, extra information is useful for us to effectively study a fuzzy system. If we cut a fuzzy object to be crisp, the extra information will disappear.

In general, risk is considered as the possibilities of the occurrence of adverse events. The probability is usually employed to measure the possibility. In many cases, it is impossible to precisely estimate the probability with respect to natural disaster risk. In fact, the probabilistic method is an extremely effective tool to study risk only in the case when a great amount of data can be collected. In other words, the probabilistic method effectively ignores fuzziness of risk assessment with incomplete data sets. Taking into account that natural disaster risk assessments are concerned with both of randomness and fuzziness, obviously, we know that, a risk system is too complex to understand by probabilistic method. Probability and fuzziness are related but different concepts. Fuzziness is a type of deterministic uncertainty. Fuzziness measures the degree to which an event occurs, not whether it occurs. Probability arouses from the question whether or not an event occurs. Moreover, it assumes that the event class is crisply defined and that the law of non-contradiction holds. That is, $A \cap A^c = \emptyset$ [1]. One day, scientists might be able to find the best models for more accurate risk predictions, however, they never eliminate the imprecision of the risk estimates within a specified error range. In this case, an alternative is to find a more effective way of expressing the vagueness and imprecision of natural disaster risk assessments and to find an acceptable way of communicating these imprecision to users. With current science and technology, a natural way to improve risk estimate is to introduce concept of fuzzy risk represented by a possibility-probability-distribution (PPD) [7] to overcome uncertainty resulting from small-sample problem.

3 Fuzzy Risk Represented by a Possibility-Probability Distribution

Scientists have used many systems engineering concepts and methods in addressing the challenges of natural disaster risk. Due to the complexity of natural disaster system, it is impossible to accurately estimate the risks of natural disasters within a specified error range. For showing the imprecision of risk assessment in terms of probabilities under the conditions of small samples, in this section we briefly introduce the concept of fuzzy risk represented by a PPD.

Definition 1. Let $M = \{m\}$ be the space of adverse events, $P = \{p\}$ be the universe of discourse of probability, and $\pi_m(p)$ be possibility that probability of m occurring is p.

$$\Pi_{M,P} = \{\pi_M(p) \mid m \in M, p \in P\}. \tag{1}$$

is called a *possibility-probability distribution* (PPD) with respect to risk.

In 1998, Huang [7] first proposed the interior-outer-set model (IOSM) derived from the method of information distribution to calculate a PPD with a small sample. In 2001, Huang, Moraga and Yuan [8] proved that IOSM could replace experts to give fuzzy probabilities for the reason that the calculation results and the subjective assessment are almost same in terms of fuzzy expected value and standard deviation. In order to simplify the combination calculus in IOSM, Huang and Moraga [9] transform the calculus into a matrix algorithm which consists of a MOVING-subalgorithm and a INDEX-subalgorithm. In 2003, Moraga [10] introduced a new version of the model with complexity in the O (n log n) class instead of complexity O (n^2).

Example 1. Suppose there is a batch of natural disaster records, the number of which is 6. The sample is too small to precisely estimate probability-risk of this disaster. We calculate a PPD with the data to replace a probability-risk.

Table 1 can show the fuzzy risk represented by a PPD of the natural disaster. From Table 1, we can see that one obvious characteristic with a fuzzy risk is that fuzzy risk is a fuzzy number which based on the universe of discourse of probability if we employ incomplete data set to estimate it. For example, for I1, we denote the corresponding fuzzy number as following,

Table 1. The PPD of a natural disaster

$\Pi_i(p) =$	p_0	p_1	p_2	p_3	p_4	p_5	p_6
I_1	0.17	0.33	1	0.5	0	0	0
I_2	0.17	0.5	1	0.33	0.17	0	0
I_3	0.17	1	0.5	0	0	0	0
I_4	0.5	1	0.17	0	0	0	0

$$\Pi_{M.P} = \frac{017}{0} + \frac{0.33}{0.17} + \frac{1}{0.33} + \frac{0.5}{0.5} \ . \tag{2}$$

where, for a/b, a is membership, b is probability.

Therefore, Fuzzy risk represented by a PPD can be employed to show the imprecision of probability estimation in risk analysis. In the practical case of risk map, it is quite difficult to interpret the often vague, imprecise, and qualitative information by probability methods. In this situation fuzzy logic is a viable alternative [11]. The question is basically how to incorporate fuzzy logic into risk mapping.

4   Challenges of Cartographical Representation of Uncertainty

Of growing interest in the cartographic community, the portrayal of uncertainty has lately been the subject of much research in the cartographic community. This brings us to the challenge of visualizing uncertainty due to incomplete-data set related to natural disaster risk assessments. However, existing methods of the display of uncertainty information related to natural disaster risk assessment has centered on the randomness in a form of exceeding-probability-risk map. For example, a popular method to make an earthquake-probability-risk map is to indicate earthquake ground motions with 10% probability of exceedence in 50 years [12]. Currently, however, the maps are used only by insurance agents to rate insurance and by parish and local governments in regulating development. There are quite a few businessmen actually do regard the risk maps as information sources and use them to support local businesses. One of the reasons is that there is no believable risk map because of the tremendous imprecision of the risk assessment. The probabilities of exceedence in a probability-risk map do not relate to any confidence in the estimate of a probability-risk, which ignores the fuzziness of natural disaster risk. Such a representation inevitably leads to inaccuracy in representing natural disaster risk. A possible means for improving the expressive ability of risk maps is to use an alternative concept in which fuzzy imprecision can be accommodated. However, efforts to the fuzziness of risk estimates have been rare. A critical issue for this research is how to incorporate fuzziness into a risk map.

A method of expression should be well suited to the nature of the information it represents. Expressive inadequacy may lead to loss of valuable information and reduce accuracy of analysis. Hence, it is crucial to find a perfect way of transforms fuzzy risks represented by PPDs into risk map, because this is of great importance on the output of the model. Taking into account that a fuzzy risk is a fuzzy number, the fuzzy α-cut technique will be used to transform fuzzy risks into risk maps.

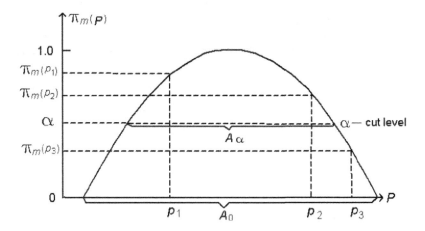

Fig. 1. Possibility-probability distribution with respect to I_j and its α-cut

The fuzzy α-cut technique is based on fuzzy logic and fuzzy set theory (introduced by Zadeh, 1965), which is widely used in representing uncertain knowledge. Fig. 1 shows the possibility-probability distribution with respect to I_j represented as a bell-shaped fuzzy number with support of A_0. The wider the support of the membership function, the higher the uncertainty. The fuzzy set that contains all elements with a membership of $\alpha \in]0, 1]$ and above is called the α-cut of the membership function. At a resolution level of α, it will have support of $A\alpha$. The higher the value of α, the higher the confidence in the probability.

The membership function is cut horizontally at a finite number of α-levels between 0 and 1. For each α-level of the output, the model is run to determine the minimum and maximum possible values of the probabilities with respect to I_j. This information is then directly used to construct the corresponding fuzziness (membership function) of the output that is used as a measure of uncertainty.

Corresponding to a non-empty α-cut, we can obtain a series of minimum probabilities and maximum probabilities with respect to I_j. By using the α-cut method, we can obtain series of probability-risk $\alpha(m)$, $\alpha \in]0, 1]$. Then, with a classical method to make a probability-risk map, we can provide a series of risk maps. For these maps, a fuzzy risk represents the imprecision. A α-cut represents some confidence in the estimate. When $\alpha = 1$, the corresponding soft risk map ought to be the same as one resulted from a classical probability method. The case means that we believe the estimated probabilities.

This kind of risk maps can represent imprecision of risk estimate and information provided by the maps is typically available as 'soft' information. Therefore, this kind of risk maps are called soft risk maps (SRM). The obvious feature of SRM is the incorporation of fuzzy information due to incomplete-data set into cartographical expression of natural disaster risks. This is a novel approach in view of the traditional method of a probabilistic representation of uncertainties. Due to the ability to represent imprecision of risk estimations that would be thrown away by probability-risk map, soft risk map can provide more information. In many cases, extra information is useful for us to effectively study a fuzzy system. If we ignore the fuzziness due to incomplete-data set in risk analysis of natural disasters, the extra information will disappear.

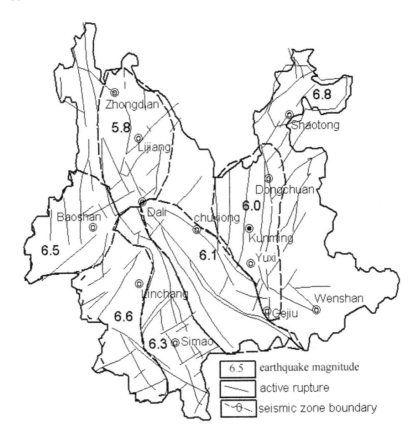

Fig. 2. Conservative risk map with ~ = 0.25 with respect to earthquakes in a region

Such a map is presented in Fig. 2 and Fig. 3. It shows that soft risk map can be adopted as a useful tool for representation and reasoning of uncertainty of risk assessments in real-world applications. Soft risk map is a kind of risk map in which each area is assigned two risk values. The double risk values represent the imprecision. The 0.25-cut represents some confidence in the estimate. More importantly it provides flexibility in the way this information is conveyed. Soft risk map can provide a better representation for risk information leading to more satisfying results. In this respect, soft risk map do meet the demands of risk map users. The author's efforts to accomplish this prompted an exploration of non-traditional forms of carto-graphic representation of natural disaster risks.

Fig. 3. Risky risk map with ~ = 0.25 with respect to earthquakes in a region

5 Conclusion and Discussion

Taking to account that natural disaster risk assessment is concerned with both ran-domness and fuzziness due to incomplete-data set, the method of probability risk map is inadequate for the representation of uncertainty related to natural disaster risk. A more advanced and effective form of cartographical representation of natural disas-ter risk can be achieved by incorporating fuzzy logic methodologies into risk map.

Soft risk map is a possible means for improving the expressive ability of risk maps which can accommodate fuzzy imprecision. More importantly it provides flexibility in the way risk information is conveyed. Soft risk map is the potential developing direction of spatially representing natural disaster risk.

Future research in this area is an extensive theoretical and experimental study on the choice of the appropriate form of transforming a fuzzy risk represented by a PPD into cartographical form for the application domain of risk map with fuzzy set methodologies incorporated in both the representation and analysis of uncertainty due to incompleteness with respect to natural disaster risk assessment.

References

1. Huang, C.F., Shi, Y.: Towards efficient fuzzy information processing — Using the principle of information diffusion, Physica-Verlag (Springer), Heidelberg, Germany (2002)
2. Huang, C.F., Shi,P.J.: Fuzzy risk and calculation, Proceedings of 18th International Conference of the North American Fuzzy Information Processing Society, New York (1999) 90-94
3. Mays, M.D., Bogardi, I., Bardossy, A.: Fuzzy logic and risk-based interpretations. Geoderma, vol. 77. (1997) 299–315
4. Zadeh, L.A.: Fuzzy sets, Information and control, Vol. 8. (1965) 338
5. Huang, C.F.: Informaion diffusion techniques and small-sample problem. International Journal of Information technology & Decision Making, Vol. 1, 2 (2002) 229–249
6. Huang, C.F., Bai, H.L.: Calculation fuzzy risk with incomplete data. Calculation fuzzy risk with incomplete data. In:Ruan, D., Abderrahim,H.A., et al.(eds.): Proceedings of the 4th International FLINS Conference, World Scientific, Singapore (2000) 180-187
7. Huang, C.F.: Concepts and methods of fuzzy risk analysis. Risk Research and Management in Asian Perspective, Beijing Normal University and et al., International Academic Publishers, Beijing (1998) 12-23.
8. Huang, C.F., Moraga, C., Yuan X.G.: Calculation vs. subjective assessment with respect to fuzzy probability. Reusch, B.(ed.): Computational Intelligence—Theory and Applications. Spinger, Heidelberg, Germany (2001) 393–411
9. Huang, C.F., Moraga, C.: A fuzzy risk model and its matrix algorithm. International Journal of Uncertainty, Fuzziness and Knowledge-Based Systems, Vol. 10,4 (2002) 347–362
10. Moraga, C., Huang, C.F.: Learning subjectvie probabilities from a small data set. Proceedings of 33rd International Symposium on Multiple-Valuee Logic, IEEE Computer Society, Los Alamitos, California (2003) 355–360
11. Koskl, B., Iaska, I.: Fuzzy logic. Sci. Am. Vol.269 (1993) 76-81
12. Wesson, R.L., Frankel, A.D. and et al.: Probabilistic seismic hazard maps of Alaska. USGS Open-File Report 99-36 (1999)

A Multi-objective Decision-Making Method for Commercial Banks Loan Portfolio[1]

Zhanqin Guo and Zongfang Zhou

Management School, University of Electronic Science & Technology of China,
Chengdu, 610054
guozhanqin@126.com, zhouzongfang@163.com

Abstract. This paper proposes a multi-objectives decision-making method for loan portfolio based on the efficient frontier. This method is based on a multi-targets decision-making model with two objective functions, one of which is to be maximized for return with regard to risk and the other minimized for risk with regard to return. We will use the method of geometry to solve this difficult problem. This method has three advantages. First, given the relative weights of each component, the risk of the portfolio, or the return of the portfolio, we can obtain the corresponding optimal loan portfolio. Second, the method is easy to understand and the calculation is simple, because it avoids reversing many matrices. Third, banks can pay adequate attention to casting credit to valued-clients and limited-clients. As a result, banks will be able to serve the debt needs of their clients well.

1 Introduction

The decision-making for the optimal loan portfolio is the process of choosing the best from a large number of loan portfolios. The current common practice in managing credit-risk in commercial banks worldwide is to set limit on the risks of single loans so that the total risks of a bank's loan portfolios can be controlled. From the points of economics, optima of single loans do not necessarily lead to the optimal portfolio, however. Therefore, it is worthwhile to further study the decision-making process in obtaining the optimal loan-portfolio.

At present, there are two important methods in managing loan-portfolio risks in the field. One is the quantitative model for loan portfolio efficient frontier developed by John Morgan (1993). This model uses industrial average ZETA fraction to represent industrial risks. It calculates the variance-covariance matrix of default through the average of ZETA. It is considered one of the most significant developments that applies Markowitz's model to solving the efficient portfolio of commercial loans, because a new method in dealing with the correlations of default was suggested. ZETA fractions, however, as we all know, only represent the fiscal ratios of a firm, but do not tell the relationships among loans directly. As a result, the accuracy of the model is greatly compromised. Moreover, the constraint that the return on a loan portfolio

---

[1] Humanities Foundation of State Education Ministry (NO.02JA790009) supports this work.

Y. Shi, W. Xu, and Z. Chen (Eds.): CASDMKM 2004, LNAI 3327, pp. 221–228, 2004.

should not be less than the stipulated return is too strong, for the more the stipulated return is expected, the higher the risks the commercial bank will face.

The other method is the model of "Commercial Loan Portfolio Analysis" proposed by Altman. It tries to find the maximum Sharpe Ratio under the constraint that the return on a loan portfolio is not less than the stipulated return. Unfortunately, this method also fails to determine a reasonable value of the stipulated return as well as a range of risk-tolerance that a commercial bank is willing to bear. A new decision-making model is suggested in reference [3] by taking both the profit and the risk a loan project may incur into consideration, based on the principle of maximum return for a unit of risk. This model only emphasizes the allocation of many loan's projects after they are approved however, but doesn't include matching up all the credits. Although the decision-making model in reference [4] takes into account the risk and return of a portfolio, it treats the minimized portfolio risk as its objective function.

We now propose a multi-target decision-making method for optimal loan portfolios based on the efficient frontier in this paper. By building a multi-targets optimal model and solving the optimization problem via the method of geometry, we can obtain the efficient frontier of a loan portfolio and the related weights quite easily.

2   The Efficient Frontier for Loan Portfolio

A rational investor always hopes to maximize his or her expected return for a given risk, or minimize the risk for a given expected return. A portfolio with such properties is considered efficient. All efficient portfolios make up an efficient set. The efficient set in the return- risk (R_p, σ_p) space is called the efficient frontier, which is also the opportunity set for rational investors. The concepts of efficient set and efficient frontier are applicable to a loan portfolio. The former is the opportunity set for a bank to optimize its loan portfolios; the latter is the combinations of maximum expected returns for given risks or minimum risks for given expected returns. Therefore, for a given loan portfolio, we may maximize its return under certain risk by changing the relative weight of every loan. In the same way, we may minimize its risk under a certain return. As a result, no matter what a risk level it wants to take, a bank can achieve its goal by adjusting its loan portfolio along the efficient frontier.

3   Multi-objectives Decision-Making Based on the Efficient Frontier for a Loan Portfolio

3.1   The Model

Suppose there are n loans for a bank to choose. Let R_i be the rate of expected return on the ith loan; let $x_i (i = 1,2,\cdots,n, x_i \geq 0, \sum x_i = 1)$ be the relative weight on the ith loan ; let σ_{ij} be the covariance of R_i and R_j; let σ_p be the standard variance of the loan portfolio; let $E(R_p)$ be the expected return of the portfolio. The model is simply:

$$\begin{cases} \min \sigma_p^2 = X^T BX, \max E(R_p) = X^T R \\ s.t. \sum_{i=1}^{n} x_i = 1 \\ 0 \le x_i \le 1, i = 1, 2, \cdots, n \end{cases} \tag{1}$$

In this expression, $R = (R_1, R_2 \cdots R_n)^T$ is the expected return vector of n loans in the portfolio, $X = (x_1, x_2, \cdots, x_n)^T$ is the relative weight vector of the portfolio and $B = (\sigma_{ij})_{n \times n}$ is the covariance-matrix.

3.2 Solution to the Model

Because of the complexity of model (1), it is impossible to solve it by traditional Lagrange multiplier. Therefore, we introduce the method of geometry here.

3.2.1 Geometric Solution

Let the relative weights of n loans be $x_1, x_2, ..., x_{n-1}, x_n (= 1 - x_1 - x_2 - \cdots - x_n)$, then the expected return R_p and variance σ_p^2 of the portfolio are stated respectively as followings:

$$R_p = x_1 R_1 + x_2 R_2 + \cdots + x_{n-1} R_{n-1} + (1 - x_1 - \cdots - x_{n-1}) R_n \tag{2}$$

$$\begin{aligned} \sigma_p^2 &= x_1^2 \sigma_{11} + x_2^2 \sigma_{22} + \cdots + x_{n-1}^2 \sigma_{n-1,n-1} + (1 - x_1 - \cdots - x_{n-1}) \sigma_{nn} \\ &+ 2x_1 x_2 \sigma_{12} + \cdots + 2x_1 x_{n-1} \sigma_{1n-1} + 2x_1 (1 - x_1 - \cdots - x_{n-1}) \sigma_{1n} \\ &+ \cdots + 2x_{n-1} (1 - x_1 - \cdots - x_{n-1}) \sigma_{n-1n} \end{aligned} \tag{3}$$

In these expressions, R_i is the expected return of the ith loan, and $R_n \ne R_i, i = 1, 2, ... n - 1$. Because the matrix of covariance is positive-definite, equation (3) represents family of isovariance hyperellipsoidal surface in the weights space in the weights space $(x_1, x_2 ..., x_{n-1})$. If we change σ_p^2, we may get a family of concentric ellipses. The "center" of the system indicates the point of minimal variance in the weights space $(x_1, x_2 \cdots; x_{n-1})$. Equation (2) expresses family of isoexpected return hyperplanes in the weights space $(x_1, x_2 \cdots; x_{n-1})$. Again, if we change R_p, we may get a family of parallel hyper-planes. Therefore, the optimal weights of the n loans are at those points where the isoexpected return hyperplanes are tangent to the isovariance hyperellipsoidal surface. All those points form the boundary of the portfolio. It is obvious that the boundary, in fact, represents the efficient frontier in the space of weights.

In equation (2), the normal vector at the point $(x_1, x_2 \cdots ; x_{n-1})$ is $(R_1 - R_n, R_2 - R_n, \cdots ; R_{n-1} - R_n)$, equation (3) shows the normal vector at the same point is:

$$((\sigma_{11} + \sigma_{nn} - 2\sigma_{1n})x_1 + \cdots + (\sigma_{1k} + \sigma_{nn} - \sigma_{1n} - \sigma_{kn})x_k + \cdots + (\sigma_{1,n-1} + \sigma_{nn} - \sigma_{1n} - \sigma_{n-1,n})x_{n-1}$$
$$+ \sigma_{1n} - \sigma_{nn}, (\sigma_{1k} + \sigma_{nn} - \sigma_{1n} - \sigma_{kn})x_1 + \cdots + (\sigma_{kk} + \sigma_{nn} - 2\sigma_{kn})x_k + \cdots + (\sigma_{k,n-1} + \sigma_{nn} - \sigma_{kn}$$
$$- \sigma_{n-1,n})x_{n-1} + \sigma_{kn} - \sigma_{nn}, \cdots (\sigma_{1,n-1} + \sigma_{nn} - \sigma_{1n} - \sigma_{n-1,n})x_1 + \cdots + (\sigma_{k,n-1} + \sigma_{nn} - \sigma_{kn} - \sigma_{n-1,n})x_k$$
$$+ \cdots + (\sigma_{n-1,n-1} + \sigma_{nn} - 2\sigma_{n-1,n})x_{n-1} + \sigma_{n-1,n} - \sigma_{nn})$$

Let:
$$P_1 = [1,0,0, \cdots, 0,0,-1],$$
$$P_2 = [0,1,0, \cdots, 0,0,-1],$$
$$\cdots \cdots$$
$$P_{n-1} = [0,0,0, \cdots, 0,1,-1]$$

$$Q = \begin{bmatrix} 1 & 0 & \cdots & 0 & 0 \\ 0 & 1 & \cdots & 0 & 0 \\ \vdots & \vdots & & \vdots & \vdots \\ 0 & 0 & \cdots & 1 & 0 \\ -1 & -1 & \cdots & -1 & 1 \end{bmatrix}, \quad W = \begin{bmatrix} x_1 \\ x_2 \\ \vdots \\ x_{n-1} \\ 1 \end{bmatrix}.$$

Then the perpendicular vector of equation (3) at the point $(x_1, x_2 \cdots ; x_{n-1})$ can be shorted as

$$(P_1 BQW, P_2 BQW, \cdots, P_k BQW, \cdots, P_{n-1} BQW) \tag{4}$$

The definition of the boundary tells that its equation is

$$\frac{P_1 BQW}{R_1 - R_n} = \frac{P_2 BQW}{R_2 - R_n} = \cdots = \frac{P_k BQW}{R_k - R_n} = \cdots = \frac{P_{n-1} BQW}{R_{n-1} - R_n} \tag{5}$$

From the above equation, we get a system of (n-2) linear equations:

$$\begin{cases} a_{11} x_1 + a_{12} x_2 + \cdots + a_{1,n-1} x_{n-1} = b_1 \\ a_{21} x_1 + a_{22} x_2 + \cdots a_{2,n-1} x_{n-1} = b_2 \\ \cdots \cdots \\ a_{n-2,1} x_1 + a_{n-2,2} x_2 + \cdots + a_{n-2,n-1} x_{n-1} = b_{n-2} \end{cases} \tag{6}$$

in which:

$$a_{ij} = \frac{\sigma_{ij} + \sigma_{nn} - \sigma_{in} - \sigma_{jn}}{R_i - R_n} - \frac{\sigma_{j,n-1} + \sigma_{nn} - \sigma_{jn} - \sigma_{n-1,n}}{R_{n-1} - R_n}, \quad b_i = -\frac{\sigma_{in} - \sigma_{nn}}{R_i - R_n} + \frac{\sigma_{n-1,n} - \sigma_{nn}}{R_{n-1} - R_n}$$

$$(i = 1, 2, \cdots, n-2, \quad j = 1, 2, \cdots, n-1) \cdot$$

3.2.2 Geometric Solution

Because the rank of equation (6) is $n-2$, it has only one fundamental solution in the basic set of solutions, and thus $x_2, x_3, \ldots, x_n$ can be expressed by x_1. So can the expected return According to the constraints and equation (6), we will obtain a range for x_1 as well as the range for R_p. Given any expected return in the range, we may obtain the optimal portfolio by combining equation (2) and (6), from which we can derive the minimum variance. Similarly, given a variance, we may acquire the optimal weight of every loan and its maximum expected return.

4   Case Analysis

4.1   The Basic Conditions of Candidate Decisions

A bank wants to optimize its loan portfolio, which includes three loans that have different expected returns. The expected returns and covariance matrix are known as:

$$R = 10^{-2} \times \begin{bmatrix} 12.3 \\ 5.4 \\ 3.7 \end{bmatrix}, \quad B = 10^{-4} \times \begin{bmatrix} 420.250 & 20.3319 & -33.825 \\ 20.3319 & 75.690 & 6.8904 \\ -33.825 & 6.8904 & 10.89 \end{bmatrix}$$

4.2   Confirmation of Efficient Frontier

Let the weights of the three loans be $X = (x_1, x_2, x_3)^T$, then a model can be built as:

$$\max E(R_p), \min \sigma_p^2$$

$$s.t. \begin{cases} E(R_p) = X^T R \\ \sigma_p^2 = X^T B X \\ \sum_{i=1}^{3} x_i = 1 \\ 0 \le x_i \le 1, i = 1,2,3 \end{cases} \tag{7}$$

The equation (6) is now:

$$23.7891 x_1 - 36.0607 x_2 = 2.8467 \tag{8}$$

From equation (7) and (8), we get:

$$X = [x_1 \quad -0.0789 + 0.6597 x_1 \quad 1.0789 - 1.6597 x_1]^T.$$

Then we need to solve the following equations:

$$\begin{cases} 23.7891 x_1 - 36.0607 x_2 = 2.8467 \\ x_1 + x_2 + x_3 = 1 \\ 0 \le x_i \le 1, i = 1,2,3 \end{cases} \tag{9}$$

Then the efficient ranges of $x_i, i = 1,2,3$ are:

$$\begin{cases} 0.1196 \leq x_1 \leq 0.6501 \\ \quad 0 \leq x_2 \leq 0.3500 \\ \quad 0 \leq x_3 \leq 0.8804 \end{cases} \tag{10}$$

Further we get:

$$E(R_p) = X^T R = 9.7215 \times 10^{-2} x_1 + 3.5658 \times 10^{-2} \tag{11}$$

Equation (11) is the expression of the efficient frontier of this loan portfolio. From $0.1196 \leq x_1 \leq 0.6501$ we obtain the range for $E(R_p)$, which is $[4.7285\%, 9.8857\%]$.

Similarly the range for σ_p^2 is $[7.3289 \times 10^{-4}, 1.9613 \times 10^{-2}]$.

Based on those results, we obtain the efficient frontier as:

$$4.7285\% \leq R_p \leq 9.8858\% \quad 10^{-4} \times 7.3289 \leq \sigma_p^2 \leq 10^{-2} \times 1.9613 \tag{12}$$

4.3 Decisions

Assuming that R_p is 5.4% in equation (11), we have $x_1 = 0.1894$. The optimal relative weights are then $X = [0.1894 \quad 0.0460 \quad 0.7646]^T$, and the minimum risk $\sigma_p^2 = 10^{-4} \times 12.6423$. Every expected return in the space of (12) can be matched up with its related optimal weights and minimum risk. Similarly, given a risk, we may find its related optimal weights and maximum return of a portfolio.

4.4 Analysis of Optimized Decision

Within the range $4.7285\% \leq R_p \leq 9.8858\%$, every expected return corresponds to a minimum risk and optimal weights, both of which may vary as the expected return varies in the following table:

Table 1. Analysis of Optimized Decision

$R_p(\%)$	4.7286	5.40	6.50	9.8848
$\sigma_p(\%)$	2.7072	3.5556	5.8253	14.0024
x_i	$x_1 = 0.1196$	$x_1 = 0.1894$	$x_1 = 0.3029$	$x_1 = 0.6500$
	$x_2 = 0.0000$	$x_2 = 0.0460$	$x_2 = 0.1210$	$x_2 = 0.3499$
	$x_3 = 0.8804$	$x_3 = 0.7646$	$x_3 = 0.5761$	$x_3 = 0.0001$

Table 1 shows that: 1) Risk of the portfolio expressed by σ_p increases rapidly with the increase of the expected return R_p ; 2) Though the expected return of the first loan is high, its relative weight could not be more than 0.6501 in view of portfolio management; 3) Diversification can decrease risks effectively. The above covariance matrix shows that when the expected return is 5.4%, the risk of a single loan is $10^{-2} \times 8.7$, while the portfolio risk is only $10^{-2} \times 3.5556$.

4.5 Optimal Decisions for Valued-Clients (or Limited-Clients)

If there are valued-clients as well as limited-clients in the portfolio, a bank should first satisfy the credit needs of the former for its own long-term health. In another word, the bank should first try to reach the relative amount of those clients (let it be x_1). The above methods can be applied to determine the optimal relative weights of portfolio $X = (x_1, x_2, x_3)^T$ as well as the maximum return and minimum risk, respectively.

5 Conclusions

This paper suggests a method to optimize commercial loan portfolios. This method illustrates directly the relationship among loans and thus results in more accurate decisions. The model meets the needs of decision-makers who have different value or risk preference. As a result, the decision-making process becomes more visual and more understandable. Given any of the risk, return, or one of the relative weights, we may obtain the only optimal loan portfolio, especially when the portfolio includes valued-clients, whose credit needs should be treated with a high priority, and limited-clients, whose needs would be satisfied later.

What will be the efficient frontier if we add risk-tolerance of a bank to the portfolio? We will further study this issue in a separate paper.

References

1. Morgan,.J.B., Ggollinger, T. L.: Calculation of an Efficient frontier for a Commercial Loan Portfolio, Journal of Portfolio Management(winter) (1993)
2. Altman,.E.I., Corporate, B., Commercial Loan Portfolio Analysis, New York: New York University Salomon Center,1997.
3. Chi ,G.T., Qin, X.Z., Zhu, Z.Y.: Decision-making Model of loans Portfolio Optimization Based on Principle of Maximum Earnings Per Risk. Control and Decision (in Chinese), 15(4) (2000) 469–472.
4. Jang, D.Z., Chi ,G.T., Lin, J.H., Decision-making Model for Optimization of Loans Portfolio Based on efficient Boundary, Journal of Harbin Institute of Technology (in Chinese)   34(5) (2002) 614–617.
5. Wang, C.F.: Risk-Management of Financial Market. Tianjin: Press of Tianjin University (in Chinese), 2001: 487–489.

6. Zhou, Z.F. and Shi Y., An algorithm in nonlinear multi-objective programming , The Proceeding of International Conference on Operations & Quantitative Management, India, 1997.
7. Zhou, Z.F., Tang X.W.: An Multi-Targets Evaluation Approaches to Customers Credit, Proceedings of 2003 International Conference on Management Science & Engineering, America, (2003) 987–990
8. Tang, X.W., Zhou, Z.F., Shi ,Y., The Research of Variable Weights in Combined Forecasting, Journal of Computers & Mathematics with Applications, 1(45) (2003) 723–730.
9. Tang, X.W., Zhou, Z.F., Shi Y.: The Errors Bounds of Combined Forecasting, Journal of Mathematical and Computer Modeling, 4(36) (2002) 997–1005
10. Zhou, Z.F., Tang, X.W.: An Multi—Targets Evaluation Approaches to Customers Credit, Proceedings of 2003 International Conference on Management Science & Engineering, Georgia, USA, (2003) 987–990
11. Zhou, Z.F., Tang X.W.: Research on Targets Evaluation for Customers Credit, Journal of Systems Science and Information, 4(1) (2003) 627–634
12. Zhou, Z.F., Tang, X.W., Mou T.Y., The optimization techniques approach to customers credit. Proceedings of ICSSSE' (2003)
13. Zhou Z.F., Tang, X.W., Mu, T.Y., An Application of Multi-Targets Evaluation in Customers Credit. Proceedings of The 5TH International Conference on Management (2004)

A Multi-factors Evaluation Method on Credit Evaluation of Commerce Banks*

Zongfang Zhou[1], Xiaowo Tang[1], and Yong Shi[2]

[1] Management school, University of Electronic Science & Technology of China,
Chengdu Sichuan, P.R. China 610054
zhouzf@uestc.edu.cn
[2] College of Information Science & Technology University of Nebraska at Omaha,
Omaha, NE 68182, U.S.A
yshi@mail.unomaha.edu

Abstract. The concept of multi-factors detached coefficients is put forth and an evaluation method is given for customer's credit in this paper. We also get the optimal multi-factors detached coefficients matrix by minimizing the estimate errors. According to this matrix, we get the scores vector of customer's credit at n factors, further the credit of the customers is evaluated and selected by commerce banks.

1 Introduction

In the respect of management and control on the credit risk, credit evaluation is an underlying task. It is a key to keep away the credit risk or credit venture, and boost the quality of the loans of commerce banks. At present, most of famous international finance institutions and investment companies and a number of scholars paid serious attention to the credit evaluation of customers and established respective evaluation models of credit[1]~[6]. However, these methods mainly depend upon historical experiences or factitious evaluation, it may give rise to deflection of the credit evaluation. In this paper, we put forth the optimal multi-factors detached coefficients matrix by minimizing the deflection of the credit evaluation. Synchronously a convenient method is got to estimate the error of credit evaluation according to optimal multi-factors detached coefficients matrix.

2 The Optimal Multi-factors Detached Coefficients Matrix

The repayment abilities of credit customers depend on some factors, the commerce banks require to use these factors to evaluate the repayment abilities of credit customers.

Assuming that the commerce bank provides a loan to a customer, to keep away the credit risk, the bank selections n credit evaluation factors $\{d_1, d_2, ..., d_n\}$ that show the repayment abilities of the customer and m credit expertise to review customers.

---

* Humanities Foundation of State Education Ministry (NO.02JA790009) supports this work.

Y. Shi, W. Xu, and Z. Chen (Eds.): CASDMKM 2004, LNAI 3327, pp. 229–232, 2004.

Suppose $\{d_1, d_2, \ldots d_{n_1}\}$ are positive evaluation factors, and $\{d_{n_1+1}, d_{n_1+2}, \ldots d_{n_1+n_2}\}$ are negative evaluation factors, and $\{d_{n_1+n_2+1}, d_{n_1+n_2+2}, \ldots, d_{n_1+n_2+n_3}\}$ are neutral evaluation factors[10],there $n_1 + n_2 + n_3 = n$. Let y_{ij}^0 $(i=1,2,\ldots,n; \ j=1,2,\cdots,m)$ are the credit evaluation values of the j-th expertise on the i-th factor, and f_i $(i=1,2,\ldots,n)$ is the critical expectations of these factors.

Let

$$e_{ij} = \begin{cases} f_i - y_{ij}^0, f_i > y_{ij}^0 \\ 0, otherwise \end{cases}, i = 1,2,\ldots, n_1, (j=1,2,\ldots,m).$$

$$e_{ij} = \begin{cases} y_{ij}^0 - f_i, y_{ij}^0 > f_i \\ 0, otherwise \end{cases}, i = n_1 +1, n_1 +2, \ldots, n_1 + n_2 \ (j=1,2,\ldots,m). \tag{1}$$

$$e_{ij} = \left| f_i - y_{ij}^0 \right|, i = n_1 + n_2 + 1, n_1 + n_2 + 2, \ldots, n.$$

where e_{ij} are the estimates errors between the expertise and critical expectations on the factors, called the estimates deflection of the credit evaluation.

On the j-th definitive expertise, the weighted sum of estimate deflection is

$$e_j^0 = \sum_{i=1}^{n} \xi_i^j e_{ij} \tag{2}$$

Where ξ_i^j $(i=1,2,\ldots,n; \ j=1,2,\ldots,m)$ are called multi-factors detached coefficients, which satisfies:

$$\sum_{i=1}^{n} \xi_i^j = 1, \quad \xi_i^j \geq 0, \quad i=1,2,\ldots,n; j=1,2,\ldots,m. \tag{3}$$

We call

$$J = \sum_{j=1}^{m} \left[e_j^0 \right]^2 = \sum_{j=1}^{m} \left[\sum_{i=1}^{n} \xi_i^j e_{ij} \right] \left[\sum_{k=1}^{n} \xi_k^j e_{kj} \right] = \sum_{j=1}^{m} (\xi^j)^T E_{(n)}^j \xi^j . \tag{4}$$

the estimate errors of credit evaluation on targets $\{d_1, d_2, \ldots, d_n\}$, where

$$\xi^j = \begin{pmatrix} \xi_1^j \\ \vdots \\ \xi_n^j \end{pmatrix}; \ E_{(n)}^j = \begin{pmatrix} e_{1j}^2 & \cdots & e_{1j}e_{nj} \\ \vdots & \ddots & \vdots \\ e_{nj}e_{1j} & \cdots & e_{nj}^2 \end{pmatrix}. \tag{5}$$

Definition 1. If the multi-factors detached coefficients vectors ξ^j ($j =1,2,\cdots,m$) are minimal about estimate errors J, $i.e.$

$$J^* = \min_{\xi^j} J = \sum_{j=1}^{m}\left[((\xi^j)^*)^T E_{(n)}^j(\xi^j)^*\right]. \tag{6}$$

J^* is called minimal estimate errors of credit evaluation on factors $\{d_1,d_2,...,d_n\}$, and $(\xi^j)^*$ is called the optimal multi-factors detached coefficients vector based on minimal estimate errors, $E_{(n)}^j$ is called the estimate deflection matrix on the j-th expertise.

After selecting credit evaluation factors $\{d_1,d_2,...,d_n\}$, from the optimization problem:

$$\begin{cases} \min J = \sum_{j=1}^{m}\left(\xi^j\right)^T E_{(n)}^j\xi^j \\ s.t. \sum_{i=1}^{n}\xi_i^j = 1; \xi_i^j \geq 0, i = 1,2,...,n; j = 1,2,...,m \end{cases} \tag{7}$$

we get the optimal multi-factors detached coefficients vector $(\xi^j)^*$ ($j=1,2,\cdots,m$) and optimal multi-factors detached coefficients matrix under minimal estimate errors:

$$\Gamma^* = \begin{pmatrix} (\xi_1^1)^* & \cdots & (\xi_1^m)^* \\ \vdots & \ddots & \vdots \\ (\xi_n^1)^* & \cdots & (\xi_n^m)^* \end{pmatrix} \tag{8}$$

The i-th row in matrix (8) shows the differences of the i-th factor under the differ expertise; and the columns reflect the weightiness of differ factor on the same expertise. Therefore this matrix describes the essentiality of these factors about repayment abilities.

According to essentiality of expertise, we take row-weighted average: $\alpha_i = \sum_{j=1}^{m}\lambda_j(\xi_i^j)^*$ ($i=1,2,\cdots,n$), where λ_j reflects the weightiness of expertise,

which satisfies: $\sum_{j=1}^{m}\lambda_j =1, \lambda_j \geq 0, j=1,2,\cdots,m.$

Definition 2. Let $\beta_i = \dfrac{\alpha_i - a}{b - a}\times 100 \in [0,100]$, ($i=1,2, \cdots ,n$), we call $(\beta_1,\beta_2, \cdots, \beta_n)^T$ the scores vector at n factors, where a and b ($a \neq b$) are supremum and infimum of α_i respectively.

If the factors scores are higher, we can think that the customer is preferable on these factors, and baddish on low-scores factors. If one or other of the low-scores factors is essentiality for repayment abilities of the customer, the bank should not provide loan to him.

Furthermore if the comparative weightiness of these factors is known, we can gain the synthetic weighted credit scores of the customers. According to the credit scores, the commercial banks gained the decision-making dependency on loans.

3 Conclusion

In this paper, we put forward the concept of multi-factors detached coefficients and optimal multi-factors detached coefficients matrix Γ^*, and give a method to determine the matrix. According to matrix Γ^*, the credit of the customers is evaluated and selected by commerce banks. We put forth the method is convenient, suppleness and handle. We can resolve the more complicated credit problems with more factors and expertise analogously by decomposing factors and combined results. We certainly believe that it can have a great potential of applications.

References

1. Wang, C.F., Wan, H.H., Zhang W.: Credit risk assessment in commercial banks by neural networks. Systems Engineering Theory & Practice, 19(9) (1999) (In Chinese).
2. Wang, C.F., Kang L. : A model based on genetic programming for credit risk assessment in commercial banks. Systems Engineering Theory & Practice, 21(2) (2001) (In Chinese).
3. Caouette, J.B., Altman, E.I., Narayanan, P.: Managing Credit Risk: The Next Great Financial Challenge. John Wiley & Sons (1998)
4. Zhou, Z.F., Shi Y.: An algorithm in nonlinear multi-objective programming. Proceeding of International Conference on Operations & Quantitative Management (1997)
5. Zhou, Z.F., Shi Y., Hao X.: An MC^2 linear programming approach to combined forecasting. International Journal of Mathematical and Computer Modeling, 29 (1999)
6. Tang, X.W., Zhou, Z.F., Shi ,Y.: The errors bound under orthogonal of combined forecasting. International Journal of Information, 5(4) (2002)
7. Zhou, Z.F., Tang ,X.W., Lu ,Y.G.: The research on variable weights in combined forecasting. Proceedings of 2002 International Conference on Management Science & Engineering (2002)
8. Tang, X.W, Zhou Z.F., Shi, Y.: The Errors Bounds of Combined Forecasting. Journal of Mathematical and Computer Modelling, 36 (2002)
9. Zhou, Z.F., Tang, X. .W.: An Multi−Targets Evaluation Approaches to Customers Credit. Proceedings of 2003 International Conference on Management Science & Engineering, Georgia, USA (2003)
10. Zhou, Z.F., Tang, X..W.: Research on Targets Evaluation for Customers Credit. Journal of Systems Science and Information, 4(1) (2003)
11. 11.Zhou, Z.F., Tang, X. W., Mou T.Y.: The optimization techniques approach to customers credit. Proceedings of ICSSSE (2003)
12. Zhou, Z.F., Tang, X.W, Mu T.Y.: An Application of Targets Evaluation in Customers Credit. Proceedings of The 5TH International Conference on Management (2004)

A Novel Hybrid AI System Framework for Crude Oil Price Forecasting

Shouyang Wang[1,2], Lean Yu[2,3], and K.K. Lai[4]

[1] Institute of Policy and Planning Sciences, University of Tsukuba,
Tsukuba, Ibaraki 305-8573, Japan
wang@sk.tsukuba.ac.jp
[2] Institute of Systems Science, Academy of Mathematics and Systems Sciences,
Chinese Academy of Sciences, Beijing 100080, China
{yulean, sywang}@mail.amss.ac.cn
[3] School of Management, Graduate School of Chinese Academy of Sciences,
Chinese Academy of Sciences, Beijing 100039, China
yulean@mail.amss.ac.cn
[4] Department of Management Sciences, City University of Hong Kong,
Tat Chee Avenue, Kowloon, Hong Kong
mskklai@cityu.edu.hk

Abstract. In this study, a novel hybrid AI system framework is developed by means of a systematic integration of artificial neural networks (ANN) and rule-based expert system (RES) with web-based text mining (WTM) techniques. Within the hybrid AI system framework, a fully novel hybrid AI forecasting approach with conditional judgment and correction is proposed for improving prediction performance. The proposed framework and approach are also illustrated with an example here.

1 Introduction

The role of oil in the world economy becomes more and more significant because nearly two-thirds of the world's energy consumption comes from the crude oil and natural gas [1]. For example, worldwide consumption of crude oil exceeds $500 billion, roughly 10% of the US GDP [2]. Besides, crude oil is also the world's most actively traded commodity, accounting for about 10% of total world trade [2]. The crude oil price is basically determined by its supply and demand, and is strongly influenced by many events like the weather, stock levels, GDP growth, political aspects and people's expectation. Because it takes considerable time to ship crude oil from a country to another country, there is often a variation of prices in different parts of the world. These facts lead to a strongly fluctuating and interacting market whose fundamental mechanism governing the complex dynamics is not well understood. Furthermore, because sharp oil price movements are likely to disturb aggregate economic activity, volatile oil prices have been considerable interest to many researchers and institutions. Therefore, forecasting oil prices is an important and very hard topic due to its intrinsic difficulty and practical applications.

Y. Shi, W. Xu, and Z. Chen (Eds.): CASDMKM 2004, LNAI 3327, pp. 233–242, 2004.

For crude oil price forecasting, most of the literature focuses only on the oil price volatility analysis (see e.g. [1, 3]) and oil price determination within the framework of supply and demand (see e.g. [4, 5]). There are only very limited number of related papers on oil price forecasting in the literature, such as [6-8]. But all the methods mentioned above belong to the range of traditional approaches. With the increase of competition, the prediction performance of traditional approaches has not met the practical needs. Therefore, it is significant to develop new forecasting models for predicting oil price by using some advanced techniques (e.g., artificial intelligence technique). In view of difficulty and complexity of crude oil price forecasting, a hybrid AI system framework is proposed in this study to integrate systematically artificial neural networks (ANN) and rule-based expert system (RES) with web-based text mining (WTM) techniques, and a hybrid AI forecasting approach with conditional judgment and correction within the hybrid AI system framework is presented for improving prediction performance.

The rest of the paper is organized as follows. Section 2 presents the general description of the hybrid AI system framework. A hybrid AI forecasting approach with conditional judgment and correction within the proposed framework is also presented in details in this section. For evaluating the proposed framework and approach, an empirical simulation in oil market is presented in Section 3. And Section 4 concludes.

2   The Hybrid AI System for Crude Oil Price Forecasting

2.1   The General System Structure of the Hybrid AI System

A superior approach is used to develop a hybrid AI system that can implement crude oil price forecasting in the volatile crude oil market. The general framework structure of the hybrid AI system is shown in Fig. 1.

From Fig. 1, the hybrid AI system for crude oil price forecasting consists of five main components, i.e., man-machine interface module, web-based text mining module, ANN-based time series forecasting module, rule-based expert system module, bases and bases management module.

2.1.1   Man-Machine Interface (MMI) Module
The man-machine interface (MMI) is a graphical window through which users can exchange information with the hybrid AI system. In details, it handles all input/output between users and the hybrid AI system. In some sense, it can be considered as open platform communicating with users and interacting with other components of the hybrid AI system.

2.1.2   Web-Based Text Mining (WTM) Module
This module is a main component of the hybrid system. Crude oil market is an unstable market with high volatility and oil price is often affected by many related factors.

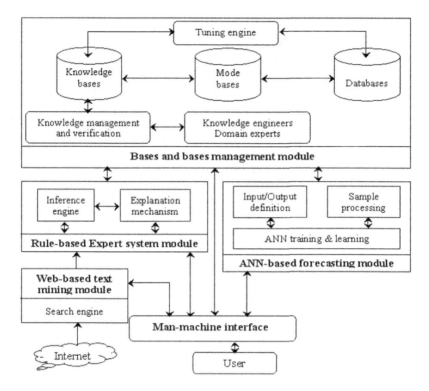

Fig. 1. The general framework structure of the hybrid AI system

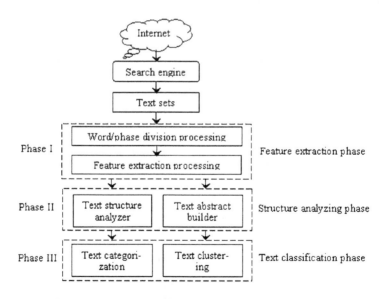

Fig. 2. The main process of web-based text mining module

In order to improve forecasting accuracy, these related factors should be taken into consideration in forecasting. It is, therefore, necessary to collect the related information from Internet. However, it is very difficult to collect the related knowledge from Internet. Collecting valuable information from Internet has received more and more attention in recent years. With the advancement of computational techniques, web -based text mining (WTM) [9] is believed to be one of the effective techniques. In this study, the main goal of web-based text mining module is to collect related information affecting oil price variability from Internet and to provide the collected useful information to the rule-based expert system forecasting module. The main process of the web-based text mining module is presented in Fig. 2.

As seen in Fig. 2, the whole process of WTM can be divided into three phases or six processing procedures. When retrieving some related information affecting the oil price variability from Internet with the web-based text mining module, the retrieved information will be send to the rule-based expert system module for further analysis.

2.1.3 Rule-Based Expert System (RES) Module

It is well known that the key of an expert system is the construction of its knowledge base (KB). In this study, KB is represented by all types of rules from knowledge engineers who collects and summarizes related knowledge and information from history and some domain experts. Thus, the main work of a rule-based expert system module is to collect and extract the rules or knowledge category in the KB. In this study, our expert system module is required to extract some rules to judge oil price abnormal variability by summarizing and concluding the relationships between oil price fluctuation and key factors affecting oil price volatility. Table 1 lists the typical factors of crude oil price variability.

Table 1. The factor classification according to the meaning of factors

Factor group	Factors	Examples
Military & political factor	War	1980-1988 Iraq-Iran war and 1991-1992 Gulf war
	Revolution	1978-1979: Iran revolution
	Terrorist attack	2001.9.11: US 911event
	Political difference	1992-1997: Iraq arms inspection program
	Sanction	1992: UN sanctions against Libya
	Hostage crisis	1979.11: Iran takes western hostage
	Strike	1994.4-9: Nigerian oil workers' strike
OPEC policy	Raise tax rate	1970.12: OPEC meeting in Caracas establishes 55% tax rate
	Nationalization	1973-74: Libya and Nigeria nationalizes foreign oil Companies.
	Embargo	1973.10-1974.3: OPEC oil embargo.
	Freeze posted price	1974.1: OPEC decides to freeze price
	Raise price	1979.4: OPEC makes 14.5% price increase
	Raise production	1989.6 and 1997.11: OPEC raise production.
	Cut production	1991.3: OPEC announce production cut to 22.3MMB/D

Table 1. (*continued*)

Non-OPEC policy	Raise production	1995:Russia and Norway raise production
	Cut production	1998.3: Norway cut production
Natural disaster	Earthquake	1990.11: Iran's oil-producing region suffers a serious earthquake
	Cold weather	1995: Extremely cold weather in the US and Europe
World economy condition	Economic crisis	1997-1998: Asia financial crisis
Other factors	Rumor or false news	2000.10: Oil price rise sharply on news of a terrorist attack on US
	Environmental protection	1999.3: US EPA statements of "cut gasoline sulfur content and tailpipe emissions"
	Oil firms merger	1999.5: Exxon and Mobil merger
	Exchange rates	1970.12: OPEC demands that posted prices be reflected changes in foreign exchange rates.
	Speculation	2000.12: OPEC chairman considers that speculation is a main cause of oil volatility.

As seen in Table 1, the main patterns that affect crude oil price volatility can be classified into six groups and 24 patterns. These patterns are used in this study.

According to the defined pattern and historical oil price, the oil price volatility rule can be concluded. Table 2 presents in details the main judgmental or forecasting rules in this study according to the extraction of historical events affecting oil price.

Table 2. The typical rules in the knowledge bases

Rule No.	Conditions	Direction movements	The range of movements (%)
1	War	Increase	5.56-45.80
2	Revolution	Increase	6.73-14.20
3	Terrorist attack	Uncertainty	16.52-33.89
4	Political difference	Uncertainty	8.73-10.97
5	Sanction	Increase	7.02-24.20
6	Hostage crisis	Increase	4.84-6.89
7	Strike	Increase	21.96-34.04
8	OPEC raise tax rate	Increase	7.55-10.39
9	OPEC nationalization	Increase	10.39-57.37
10	OPEC embargo	Increase	67.29-134.57
11	OPEC freeze posted price	Increase	35.11-53.36
12	OPEC raise price	Increase	14.50-58.14
13	OPEC raise production	Decrease	15.09-34.29
14	OPEC cut production	Increase	6.95-10.40
15	Non-OPEC raise production	Decrease	5.81-6.47
16	Non-OPEC cut production	Increase	2.80-9.05
17	Earthquake	Increase	16.68-18.15
18	Cold weather	Increase	5.21-8.28
19	Economic crisis	Decrease	8.79-13.83
20	Rumor and false news	Uncertainty	10.19-15.55
21	Environmental protection	Increase	18.28-48.14
22	Oil company merger	Uncertainty	4.46-13.07
23	Foreign exchange rates	Uncertainty	10-40
24	Speculation	Uncertainty	14.05-28.11

In addition, in the rule-based expert system module, the inference engine (IE) and explanation mechanism (EM) are presented to interact with users via MMI module. The function of IE and EM is to provide automatic criteria comparison and interpretation of rules. With the help of this information, one can judge the range of oil price movements with the RES module.

2.1.4   ANN-Based Time Series Forecasting Module

As mentioned previously, the ANN-based time series forecasting module adopts ANN techniques. Recently, ANNs have gained popularity as an emerging computational technology and offer a new avenue to explore the dynamics of a variety of practical applications. The ANN used in this study is a three-layer back-propagation neural network (BPNN) incorporating the Levenberg- Marquardt algorithm for training.

In this study, BPNN traces previous and present values and predicts the future values using the historical data. The crude oil price data used in this paper are monthly spot prices of West Texas Intermediate (WTI) crude oil, covered the period from January 1970 to December 2002 with a total of $n = 396$ observations. For the purpose of this study, the first 360 observations are used in-sample data (including 72 validation data) as training and validating sets, while the reminders used as testing ones.

For an univariate time-series forecasting problem, the inputs of the network are the past lagged observations of the data series and the outputs are the future values. Each input vector is composed of a moving window of fixed length along the data sets. That is, the BPNN time-series forecasting model performs a nonlinear mapping as follows.

$$y_{t+1} = f(y_t, y_{t-1}, \cdots, y_{t-p}) \tag{1}$$

where y_t is the observation at time t, $f(\bullet)$ is a nonlinear function determined by the network structure and connection weights, and p is the dimension of the input vector or the number of past observations related to the future value, y_{t+1}. The BPNN used for time series forecasting is a general nonlinear autoregressive (NAR) model.

2.1.5   Bases and Bases Management Module

The bases and bases management module is the important part of the hybrid AI system because the other modules of the hybrid AI system have a strong connection with this module. For example, ANN-based forecasting module utilizes MB and DB, while the rule-based expert system mainly used the KB and DB, as illustrated in Fig. 1.

To summarize, the hybrid AI system framework, as mentioned previously, is developed through integration of the web-based text mining, rule-based expert system and ANN-based time series forecasting techniques. Within the framework of hybrid AI system, a novel hybrid AI forecasting approach is proposed to improve oil price forecasting performance in the following.

2.2 The Proposed Hybrid AI Forecasting Approach

Based on the general framework of a hybrid AI system and the above detailed descriptions of their modules, a novel hybrid AI forecasting approach to oil price forecasting is proposed. The flow chart of the hybrid AI forecasting approach is shown in Fig. 3.

As can be seen in Fig. 3, the proposed hybrid AI forecasting approach generally consists of four main steps. First of all, using web-based text mining technique, we can obtain some recent information affecting oil price. Next, by comparing the retrieved or collected information with the predefined patterns, we can judge whether the important events affecting oil price volatility exist or not. Subsequently, if there are no related patterns, then we can directly implement ANN-based time series forecasting module for oil price prediction using the historical data series. If there are important events in retrieved information, then we turn to the next step. In the last stage, we use ANN-based time series forecasting module for oil price series prediction, and use rule-based expert system module for oil price volatility prediction based on some important factor affecting oil price variability. By implementing the two modules, the oil price predicted value could be obtained.

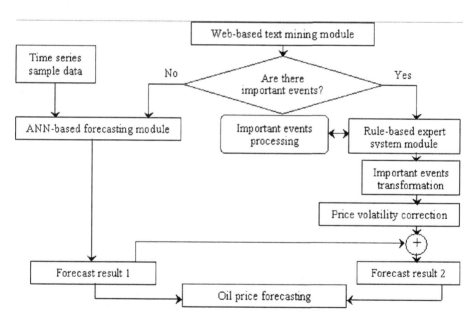

Fig. 3. The overall computational flow chart of the hybrid AI forecasting approach

According to the previous descriptions and Fig. 3, we can conclude a computational equation as follows. Assume that: S: {Related important event information base in KB defined beforehand}; S_t: {Related event information retrieved by web-based text mining module at time t}; $\hat{P}_{t+1}^{ANN}$: The forecasting result with ANN-based forecasting module at time $t+1$; $\hat{P}_{t+1}^{Corr}$: The correction term with rule-based expert system module at time $t+1$; $\hat{P}_{t+1}$: The final forecasting result of oil price at time $t+1$. Then the computational equation is represented as

$$\hat{P}_{t+1} = \begin{cases} \hat{P}_{t+1}^{ANN}, & \text{if } S_t \notin S; \\ \hat{P}_{t+1}^{ANN} + \hat{P}_{t+1}^{Corr}, & \text{if } S_t \in S. \end{cases} \tag{2}$$

Thus, a novel hybrid AI forecasting approach to oil price prediction is formulated. In order to verify the efficiency and effectiveness of the proposed approach, a simulated experiment is reported in the next section.

3 A Simulation Study

Using the proposed hybrid AI forecasting approach within the framework of hybrid AI system, a simulation experiment is made. The corresponding results are summarized in Table 3. Accordingly, the evaluation criteria are the root mean square error (*RMSE*) and direction change statistics (D_{stat}). For a comparison, the full evaluation period is divided into three sub-periods in terms of chronology. In addition, the individual ANN forecasting method is used as a benchmark model here.

Table 3. The forecasting results of crude oil price (Jan. 2000 - Dec. 2002)*

Evaluation	Full period (2000-2002)	Sub-period I (2000)	Sub-period II (2001)	Sub-period III (2002)
ANN method				
RMSE	3.413	3.405	3.020	3.324
D_{stat} (%)	61.11	50.00	66.67	66.67
Hybrid AI method				
RMSE	2.369	3.000	2.040	1.916
D_{stat} (%)	80.56	75.00	83.33	91.67

* *RMSE*: root mean square error; D_{stat}: direction change statistics.

Table 3 shows the detailed results of the simulated experiment. It can be seen that the hybrid AI method outperforms the individual ANN method in terms of either *RMSE* or D_{stat}. Notably, the values of D_{stat} of our hybrid AI forecasting method for each evaluation period exceed 70%, indicating that the proposed hybrid AI forecasting approach has good performance for the crude oil price forecasting considering the complexity of the crude oil market.

Focusing on the *RMSE* indicator, in the case of individual ANN method, the second sub-period (i.e., 2001) performs the best, followed by 2002 and 2000. While in the case of the hybrid AI method, the results of 2002 outperform those of the other evaluation period. The main reason is that many important events affecting oil price volatility happened. The information of those important events could be obtained and analyzed by the web-based text mining technique. Table 4 presents these events that affect the oil price. As can be seen in Table 4, the number of events in 2002 is obviously larger than those of years 2000–2001.

Table 4. The important events affecting oil price from Jan. 2000 to Dec. 2002[*]

Year	Month	Important events affecting oil price in the world
2000	01	Energy companies and countries care about "Y2K Bug".
	02	No important events.
	03	Vladimir Putin is elected Russian president and OPEC increases production.
	04	No important events.
	05	The Environmental Protection Agency (EPA) proposes a rule to reduce sulfur levels in diesel fuel by 97% over the next five years
	06	OPEC oil ministers (Vienna) agree to raise crude oil production
	07	No important events.
	08	The Energy Information Administration (EIA) reports that crude oil stock levels in the United States have fallen to their lowest level since 1976.
	09	OPEC raise oil production and President Clinton authorizes the release of 30 million barrels of oil from the Strategic Petroleum Reserve (SPR) over 30 days to bolster oil supplies, particular heating oil in the Northeast.
	10	Oil prices rise sharply on news of a terrorist attack on an American warship.
	11	OPEC oil ministers, meeting in Vienna, announce a decision to put any further production increases on hold until their next meeting scheduled for Jan. 2001.
	12	The US suffered energy shortages due to cold weather in the area and Saudi oil minister Ali Naimi says that OPEC will cut production in next OPEC meeting.
2001	01	No important events.
	02	No important events.
	03	No important events.
	04	The oil demand of US increase according to administration's energy plan.
	05	No important events.
	06	No important events.
	07	Faced with declining oil prices, OPEC ministers agree to cut crude oil production quotas by about 4%
	08	No important events.
	09	The largest terrorist attack in world history occurs in the US.
	10	The supply of natural gas in US increases
	11	No important events.
	12	OPEC oil ministers meeting in Cairo agree to reduce their oil output quotas.
2002	01	The OPEC oil production quota cuts of 1.5 million barrels per day.
	02	Iraq says that it will not allow U.N. arms inspectors to return to Iraq.
	03	OPEC and non-OPEC countries cut oil production.
	04	A general strike of Venezuela oil workers
	05	Russia raise oil production and extend crude oil export.
	06	Non-OPEC countries continue cut oil production.
	07	The California State Legislature passes legislation and US Depart of Energy increases SPR, and a strike in Nigeria happens.
	08	The US Environmental Protection Agency requires diesel trucks and buses to reduce emissions by 90% by 2007 and Mexico limits its crude oil exports.
	09	OPEC, meeting in Osaka, Japan, decides keep current oil production and price
	10	No important events.
	11	The US SPR increases and the U.N. adopts Resolution 1441.
	12	A strike happens in Venezuela and US Secretary of State Colin Powell declares that the Iraq fails to meet the resolution's requirement of U.N.

From a practitioners' point of view, indicator D_{stat} is more important than the indicator *RMSE*. This is because the former can reflect the movement trend of oil price and can help traders to make good trading decisions. For the test case of our hybrid AI approach and from the view of D_{stat}, the performance of 2002 is much better than that of 2000 and 2001, as shown in Table 3.

By Table 3, we observe that a smaller *RMSE* does not necessarily mean higher D_{stat}. For example, for the test case of the individual ANN method, the *RMSE* for 2000 is slightly smaller than that for full-period (i.e., 2000-2002), while the D_{stat} for 2000-2002 is larger than that for 2000.

However, the overall prediction performance of the proposed hybrid AI approach is satisfactory because the *RMSE* for each evaluation period is smaller than 3.00, and the D_{stat} for each evaluation period exceeds 70%. This indicates that there are some profit opportunities if traders use the proposed approach to forecast oil price.

4   Conclusions

In this study, a hybrid AI system framework integrating web-based text mining and rule-based expert system with ANN-based time series forecasting techniques is proposed for crude oil price forecasting and a corresponding hybrid AI system is also developed. A fully novel hybrid AI forecasting approach within the framework of the hybrid AI system is presented for crude oil price forecasting.

To verify the effectiveness of proposed approach, a simulation study is presented. The simulation results show that the proposed approach is significantly effective and practically feasible. Hence, the novel hybrid AI forecasting model can be used as an appropriate tool for crude oil price forecasting to improve forecasting accuracy.

References

[1] Alvarez-Ramirez, J., Soriano, A., Cisneros, M., Suarez, R.: Symmetry/anti-symmetry phase transitions in crude oil markets. Physica A, 322 (2003) 583-596
[2] Verleger, P.K.: Adjusting to volatile energy prices. Working paper. Institute for International Economics, Washington DC (1993)
[3] Watkins, G.C., Plourde, A.: How volatile are crude oil prices? *OPEC Review*, 18(4) (1994) 220-245.
[4] Hagen, R.: How is the international price of a particular crude determining? OPEC Review, 18 (1) (1994) 145-158
[5] Stevens, P.: The determination of oil prices 1945-1995. Energy Policy, 23(10) (1995) 861-870
[6] Huntington, H.G.: Oil price forecasting in the 1980s: what went wrong? The Energy Journal, 15(2) (1994) 1-22
[7] Abramson, B., Finizza, A.: Probabilistic forecasts from probabilistic models: a case study in the oil market. International Journal of Forecasting, 11(1) (1995) 63-72
[8] Morana, C.: A semiparametric approach to short-term oil price forecasting. Energy Economics, 23(3) (2001) 325-338
[9] Shi, Z.: Knowledge Discovery. Tsinghua University Press, Beijing (2002)

A Neural Network and Web-Based Decision Support System for Forex Forecasting and Trading

K.K. Lai[1], Lean Yu[2,3], and Shouyang Wang[2,4]

[1] Department of Management Sciences, City University of Hong Kong,
Tat Chee Avenue, Kowloon, Hong Kong
mskklai@cityu.edu.hk
[2] Institute of Systems Science, Academy of Mathematics and Systems Sciences,
Chinese Academy of Sciences, Beijing 100080, China
{yulean, sywang}@mail.amss.ac.cn
[3] School of Management, Graduate School of Chinese Academy of Sciences,
Chinese Academy of Sciences, Beijing 100039, China
[4] Institute of Policy and Planning Sciences, University of Tsukuba,
Tsukuba, Ibaraki 305-8573, Japan
wang@sk.tsukuba.ac.jp

Abstract. This study presents a neural network & web-based decision support system (DSS) for foreign exchange (forex) forecasting and trading decision, which is adaptable to the needs of financial organizations and individual investors. In this study, we integrate the back-propagation neural network (BPNN)-based forex rolling forecasting system to accurately predict the change in direction of daily exchange rates, and the Web-based forex trading decision support system to obtain forecasting data and provide some investment decision suggestions for financial practitioners. This research reveals the structure of the DSS by the description of an integrated framework, and meantime we find that the DSS is integrated, user-oriented by its implementation, and practical applications reveal that this DSS demonstrates very high forecasting accuracy and its trading recommendations are reliable.

1 Introduction

Decision support system (DSS) is a powerful tool which can be used to support decision makers in making strategic decisions [1]. One of their objectives is to improve management judgment by fostering understanding and insights and by allowing appropriate access to relevant information [2]. The ability to forecast the future, based only on past data, leads to strategic advantages, which may be the key to success in organizations. In real life, one would be interested not only in efforts in forecasting, but also in practical trading strategies with possibility of taking positions in the foreign exchange (forex) market. Furthermore, Tsoi et al. in their earlier studies have shown that the direction of the forecast is more important than the actual forecast itself in determining the profitability of a forecasting and trading system [3]. In addition, the forex market is a rather complicated environment, and good predictions for

Y. Shi, W. Xu, and Z. Chen (Eds.): CASDMKM 2004, LNAI 3327, pp. 243–253, 2004.

its developments are key to successful trading. Traders must predict forex price movements in order to sell at top range and to buy at bottom range. Forecasting often plays an important role in the process of decision-making. Hence, forecasting system is always connected with the DSS to improve decision-making.

However, there is currently no integrated DSS approach that combines the ANN-based forecasting and web-based decision implementation to support predicting and trading decision in forex markets. We therefore propose an integrated framework approach that can implement the forex forecasting and present trading strategies in forex trading. Our approach, based on the framework, is as follows: first, the BPNN-based forex rolling forecasting system (BPNNFRFS) provides the prediction results of main international currencies employing burgeoning artificial intelligence technology to forex trading decision support system; second, the web-based forex trading decision support system (WFTDSS) is developed to provide some trading signals or trading suggestions for investors according to some corresponding decision criteria. In addition, the BPNNFRFS is constructed using artificial neural networks, while the WFTDSS uses various decision techniques and web technologies. Moreover, the integrated forex rolling forecasting and trading decision support system (IFRFTDSS), which integrates BPNNFRFS and WFTDSS, is designed to provide investors with daily trading suggestions on the forex markets. In the following section, we start with a brief introduction to the integrated framework of IFRFTDSS. Then we describe how a BPNNFRFS and a WFTDSS can be built around the framework. We also show how to incorporate two individual systems into an integrated DSS with support for financial institutions and individual investors. At the same time, we provide a brief description of IFRFTDSS, and show the implementations of the IFRFTDSS. Finally, some conclusions are made.

2 The Proposed Framework for IFRFTDSS

This section first describes the general integrated framework of IFRFTDSS, and discusses the two subsystems — BPNNFRFS and WFTDSS — which will be employed in the proposed integrated framework. The integrated system in the framework, IFRFTDSS, will be described in next section.

2.1 The General Integrated Framework

The integrated framework of IFRFTDSS proposed in this study will be developed to support decision making in forex trading with the use of the forex rolling forecasting results and various trading decision criteria. That is, it is designed to generate sell/buy/hold signals to support forex trading decisions. Based on this framework, we develop an IFRFTDSS for main international currencies. IFRFTDSS consists of two subsystems: one is the BPNN-based Forex rolling forecasting system (BPNNFRFS), which is the off-line training and forecasting unit; the other is the web-based forex trading decision support system (WFTDSS), which is the daily on-line prediction and decision unit. The former can provide database support for the latter. That is to say, they couple with the data that is produced by the BPNNFRFS. The general frame-work we propose is shown in Fig. 1.

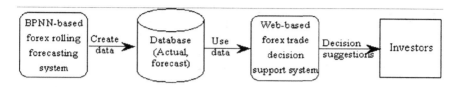

Fig. 1. The general integrated framework

2.2 The BPNN-Based Forex Rolling Forecasting System — BPNNFRFS

Studies [1, 3, 4, 5, 6-9] reveal that there are many applications for forex forecasting with BPNN, but it is hard to find a whole forecasting system based on BPNN tech-niques in the literature. Furthermore, most existing forecasting methods and tools do not have good interaction or flexibility, as the practitioners are required to have a thorough theory background in order to understand the methodologies and models. Hence, it is difficult to achieve good decision alternatives based on these models and tools. Although methods and tools used in their works are quite diverse, satisfactory forecasting results have not been obtained so far. Thus, this study aims to develop a whole forex forecasting system to forecast a change in direction or trend in forex movements for some main international currencies employing burgeoning artificial intelligence technology. The rolling forecasting technique is also introduced to im-prove forecasting accuracy in this forecasting system. Thus, the BPNN-based Forex rolling forecasting system — BPNNFRFS — is generated. The main user interface of the BPNNFRFS is shown in Fig. 2.

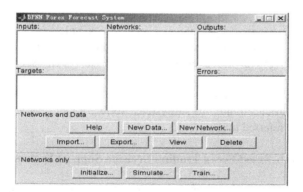

Fig. 2. The user interface of BPNNFRFS

The BPNNFRFS is built using the Matlab software, which is produced by Math-works Laboratory Corporation. The main flows in this system contain eight key stages, i.e., sample selection, data division, data preprocessing, determination of network architecture, initialization, sample training, sample validation, and simulation and forecast, as shown in Fig. 3.

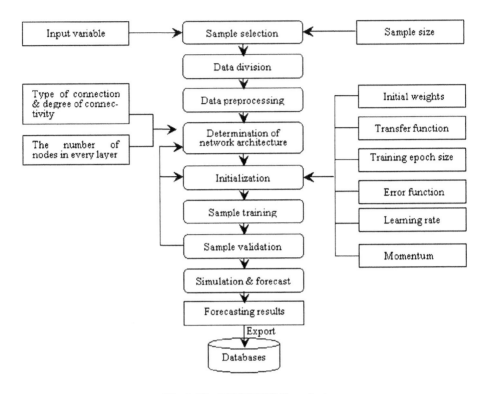

Fig. 3. The BPNNFRFS flow chart

From Fig.3, we can see that this is a relatively complex process. However, easy operating is an important measurement of software system. In order to facilitate forecasters and investors, we develop this easy-use subsystem (see Fig.2) for forex prediction. Especially, this system can be used independently as a forecasting system.

In order to improve prediction accuracy and performance, rolling forecasting techniques are introduced into this subsystem. Rolling forecasting techniques with neural networks are referred to [8].

2.3 The Web-Based Forex Trading Decision Support System — WFTDSS

WFTDSS is developed to support decision making in forex trading. It is designed to convert forex price information that is presented by BPNNFRFS into forex movement tendency information, thus generating sell/buy/hold signals directly for investors. In this system, four trading rules are presented for users' choice. Different trading rules may result in different trading strategies. In order to introduce these judgment rules, the forex actual and predicted values at time t, x_t and $\hat{x}_t$, are defined here.

The *first* rule is a simple price comparison judgment criterion. In general, this criterion is the simplest of all, and includes the following three rules.

Rule I: If $(\hat{x}_{t+1} - x_t) > 0$, then the forex price trend is *"upward"* and the current trading strategy is *"buy"*.

Rule II: If $(\hat{x}_{t+1} - x_t) < 0$, then the forex price trend is *"downward"* and the current trading strategy is *"sell"*.

Rule III: If $(\hat{x}_{t+1} - x_t) = 0$, then forex price is *"unchangeable"* and the current trading strategy is *"hold and deposit"*.

It is worth noting that use of this rule has no man's participation (i.e., parameter specification), but the forex trading strategies can still be generated automatically.

The *second* rule is a cost-adjusted filter judgment criterion. This rule introduces cost as adjusted bands. The objective of the band is to reduce the number of buy (sell) signals by eliminating weak signals when the predicted value $\hat{x}_{t+1}$ and the actual value x_t are very close. After considering funding costs and transaction costs, some trading is not worth executing. Thus, this rule can help a trading system eliminate unnecessary trading and gain more profits. Mathematically the trading rules in their simplest form can be expressed as follows.

Rule I: If $(\hat{x}_{t+1} - x_t) > c$, then the current trading strategy is *"buy"*.

Rule II: If $(\hat{x}_{t+1} - x_t) < c$, then the current trading strategy is *"sell"*.

Rule III: If $(\hat{x}_{t+1} - x_t) = c$, then the current trading strategy is *"hold and deposit"*.

where c denotes cost, including all transaction costs and funding costs.

The *third* rule is a probability-based threshold judgment criterion. The trading probability based on the predicted forex price return is the basis of this trading judgment criterion. Its procedures include three steps as follows.

Firstly, let the forex price and forex price return at day t be denoted by x_t, and R_t. Based on the predicted value $\hat{x}_{t+1}$ that is produced by BPNNFRFS, the forex price return can also be calculated by

$$\hat{R}_{t+1} = (\hat{x}_{t+1} - x_t)/x_t \tag{1}$$

Secondly, let the "buy" and "sell" probability of the forex price return be denoted by $B_{t+1(j)}$, $S_{t+1(j)}$, respectively. As the forex price is a stochastic process, the probability $B_{t+1(j)}$ and $S_{t+1(j)}$ for the next day are calculated, respectively, by

$$B_{t+1(j)} = P\{R_{t+1(j)} > 0\} \quad (j=1, 2,..., N) \tag{2}$$
$$S_{t+1(j)} = P\{R_{t+1(j)} < 0\} \quad (j=1, 2,..., N) \tag{3}$$

where j denotes the number of forex candidates.

In the "buy" case, the basic rule is that the predicted forex price of the next day is higher than the current price, i.e. the predicted forex price return is larger than zero. In the "sell" case, the basic criterion is that the predicted forex price of the next day is lower than the current price, i.e. the predicted forex price return should be smaller than zero. It is worth noting that in the "buy" case, the forex with the largest trading probability $B_{t+1(max)}$ is chosen from the trading probability $B_{t+1(j)}$ of all N forex candidates by

$$B_{t+1(max)} = \max\{ B_{t+1(1)}, B_{t+1(2)}, ..., B_{T+1(N)} \} \tag{4}$$

Thirdly, the thresholds for buying and selling, θ_B and θ_S, are set in advance.

Up until now, the corresponding trading judgment rules are given by:

Rule I: If $B_{t+1(max)} \geq \theta_B$, then the trading strategy is "*buy*".

Rule II: If $S_{t+1(j)} \geq \theta_S$, then the trading strategy is "*sell*".

In this criterion, once the users or decision-makers specify a certain threshold, the optimal trading strategies will be presented explicitly.

The *fourth* criterion is risk-adjusted forex trading judgment criterion, which originated from the work of Chen and Leung [9]. Their work assumed that the forex market investment returns are determined by three features: forex appreciation, forex depreciation, and interest received from the money market. Let r and r^* be the daily domestic and foreign money market rates, and x_t and $\hat{x}_{t+1}$ be the observed exchange rates at day t and the forecast of exchange rate at day $(t+1)$ respectively. Given the notion that an investor is risk averse and can earn risk free interest from the domestic money market, we need to discount the expected rate of return based on a long or a short position by a risk aversion factor, γ. The risk aversion factor γ can take on any real value greater than negative one ($\gamma > -1.0$). For the risk neutral case, γ is zero ($\gamma = 0.0$). The value of γ is greater than zero ($\gamma > 0.0$) if the investor is risk averse. On the other hand, the value of γ is between zero and negative one ($-1.0 < \gamma < 0.0$) if the investor is a risk lover.

Based on this logical framework, we develop a risk-adjusted forex trading rule. The detailed expressions are as follows (for derivation of these conditions, refer to [9]).

Rule I: If $\ln\left(\dfrac{\hat{x}_{t+1}}{x_t}\right) < (r^* - r)(1+\gamma)$ and $(r^* - r)(1+\gamma) < 0$, then trading strategy is "buy".

Rule II: If $\ln\left(\dfrac{\hat{x}_{t+1}}{x_t}\right) \leq \dfrac{(r^* - r)(1+\gamma)}{2}$ and $(r^* - r)(1+\gamma) \geq 0$, then the strategy is "buy".

Rule III: If $\ln\left(\dfrac{\hat{x}_{t+1}}{x_t}\right) > \dfrac{(r^* - r)(1+\gamma)}{2}$ and $\ln\left(\dfrac{\hat{x}_{t+1}}{x_t}\right) > 0$, then the trading strategy is "sell".

Rule IV: If $\ln\left(\dfrac{\hat{x}_{t+1}}{x_t}\right) \geq (r^* - r)(1+\gamma)$ and $\ln\left(\dfrac{\hat{x}_{t+1}}{x_t}\right) \leq 0$, then the trading strategy is "hold and deposit".

Compared with the previous three criteria, this criterion seems to be relative complex. However, once the values of r^*, r and γ are specified by users or decision-makers, the optimal trading strategies will also be generated automatically regardless of paying attention to meaning of optimal conditions.

Of course, we can also implement more complex pre-defined or user-defined conditions and more complex judgment rules, and thus more optimal trading criteria and trading strategies will be generated. In our DSS, the knowledge base (KB) is formed by these rules and other judgment criteria. Besides these rules and criteria, there are many heuristic methodologies that deal with univariate time series data, e.g. how to convert univariate forex time series into input matrix vector for BPNN training, the allocation size in each traded currency. Thus the model base (MB) is generated by these models.

Based on the KB and MB, plus the database (DB) already produced by the BPNNFRFS, the web-based forex trading decision support system (WFTDSS) is constructed with the aid of popular web technology. Fig. 4 shows the basic architecture of this subsystem and the data flow between user interface, KB, MB and DB. Basically, this system contains the following components.

User-Friendly Interface. Used by decision-makers and investors to input some data and query conditions, and to select some trading decision methods and retrieve answers from related services. It also displays to the users and allows them to interact with the system to arrive at satisfactory solutions.

MB. Used to handle models of the many different types, which may be chosen.

KB. Used to judge the forex change tendency and determine forex trading decisions.

DB. Used as a repository of historical data and forecasting data for all model programs. In the meantime, it provides data support for the KB and MB needed.

Security System. Not only used for user protection purposes, but also checks for user access levels to determine the level of flexibility and interaction that the system would allow or provide.

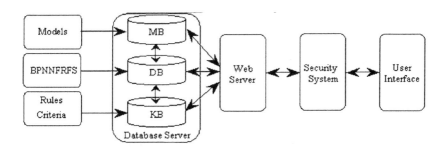

Fig. 4. The basic architecture and data flow of the WFTDSS

According to the previous WFTDSS architecture and data flow, we develop the web-based forex trading decision system adopting popular web technology and using the browser/server mode, which contains a three-tier structure. The basic construction of three-tier structure is shown in Fig. 5.

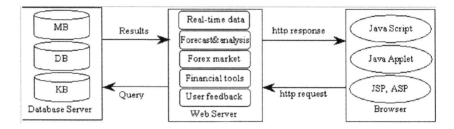

Fig. 5. Three-tier structure of WFTDSS

For explanation, WFTDSS partial user interfaces are shown in Fig. 6. Fig. 6(a) shows the interface of the trading decision criterion selection, which presents four types of decision criteria alternatives. Of the four, only one is selected by users every time. As shown in Fig. 6 (b), the interface of the fourth trading criterion mentioned previously is presented. In the interface, the corresponding optimal trading strategies will be generated by the WFTDSS as long as users or decision-makers can input certain real values or select certain "option buttons". In the same way, WFTDSS is also used as an individual system.

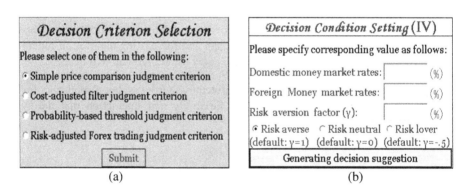

Fig. 6. WFTDSS partial user interface

3   The Formation of IFRFTDSS

Based on the general integrated framework and the description of two subsystems previously, we construct an integrated forex rolling forecasting and trading decision support system (IFRFTDSS) that incorporates BPNNFRFS and WFTDSS for users' convenience. Generally, the BPNNFRFS provides forex forecasting data; the WFTDSS provides trading rules and trading decisions using prediction results that are presented by the BPNNFRFS. As a whole, the formation of IFRFTDSS is the integration of the BPNNFRFS and WFTDSS. The integration process is that the BPNNFRFS is embedded into the WFTDSS.

The BPNNFRFS is a forex forecasting system that is developed by Matlab software with the use of the neural network toolbox. This system adopts the client/server (C/S) mode here. The advantage of this mode is that the server's function can be exerted as it can in terms of either program execution efficiency or program interaction as Fig. 2 indicates, but its main disadvantage is that the client program must be installed in the every client, which lowers the holistic efficiency of the software system. In BPNNFRFS, the input data is the univariate forex time series. These sample data are transformed into appropriate input matrix vectors by corresponding rules and heuristic algorithms. Empirical results reveal that we can obtain better forecasting results than those of other statistical models [8]. Thus, the BPNN model can be used as an alternative forecasting tool for exchange rates to achieve greater forecasting accuracy and improve the prediction quality further.

In order to facilitate using the forecasting results presented by BPNNFRFS and translating the forecasting results into corresponding trading decision information, the WFTDSS is constructed. The WFTDSS can be seen as an extension of BPNNFRFS to some extent. In the same way, the BPNNFRFS is considered to be an embedded system and has been a part of WFTDSS in this integrated framework. Based on some models and knowledge bases and databases, we develop WFTDSS with a three-tier structure adopting popular web technology and using the popular browser/server mode. The advantage of this mode lies in easy operating and easy maintenance because all programs are installed in the server site. Moreover, programs can be edited and revised remotely in the client site if access is authorized. Its disadvantage is that the program execution efficiency will be low when a large number of computations exist.

Based on BPNNFRFS and WFTDSS with their three-tier structure, the IFRFTDSS is generated naturally in order to overcome the drawbacks of the two subsystems. BPNNFRFS is seen as an embedded system and has already been combined with WFTDSS in the integrated system. In the IFRFTDSS, the operations are as follows. When entering the WFTDSS, we can click the "BPNNFRFS" button; then the BPNNFRFS will run in the server site according to the corresponding program design, and meanwhile the forecasting results obtained will be transmitted into the corresponding DB of the database server. Fig. 7 shows an IFRFTDSS interface when the first trading judgment criterion is selected by users.

By implementation of IFRFTDSS and practical application, we find that the DSS is integrated, user-oriented, the forecasting performance is high and thus their decision suggestions are reliable by practical testing.

4 Conclusions

This study briefly introduces an integrated framework for forex rolling forecasting and trading decision, and implementation of the framework. Based on the proposed framework, we construct an integrated forex rolling forecasting and trading decision support system (IFRFTDSS), which not only incorporates BPNNFRFS and WFTDSS, but also improves the overall performance of forecasting and decision process as well as providing a more organized and user-friendly interface specifically oriented for decision making in forex market investments.

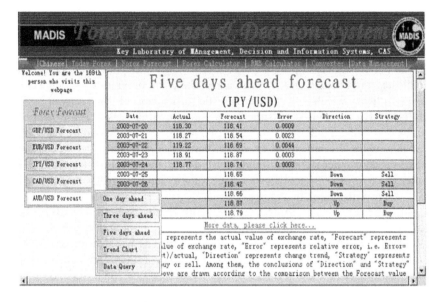

Fig. 7. The implementation of IFRFTDSS

IFRFTDSS is based on our proposed framework, which supports the flexible and interactive approach in system design and implementation, since users can visit the IFRFTDSS website and obtain real-time information and trading recommendations to adjust their own investment strategies. This system provides ease of use as well as a fast response time, which we believe is critical to all users, especially executive decision makers. At the same time, this system also provides a multidimensional data view and graphic display to help aid users' analysis. Furthermore, practical applications of the integrated system reveal that forecasting accuracy of this integrated system is very high and its trading recommendations are reliable.

Acknowledgements

The work described in this paper was fully support by grants from the Chinese Academy of Sciences and City University of Hong Kong (Project No. 7001677).

References

[1] Quah, T.S., Tan, C.L., Raman, K.S., Srinivasan, B.: Towards integrating rule-based expert systems and neural networks. Decision Support Systems, 17 (1996) 99-118
[2] Kean, P.G.W., Scott Morton, M.S.: Decision Support Systems: An Organizational Perspective. Addison- Wesley, Reading (1978)
[3] Tsoi, A.C., Tan, C.N.W., Lawrence S.: Financial time series forecasting: Application of artificial neural network techniques. Working paper (1993)

[4] Faraway, J., Chatfield, C.: Time series forecasting with neural networks: a comparative study using the airline data. Applied Statistics 47 (2) (1998) 231-250

[5] Kaastra, I., Boyd, M.S.: Forecasting futures trading volume using neural networks. The Journal of Futures Markets 15 (8), (1995) 953-970

[6] Freeman, J.A., Skapura, D.M.: Neural Networks: Algorithms, Applications and Programming Techniques. Addison-Wesley, MA (1991)

[7] Maier, H.R., Dandy, G.C.: Neural networks for the prediction and forecasting of water resources variables: a review of modeling issues and applications. Environmental Modelling & Software, 15 (2000) 101-124

[8] Yu, L.A., Wang, S.Y., Lai, K. K.: Exchange rates rolling forecasting using neural network model with parameter adaptive control. In: S. Chen et al. (Eds), Financial Systems Engineering, Global-Link Publishers, Hong Kong, (2003) 330-346

[9] Chen, A.S., Leung, M.T.: Regression network for error correction in foreign exchange forecasting and trading. Computers & Operations Research, 31(7) (2004) 1049-1068

XML-Based Schemes for Business Project Portfolio Selection*

Jichang Dong[1], K. K. Lai[2], and Shouyang Wang[3]

[1] GS School of Management, Chinese Academy of Science,
Beijing 100039, China
jcdonglc@gscas.ac.cn
[2] Department of Management Sciences, City University of Hong Kong,
Tat Chee Avenue, Kowloon, Hong Kong
mskklai@cityu.edu.hk
[3] Institute of Systems Science, Chinese Academy of Sciences,
Beijing 100080, China
swang@mail.iss.ac.cn

Abstract. Many methodologies have been introduced to deal with project portfolio selection problem including some techniques that help to evaluate individual projects, or to select a portfolio among available projects. This paper, however, provides several XML-based schemes for building efficient and flexible project portfolio selection systems based on an integrated portfolio selection model proposed. In additional to provide an interactive and adaptable portfolio selection management framework for the organizations, we also stress the use of XML to standardize the data representation for developing Web-based decision support systems with heterogeneous data sources and multiple decision models.

1 Introduction

Project portfolio selection is the periodic activity involved in selecting a portfolio of projects, that meets an organization's stated objectives without exceeding available resources or violating other constraints [2]. Choosing the right projects to invest in can make the difference between corporate survival and failure. Some of the issues that have to be addressed in this problem are the organization's objectives and priorities, financial benefits, intangible benefits, availability of resources, and risk level of the project portfolio.

Many methodologies have been developed for dealing with this problem, including techniques which evaluate individual projects or which select a portfolio from among available projects [3]. Also, there exist some process frameworks for project portfolio selection which is adaptable to the needs and preferences of the corporation, and which provides an approach to selecting a portfolio that meets the organization's requirements.

---

* Supported by NSFC, CAS, RGC of Hong Kong and Foundation of GSCAS (yzjj 200307).

Y. Shi, W. Xu, and Z. Chen (Eds.): CASDMKM 2004, LNAI 3327, pp. 254–262, 2004.

However, there does not exist a well-formed framework using Web service technologies for project portfolio selection. In this paper, we focus on developing a framework for project portfolio selection through XML-based decision support system. This method is proved to be simple, flexible, and adaptable based on our study.

Efficient project portfolio selection process requires the interchange of inter-organizational electronic data that may be from different resources with different formats to deal with the different representations of the same data, when evaluating a project or constructing a portfolio optimization model. Also, there is a need for electronically interchanging different structured data between the involved organizations. Moreover, as the development of Web services technology, the sharing of the portfolio optimization model is prevalent and profitable.

The extensible, structural and validated nature of XML provides standard data representation for efficient data interchange among diverse information resources on the Web, therefore, leads to its growing recognition in e-commerce and Internet-based information exchange. In this paper, we stress the adoption of XML technology in developing efficient and flexible Web decision support systems with standard data representation for sharing and exchanging heterogeneous data sources and multiple decision models. We present XML-based schemes for project portfolio selection systems following the proposal of an integrated portfolio selection framework.

In the following, we introduce an integrated framework to project portfolio selection firstly. Then, we expand our discussion on applying XML to the portfolio selection framework provided. Finally, we further explore the issues on handling diverse data sources and sharing of heterogeneous decision models, emerged by the use of XML technology.

2 An Integrated Project Portfolio Selection Management Model

In order to solve an optimization problem to gain maximum acceptance and cooperation from the decision makers, here, we provide a five-step integrated model for efficient and flexible project portfolio selection management, which combines *Resource Allocation*, *Project Analysis*, *Project Selection*, *Portfolio Optimization*, and *Reassessing* processes.

Resource allocation. This first step involves activities such as, determination of strategic focus, setting resource constraints, selecting the techniques to use for portfolio selection, and pre-screening the projects. This stage provides high-level guidance to the whole portfolio selection management process. Strategy development may consume lots of managerial time, and resource allocation to the particular project category also involves high-level decisions. The organization's experience, culture, problem solving style, and project environment must also be considered in the stage. Moreover, in this stage, the projects selected must fit in with the strategic focus of the portfolio, and undergo a preliminary analysis.

Project analysis is an important stage, which enables a decision-maker to conduct an analysis of projects that may be under consideration for inclusion in a portfolio. A common set of parameters, such as risk, net present value or return is calculated for each project.

In the **project selection** stage, project attributes from the previous stage are examined. Any projects, which don't meet pre-set criteria such as return and risk limit, are eliminated except for those projects that are mandatory or required.

Portfolio optimization is a major stage in project portfolio selection. This stage is to ensure optimal objectives by analyzing the portfolio and managing the projects. The resource limitations, timing, project interdependencies and other constraints must be considered into a optimization model. Some comparative optimization models can be considered in this stage, such as Analytical Hierarchy Process (AHP). As an important part of the integrated solution provided, portfolio optimization can be further break down into several sub-processes, which allow decision-makers to assess how close to the optimum their portfolios are performing.

Re-assessing is an optional stage of portfolio selection. In this stage, decision-makers apply their knowledge and experience to reassess the portfolio and make adjustment, or make decisions as to employ or dispose the particular project. This adjustment can help to achieve balance among the projects selected.

3 XML-Based 3-Tier Scheme for Project Portfolio Selection

3.1 Design of the DSS

Fig. 1 presents an XML-based 3-tier structure following the integrated project portfolio selection model introduced in earlier section. Our main goal is to provide a user-friendly interface with interactive feedback and ease of use with rapid response, which is critical to all users especially executive decision makers. The three tiers of our solution are the clients, the middleware servers, and the back-end applications. The Java client, part of the middle tier and the back-end systems can be written in Java and run on multiple platforms without modification.

Clients. It displays results to the users and allows them to interact with the system to arrive at satisfactory solutions. The user interface is used by decision-makers to input data and decision preferences, and to retrieve answers from related services in the clients. The clients can also run as applets in java-enabled browsers.

Middle tier. The middle tier mainly includes standard Web servers, application logic, modelbases, data services, and XML modules. A project portfolio selection framework is used to aid the users to expedite their decision-making processes in a more organized fashion. A modelbase is used to deposit and handle portfolio models of the many different types, -which may be chosen. The middle server is responsible for: receiving requests from the clients, accessing the data source, authenticating users and performing session management, formatting the received results into XML if necessary and returning them to the clients, as well as providing decision models.

Back-end applications. The third tier consists of persistent data stores, legacy systems, and data sources. The historical data is in the database for all model programs and data analysis services.

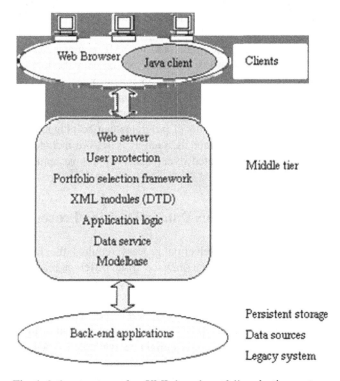

Fig. 1. 3-tier structure of an XML-based portfolio selection system

3.2 Interactions and Implementation

On the client side, the Web browser and Java applet handle the user interface and the presentation logic. The Web server gets all HTTP requests from the Web user and propagates the requests to the application server that implements the logic of all the services for portfolio selection. Communication between the Web server and the application logic can be achieved through the CGI, ASP or other gateway tools. An application server sends a query to the data source and gets the result set. The application server can format the result into XML if necessary and provide the XML document to the client. The Java client receives an XML page, parses it and generates Java objects that are then graphically displayed by the applet. At the third tier, all kinds of data are stored in the database by RDBMS. Portfolio optimization models can be maintained in a separate database.

Regarding to the design of Java client, it becomes clear that we need develop a better interface to the middle server that allows the (Java) client to access the data in a more comprehensible way. We can use an HTTP/XML-based approach, and construct a document type definition (DTD) for data structures. The DTD describes how certain objects are described in XML using a specific tag set, and thus allows the client to validate response against the DTD. The server script simply fetches the requested objects from the database and transforms the python objects into XML-tagged output. The Java applet is based on publicly available XML software for Java. We can develop the interface between the applet and its XML components by the Simple API for XML (SAX), which connects the XML parser with the main application via a specific method XML-parser. We use the document object model (DOM) to provide standard objects for accessing parsed XML documents.

A modelbase is used to support variety of modeling techniques for portfolio selection optimization. Optimization model programs can be plugged into the modelbase for the system to use. Popular models, such as AHP, are included in the modelbase. The decision results are generated dynamically by a Java applet from information retrieved from database.

4   XML for Heterogeneous Data in Decision Process

In general, project portfolio selection process requires the interchange of inter-organizational electronic data that may be from different resources with different formats to deal with the different representations of the same data, evaluate a project or construct a portfolio optimization model. Also, there is a need for electronically interchanging different structured data between the involved organizations. These data may be saved in heterogeneous databases and presented in different formats. Especially, heterogeneous data sources might be available for posting a single request constantly. In this section, we present a 3-tier structure based on XML and Java that is relevant to the problem of heterogeneous databases in project portfolio selection process (Fig. 2).

We provide an illustration of the structure of the proposed system in Figure 2. The main components are data sources, agents, switchers, application logic, and Java client (Java applet).

Data sources. Data sources include legacy systems such as conventional RDBMS (e.g., SQL Server and Oracle) and can be used as a repository of data for all model programs and search requests.

Agents. They are used to control the interaction with specific data sources. Access to the data sources is accomplished through well-established protocols such as Microsoft's ODBC or OLE DB, JDBC, and ADO. Agents can also operate like typical Web spiders. The role of an agent is to establish a two-way connection with a specified data source, and server requests arriving from one more switchers.

Switchers. The switcher component is responsible for converting the received results in XML format and returning them to the gateway tools, relaying requests from application logic to agents and controls the flow of results in the reverse direction. Switchers have a multi-thread architecture, which allows simultaneous communication with multiple agents. They are information brokers which receive specific requests from Web clients, determine the proper agent for their execution, relay requests, combine results coming from more than one agent, and provide for session management.

Java applet. A Java applet handles the user interface and the presentation logic, receives a XML page, and parses it.

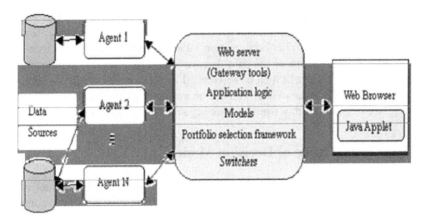

Fig. 2. 3-tier structure for integrating heterogeneous data

```
<!ELEMENT commodityType (organization, code, (commodity)*)>
<!ELEMENT country CDATA>
<!ELEMENT code CDATA>
<!ELEMENT commodity
  (date, price, name?, volume?, industry?, turnover?, maker?)>
    <!ATTLIST commodity symbol ID #REQUIRED>
<!ELEMENT date CDATA>
<!ELEMENT price CDATA>
<!ELEMENT name CDATA>
<!ELEMENT volume CDATA>
<!ELEMENT industry CDATA>
<!ELEMENT turnover CDATA>
<!ELEMENT maker CDATA>
```

Fig. 3. XML DTD for commodity information exchange

In the 3-tier scheme presented, agents handle individual information sources such as RDBMS, and the schemata model of each individual source mapped to a generic representation known to both agents and switchers. Switchers operate behind classical Web server using interfaces such as CGI or other gateway tools. Switchers map meta-information as well as the actual data to a proposed XML DTD. XML streams are transmitted to clients using regular HTTP dialogues, and XML is received and processed by a Java applet. After the applet's invocation, communication with the server is still performed using the HTTP protocol but the HTTP response message always contains XML code in its body. The applet, besides formulation of the appropriate user interface for posting queries and viewing results, incorporates an XML parser.

To ensure the generality of the agent, the problem of different data types and different data-type inner representations have to be dealt with. For example, some data may be collected from another organization taking deferent format with local, so we need to define the structure of the data that we would like to receive by using XML DTD file. This DTD file will then be referenced by Switchers to translate source data into XML format. For example, we can define a simple XML DTD to specify the tags and structure of a commodity from another organization as shown in Fig. 3.

5   Open Interchange of Decision Models

In the process of project portfolio selection, portfolio optimization model is a key component, and the modeling process is knowledge-intensive and time-consuming. There are many researches on sharing models that may be in different environments now. In order to support modeling processes and related activities, many researches on modeling environments (ME) [1, 4] have been made. To implement such a ME, a conceptual modeling framework is important for representing and managing decision models. In general, a closed architecture for interchange of models and data may produce a tangle of import and export point translators. An open exchange standard improves the shortcomings of closed architecture. Having a standard syntax for creating and exchanging data structures is obviously important for this type of integration. XML provides such a framework for describing the syntax. The distinctive characteristics of XML can satisfy some of the new requirements for modeling tools and technologies in the age of the Internet, such as simplicity, extensibility, interoperability and openness. There are many approaches and systems that involve XML in the standardization of data exchange and presentation, such as CML (Chemical Markup Language), MathML (Mathematical Markup Language), and ebXML, reflects the growing requirements and importance of XML.

We can adopt XML as a meta-language and construct a Web-based structure (shown in Fig. 4) for open interchange of portfolio optimization models in different environments. An XML-based language (a central switcher in Fig. 4), formally defined by a simple XML DTD, for the representation, sharing and management of different portfolio optimization models in open architecture, is required. The language is able to allow applications to access models obtained from multiple sources without having to deal with individual differences between those sources. The modeling environments are based on the Web for sharing modeling knowledge. In this open architecture, we can use Markov decision process or fuzzy technology to optimize load balancing for multi-computer system. Hereto, although we describe the systems shown as Fig. 1, Fig. 2, and Fig. 4 respectively, we can unite them as an integrated system.

We can give a generalized XML DTD definition to describe heterogeneous portfolio optimization models. As shown in Fig. 5, a model has its own unique name and pre-defined format for parameters passed in and out. The type of parameters for a model, in this case, can be of "SI" for system-generated input; "UI" for user input; or "O" for output parameters.

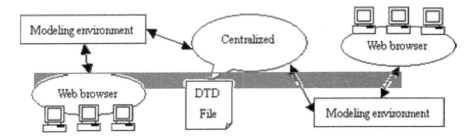

Fig. 4. Architecture for model sharing based on an XML-standard

```
<!ELEMENT model (name, parameter+)>
<!ELEMENT name (#PCDATA)>
<!ELEMENT parameter (name, type)>
    <!ATTLIST parameter ptype (SI|UI|O) #REQUIRED>
<!ELEMENT type (#PCDATA)>
```

Fig. 5. XML DTD for portfolio optimization model

6   Advantages to Decision Process

In this paper, we provide an integrated framework for project portfolio selection that is adaptable to the needs of financial organizations and individual investors. From previous discussion, we can see that portfolio selection process can be more flexible and organized once we break it down into several stages.

Using of XML, the system can re-distribute processing load from the server to the Web clients. The client can do many things that were originally done by server, which can improve the performance of the system and save time during which programmers might otherwise have to update the system. In a distributed modeling environment, the highly structured delivery of data of XML enables open interchange between servers and clients, and potentially between servers themselves. In distributed HTML-based modeling environments, the model manipulation and output generation is performed on the server side.

In the project portfolio selection process, data validation is very important to guarantee efficient decision-making. XML incorporate data validation through the DTD of an XML message and XML method is not complex. What is more, by making use of XML, the programmer can save lots of times that might previously have been used to develop a validity-checking mechanism.

In the project portfolio selection process, various types of data may be used. These data may be saved in heterogeneous databases with deferent structure according in the portfolio selection process. Using a XML method to access data source may be much better because of the advantages of XML. This method makes the design of the system more conveniently and easily, and makes interaction of system more efficiently.

Finally, we can adopt XML as a meta-language and construct a Web-based structure for open interchange of portfolio optimization models in different environments conveniently and easily.

7 Conclusions

In this paper, we discuss XML and its application to the Web-based information systems. Several XML-based schemes following our proposed portfolio selection model for Web DSS are presented. We also provide design and discussion on the adoption of XML for heterogeneous data sources as well as sharing decision models in portfolio selection process. The use of XML for constructing the 3-tier structure of a portfolio selection system is considered extremely advantageous. Although XML offers many benefits to Web applications including portfolio selection DSS, it is also important to be aware that many of its benefits may at the same time impose the weakness. For instance, XML's openness leads to the problem of lack of security; its tree-like hierarchical data structure represents the real-world objects naturally, but creates difficulty in communicating with existing databases that are relational or hierarchical.

References

1. Geoffrion, A.M.: Computer-based modeling environments. European Journal of Operational Research 41 (1989) 33-43.
2. Ghasemzadeh, F., Archer, N.P.: Project portfolio selection through decision support. Decision Support Systems 29 (2000) 73-88.
3. Archer, N.P., Ghasemzadeh, F.: A decision support system for project portfolio selection. International Journal of Technology Management 16 (1998) 105-115.
4. Park, S.J., Kim, H.D.: Constraint-based meta-view approach for modeling environment generation. Decision Support System 9 (1993) 325-348.

Author Index

Lecture Notes in Artificial Intelligence (LNAI)